W9-AZZ-627

INSIDERS' GUIDE® SERIES

INSIDERS' GUIDE® TO
MEMPHIS

SECOND EDITION

NICKY ROBERTSHAW

INSIDERS' GUIDE®

GUILFORD, CONNECTICUT
AN IMPRINT OF THE GLOBE PEQUOT PRESS

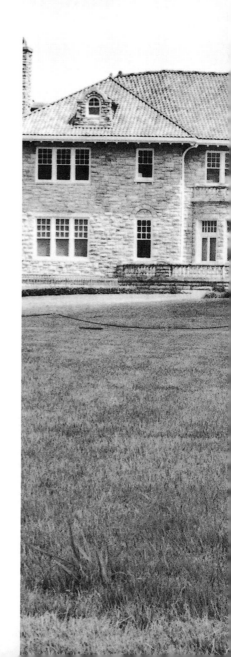

INSIDERS' GUIDE®

Copyright © 2002, 2005 by The Globe Pequot Press

Text design: LeAnna Weller Smith
Maps: XNR Productions, Inc. © The Globe Pequot Press

ISSN: 1542-8451
ISBN: 0-7627-3454-X

Manufactured in the United States of America
Second Edition/First Printing

Pink Palace Mansion and Museum. BONNIE TATE

AutoZone Park, home field of Memphis Redbirds. BONNIE TATE

Skyline. MEMPHIS CONVENTION & VISITORS BUREAU

House in Victorian Village. BONNIE TATE

Memphis Zoo. MEMPHIS CONVENTION & VISITORS BUREAU

Stax Museum of American Soul Music. BONNIE TATE

Sun Studio. BONNIE TATE

[Top] *Graceland.* MEMPHIS CONVENTION & VISITORS BUREAU
[Bottom] *Pyramid Arena.* MEMPHIS CONVENTION & VISITORS BUREAU

[Top] *Gibson Guitar Factory.* MEMPHIS CONVENTION & VISITORS BUREAU
[Bottom] *Memphis Motorsports Park.* MEMPHIS CONVENTION & VISITORS BUREAU

Orpheum Theater. BONNIE TATE

[Top] *W. C. Handy House on Beale Street.* BONNIE TATE
[Bottom] *National Civil Rights Museum (formerly the Lorraine Motel).* BONNIE TATE

The Peabody Hotel. BONNIE TATE

Memphis Brooks Museum of Art. BONNIE TATE

Memphis Botanic Garden. MEMPHIS CONVENTION & VISITORS BUREAU

CONTENTS

Preface xxiii

Acknowledgments xxiv

How to Use This Book 1

Area Overview 3

Getting Here, Getting Around 13

History 19

Accommodations 31

Restaurants 51

Nightlife 82

Memphis Music 98

African-American Heritage 110

Shopping 117

Attractions 131

Kidstuff 151

Annual Events 162

The Arts 171

Parks and Recreation 184

Spectator Sports 210

Day Trips and Weekend Getaways 217

Casinos 229

Relocation 233

Health Care and Wellness 246

Education 257

Retirement 269

Media 275

Worship 285

Index 289

About the Author 305

CONTENTS

Directory of Maps

City of Memphis xix

Downtown Memphis xx

Memphis Area Neighborhoods xxi

Memphis and Surrounding Area xxii

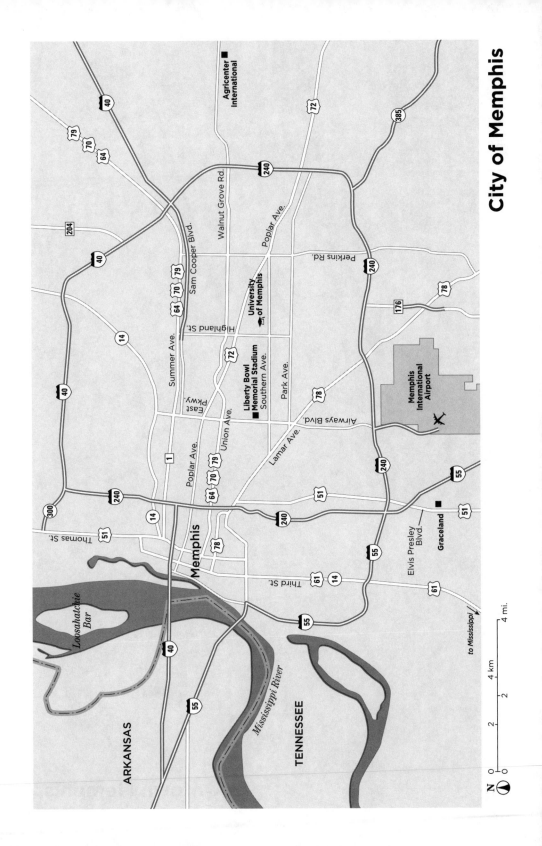

City of Memphis

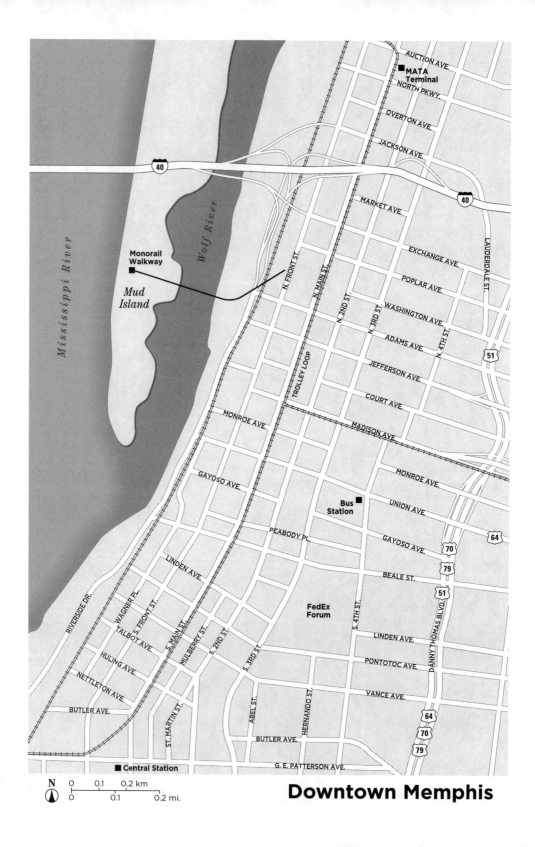

Downtown Memphis

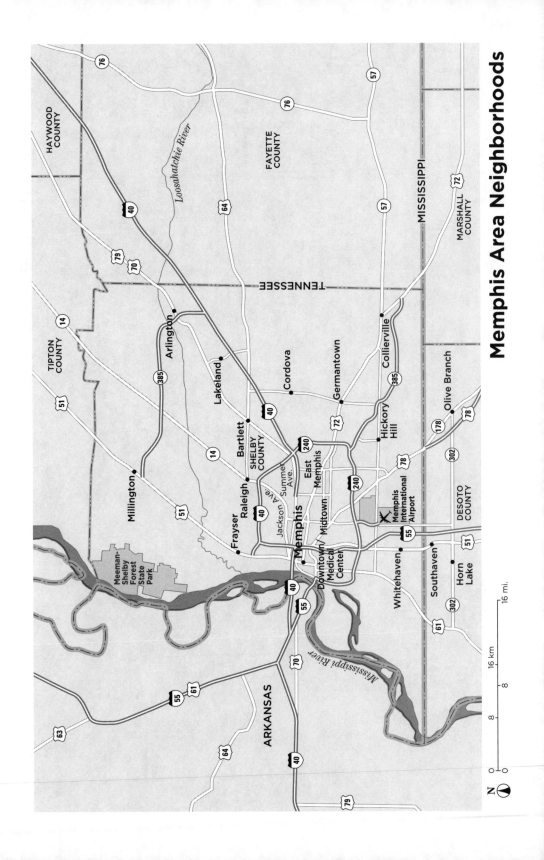

Memphis Area Neighborhoods

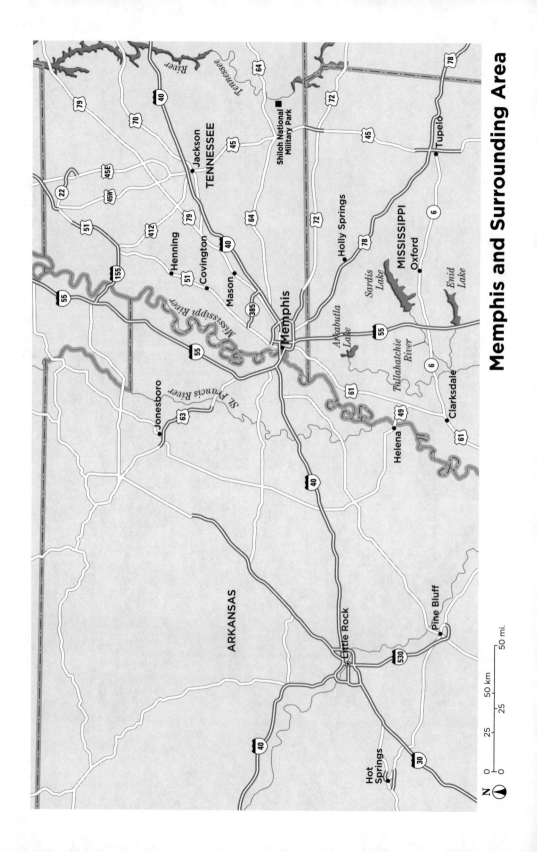

Memphis and Surrounding Area

PREFACE

Welcome to Memphis! Memphis is one of those mythical places in the minds of those who love rock and roll, blues, and other American music. Even if you couldn't find it on a map, you have undoubtedly heard Memphis in songs (the city's name is in the title or lyrics of some 400 songs). You probably already know that this is Elvis Presley's hometown.

It has been more than 50 years now since the King first recorded "That's All Right (Mama)" at Memphis's Sun Studio, an event widely celebrated as the birth of rock and roll. Even as Memphis pays tribute to its musical past—both rock and roll and the city's rich blues legacy—the city is changing fast as it moves boldly into the future. FedExForum, the downtown arena built for the Grizzlies NBA team, now takes its place in the Memphis skyline. New musical talent is coming out of Memphis, including performers as diverse as the blues/Southern rock band North Mississippi Allstars, rappers Three 6 Mafia, pop star Justin Timberlake, and bluesman Alvin Youngblood Hart. In addition, plans are afoot to redevelop the heart of the downtown and make it more accessible, a step that brings the city full circle. After all, this famous river town first came into being and thrived because of its location

on the banks of the Mississippi. As becomes a city in the Deep South, it's also full of friendly people with Southern drawls, for whom genuine hospitality is second nature. Of course, you'll find plenty of flatter American accents, and foreign accents as well, a sign that Memphis has attracted visitors and new residents from all over the world.

Memphis is a laid-back, easygoing place where you can relax and enjoy great music on or off Beale Street, indulge in delicacies ranging from barbecue sandwiches to outstanding eclectic American cuisine, and enjoy a wide range of sights, arts, and sports.

Insiders' Guide to Memphis was written to help you find your way around this multifaceted city, whether you are visiting the city on vacation or business, or planning to move here and looking for information on neighborhoods, schools, and the like. The book is an equally useful tool for people who already live here, with its listings of restaurants, shops, and sporting events. You'll also find ideas for entertaining the kids and the lowdown on the area's best golf courses, mountain-biking trails, and fishing spots.

So have a great time in Memphis, and see for yourself what everyone is singing about.

ACKNOWLEDGMENTS

This book would not have been possible without the help of many people.

First of all, I'd like to thank my husband, Chris, for his incredible support during the writing and updating of this book. I also want to thank him for his great work on the book, particularly the golf section (somebody had to test all those golf courses!). And thanks to my two-year-old daughter, Maddie, for being a good sport, and to Dina Upton for keeping her happy while Mom was busy with her book. I also want to thank other friends and family, including my sister Sylvia and brother Frank, for their support.

The book would not be the same without mom and innkeeper Jamie Baker's great eye for kidstuff, or Bob Phillips's insight into Memphis's new role as a happening sports town. Many thanks, too, to Jonathan Scott, a native Memphian with a great feel for the city's history, and historian Dr. Charles W. Crawford at the University of Memphis. I want to thank Scott Shepherd at the *Memphis Business Journal,* who probably knows more than anyone about Memphis health care and education. Thanks to Chris Herrington, music writer at the *Memphis Flyer,* for his help on the Memphis music and nightlife chapters. Thanks also to Julie Clary, Amber Shaw, and Catherine Curtis, who helped with the massive task of updating an entire book.

I also want to thank the Memphis Convention & Visitors Bureau, and Cary Hull at The Globe Pequot Press. I'd also like to thank all the editors who, throughout the years, have helped me develop as a writer.

Lastly, thank you, Memphis, for being such a great place to live and play. You make my job easy.

HOW TO USE THIS BOOK

Memphis truly is, as the tourism slogan goes, the Home of the Blues and the Birthplace of Rock and Roll. But even if you aren't a music fan, you'll find plenty to enjoy in this friendly city on the bluffs overlooking the Mississippi River, whether it's world-famous pork barbecue, the bright lights of Beale Street, or Graceland Mansion.

Consider this book as your personal tool for enjoying the best of what Memphis has to offer, whether you're in town for a few days of sightseeing or moving here for an extended stay.

This book is divided into self-contained, stand-alone chapters, each about a specific aspect of Memphis, such as nightlife or restaurants. We begin with an overview of the city, where you can learn what makes Memphis a unique place. You may be surprised to learn, for example, that Memphis is still called the hardwood capital of the world, is home to the world's busiest airport (thanks to FedEx), and has a gigantic glass pyramid next to the Mississippi River. You can get your bearings by reading the Getting Here, Getting Around chapter.

If you're looking for a place to stay, check out the Accommodations chapter for listings of hotels, bed-and-breakfast inns, and other options. If you're looking for a great meal or just a nosh, flip to the Restaurants chapter. We list restaurants by type of cuisine, including barbecue, so you can find out where to get the best versions of this legendary Memphis specialty, as well as old-fashioned Southern home cooking.

Memphis music is the reason many people visit Memphis, and you'll find out where to hear it, both on and off Beale Street, in the Nightlife chapter. Check out the Memphis Music chapter for an extensive look at

how American music, including the blues, rock and roll, and soul, grew out of Memphis, and how new music still bubbles up from the city's rich musical heritage.

When you're ready to see the town, turn to the Attractions chapter, where you'll get the skinny on Graceland, the National Civil Rights Museum, Sun Studio, and other sights. You'll find more choices in the Kidstuff chapter, where you can get the kid-friendly skinny on basic attractions including Beale Street. For other diversions check out the Parks and Recreation, Spectator Sports, Annual Events, and Day Trips and Weekend Getaways chapters. To learn more about Memphis's African-American heritage, turn to the chapter bearing that name.

If you're planning to make Memphis your home, flip to the back of the book and learn more about daily life in Memphis. You'll find chapters on relocation (real estate and neighborhoods), education, media, health care, retirement, and worship.

Throughout the book you'll find Close-ups, which highlight some noteworthy aspect of the city, and Insiders' tips—look for the **i** —nuggets of information you might not find anywhere else.

We hope you will make good use of this book as you explore Memphis, but remember to put it away, too. Just hanging out is one of the pleasures of being here, and if you're too much the "tourist on a mission," you'll miss that aspect. Memphis is a laid-back, friendly place, so take time to relax and enjoy watching the river, listen to some blues, and make some new friends.

Bear in mind that things can change quickly even in a laid-back city like Memphis. We doubt that the Mississippi River will stop flowing or that Graceland Mansion will close its doors to visitors, but before you know it, a restaurant could move to the suburbs, an attraction change its hours, or a nightclub close its doors. It's always a good idea to call ahead before you visit the places we list here.

We've made every effort to include accurate, up-to-date information, but nobody's perfect. Let us know if we've goofed, or if you discover a great little barbecue joint or blues club that escaped our notice. This guide is periodically updated, and your input will help to improve the next edition.

Write to us at *Insiders' Guide to Memphis,* The Globe Pequot Press, P.O. Box 480, Guilford, CT 06437-0480 or at editorial@GlobePequot.com.

We hope you have a great time in Memphis. You'll see why people come here for school, a work assignment, or a short visit and find they're still here five years later enjoying the mellow Memphis lifestyle.

AREA OVERVIEW

There's more to Memphis than first meets the visitor's eye.

True, it's the birthplace of rock and roll, Elvis Presley's hometown, the pork barbecue capital of the world, and an important Mississippi River port. Visitors can see Graceland, take in some blues on Beale Street, enjoy outstanding barbecue ribs, and gaze out at Old Man River. The people you encounter are likely to be very friendly and only too happy to give directions or recommend a personal favorite. It's very laid-back—no need to rush around unless that's what you want to do.

Look a little deeper, however, and you'll find more in this city that got its start as a rowdy river town. Memphis has a family-friendly attitude, an employment rate that's often better than the national average, and a diversified economy that makes the city resilient to downturns. Memphis throughout the years has spawned innovations that change the way we live. These include the modern supermarket (Piggly Wiggly, 1916), the modern hotel chain (Holiday Inn, 1952), and overnight package delivery (FedEx, 1972).

The city has its share of paradoxes. Despite a basically conservative atmosphere, the city has produced musical revolutions that shaped the complexion of American music. Remember how shocking Elvis's gyrations were considered in the 1950s, yet his act originated in the conservative Southern city of Memphis. And despite the extreme poverty within much of the black community and the fact that Dr. Martin Luther King Jr. was assassinated here in 1968, Memphis is attracting a good share of blacks moving south as part of the reverse migration currently taking place in the United States. In fact, the city rated as one of the best places in the United States for African Americans to live in 2001, according to *Black Enterprise* magazine.

The city also has a low cost of living, has affordably priced homes, and ranks among the best cities in the country for starting a small business. In Memphis, as becomes a city in the midst of the Bible Belt, many are churchgoing citizens, often building their personal lives around the church or temple of their choice.

Memphis is also one of the country's most important distribution centers, a growing center for medical research (St. Jude Children's Research Hospital won a Nobel Prize), and the southern hub for Northwest Airlines. In addition, Memphis remains a strong river port and a center for marketing of U.S. cotton crops, the businesses that first put Memphis on the map in the 1800s.

But there's something intangible about Memphis that grows on you. Just ask around, and you'll likely encounter more than a few people who came to Memphis intending only a short stay. Yet here they are five or ten years later, feeling very much at home but not really sure how it happened. You might also be surprised at how many native Memphians choose to stay here. While many are proud of their city and delight in its successes, there's an unfortunate propensity among some native Memphians to complain that the city isn't Manhattan or Atlanta. Yet even these malcontents find a place for themselves in Memphis; after all, flights leave daily for New York and Atlanta, and they're still here.

A big part of the city's charm has to do with Memphians. They are a hospitable bunch, and generous, too. In fact, the city ranked as the fifth most generous urban area, according to a study by the *Chronicle of Philanthropy*.

It's an exciting time to be in Memphis, as long-held dreams, including the revival of downtown Memphis and professional sports, have become a reality. Now attention is being focused on redeveloping the city riverfront in such a way as to make it more accessible to visitors and residents alike. Economic-development activity continues, as new businesses come to town and existing ones expand their operations.

For more information check out these Web sites: www.cityofmemphis.org (City of Memphis), www.memphischamber .com (Memphis Regional Chamber), www.memphistravel.com (Memphis Convention & Visitors Bureau), and www .commercialappeal.com (the Commercial Appeal, the city's daily newspaper).

THE MEMPHIS CITYSCAPE

Graceland Mansion may be the city's most recognizable building, but in fact most of the city looks very different from the Presley home.

Built on flat, sometimes rolling, terrain and dotted with parks and stately oaks, magnolias, and other trees, the Memphis cityscape includes a variety of architectural styles, ranging from antebellum homes and 1800s commercial buildings to skyscrapers and modern shopping centers. It's eclectic, to say the least, so you can't really point to a Memphis style that's as distinctive and characteristic as what you'd find in other Southern towns such as New Orleans or Savannah.

Memphis does boast a large number of historic buildings, particularly in the downtown area, more than you'd find in Charlotte, Atlanta, and other Southern cities where many more older buildings were cleared to make way for progress.

Downtown is also where the variety is most pronounced; within 10 to 20 blocks you find austere government buildings from the 1960s, restored Victorian homes, a few antebellum structures, and several skyscrapers. There are many lofty commercial buildings dating from the early 1900s, many of which have been put to new uses.

Among them is a former Kress Variety Store with a colorful, beautifully preserved glazed terra-cotta facade. It's now a hotel. Just across the Auction Bridge on Mud Island is Harbortown, a residential neighborhood begun in the 1980s. It includes sometimes pricey award-winning new homes that incorporate many elements of traditional Southern architecture.

As you leave the downtown area on the main thoroughfares such as Union or Poplar and move into midtown, you'll see a few of the stately homes that formerly lined these streets, now interspersed with commercial and medical buildings, gas stations and fast-food joints, apartment buildings, churches, and strip shopping centers. Central and Peabody Avenues in midtown have remained residential, and here you can still see many of the city's beautiful old homes, particularly in the Central Gardens area.

Memphis prides itself on its beautiful old oaks and other trees, so it was heart-wrenching in 2003 when a strong "inland hurricane" storm destroyed about one-third of them. But the survivors are as stately as ever, even if some are a bit misshapen as a result of the storm damage.

If there's any such thing as a typical Memphis building, it has to be the bungalow, a style of middle-class home with a front porch and extended eaves popular in the 1910s and 1920s. You'll see many bungalows in midtown neighborhoods, as well as "foursquares," so called because each floor has four big rooms. Once you reach East Memphis, residences are mostly tract housing from the 1950s through the 1980s, whereas commercial buildings include shopping centers, low retail and office buildings of up to four floors, and a few high-rise buildings. The far suburbs such as Germantown and Collierville have some historic buildings, including Collierville's picturesque town square, but otherwise homes, apartment complexes, office buildings, and shopping centers are typical modern suburban in their design. Standouts include the FedEx World Headquarters campus in Collierville.

A SENSE OF PLACE

To understand what makes Memphis the city it is today, you must start with its location. Perched above the Mississippi River on what is known as the Fourth Chickasaw Bluff, it's safe from flooding yet benefits from the remarkably rich soil created by annual flooding in surrounding areas. Memphis started as a shipping and marketing center for locally grown cotton and other crops in the early 1800s and continues to be active in bringing cotton to market. Memphis also is still an active river port, and although port operations have been moved south of downtown, you can see barges and towboats plying the Mississippi.

Memphis rests in the southwest corner of Tennessee, several hundred miles away culturally and geographically from the Great Smoky Mountains of east Tennessee. Memphis is the capital of the Mid-South, a region that includes west Tennessee, northern Mississippi, eastern Arkansas, and the Missouri boot heel. As in years past, Memphis continues to be big lights, big city for that part of the country.

Because it sits on the top of the state of Mississippi and draws many residents from that state, Memphis has traditionally been viewed as the capital of Mississippi. Southern writer David Cohn famously underscored that point in the 1930s when he wrote that the Mississippi Delta begins in the lobby of The Peabody hotel in Memphis.

Delta people have traditionally come to Memphis not only to socialize at The Peabody (still a favorite pastime) but also to shop, do business, and to amuse themselves, whether it's fine dining, the clubs on Beale Street, a Redbirds game, or a touring Broadway show.

Mid-Southerners also flock here to live, attend college, find work, or otherwise get away from their small towns and farms.

At present, in terms of the city's economy, location is just as important as it was in the 1800s, but in a different way. Because Memphis is centrally located in the North American continent and within a

day's drive of most of the U.S. population, it has become a major distribution and transportation hub, with cargo traveling via rail, truck, and air as well as by river barge. Memphis is far enough south that it's rarely snowed in, an important reason that Memphian Fred Smith decided to base his Federal Express operations here. FedEx is the city's largest employer and has helped Memphis International Airport hold its position as the world's busiest air-cargo airport since 1992. The presence of FedEx continues to attract companies to set up their own distribution centers here for the quickest possible delivery to their customers.

The annual average temperature here is 62 degrees, with the temperature averaging 41 degrees in January and 81 degrees in July. Humidity averages 69 percent. Summers can be scorchers with highs often in the upper 90s, especially in late July and August (luckily, air-conditioning is ubiquitous). May and October generally have the best weather. In winter Memphis sometimes gets ice storms, and temperatures are sometimes in the 20s or even the teens. But it's also prone to winter warm spells, so you're just as likely to find Memphians wearing shorts as down jackets in February.

Rainfall averages 49 inches, and snowfall averages 5.3 inches a year, although many years there are only flurries. Memphis often is a standout on national weather maps because it's situated where the plains to the west end and the mountains to the east begin. Memphians were reminded of that in July 2003, when a storm some describe as an inland hurricane struck the city without warning, packing winds up to 100 mph. The storm, virtually ignored by the national press, left Memphians without power, some for as long as two weeks, and destroyed about a third of the city's trees. Thunderstorms here are dramatic, a far cry from the misty rains of Seattle. Tornadoes also threaten and sometimes strike Memphis and the surrounding area.

Another geographical quirk is that the city sits on the Memphis Sand Aquifer, an enormous underground reservoir of naturally purified water that's retrieved through drilled wells for the city water supply. Memphis is the largest city in the world to rely exclusively on artesian wells for its water supply.

DEMOGRAPHICALLY SPEAKING

Memphis is Tennessee's largest city, situated in the extreme southwest corner of Tennessee in Shelby County, the state's most populous county. It's the 18th-largest city in the country, with 650,100 people, according to the 2000 census. The Memphis MSA (metropolitan statistical area) is the 44th largest and consists of five counties in three states: Shelby, Tipton, and Fayette Counties in Tennessee, DeSoto County in Mississippi, and Crittenden County in Arkansas. More recent estimates set the MSA population at 1,144,470; but in 2000 it was 1,135,614, an almost 13 percent increase over 1990, according to 2000 census figures. In contrast the population of Nashville is 569,891, according to the 2000 census. During the 1990s the Nashville MSA grew by 25 percent compared with Memphis's 13 percent growth; as a result Nashville overtook Memphis as the most populous MSA, with 1,251,509, according to the 2000 census.

Most of the current growth in population is in the suburbs, although downtown Memphis saw a huge increase in population during the 1990s as new homes and apartments were built and some historic buildings were renovated into apartments. The strongest suburban growth during the 1990s took place in DeSoto County, Mississippi, with a 58 percent increase in population; Tipton, with 36 percent growth; and Fayette County, with 13 percent growth. In Shelby County the hot 1990s growth spots were Collierville, which grew by 120 percent, and Lakeland, which grew by more than 400 percent.

The city continues to build out to far eastern Shelby County towns including Oakland, Arlington, and Eads, and north to Tipton County towns such as Atoka and Covington. In DeSoto County, Mississippi, further development is expected in Olive Branch and Hernando. See the Relocation chapter for more details.

It shouldn't surprise anyone that the demographics of Memphis differ dramatically from those of Tennessee as a whole. After all, Tennessee stretches some 500 miles over the top of the states of Mississippi, Alabama, and Georgia, and because of its extreme width, west Tennessee (where Memphis is), middle Tennessee (where Nashville is), and east Tennessee (home to Knoxville and Chattanooga) are so distinct they could easily be three separate states.

For example, Memphis has higher concentrations of minority populations than the state as a whole. As of 2000, the Memphis MSA population was 51.2 percent white, 43.2 percent black, 2.4 percent Hispanic, and 1.4 percent Asian, according to census figures. In contrast Tennessee's population is 80.2 percent white, 16.4 percent black, 2.2 percent Hispanic, and 1 percent Asian. Although figures for the Memphis MSA and Shelby County show that whites slightly outnumber blacks, in the city of Memphis the black population exceeds the white population.

Per-capita personal income for the Memphis MSA was $30,559 for 2001, a figure that's just above the national per-capita figure of $30,413, according to government statistics. The city's cost of liv-

Did you know that Memphis was the home of the first Welcome Wagon in 1928? The home of the first Greyhound and Continental Trailways bus lines? It's also home to the world's largest producer of Christmas wrapping paper and was named the cleanest city in the nation, according to National City Beautiful Commission, and the only city that's a five-time winner of that award.

ing is lower than the national average, according to the American Chamber of Commerce Researchers Association, which calculated that as of September 30, 2001, Memphis's cost of living was about 90 percent of the national average.

In terms of the job market, unemployment levels for the Memphis MSA had been lower than the national average through most of the 1990s and earlier in this decade. Lately, it has been more in line with the national average. As of January 2004 local unemployment was 5.9 percent, compared with 5.6 percent for the country as a whole.

DOING BUSINESS: FROM COTTON TO E-COMMERCE

Memphis is an economically diverse city, a characteristic that helps the city to weather the ups and downs in the economy. One reason is that manufacturing accounts for about 9 percent of local employment, a key factor because manufacturing is hit hardest by tough times. Instead, most jobs are in the more resilient service sector, where large employers include FedEx, the health-care industry, retail, and other transportation/distribution companies.

FedEx is the city's largest employer, with about 30,000 Memphis employees, so it's an important engine to the local economy. The company's headquarters are here, and a huge number of the company's worldwide package volume comes through Memphis. FedEx is a big reason that Memphis International Airport is the world's busiest air-cargo airport, handling 3.4 million tons in fiscal 2002.

It's also a big reason companies continue to flock to Memphis to open their own distribution centers. Among these are Internet and catalog retailer Williams-Sonoma and numerous other companies, including Nike, Pfizer, and the computer hardware and software company Ingram Micro.

Other modes of transportation are strong here, including railroad, river, and trucking. Memphis is the country's third-largest rail center, its fourth-largest inland port, and home to more than 200 trucking companies. Because of the city's central location, products moved by truck and rail can reach two thirds of the U.S. population within 24 hours.

Memphis has exported cotton and other products to overseas markets since the early 1800s and continues to do so, selling several billion dollars worth of goods each year for export.

Although not the reigning economic king it once was, cotton continues to be an important part of the local economy. The Mid-South cotton industry (from farming to textiles) generates some $7.5 billion in revenues, and Memphis-based merchants market more than half of the total U.S. cotton crop. Memphis is home to the largest spot cotton-trading market in the world and cotton-trading-giant Dunavant Enterprises as well as the National Cotton Council and other cotton organizations. Memphis is also home to the National Hardwood Lumber Association and is still called the hardwood capital of the world, even though a century has passed since the days when the area produced one billion feet of lumber per year.

Memphis is also strong in health care, given the two large hospital systems as well as St. Jude Children's Research Hospital and the University of Tennessee Health Science Center. The retail industry is also a big player in the local economy because Memphis is where the Mid-South comes to shop. The federal and local governments also are large employers, as are the city and county school systems.

Memphis economic development has been on the rise. Each year since 1997 there has been at least $1 billion in capital investment through major projects, while Memphis economic development is estimated to account for about one quarter of total economic development within the entire state, according to the Memphis

Memphis Vital Statistics

Founded: In 1819 on the Fourth Chickasaw Bluff overlooking the Mississippi by Andrew Jackson, James Winchester, and John Overton

Nickname: Bluff City

Mayors/Governor: Memphis: Mayor W. W. Herenton; Shelby County: Mayor A C Wharton Jr.; Tennessee: Governor Phil Bredesen

Population: Memphis: 660,960; Shelby County: 905,678; Memphis metropolitan statistical area (MSA): 1,144,470; Tennessee: 5,797,289

Area: Memphis: 296 square miles; Shelby County: 772 square miles; Memphis MSA: 3,012 square miles

Counties in the Memphis MSA: Shelby, Tipton, and Fayette Counties in Tennessee, Crittenden County in Arkansas, and DeSoto County in Mississippi

Average temperatures:
  January: 41° F;
  July: 81° F;
  Annual: 62° F

Average annual rainfall: 48.6 inches

Average snowfall: 5.3 inches

Major airport: Memphis International Airport, the world's busiest cargo airport since 1992 thanks to FedEx, and the southern hub for Northwest Airlines

Major interstates: I-40 (east-west) and I-55 (north-south)

Maritime and railroad activity: Memphis is the fourth-largest inland port in the United States (second-largest on the Mississippi) and the third-largest rail hub in the United States.

Major colleges and universities: University of Memphis, University of Tennessee Health Science Center, Christian Brothers University, Rhodes College, and LeMoyne-Owen College

Important dates in Memphis history:

1541:   Hernando DeSoto and his party are the first white men to view the lower Mississippi and may have been the first white men to visit the Fourth Chickasaw Bluff.

1739:   The French build a fort on the Fourth Chickasaw Bluff.

1795:   The Spanish build Fort San Fernando on the Fourth Chickasaw Bluff, which lasts only two years until the Americans build Fort Adams on its ruins.

1819:   Memphis is founded.

1826:   Memphis is incorporated as a town.

1857:   The Memphis-Charleston Railroad is completed, launching the city's position as an important rail hub.

1862:   Memphis falls to Union forces but continues to operate as a major center of commerce for both sides.

1879:   Memphis declares bankruptcy and loses its charter after a series of yellow-fever epidemics kill or drive off most of its population.

1880s: Memphis becomes the largest hardwood market in the world.

1893: Memphis regains its charter.

1899: Church Park and Auditorium are built for the city's African Americans by black millionaire Robert Church, cementing Beale Street as the center of African-American culture and commerce.

1909: Beale Street bandleader W. C. Handy publishes the first blues music, becoming "father of the blues" for his role in bringing this style of music to the American mainstream.

1916: The first self-service grocery store in the country opens in Memphis under the name Piggly Wiggly, which evolves into the modern supermarket.

1948: WDIA becomes the first radio station to adopt an all African-American format, launching the careers of B. B. King, Rufus Thomas, and others.

1952: "Rocket 88" is recorded at Sun Studio by Jackie Brenston and the Delta Cats, considered by some to be the first rock-and-roll recording.

1952: Memphis entrepreneur Kemmons Wilson opens his first Holiday Inn, pioneering the modern hotel/motel chain.

1954: Elvis Presley records his first hit, "That's All Right (Mama)," at Sun Studio, quickly becoming an international superstar.

1960: Stax Records has its first major hit, "Cause I Love You," by Rufus Thomas and his daughter Carla Thomas, to be followed by many more hits by Otis Redding, the Staple Singers, Isaac Hayes, and others.

1968: Dr. Martin Luther King Jr., in town to support striking African-American garbage workers, is assassinated at the Lorraine Motel.

1972: Frederick W. Smith starts Federal Express Corp. in Little Rock, soon moving the operation to Memphis.

1977: Elvis Presley dies at his south Memphis home Graceland at age 42.

1980s: Memphis tourism heats up as The Peabody hotel is reopened, Beale Street is revived, and Graceland and Sun Studio are opened to visitors.

1992: The city elects its first African-American mayor, City Schools Superintendent W. W. Herenton.

1994: Memphis International Airport, already a major Northwest Airlines hub, begins direct international service when KLM Royal Dutch Airlines launches its Memphis-to-Amsterdam flight.

2000: The AAA Redbirds baseball team opens its first season at a new downtown ball park.

2001: Memphis lands an NBA team, the Grizzlies, from Vancouver, which begins its first season here.

2002: A C Wharton Jr. is elected mayor of Shelby County, the first time both the city and county have had an African-American mayor.

2003: Two giant pandas, Le Le and Ya Ya, arrive at the Memphis Zoo from China, making the city's zoo one of only four zoos in the country to have pandas.

2004: The brand-new arena FedExForum opens in downtown Memphis as home to the Memphis Grizzlies.

Major area employers with more than 5,000 employees: FedEx, U.S. Government, Memphis City Schools, Methodist Healthcare Corp., Baptist Memorial Health Care Corp.,

City of Memphis, Shelby County Government, Wal-Mart Stores, Tennessee State Government, Shelby County Schools

Memphis companies with more than $1 billion in annual revenues (2002):
FedEx Corp. (express delivery), AutoZone (auto parts retailer), First Horizon National Corp. (financial services), Thomas & Betts (electrical components), Fred's Inc. (discount retailer), TCB Corp. (tires), and Accredo Health (specialized pharmacy services)

Famous sons and daughters: Actors Cybill Shepherd, Kathy Bates, and Morgan Freeman, pop star Justin Timberlake, DJ Rick Dees, basketball player Penny Hardaway, game-show host Wink Martindale, musicians Isaac Hayes, Elvis Presley, and Machine Gun Kelly, Confederate general Nathan Bedford Forrest, sportscaster Tim McCarver

Famous Memphis residents: Historian Shelby Foote, soprano Kallen Esperian, Debbi Fields Rose (Mrs. Fields' Cookies), civil rights leader Benjamin Hooks, preacher/musician Al Green, Nobel Prize–winning researcher Peter Doherty, entertainer Jerry Lee Lewis

Major American music innovations from Memphis: 1910s: the blues, first published by W. C. Handy; 1950s: rock and roll, first recorded at Sun Studio; 1960s–early 1970s: Southern soul, recorded at Stax Records

Public transportation: Memphis Area Transit Authority operates bus lines, the downtown trolley, and an airport shuttle service for downtown hotels.

Military bases: Naval Support Activity Memphis in Millington, Tennessee, home of the Bureau of Naval Personnel

Driving laws: Speed limits are usually 35 mph on the city's main streets unless marked otherwise. Turning right at a red light is allowed unless signs say otherwise. Where you see an HOV lane, travel in that lane is limited to cars with at least two passengers during the rush hours posted on the signs.

Alcohol laws: You must be age 21 or older to drink alcohol. Liquor may be served until 3:00 A.M. except on Beale Street between Second and Fourth Streets, where establishments have permission to serve until 5:00 A.M. Only in this section of Beale Street is it legal to carry an open container of alcohol. Under Tennessee law, drivers are considered to be illegally impaired if their blood alcohol level reaches .08.

Daily newspaper: The *Commercial Appeal*

Taxes: Sales tax: 9.25 percent (7 percent Tennessee tax, 2.25 percent local tax); hotel-room tax: 15.95 percent (includes sales tax; may vary outside Shelby County)

Regional Chamber. In 2003, 16 major companies announced relocations to Memphis, while 123 Memphis companies announced major expansions. While the Memphis economy suffered from the fallout of September 11, the effects seem to have been short-lived. Such resiliency is in keeping with the city's history of being better able than many other cities to weather downturns in the economy. One reason is that the Memphis business community is pretty conservative, so expansion doesn't get out of hand during good times. That means there's not as far to fall when business slows down. Its relatively low level of manufacturing also protects the city economy during bad times, even though that also means that economic booms here are not as great as in cities with a larger portion of manufacturing.

The job market lately has been close to the national average. At times, low unemployment rather than high unemployment has been the problem, as employers struggle to find enough people to man lower-paying jobs and the skilled people necessary for high-tech and other jobs. Cognizant of this challenge, city leaders have focused their attention on improving the local education system as a way to produce more skilled workers.

Despite the city's economic resilience, its tourism, aviation, and convention industries keenly felt the effects of the slowdown in travel that occurred after September 11. In recent years, though, things have improved as travel has resumed and as the $100-million-plus expansion and renovation of the Memphis Cook Convention Center was completed in 2003.

The city is making great progress toward its goal of creating a strong downtown, and in fact it's one of the fastest-growing urban areas in the Southeast. In 2004 there was some $2.4 billion in development dollars being spent for projects under way or recently completed, including the extension of the Main Street trolley and FedExForum.

MEMPHIS AT PLAY

Downtown Memphis has become the main drawing card for leisure activities as well, particularly in the area of professional sports. The arrival of the Grizzlies, Memphis's first NBA team, in 2001, and the 2004 completion of FedExForum, their glitzy new home just north of Beale Street, have been exciting developments, and Memphians have shown their support by attending the games in record numbers. To the north, AutoZone Park is a beautiful baseball park designed along the lines of Baltimore's Oriole Park in Camden Yards, and is home to the Triple A Memphis Redbirds. Since this Cardinals farm team started playing there, its games have enjoyed some of the highest levels of attendance in its league.

The area in between the two venues and a bit to the west is where you'll find Peabody Place, a shopping and entertainment complex featuring Jillian's, a small shopping mall, a large movie theater, and other diversions. A few blocks away, South Main Street has become the gallery district for the city, with galleries as well as chic shops.

There are plenty of restaurants and bars of all kinds downtown, so visitors can easily have a meal or drinks before or after the game, the movies, and other entertainments.

Beale Street is a huge destination for visitors, locals, and residents of nearby towns and farms, drawing more visitors than any other attraction in the state.

Feeling lucky? Tennessee recently instituted a lottery that includes instant games as well as drawings for multimillion-dollar jackpots. You can buy tickets at convenience stores and other retail outlets. Look for the green and purple logo featuring a capital T with stars, or you can learn more by visiting www.tnlottery.gov.

Good local blues and other live music can be found on the street every night, and sometimes national acts that have included B. B. King, Alvin Youngblood Hart, and Buckwheat Zydeco. Outside of Beale Street you'll find all kinds of live music, ranging from big concerts by stars such as hometown boy Justin Timberlake and Pearl Jam at the Pyramid Arena to club performances ranging from heavy metal to jazz, blues to bluegrass.

Beyond downtown Memphis you'll find good shopping, numerous parks including 5,000-acre Shelby Farms, and many places to enjoy your favorite activity, whether it's skateboarding, bowling, hanging out in bookstores, or catching the game at a local bar. Check out the Nightlife, Parks and Recreation, and Shopping chapters for a full rundown, not to mention our listing of Annual Events.

GETTING HERE, GETTING AROUND

Memphis is near the geographical center of the country and is well connected by highway, air, railroad, and even the Mississippi River for passengers on riverboats or passenger barges. Northwest Airlines/KLM makes the city easily accessible from Europe and beyond, flying daily to and from Amsterdam. Once here, unless you are staying downtown (where there's the Main Street Trolley and cab stands) and plan to spend most of your time there, you'll want to have a car. True, Memphis has a well-run bus system, but relying on the bus can prove time-consuming and not always very convenient. For a taxi you must call a cab company to arrange your rides, as it's generally not possible to hail a cab on the street.

To get your bearings from downtown, face the Mississippi River, which is west, looking into Arkansas. To the left is south Memphis, where you find Graceland and the airport, and just beyond, the state of Mississippi. Much of the city's residential and commercial growth throughout the years has been to the east, so that's where you'll find many of the city's homes, restaurants, hotels, and shopping centers.

For driving Memphis could be called a 20-minute city, since by taking the I-240 loop around the city, you can get just about anywhere except the far suburbs within 20 to 25 minutes. Avenues run east and west, including Poplar and Union, and streets run north and south, with the dividing line between north and south at Madison Avenue. Of course, traffic is always a wild card, and if it's bad, it can add considerably to the length of your trip.

Remember, if you get lost or need assistance in finding your way, don't hesitate to ask someone for help. You'll find that Memphians are very friendly and glad to give you directions.

Memphis isn't very well set up for biking. The city recently added a series of marked on-road bike-tour routes that, while useful for planning rides, have done little to increase cyclist safety. Memphis thoroughfares rarely have bike lanes, and local drivers aren't used to accommodating bicycles. Stick to the smaller streets, park bike paths, and less-busy thoroughfares (such as Jefferson and North Parkway) if you must rely on your bike to get around.

GETTING HERE

By Roadway

Two major interstate arteries cross at Memphis: I-40, which runs east and west, and I-55, which runs north and south. From the west and north, they converge in West Memphis, Arkansas, a town just across the river that seems like a huge truck plaza, given all the commercial traffic. Two highway bridges bring cars across the Mississippi into Memphis: the I-40 bridge, which crosses the Mississippi near the Pyramid Arena at the northern end of downtown, and the I-55 bridge, from which you take Riverside Drive to get downtown. I-40 East comes in past Wolfchase Galleria, the city's newest regional shopping mall, and feeds into the I-240 loop around Memphis. To go directly into the heart of the city from I-40 East, take Sam Cooper Boulevard. If you're coming in from Mississippi on I-55, you'll be well inside the city before you link up with Riverside for direct access into downtown (and a great view of the river). Alternatively, from I-55 you can take the I-240 loop near Graceland to reach other parts of the city.

Whichever route you take, you're likely to find a welcome center or visitor center on the way in. If you are coming in on I–55 North or I–40 East, you'll end up on Riverside Drive in downtown Memphis, where you'll find the Tennessee State Welcome Center. If you are driving on I–40 West, look for the Memphis/Shelby County Visitors Center at Arlington (exit 25) as you approach the city. South of Memphis is a welcome center on I–55 right at the Mississippi-Tennessee state line.

By Air

Memphis is well served by commercial airlines, with more than 600 departures and arrivals each day and an excellent on-time arrivals record; if anything, flights sometimes arrive early. Because Memphis is a Northwest Airlines hub, Memphis has direct flights to and from just about any U.S. city. At least seven other airlines serve the Memphis airport as well, and Northwest Airlines/KLM connects Memphis to Europe and beyond, flying daily to and from Amsterdam. On the cargo side Memphis International Airport has been the world's busiest cargo airport for the past decade by virtue of Federal Express, moving some 3.4 million tons of cargo in fiscal 2002. This hometown company has its SuperHub package-sorting facility at the

airport, and many companies have opened distribution centers near FedEx to expedite shipments. Memphis International Airport, attentive to future needs, has spent some $600 million during the last decade on capital improvements to runways, terminals, parking, and other areas.

The airport has three terminals, designed with a triangular pattern on the exterior so that from afar they resemble trays of martinis. Each has baggage claim on the ground floor and ticket counters, gates, shops, and restaurants on the second level.

When you fly out of Memphis International, it's generally a good idea to arrive an hour and a half early so there's plenty of time to get through security (as is the case with most major airports since September 11). Call your airline to find out exactly how much time they recommend that you allow. The wait at Memphis airport's security checkpoints can vary quite a bit, so if you breeze through in five minutes when taking one flight, don't assume that will be the case the next time you fly.

When your flight arrives at the airport, follow signs to the baggage-claim area on the ground floor. Skycap porters are available to handle your luggage for a minimum of 50 cents per bag; baggage carts are available from a vending machine ($3.00 in cash or paid with a major credit card, with a 25-cent reward for returning

---

Airlines Serving Memphis

AirTran, (800) 247-8726,
www.airtran.com

America West, (800) 235-9292,
www.americawest.com

American Airlines, (800) 433-7300,
www.aa.com

Continental Airlines, (800) 523-3273,
www.continental.com

Delta Air Lines, (800) 221-1212,
www.delta.com

Northwest Airlines/KLM,
(800) 225-2525, www.nwa.com

United Express, (800) 864-8331,
www.united.com

U.S. Airways, (800) 428-4322,
www.usairways.com

Note: Some operate commuter aircraft on certain flights.

the cart to the machine) in each terminal's baggage-claim area and throughout the terminals and parking areas.

Most of the stores, restaurants, and food stands are in Terminal B, but after mid-2005, you'll find a dramatically different lineup of places to eat and shop. That's because the airport and its vendors are completely reworking and updating the concessions, to the tune of $25 million. When it's finished, the main area will have a Memphis-style new look and an emphasis on local restaurants, including the hamburger-joint Huey's, bigger and better outlets for Interstate Bar-B-Q and Corky's Ribs & BBQ, and Grisanti's Bol a Pasta (see the Restaurants chapter for details on these Memphis favorites). Other food choices will include well-known names such as Ben & Jerry's Ice Cream and Einstein Bros. Bagels. There will be smaller concession areas with similar decor and offerings in Terminals A and C as well.

Meanwhile, until the concessions upgrades are complete, the choices are mostly fast-food restaurants and bars. And if you did not get your barbecue fix already, check out Interstate at gate B14, or Da Blues Memphis (featuring Corky's) near gate B34. That's where you can find these barbecue legends until they move to their new homes at the airport. Among the purveyors of coffee drinks is Starbucks, located near gate B8 and elsewhere.

Airport shopping, too, is changing, with a focus on Memphis attractions such as Sun Studio, the Memphis Zoo, local sports teams, and, of course, Elvis. National retailers include Godiva Chocolatier and PGA Golf Shop. A whole slew of services, including a hair salon, a travel agency, and a business center, are also available at the airport. Northwest Airlines has its World Club near the security checkpoint at Terminal B (for members only). For a complete listing of airport amenities, check out www.mscaa.com.

Smoking is not allowed in the airport terminals, except in the Bud Bar & Restaurant in Terminal B. P. J. O'Rourke's bar is making its home in the Terminal B ticket

Memphis International Airport's Blue Suede Service program dispatches a team of volunteers into the terminals to help passengers with directions, information about amenities, translation services, and other needs. Look for them dressed in khakis and blue vests. Call them at (901) 922-8000 or e-mail director Ruth Greene at Ruthg@mscaa.com with questions or requests.

lobby, and it, too, will allow smoking. Otherwise, smokers must go outside the terminal and at least 20 feet away from the public entrances to smoke.

GETTING FROM THE AIRPORT TO THE CITY

A taxi stand, courtesy shuttles, and other transportation are located outside the lower-level exits. If you are renting a car or intend to use your hotel's shuttle service, look for free indoor courtesy phones, just inside the door of each terminal's baggage-claim area. Call your hotel to let them know you arrived or to make reservations. At some point the airport will be working on the roadways and the areas outside the terminals, which may change traffic patterns.

CAR RENTAL

Car-rental agencies, which are located just off the airport property, have free shuttles that stop in the far lane outside the baggage area.

Alamo/National, (901) 332-8412
Avis, (901) 345-2847
Budget, (901) 398-8888
Dollar, (800) 800-4000
Enterprise, (901) 396-3736
Hertz, (901) 345-5680
Thrifty, (901) 345-0170

TAXIS AND HOTEL SHUTTLES

Taxis cost $1.60 for the first 1/8 mile, then 20 cents for each additional 1/8 mile, plus

50 cents for each extra passenger or luggage. A cab ride downtown costs about $23 plus tip. Try Yellow Cab or Checker Cab (901-577-7777) or Metro Cab (901-323-3333).

If you're staying downtown, a special airport shuttle (DASH) provides service to the downtown hotels for a cost of $20 round-trip or $12 one way. Many hotels operate free shuttles for their guests. Ask when you make your reservations or try the courtesy telephones in the airport baggage-claim area.

As for transportation back to the airport, ask your hotel's front desk for their recommendation. Often they have a shuttle or other arrangements for getting guests to the airport. You can call a taxi, but taxis don't always arrive on time, which can be pretty nerve-racking if you have a plane to catch. If you are dropping off a rental car, you'll probably want to allow an extra 15 minutes for the shuttle ride from the agency to the airport terminal.

By Train

Amtrak's *City of New Orleans* train stops in Memphis's Central Station on South Main Street, with service to New Orleans or Chicago. If you don't already have your tickets, it's best to arrive an hour early to buy them (the entrance is on Main Street). The northbound train leaves at 10:40 P.M. and arrives at 9:00 A.M., so you may want to invest in a sleeper car for a more comfortable trip. The southbound train leaves at 6:50 A.M. and arrives in New Orleans at 3:40 P.M. Call (800) 872-7245 or check out www.amtrak.com for more information. It's a good idea to call the station (901-526-0052) beforehand to make sure the train is on schedule.

By Bus

Greyhound Bus Lines offers service between Memphis and destinations across the country. The phone number for the downtown bus station is (901) 523-9253; or for reservations call (800) 231-2222. *Note:* The Greyhound bus station, which operates at 203 Union Avenue, will eventually move to a new location in south Memphis near the airport.

By Boat

The Delta Queen Steamboat Company operates paddle-wheel steamboat cruises on the Mississippi aboard the *Delta Queen* or one of her sisters, which stop in Memphis. For information call (800) 543-1949 or check out www.deltaqueen.com. River-Barge Excursion Lines (888-456-2206, www.riverbarge.com) operates barge cruises between Memphis and New Orleans or St. Louis (and other destinations starting in 2005).

General Aviation

Memphis International Airport has two fixed-based operators, Wilson Air Center (901-345-2992) and Signature Flight Support (901-345-4700). Both provide services to private and corporate aircraft, including fuel, repairs, hangar, and tie-down.

In addition, the airport authority operates two secondary general-aviation airports. General DeWitt Spain Airport is just north of downtown Memphis, and Charles W. Baker Airport is 22 miles north of Memphis International in Millington. Call (901) 873-1768 for information on services.

GETTING AROUND
By Car

Memphis likes to name its highways, but for some reason people never use the names. Although segments of the loop around the city have names including Avron B. Fogelman Expressway and Martin Luther King Expressway, locals always refer to it as I-240, 240, or the Expressway. Tourism officials have named I-40 between Memphis and Nashville Music Highway, but everybody else calls it I-40, or the Interstate. The leg of Highway 385 from East Memphis to Collierville was renamed Bill Morris Parkway, but everybody still calls it by its original name, Nonconnah Parkway, just plain Nonconnah, or sometimes 385. This no-nonsense freeway makes for a quick trip to southeast Memphis or Collierville.

If someone recommends that you take Sam Cooper Boulevard, they're referring to the newly widened freeway that connects midtown Memphis to I-40 East. This is a popular shortcut favored by midtowners to get out east. Another eccentricity in midtown and downtown is streets that stop and start. If you're in the 200 block of Jefferson Avenue in downtown Memphis, you can't drive straight east on Jefferson to reach an address in the 2000 block.

The main east/west arteries out of downtown are Union, Madison, and Poplar (locals always call them by their "first names," never adding Avenue). Union (not to be confused with Union Extended, a different street) turns into Walnut Grove Road, continuing east across I-240 to Shelby Farms Park, the International Agricenter, and Germantown. Madison dead-ends into East Parkway, just east of Overton Square, but a quick left, then right at the first light puts you onto Poplar. Poplar continues past I-240 through Germantown to Collierville, where it's renamed West Poplar and then turns into U.S. 72. (Any address with West Poplar is in Collierville.) Arteries that run north/south include Danny Thomas Boulevard just past downtown; Eastern Parkway in midtown; Highland just past midtown; Perkins, Mendenhall, White Station, and Ridgeway in East Memphis; and Germantown Parkway in Germantown.

Bear in mind that the law requires the use of seat belts for passengers and child-safety seats for children younger than age four. It's legal to turn right on red at an intersection, as long as you come to a

complete stop first. Look for signs, for turning right on red is prohibited at specified intersections. The speed limits vary, usually between 35 mph and 55 mph. Remember that if the stoplights aren't working at an intersection, it should be treated like a four-way stop.

Also, during the 2004–2006 time frame, parts of the interstate system in and around Memphis will be under construction. Spots to watch are the I-40/I-240 interchange between midtown and downtown, the section just south of that exchange to I-55, and the section between Highway 385 and Walnut Grove Road. In 2006 crews will be working on the I-40/I-240 interchange east of the city. Also east of the city there will be construction around U.S. 64, as crews build what will basically be an outer semiloop around the city. The work will be on the segment of Highway 385 between Collierville and I-40.

As you drive into town, look for detailed signs on how to avoid trouble spots. We recommend that before you come to Memphis, check out www.tennessee.gov/tdot for an update on construction and recommendations on how to avoid congested areas. The site also has information on weather-related conditions.

Also be aware that I-40 and I-55 have HOV lanes east and south of the city during rush hour to help manage traffic. During the posted hours the lanes are limited to vehicles with at least two passengers.

PARKING

Parking is free in most of the city, with the exception of downtown. While there's

The Tennessee Department of Transportation is a great resource for up-to-date maps of the state as well as cities and counties. The state map is free, but there's a charge for detailed city and county maps. To order a map, call (615) 741-2195 or log on to www.tdot.state.tn.us/maps.htm.

some parking on the streets (with meters), it's snatched up quickly, so parking lots in the area are usually your best bet. Downtown lots cost $2.00 to $7.00, except during big events, when the capitalist spirit pushes prices to $10.00 or whatever the market will bear. Parking meters are in use only during weekdays until 6:00 P.M., so don't worry about feeding the meters at other times. Pay attention if you park on the street during Redbirds games, when there are additional parking restrictions.

By Public Transportation

MATA BUSES

The Memphis Area Transit Authority operates air-conditioned buses throughout the city and the immediate suburbs. The base fare is $1.25 one way (exact change required; 10 cents extra if you transfer to another route). To find out how to get to a destination, call the MATA Hotline (901–274–6282) Monday through Saturday and press "0" to reach someone who will tell you exactly which bus or buses will take you there. You can also visit the MATA North End Terminal, 444 North Main Street (at the corner of Auction Avenue), for a map or directions. Disabled passengers can arrange transportation by calling MATAplus at (901) 722-7171.

MAIN STREET TROLLEY

The downtown trolley operates along Main Street and loops along the riverfront. A 2-mile extension takes you east along Madison Avenue past the medical center. The Riverfront Loop allows for an excellent panorama of the Mississippi River and also stops at the Tennessee Welcome Center and the Pyramid Arena. (For more details on the Main Street Trolley, see the Kidstuff chapter.)

Tickets are 50 cents per ride for all ages, except seniors and disabled persons, who pay 25 cents. You can also get a $2.50 daylong pass or a $6.00 three-day pass. Exact change is required. Call (901) 274-6282 for more information.

HISTORY 🏛

Location and transportation: These are the two main elements responsible for the founding of Memphis and its development and which continue to influence this Mississippi River city today.

This was true more than 1,000 years ago when Native Americans used crude stone tools to build a village on one of the high bluffs of the river and brought their canoes to navigate the waterway. It remains true now as this diverse multicultural community uses the latest high-tech equipment to move information, people, and services around the globe.

Between then and now, the city has repeatedly bounced back and forth between prosperity and ruin and has served as the capital of an area known as the Mid-South. This region can be defined as the area stretching 200 miles on all sides of the city. Throughout Memphis's history fascinating and legendary people have made their mark in the worlds of civil rights and politics (Ida Wells and Benjamin Hooks), literature (William Faulkner), entertainment (Elvis Presley and B. B. King), and business (Fred Smith with FedEx and Kemmons Wilson with Holiday Inns).

As frequently happens, this development occurred by chance because of the natural amenities provided by a small patch of land situated along a mighty river. People could either traverse the waterway or, due to the safety afforded by the bluffs from the catastrophic floods, settle here. This patch of land was known as the Fourth Chickasaw Bluff.

BIRTH OF THE BLUFF CITY

Hundreds of years before European explorers claimed the land upon which Memphis would eventually rise, Native Americans had a thriving culture. Evidence of this culture can be found at Chucalissa, an Indian village located just 6 miles south of where downtown Memphis bustles today. Although abandoned in the 1500s, Chucalissa was reconstructed in the late 1950s and now remains open as the Chucalissa Archaeological Museum and Reconstructed Indian Village. Guided tours provide a glimpse into what life was like for the area's first permanent settlers. (See the Attractions chapter for details.)

Like the people of European descent who would follow in their footsteps, the Native Americans built permanent settlements in the area because the high bluffs protected their shelters from floods. From the many remnants of graves, tools, weapons, and pottery found at Chucalissa, it is obvious that the Mid-South flourished as a center for trading, hunting, and farming for Indians for hundreds of years, but that began to change in the 1500s.

In 1541 Hernando DeSoto led his army to the Mississippi River, although exactly where along the river is still debated to this day. Most historians, however, agree that DeSoto's party was the first group of Europeans to view the lower half of the river and that they made camp somewhere near Memphis. Although DeSoto claimed this area for Spain, for the next 200 years the ownership of the Memphis area changed hands and was held by the English and the French as well. Eventually it was made the westernmost border of North Carolina, and in 1796 this area was included as part of Tennessee, the 16th state admitted to the Union.

An interesting footnote is that when the Fourth Chickasaw Bluff was home to an American frontier outpost known as Fort Adams, its commandant, Capt. Meriwether Lewis, was visited by a friend named William Clark. Little did they know that five years later the two men, at the request of President Jefferson, would come to the banks of the Mississippi River again—although farther north—to begin their famous expedition.

Even though various outposts were built on the Fourth Chickasaw Bluff, the city of Memphis didn't come into existence until the 1800s. In 1818 the Chickasaw Indians sold the land encompassing Memphis to the United States, resolving once and for all the question of ownership. That same year, three entrepreneurs decided to become absentee landlords of their own city, which they decided to name Memphis.

Future president Andrew Jackson joined with two other middle Tennesseans, John Overton and James Winchester, and together this trio of entrepreneurs not only recognized the two natural geographical advantages—high bluffs and harbor access created by the convergence of the Wolf and Mississippi Rivers—but also were foresighted enough to see the financial possibilities of erecting a city there. In May 1819 the three founders ordered a survey of a 5,000-acre tract on the banks of the river, which would form the heart of downtown Memphis. A mere five months after this survey, a new county named Shelby was carved into the southwest corner of Tennessee. (Within a few years Andrew Jackson sold his share to a fourth entrepreneur, John G. McLemore, who later became president of the first railroad built in Memphis.)

The state may have had a new county, but this county still needed a name for its laid-out-on-paper city. Like many of the nation's early settlers and founders, the fathers of this new city turned to their history books to find a name suitable for this new river town. In these books they settled on the name "Memphis," which seemed especially appropriate as it was originally the name of a once-thriving metropolis on the banks of the Nile River in ancient Egypt. The Egyptian word translates roughly as "place of good abode."

By naming the new city Memphis, the founders conjured images of a great cosmopolitan town for this fledging community. Of course, during its first decades, Memphis was anything but a thriving, progressive city. The city was officially incorporated in 1826, and shortly before that, when the first census was conducted in 1820, Memphis was a small village of only 663 residents. At the time Memphis wasn't much more than a rowdy settlement for transients. Many viewed the city as little more than an outpost as they passed through Memphis on their way to explore the Wild West, which started just across the river in Arkansas. Memphis was also frequented by river men, who stopped for a night or two as they dropped off or picked up goods for their steamboats or flatboats.

Memphis may have been a backwater hamlet, but it was on the verge of a boom: The city's population nearly tripled by the time the 1840 census came around.

The primary economic force responsible for this population explosion was the so-called "white gold." Cotton was quickly becoming king of the Mid-South's agrarian economy. Built on the backs of slave labor, the cotton trade was so profitable that ambitious planters quickly moved in and planted thousands of acres. In 1825, 300 bales of cotton were recorded in Memphis. Just 15 years later cotton merchants reported 35,000 bales shipped from Memphis. By 1850 Memphis was acknowledged as the largest inland cotton market in the world. In 1859, the eve of the Civil War, more than 400,000 bales of cotton were transported out of Memphis. In the time since its birth on the banks of the Mississippi River just four decades earlier, Memphis had become one of the nation's busiest river ports, rivaling New Orleans to the south and St. Louis to the north. The Bluff City's population had grown from nothing more than a crowd to a lively metropolis of more than 22,000. Most of the growth was due to the valuable commodity known as cotton. But Memphis's economic success came at a high price. It had been built on an inhuman foundation of slavery, and this foundation was about to crumble. In the process, the young nation was ripped apart.

THE CIVIL WAR YEARS

With its strategic location on the Mississippi River, its strong economy, and its designation by the 1860 federal census as the 38th-largest city in the nation, Memphis would prove to be a valuable asset to whichever side—the Union or the Confederacy—had possession of it.

Of course, given its location in the Deep South, once the Civil War began in earnest, Memphians were firmly on the side of the Confederacy. When shortly after the war began there was a vote on the matter, the voters of Memphis spoke unanimously: A mere five voters in Memphis cast ballots against secession.

In 1861 a Confederate army headquarters and supply depot was established in Memphis. Many of the city's 22,600 people signed up to join the Army of the Confederacy. Some 72 Confederate companies were formed by the Memphis recruits. Initially, Memphians were confident the war would end quickly and favorably for the Confederacy. That point of view, however, proved short-lived.

In 1862 Union naval forces gathered on the river not far from Memphis, and the Confederate gunboats prepared to defend the city. As daylight broke across the river on June 6, hundreds of Memphians lined the bluffs to witness what they were sure would be the swift defeat of the Union forces. Yet just two hours after the first shots were fired, the Union vessels had soundly defeated the Confederates. That afternoon, the Confederate flag was lowered, and the U.S. flag once again flew over the city. Memphis had returned to the Union only 363 days after its residents had voted to secede.

The Confederate army headquarters and supply depot quickly became a Union headquarters and supply depot. Memphis also became a prisoner-of-war center. The victorious Union leaders soon learned that a military occupation of Memphis was not the same as a city voluntarily rejoining the United States. First Gen. Ulysses S. Grant and then Gen. William T. Sherman found out for themselves how hard it was to actually retain control over the citizenry. Memphis merchants quickly adapted to the occupation and discovered that Union money was as good as, if not better than, Confederate money since many Yankees paid in gold and silver. Although they may have been under Union occupation, many members of the local business community remained loyal to the Confederacy. Thus, much of the money businesses earned by Memphians trading with the Union ended up back in the hands of the Confederates, which the Southern army then used to buy the supplies that allowed it to continue its war with the Union. Although Grant and Sherman tried one initiative after the other to stop the flow of money and/or contraband from Memphis to the Confederacy, neither one had much success.

One of the most stubborn supporters of the Confederacy was a local newspaper, *The Appeal* (forerunner of today's *Commercial Appeal*). Following the fall of Memphis in 1862, the newspaper operators gathered up their presses and fled to Mississippi. In order to continue to provide the news from a Confederate point of view and avoid capture, the newspaper staff was forced to relocate continually throughout the Civil War.

It wasn't until the final weeks of the war that the support for the Confederate army waned in the Memphis community. By this time it was clear that the South was going to lose the war, and the Memphis economy was gradually grinding to a halt.

When the war ended in 1865, Memphis had managed to avoid the serious damage experienced by many of its sister cities in the South. For instance, it wasn't torched like Atlanta, and, because the battle for Memphis was over so quickly and took place only on the river, the city wasn't terrorized by artillery fire like Richmond, Virginia, or Vicksburg, Mississippi. Although a horrific four-year-long civil war left little mark on Memphis, a tiny mosquito was about to harm the city in ways that the war did not.

CLOSE-UP

An Early Experiment: The Nashoba Plantation Colony

Although not generally regarded as a hotbed of progressive politics or a haven for freethinkers, Memphis was the site of one of the nation's earliest interracial communes. And, of all things, the founder of this utopian colony was a woman.

Frances Wright, a native of Scotland, was a freethinker and someone who was years ahead of her time. She left Scotland and traveled around much of the United States in the 1820s, observing the people and absorbing the culture of this new nation. She made a favorable impression on many of the leading intellectuals of the day, including Ralph Waldo Emerson.

One aspect of this new nation that truly appalled her was the institution of slavery. Wright eventually made her way to an area located near what would soon become Memphis, Tennessee (and presently is in Germantown, Tennessee), and there in 1825 she founded the Nashoba Plantation Colony.

Wright's plan was to establish a community where slaves could earn their freedom by living and working on this plantation. Her long-range goal was to have others replicate this colony in other parts of the country so that over time, slavery would eventually disappear.

Before this radical Nashoba Plantation concept could move much beyond the planning stages, however, Wright was forced to return to Scotland due to illness. Although others had promised to fulfill Wright's dream, the colony foundered without the strong leadership and vision provided by Wright herself.

The Nashoba experiment was abandoned, but the name "Nashoba" is still used by developers and businesspeople in Germantown.

YELLOW FEVER

Memphis's location along the Mississippi River may be responsible for the city's founding and success, but it also harbored the cause of a disease that would almost destroy the city. Along with its desirable bluffs, Memphis had swampy areas and lowlands that flooded. Both types of terrain formed ideal breeding grounds for mosquitoes. The unsanitary conditions of the formative decades of Memphis had made the city prone to diseases such as cholera, dengue, dysentery, and smallpox. Worst of all, however, was the mosquito population that spread yellow fever, or as it was commonly called, yellow jack.

The first reported yellow-fever epidemic to strike Memphis occurred shortly after the city was incorporated in 1826, and it returned every few years. While these earlier epidemics were responsible for the deaths of hundreds of Memphians, it wasn't until after the Civil War that the city found out just how devastating yellow fever could be.

During the 1873 epidemic 5,000 cases were reported, and 2,000 deaths were attributed to yellow fever. But yellow jack would prove even more deadly five years later. In 1878 it seemed as if the mosquitoes would not be content until they had wiped out the human population of the city. Records of that year indicate that

17,600 cases of yellow fever were treated in Memphis. Of these, however, 5,150 perished. The next year, the city experienced yet another bout of yellow-fever cases, although on a lesser scale. A mere 2,000 cases were treated, and only 600 yellow-fever deaths were reported. By the time of the climactic 1878 yellow-fever epidemic, so panicked were the citizens of the city that one month after the first yellow-fever death was reported, fewer than 20,000 residents remained in the city. Most of those who were able fled the city.

Memphis had been hit so hard by the sickness and death that the city's economy was a catastrophe. The city was forced to declare bankruptcy and surrender its charter, thereby being reduced to a state taxing district in 1879.

By this time the population no longer had a city, but the leaders of the community now knew what was needed to return Memphis to the thriving metropolis it once had been: a massive upgrading and sanitizing of the city's water and sewer system. Memphis may have been at its lowest point in its 60-year history. But it was repositioning itself to be revitalized and ready for the modern 20th century that was just around the corner.

MEMPHIS REBORN

As the 19th century came to a close, so did Memphis's economic hard times and its reputation as an unsanitary and disease-ridden community. The Bluff City still contained some untamed, crime-infested pockets, and the white, male leaders certainly retained plenty of the conservative, often racist views shared by their counterparts in many other Southern cities (especially their views of African Americans). Nevertheless, compared with the squalid conditions and backward, corrupt political systems in Memphis just a few short years before, the city in 1900 was entering one of its most progressive periods.

Following the devastating yellow-fever epidemics of the 1870s, Memphis officials could no longer ignore the importance of providing clean water and a sanitary sewer system, so in the 1880s, the city began a major push to make the community more sanitary. It built a sewer system and began testing the water supply located deep beneath the city. Memphis began supplying its residents and businesses with clean, safe drinking water through artesian wells. The city's ample supply of pure artesian-springs well water continues to serve as a key economic development tool to city officials in the 21st century.

A number of other infrastructure-improvement projects began in the 1890s that helped boost the city's reputation in the nation and made it more attractive to businesses and families. The first electric streetcar was inaugurated. The Frisco Bridge was completed in 1892, thereby becoming the first bridge to span the Mississippi River south of St. Louis. A public library was opened, a new general hospital was built, and competing street rail lines entered the Memphis market. In 1895 the city's first steel skyscraper, the Porter Building, was such a wonder to the local community that many residents eagerly paid 10 cents to ride on the "high-speed" elevator. The 11-story structure remains in use downtown.

Another important improvement program involved the community's investment in public education. Between 1890 and 1910, 23 new schools were constructed, including 4 for black students. Providing public schools for blacks is notable for a number of reasons. Since 1864, the city had provided a public education for African Americans and was finally making a financial commitment as well. Also, these new schools reflected the steadily growing number of blacks moving into Memphis. This agrarian-based community had relied on slave labor in its formative years, but with the Civil War and its subsequent reconstruction era, Memphis became popular with freed blacks. The city's minority population swelled even more when mechanization forced thousands of black farmers and farmhands to move to the city to find jobs. Through the first half of the 20th century, African Americans continued to find Memphis a fairly agreeable city in which to enjoy a modest, if second-class, quality of life.

Of course, although there were rare exceptions, by and large, blacks were denied leadership roles in the community. Robert Church became a millionaire and city leader, but for every successful black businessperson such as Church, thousands of other minority store owners and operators were ignored by white business leaders. And for every social reformer such as Ida B. Wells, hundreds of other civil rights advocates in the black community were never given an opportunity to raise their voices. Still, the cultural and economic impact of this burgeoning segment of the population cannot be underestimated. During this time blues and jazz were born, and the sounds of these new musical genres could be heard on Beale Street and other parts of Memphis where blacks congregated for social interaction. (See the African-American Heritage and Memphis Music chapters for more details on these subjects.)

By 1900 the city's population hit 102,320, topping the 100,000 mark for the first time and making it a top-tier Southern metropolis. The city also had managed to have its charter, which was lost in 1879, restored in 1893. In this atmosphere of change, a young man named Edward Hull Crump from north Mississippi walked onto the political stage of Memphis. He wouldn't budge from this stage for nearly 50 years, and faint traces of his fingerprints can still be found on the city.

THE CRUMP YEARS (1909–1954)

E. H. Crump, or "Boss Crump" as he is most often referred to, established a political machine that managed to implement some much-needed public improvements. Yet he often relied on questionable political tactics to do so.

Crump was elected mayor of Memphis in 1909 and was ousted from the mayor's office just six years later. Yet, for more than three decades after he left his position as mayor, Crump still pulled the political strings in Memphis and Shelby County. Until his death in 1954, Crump was a powerful political force in local, state, and even national politics.

When he was elected mayor of Memphis, Crump touted himself as a reformer. At that time Memphis was infamously known as the "murder capital" of the nation after a 1912 study found that the city had 47.1 homicides per 100,000 population compared with the national average of 7.2 homicides per 100,000. (Later, Prudential Insurance Co. of America found that in 1916 Memphis had a jaw-dropping 89.9 homicides per 100,000, more than twice as many as its nearest competitor.)

Crump pledged to clean up the city by clamping down on saloons, gambling halls, and houses of ill repute. He managed to get elected mayor, but only by a margin of 78 votes. Sure enough, shortly after taking office, Crump did crack down on the dives, crap games, and prostitutes. It is worth noting, however, that during his time as mayor, the murder rate of Memphis continued to climb. It was not by accident that whenever election time approached, Crump would loosen his grip on the enforcement of these laws, and once again the booze would flow, the dice would roll, and the streetwalkers would stroll. Ironically, while Crump was elected as someone who would rid the city of vice, he ended up being ousted from the mayor's office by an act of the state legislature on a charge that he wouldn't enforce the state liquor laws.

Even though he was forced out of the mayor's office in 1916, by some shrewd political maneuvering he had the city commissioners appoint his hand-picked successor to the office. Just six months after resigning as mayor, Crump was elected County Trustee, and, some years later, he was elected to two terms to Congress. Whether in an elected office or out, Crump ran a highly organized political machine.

Crump not only influenced who got elected in Memphis and Shelby County, but his ability to "deliver" the voters of the city and county in state and federal races also allowed him to have an effect on races for governor and Congress.

During the Crump era Memphis did enjoy much prosperity and growth. One of Crump's most hard-fought initiatives and proudest accomplishments was wresting control of the utility services from the private sector into the hands of local government. The repercussions of this Crump achievement are enjoyed by every resident and business in Memphis today in the form of high levels of service and some of the lowest costs in the United States, because the city continues to own and operate Memphis Light, Gas & Water, the largest three-service municipal utility in the nation.

The Crump era began shortly before World War I and ended shortly after World War II. Like other American cities during these wars, Memphians rallied to the defense of the nation as patriotic pledges were renewed.

Anti-German sentiments grew so strong during World War I that the city of Germantown, essentially a suburb of Memphis, temporarily changed its name to Nashoba. In Millington, a city just north of Memphis, Park Field was used as a training field for World War I pilots. When World War II came along, Park Field officially became the Millington Naval Air Base.

Between the world wars many Memphians participated in the prosperous years of the 1920s. However, even more Memphians participated in the economic downturn period known as the Great Depression. When the stock market crashed in 1929, the price of cotton fell as well. Since much of the city's economy was still tied to the cotton industry, businesses throughout Memphis were hurt. With the financial means of the private sector severely limited, the federal government stepped in to pump money into the local economy. During the 1930s some $20 million in work-relief construction projects were started in the city.

The cotton market improved when World War II erupted, and that meant the Memphis economy was regaining its strength. Once again the city mobilized in support of the war effort. Its young men signed up for the various branches of the armed services, and the civilians at home did their part by supporting war-bond drives. Several defense-related industries had started operating in Memphis even before the war started, but once the United States entered the war, these businesses flourished. The city's economy also got a boost as a result of the thousands of naval personnel who were stationed at the Millington base. World War II also provided Memphis with one of its most enduring symbols—the *Memphis Belle*. The *Memphis Belle* was the first B-17 to complete 25 missions. The bomber and its crew logged more than 20,000 combat miles and dropped more than 60 tons of bombs during World War II. All missions were completed without a single casualty. This famed bomber, named for Memphian Margaret Polk, is considered the most celebrated bomber of the war.

Although World War II ended, the boom in the Memphis economy didn't. Crump continued to push for economic development and was not satisfied to wait for industry to come to the city; instead, he took a proactive approach to business recruitment. One of the last Crump initiatives was the development of Presidents Island, a peninsula jutting out into the Mississippi River just south of the downtown section of the city. This area remains the most industrialized corner of Memphis.

It's interesting to note that in the 1950s, Memphis had a slightly larger population than Atlanta (Memphis had 396,000 inhabitants compared with 331,314 for Atlanta, according to the 1950 census). The subsequent development of Atlanta into the Capital of the New South, with a metro population of more than four million people compared with little more than one million in the present-day Memphis metro area, has been thought-provoking for city leaders, and has led some to question whether Memphis might not have pushed harder during that time to attract more new industry.

Although the Crump political era did eventually fade, the Memphis business community has steadily moved forward at its own pace.

A BRIEF HISTORY OF MEMPHIS BUSINESS

As the local adage affirms, cotton was certainly king in Memphis and was instrumental in the city's development. This commodity continues to provide hundreds of jobs and millions of dollars to the community, but other products and services have played an equally important role in the city's economy.

For example, after the Civil War Memphis became home to one of the nation's largest hardwood lumber industries. By the start of the 20th century, Memphis officials adopted the slogan that the city was the "First Hardwood Market" in the nation. At that time more than 500 lumber mills operated within a 100-mile radius of Memphis, producing more than one billion feet of lumber a year. Naturally, with all the lumber in the region, spin-off industries blossomed, including furniture manufacturers. The Mid-South continues to be a center for furniture production in the United States in the 21st century.

Manufacturing thrived in Memphis for about 100 years after the Civil War. The city became an attractive place in which to relocate a plant from the North for two reasons: a cheap labor market and a centrally located distribution network.

Because it was surrounded by hundreds of miles of rural farmlands, Memphis attracted workers, black and white, from throughout the Mid-South who were losing their jobs due to the mechanization of farming. These unskilled laborers were willing to work for wages much lower than their counterparts in many other parts of the United States. Memphis economic-development officials never hesitated to

tout the cost savings a company could realize by moving their production lines to the Bluff City.

With the river at its doorstep, Memphis has always been attractive to businesses that needed to move their goods by water. Today, of course, a strong, well-developed infrastructure of air, rail, and trucking transportation provides other equally desirable means of moving cargo and makes Memphis an important hub for intermodal transport.

From the riverboats of yesteryear to the barges of today, Memphis has consistently been one of the busiest inland ports in the nation. It has the fourth-largest inland port in the nation, and the Memphis harbor contains 44 private terminals and 8 public terminals.

With the advent of the locomotive, rail lines tended to traverse Memphis, once again enhancing the city's transportation amenities. It was out of Memphis, of course, that the legendary Casey Jones made his final run on the Illinois Central. Today, this is still one of the top U.S. cities for railroad traffic. The city continues to be served by passenger rail service, too, with Amtrak's *City of New Orleans* running daily between New Orleans and Chicago.

Once automobiles became the rage and a highway system was developed, Memphis found itself a key crossroads for the nation. The nation's major north/south interstate route for the central United States, I-55, runs through Memphis, as does I-40, the nation's major east/west route across the country. Another seven U.S. highways converge in Memphis, and one of the nation's most ambitious new road projects, I-69, will pass through Memphis as it connects Toronto, Canada, with Monterrey, Mexico.

Naturally, this combination of a central location and confluence of major highways and interstates has proved to be a fertile breeding ground for truck companies. At last count more than 300 motor-freight companies are operating in Memphis.

Finally, with the dramatic growth in air transportation, especially air cargo, in the

Clarence Saunders, the Founder of the Modern Supermarket

Few people realize it, but Memphis is the birthplace of the modern supermarket.

In 1916 entrepreneur Clarence Saunders opened the first Piggly Wiggly grocery store on Jefferson Avenue, between Front and Main Streets, in downtown Memphis. The store contained a feature that few shoppers had ever seen before: self-service. Previously, shoppers would typically enter a store with a list, tell clerks what they wanted, and clerks would pick the merchandise for them from the store shelves and bins. At Piggly Wiggly they picked the items themselves. Saunders took his modern approach a step further. He figured out how best to accommodate shoppers and patented his own "traffic-flow pattern."

Whatever he did worked. By 1923, just seven years later, 2,600 Piggly Wiggly grocery stores dotted the nation.

Saunders became a millionaire, and in the early 1920s he started building a 22-room mansion to be constructed with pink marble. He spent about $1 million on his grand home, which would feature such lavish elements as an indoor swimming pool and a bowling alley.

Saunders's prosperity did not last. In 1923 he lost the company and found himself penniless. As a result, he also lost the mansion, dubbed the Pink Palace because of the pink-marble construction. Saunders tried other ventures over the years, notably, a grocery store with an electronic picking system called Keedoozle, but none met with the success of Piggly Wiggly.

The city of Memphis now owns his home, still known as the Pink Palace, where an IMAX theater, a planetarium, and a popular museum make their home. Appropriately, the museum contains a permanent exhibit that features a replica of Saunders's pioneering self-service Piggly Wiggly grocery store.

past 50 years, Memphis has found itself ideally suited to take advantage of its location in the central part of the United States. While many cargo airlines operate in Memphis, the internationally renowned FedEx was founded here in 1972 by Fred Smith. At present, FedEx is the city's largest employer with some 30,000 locally based employees.

FedEx's enormous volume of packages plus the concentration of air cargo companies make Memphis International Airport the world's busiest cargo airport. So, it's no surprise that companies as diverse as Williams-Sonoma, SBC Datacomm, and Pfizer have opened distribution centers here to take advantage of these outstanding transportation resources.

THE CIVIL RIGHTS ERA

The city's unique location and transportation advantages have certainly served as the backbone of the Memphis economy for decades, but these two natural elements have also served as a key backdrop to what is perhaps this area's unifying feature when it comes to its people: the struggle for racial equality and harmony.

The city's population has almost always had a large percentage of black residents, and after the Civil War, this segment of the community gradually increased. During the Jim Crow era of the 1880s to the 1950s, within the city limits of Memphis were, essentially, two cities: one for whites and one for blacks. Whites may have held all the elected positions and other leadership positions generally recognized by the white media, but within the black community, neighborhood, education, business, and religious leaders have played important roles. Yet few of these black leaders were recognized by the white establishment, and blacks were forced to remain second-class citizens, a situation that began to change after World War II.

From the pulpits of black churches, and, eventually, to the ballot boxes, community centers, and union halls, a call for equality started to be heard. While the civil rights movement was gaining momentum in other large urban centers in the South in the late 1950s and early 1960s, Memphis seemed to avoid stepping onto that emotional and all-too-often dangerous stage. Yet by the mid-1960s, black leaders in Memphis had managed to quietly and nonviolently integrate many of the city's public facilities. Then the city's racial struggles took center stage, as the city's black sanitation workers went on strike, and Rev. Martin Luther King Jr. came to Memphis in 1968 to support their cause. The city's black sanitation workers had walked off their jobs in protest of what they claimed were discriminatory work conditions and wages.

While in Memphis, Dr. King was shot down in front of the Lorraine Motel on April 4, 1968. The assassination of King shocked the nation, set off riots in many major cities, and shook the morale of Memphis, particularly in the black community. The city was forced to confront the complicated issues associated with racial intolerance and inequality unlike it had at any other time in its history. (See the African-American Heritage chapter for more details.)

Yet, during the 1960s in Memphis, anyone who stepped outside of City Hall and simply turned on the radio would have heard less political rhetoric about integration and instead discovered the sound of integration in practice. The black and white musicians in places such as Stax Records and Sun Studio showed Memphis and people all around the world what a beautiful noise could be made when they worked it out together. (See the Memphis Music chapter for more information about the golden era of music making in Memphis.)

As the inspired and talented people at Stax and Hi Records were amassing an enormous music catalog during the late 1960s and early 1970s, Memphis itself was expanding its catalog of new neighborhoods. Every few years city officials were gobbling up more neighborhoods as the community grew eastward. With the river on the west and the Mississippi state line to the south, about the only direction the city could move was east. People moved farther east at a rapid pace, and as they did, the jobs followed.

As a result, the once-vibrant downtown section of Memphis, like many other urban centers around the nation, was all but abandoned.

MODERN MEMPHIS TAKES SHAPE

During the late 1960s and early 1970s, the political landscape and the community began to change. The public schools were integrated during this time, and while there were heated arguments and hints of violence when they were forced to integrate, the so-called "busing" program was implemented with far more ease than integration efforts in many other urban cities such as Boston and Little Rock.

At the same time the city's African-American political leaders began to rise to the top. Blacks started being elected, first to local political bodies such as the school board and city council, and then to national offices. Beginning in the 1970s the machine politics formerly so common in the white community became popular in the black community with the emergence of the Ford family. Harold Ford Sr. and his brothers began getting elected to local, state, and national offices in the early 1970s. During this time a political dynasty was formed that continues to this day.

On the surface little seemed to happen in Memphis during the 1970s. Instead of progress, many of the best attributes of the city seemed to be dying. The hugely popular and influential Memphis sound grew faint with the closing of Stax Records. Beale Street's lascivious luster had long since faded. Downtown was on life support, and the city even lost its most famous son when Elvis Presley died in 1977 at age 42.

But just as Elvis's career was to rise after his death, Memphis was about to launch its own comeback. During the 1970s a new vision for the city came into view. Community leaders agreed on the need to revitalize downtown and bring back Beale Street. Once-glamorous, The Peabody hotel had been shuttered, but it was about to get new owners and a new life. And a little overnight delivery company named Federal Express was founded, which was destined to remake the city's economy and bring Memphis closer to the rest of the world.

As Memphis moved into the 1980s, city leaders began to finally realize the enormous appeal of Memphis's one-of-a-kind music history and began to build the tourism business around this unique advantage. Graceland and Sun Studio were opened to the public as tourist attractions. Money was pumped into Beale Street redevelopment. Capitalizing on its odd Egyptian namesake, city leaders decided to fund the construction of a new pyramid-shaped arena that would rise from the banks of the river.

The city managed well during the economic recession of the late 1970s and early 1980s (and those that followed in later years), mainly because it has such a diverse base of businesses. Because Memphis has this mix of medical, government, agriculture, distribution, manufacturing, retail, and tourism industries, it never suffers too seriously during an economic downturn. On the other hand, during the periodic boom periods experienced by many other parts of the country, the Memphis economy never seems to explode either.

While the city's business economy remained relatively stable in the 1980s and 1990s, Memphis's political landscape changed drastically.

In 1992 the city's former school superintendent, Willie Herenton, surprised virtually all the local election prognosticators by unseating Dick Hackett, Memphis's popular white mayor, and becoming the first elected black mayor in the city's history. Herenton's first dramatic mayoral victory was achieved with fewer than 200 votes. In three subsequent city elections, however, Herenton has been reelected by wide margins, proving how popular he has become with both white and black voters.

In 1996 U.S. Representative Harold Ford Sr. retired from Congress, but his son, Harold Ford Jr., was elected in his place. Representative Ford Jr., now in his 30s, is viewed as one of the most astute young political leaders in the nation today and appears poised for much success in the future.

A 21ST-CENTURY CITY

Memphis has momentum as it enters the 21st century. The 2000 U.S. Census reveals a city of more than 650,000 that not only has about the same percentage of white and black residents but also a population that is becoming much more culturally diverse. The city's Hispanic and Asian-American populations are rapidly expanding, and business and community leaders from both these segments are emerging. With the election in 2003 of attorney A C Wharton Jr. as Shelby County mayor, blacks continue to play a key role in area politics and government.

Read about Memphis History

For more information on the history of Memphis, you may want to check out these books, which provide some of the information for this chapter:

- *Memphis during the Progressive Era 1900–1917,* by William D. Miller; the Memphis State University Press, Memphis, Tennessee; the American History Research Center, 1957.
- *Metropolis of the American Nile,* by John E. Harkins; the Guild Bindery Press, 1982.
- *Mr. Crump of Memphis,* by William D. Miller; Louisiana State University Press, 1964.
- *Yesterday's Memphis,* by Charles W. Crawford; E.A. Seeman Publishing, Inc., 1976.

Other books about Memphis history:

- *At the River I Stand: Memphis, the 1968 Strike and Dr. Martin Luther King, Jr.,* by Joan Turner Beifuss; Carlson Publishing, 1989.
- *Memphis: In Black and White,* by Beverly G. Bond and Janann Sherman; Arcadia Publishing, 2003.
- *Memphis Memoirs,* by Paul R. Coppock; Memphis State University Press, 1980.
- *Race, Power, and Political Emergence in Memphis,* by Sharon D. Wright; Garland Publishing, Inc., 2000.

The city's efforts in reviving downtown Memphis after decades of neglect and economic stagnation are paying off. The city's downtown is now thriving. Not only are businesses returning to the oldest section of Memphis, but new residential development also is attracting hundreds of new homeowners and apartment dwellers to downtown. The city continues to expand outward as well. Memphis's rich musical heritage still attracts visitors, while its music scene continues to produce great performers, most recently, pop star Justin Timberlake, rap group Three 6 Mafia, and a critically acclaimed comeback CD by soul legend Al Green. Memphis recently completed construction of FedExForum, a downtown arena home for the NBA's Grizzlies team, which moved to Memphis in 2001. The Redbirds' stadium continues to bring families and other baseball fans downtown during the season. The next downtown focal point is the riverfront. Officials are discussing the investment of some $300 million in a revitalization of the city's historic riverfront area under the watchful eye of a citizens group that includes descendants of Memphis founder John Overton. Plans also are well under way to build a multimillion-dollar biotech research park in the city's medical-center area, where it will join the University of Tennessee's medical school and a number of hospitals.

Given its diverse economic base, reenergized downtown, prospering suburban communities, and improved racial and cultural environment, Memphis appears headed toward a healthy future.

ACCOMMODATIONS

emphis has some 20,000 hotel rooms at all price levels. At the top are The Peabody, one of the South's premier grand hotels, and the Madison Hotel, a swank luxury hotel. You'll find plenty of comfortable accommodations here, including a handful of bed-and-breakfast inns, but for the most part, it isn't a travel destination you would choose for its quaint inns (such as St. Augustine, Florida) or fabulous hotels (such as San Francisco).

Memphis is the birthplace of the modern hotel. The whole concept of standardized lodging originated here in 1952, when local entrepreneur Kemmons Wilson opened the first Holiday Inn. Even though the idea of a brand-name hotel chain, with hotels that are the same from city to city, is commonplace today, at that time it was radical. As befits the birthplace of the chain hotel, the city has many familiar lodging names representing every major hotel company. You'll notice more Hampton Inn properties here than in most cities this size, because its parent company was once headquartered here.

In this chapter we list hotels in five areas of the city: downtown, medical center/midtown, East Memphis, southeast Memphis, and the Graceland/airport area (south Memphis). Downtown is home to most tourist attractions, including Beale Street, but if you choose to stay outside this area, you still won't be too far away. By taking the I-240 loop around the city, no destination is more than 20 or 25 minutes away, except the far suburbs. It can sometimes take longer, as Memphis has its share of traffic problems.

We don't list hotels in the far suburbs, although you'll find many chains represented at the exits along I-40 and I-55 as you come into town. If you come in from Arkansas via I-40 West and I-55 North, most of the hotels you'll see cater to truck-

ers rather than leisure travelers. Along I-40 East familiar chain hotels are clustered around the exits, particularly Sycamore View (exit 12), Germantown Parkway (exit 16), and U.S. 64/Bartlett (exit 18). Exits 16 and 18 are convenient to Wolfchase Galleria, the city's best regional mall, and other shopping, as well as the Agricenter International, where events such as the Ducks Unlimited Great Outdoors Festival take place. You'll find Wingate Inn (800-228-1000), Comfort Inn (800-228-5150), and LaQuinta Inn (800-531-5900), among others, at Germantown Parkway and at U.S. 64, Holiday Inn Express (800-HOLIDAY), Country Inn & Suites by Carlson (800-456-4000), and others. The Sycamore View exit has Baymont Inn and Suites (877-229-6668), Holiday Inn (800-HOLIDAY), and other options. If you don't see your favorite hotel chain listed, check out its Web site or call its reservations number.

Near the airport at the Millbranch Road exit of I-240, you'll find Baymont (877-BAYMONT), Best Western (800-780-7234), and Hampton Inn (800-HAMPTON), although they're in a gritty industrial area. In the neighboring office-park area of Nonconnah Boulevard, you'll find Courtyard by Marriott (800-321-2211) and Homestead Studio Suites (800-STAYHSD), both well-maintained hotels that offer good values on weekends if you don't mind an office-park setting.

Although bed-and-breakfast inns are rare within the city limits, they can be found, along with at least one country inn, farther out. We list a few, but you can also check our Day Trips chapter or your favorite B&B Web site or directory for other options near Memphis.

Downtown Memphis is the most convenient place to stay if you're taking in the sights, partying on Beale Street, or attending an event on the riverfront or at the

Memphis Cook Convention Center. You can walk or take the Main Street Trolley to Beale Street, the convention center, and top attractions, including the Rock 'n' Soul Museum, National Civil Rights Museum, and The Peabody with its famous ducks—a plus that easily outweighs the fact that some downtown guest rooms are a bit smaller and more expensive than their sub-urban counterparts. Downtown is by far the most pedestrian-friendly place to stay, and probably the only area where you won't miss having a car. It's also the most popular.

As you go east, you'll find a few options in the medical-center and midtown areas. Basically, though, there's a gap of about 10 miles as you go east on Poplar between the downtown cluster of hotels and the next concentration of rooms at or near I–240 in East Memphis.

East Memphis offers many lodging choices, including apartment-like digs at extended-stay hotels. Many are clustered around the intersection of Poplar Avenue and I–240, easily accessible by car, taxi, or the hotels' free airport shuttles. They're convenient to events such as the FedEx St. Jude Classic.

The area also has great restaurants and shopping at Oak Court Mall and other cen-ters. It's home to many schools, so on the weekends the hotels draw student sports teams and their families in town for games and tournaments.

Southeast Memphis is within a few miles of the airport and Graceland. You'll find some lodging options clustered at the Perkins Road exit of I–240, including a spiffy full-service Marriott.

The Graceland/Memphis International Airport area is a good bet for visitors with limited time in Memphis who mainly want to see Graceland. A number of south Memphis hotels operate within a few blocks or a few miles of both the popular tourist attraction and the airport, including a handsomely renovated Holiday Inn Select. Sadly, the surrounding neighbor-hood, one of the best areas of town when Elvis bought Graceland, has become

extremely run-down. We recommend a few hotels and an RV park there but have chosen to skip the other properties in the area. We would caution you that if you see hotel deals in this area that sound too good to be true, pay attention, as they may put you too close for comfort to the seedy side of the city. That's equally true of the general area near the airport, an industrial part of town with a scattering of strip joints.

The prices we quote are the basic off-the-street rates known in the industry as rack rates; they do not include tax, tips, and extra charges. It's always worth asking if you qualify for a better rate, and some-times just the fact you're staying on the weekend will lower the price. Of course, you can always check your favorite online service such as expedia.com or priceline.com. Don't forget to inquire about weekend packages that sometimes include extras such as a bottle of champagne or passes to local attractions. Unless we note otherwise, all the listed hotels accept major credit cards. Bear in mind that some hotels will up their rates for the busiest weekends.

In general, Memphis hotels all have nonsmoking rooms and wheelchair-accessible rooms. Most do not accept pets, and the ones that do often require a non-refundable deposit. Hotels usually allow children younger than age 18 to stay free with their parent or parents but charge an additional $5.00 to $10.00 for an extra adult in the room. Virtually all properties have coffeemakers, hair dryers, ironing boards and irons, dataports, air-conditioning, cable television with a free movie channel in the guest rooms, and at least one free newspaper. We note the exceptions in the individual hotel write-ups. These amenities are not ubiquitous among country inns and bed-and-breakfast inns, however.

Free parking is a standard hotel amenity in all parts of the city except downtown. We'll note which hotels charge extra for parking. DASH, an airport shuttle service operated by Memphis Area Transit

Authority, serves the downtown hotels (see the Getting Here, Getting Around chapter for details), and many other hotels operate free airport shuttles for their guests.

Remember that hotels, especially those downtown, fill up fast during the May weekends when annual Memphis in May events such as the Beale Street Music Festival take place, the busy summer tourist season, Elvis commemorations, popular sporting events, and large conventions. (See the Annual Events chapter.) Rooms are particularly hard to find during the huge Church of God in Christ convention that takes place the second week of November. If you have trouble finding a room, try the suburbs, especially the hotels along I-40 east of the city proper.

PRICE CODE

The following price code is the average cost of a double-occupancy room (two adults) during peak season. For hotels with a substantial number of suites, the price is a range that includes the cost for a room and for a suite. Prices do not include a 15.95 percent tax (9.25 percent for state sales tax, 6.7 percent for room and local tax) charged for hotel rooms in Memphis. The tax varies slightly in areas outside the city limits.

$	Less than $90
$$	$90 to $119
$$$	$120 to $149
$$$$	$150 and up

HOTELS AND MOTELS
Downtown

Comfort Inn Downtown   **$$**
100 North Front Street
(901) 520-0583, (800) 228-5150
www.choicehotels.com
This super-friendly 71-unit hotel, which rates high within the Comfort Inn chain, offers basic rooms within easy walking distance of Mud Island River Park and

other downtown attractions. The hotel offers a number of free amenities, including indoor parking, Internet access, and a deluxe breakfast. The lobby and room decor is nothing special, but if you're staying on an upper floor facing west, you'll have a great view of the river. There's also an outdoor pool, a fitness facility, and a tiny Greek-American restaurant on the ground floor facing Adams Avenue.

Hampton Inn & Suites at
Peabody Place   **$$$$**
175 Peabody Place
(901) 260-4000, (800) HAMPTON
www.hampton-inn.com
This 144-unit accommodation is as close as you can stay to Beale Street unless you decide to sleep in W. C. Handy Park. It is one of the most luxurious Hampton Inns in that chain, built by the owners of The Peabody as an alternative for visitors when the grand hotel is full. The nicely appointed Hampton lobby may not have ducks, but it does have bronze-toned stone floors, plush sofas and chairs, a small business center, and a large, cheerful breakfast bar. A small indoor swimming pool and modern fitness center are around the corner. The Hampton has 108 modest-size guest rooms and 36 suites. The king suite features a kitchen outfitted with basic cooking and serving items, microwave, full-size refrigerator, dishwasher, and breakfast bar. It also has four phones, a large work area and three recliners, and plenty of room. All rooms include the usual amenities, plus pay-per-view movies and Nintendo. The property has its own parking garage, available for $10 a day. Some of the biggest amenities are just outside the hotel: Beale Street a block to the south, Peabody Place Entertainment Center across the street to the north. Most guests like being close to the action, but as the street often goes all night on the weekends, it can be a bit noisy. If you're susceptible, ask for a room facing the courtyard, and remember that earplugs are available at the front desk.

The Memphis Convention & Visitors Bureau's excellent Web site includes an extensive and frequently updated listing of hotels. You can even book a room online at some Memphis hotels. The Web address is www.memphis travel.com.

Holiday Inn Select Downtown $$$$
160 Union Avenue
(901) 525-5491, (888) 300-5491
www.hiselect.com/memdowntown

Its central location across the street from The Peabody is a good reason to select this full-service hotel, which was converted into a Holiday Inn and completely renovated in 1996. The spacious, carpeted lobby features a marble fireplace and marble cornices around the elevators plus a tiny business center with fax machine and computer. The 15-story hotel has 192 rooms, each with big windows and mahogany-finish furniture. Each room includes the usual amenities, and for an extra charge there are in-room Nintendo and movies available. The hotel also has what it calls Executive Edition rooms, which cost $30 extra per night. These slightly larger corner rooms come with a sleeper sofa (in addition to the bed) as well as such extras as a minifridge, a microwave, and terry bathrobes. The hotel's fourth-floor outdoor pool feels private and relaxed. (Hint for swimmers: Ask for a fourth-floor room with direct access to the pool.) Holiday Inn Select Downtown has two restaurants. The Union Café serves a buffet breakfast (not included in room rates) every morning and offers basic American fare for other meals plus a full bar. There's also Sekisui, a popular Japanese eatery featuring a sushi bar. Food from both restaurants is available for room service. Parking is $6.00 a day.

Kress Suites $$-$$$
9 North Main Street
(901) 522-2100, (888) 287-9400
www.springhillsuites.com

The historic Kress Building, with its colorful, original terra-cotta facade, literally was a Kress Dime Store for many years and now is being renovated into a 48-suite hotel. This chain of stores was once famous for decorating its storefronts' exteriors with extravagant, multicolored terra-cotta ceramics, and this building has one of the best-preserved Kress facades in the country. The exterior of this building is being carefully restored. When it is completed in the mid-2000s, each suite will have a work area and modest kitchen area as well as either two queen-size beds or one king. Other amenities on the premises include free high-speed Internet and meeting rooms. However, guests must go to the SpringHill Suites property next door for front-desk services, the free continental breakfast, and access to the swimming pool and small fitness center. Parking is $5.00 per day.

Madison Hotel $$$$
79 Madison Avenue
(901) 333-1200, (866) 44-MEMPHIS
www.madisonhotelmemphis.com

The Madison Hotel has just one goal: to be the finest hotel in Memphis. Opened in 2002 by a former Peabody general manager, this luxury boutique hotel has spared no expense in furnishing the rooms and common areas. The 16-story former bank building, built in 1905, was gutted then renovated into a European-style, small luxury hotel (affiliated with the Small Luxury Hotels of the World group). The Madison offers excellent service and is rich in well-chosen details, from the colorful prints and original sculpture in the lobby to the luxurious down duvets on the beds and upscale toiletries in the bathrooms. The swank art deco lobby also features plush sofas and chairs, a musical motif, and cocktail service. Just east of the lobby, you'll find the hotel's Grill 83, one of the best-looking restaurants in the city. A popular spot with Memphians and visitors alike, Grill 83 serves an uptown menu (don't miss the Kansas City filet), and at the bar you can enjoy elegant cocktails. A free continental breakfast and afternoon happy hour take place on the mezzanine. The 110 rooms and suites feature granite-topped wet bars with refrigerators, microwaves, coffeemakers, and an honor bar. All feature high-speed Internet. The top rooms have great views of the river, and 28 rooms have Jacuzzis. The hotel also has two presidential suites available for $900 a night. Valet parking is available for $10 a day.

Memphis Marriott Downtown $$$$
250 North Main Street
(901) 527-7300, (800) 557-8740
www.marriott.com/memdt
The Memphis Marriott Downtown has become the city's largest hotel, with 600 rooms, now that it has added a 13-story tower. Across Main Street from Memphis Cook Convention Center, this hotel is very popular with visitors attending events and conventions at the center as well as other business travelers. Marriott has spent some $50 million on the property during the last decade. The investment is driven by the recent $100-million-plus expansion of the convention center. The hotel has all the amenities you would expect from a full-service Marriott hotel, including room service, a spacious, well-equipped fitness center, an indoor pool, a whirlpool, and a sauna. The lobby is a lofty atrium with white marble floors, tall large windows looking out onto Main Street, and a number of sitting areas. An escalator goes up to the meeting rooms as well as to the covered crosswalk over to the convention center. The rooms, which seem bigger and fresher than most downtown rooms, are outfitted in cheerful furnishings. Three concierge floors feature slightly more expensive rooms with added amenities such as terry robes and bottled water as well as access to a lounge that serves a free continental breakfast in the mornings and honor bar and hors d'oeuvres in the early evenings. The hotel lobby restaurant, Magnolia Grille, serves a Southern menu and daily breakfast buffet, whereas Trolley Stop Bar features appetizers and snacks

plus a full bar. Valet parking is available for $12.00 (unlimited in and out); self-parking is $7.00 for each entry.

The Peabody $$$$
149 Union Avenue
(901) 529-4000, (800) 732-2639
www.peabodymemphis.com
This gracefully restored historic downtown hotel promotes itself as the South's Grand New Hotel, and with good reason. It preserves traditional charms such as the Italianate fountain with its famous ducks while offering attentive service and modern amenities such as excellent meeting and convention facilities, a fitness center, and all the conveniences today's executive travelers expect. The Peabody, first established in 1869, was closed in the 1970s amid the urban decline of the downtown area. Its restoration—to the tune of $25 million—and reopening in 1981 were the opening salvo of the battle to return downtown Memphis to prominence. Over the years writer William Faulkner, U.S. presidents from Andrew Jackson to Bill Clinton, the Rolling Stones, Barbara Streisand, and Cary Grant have all stayed here. The Peabody has always been the social and commercial hub of the city and the surrounding Delta region. Mississippi writer David Cohn in 1935 wrote that "the Delta begins in the lobby of the Peabody Hotel and ends on Catfish Row in Vicksburg. The Peabody is the Paris Ritz, the Cairo Shepheard's, the London Savoy of this section." Other hotels offer luxurious accommodations and nice lobby areas, but The Peabody Lobby, where visitors and locals alike meet for drinks or afternoon tea, is peerless.

Railroad builder Col. Robert C. Brinkley opened The Peabody shortly after the Civil War, naming it after philanthropist George Peabody. At that time the hotel charged $3.00 to $4.00 a night (including meals but charging extra for fire and gaslight) for the 75 rooms, each with a private bath. Its saloon was the site of high-stakes poker games, at which plantations were won and lost, according to local lore. In 1925 The Peabody moved to its present location.

Built in the colonnaded Italian Renaissance style, it features a two-story lobby with a fountain carved from a single piece of marble. Subsequent renovations have carefully preserved this design.

As for restaurants, The Peabody's culinary jewel is Chez Philippe, one of the city's finest haute-cuisine restaurants. There's also Capriccio Grill, a Northern Italian eatery. (For more information see the Restaurants chapter.) Room service is available around the clock. The hotel has a day spa (services range from haircuts and facials to massages) and a decent-size fitness center on the lower level as well as a small but elegant indoor swimming pool, sauna, and whirlpool spa. Shops line the Union Avenue side of the ground floor, selling souvenirs, T-shirts and finer apparel, jewelry, and artwork. Next door is Peabody Place Entertainment Center, which includes Jillian's, a multiscreen movie theater, and other shops and hangouts. The roof of The Peabody features an art deco–style Skyway and a well-groomed terrace, and it's always worth asking if you can go up there to enjoy the great views of the Mississippi and perhaps visit the famous Peabody Ducks in their off-hours digs, the Duck Palace.

The Peabody's 468 guest rooms range from lavish $1,000-plus-a-night luxury suites to modest-size standard rooms around $200. Because of the building's quirks, no two rooms are alike. They're decorated in muted pastel tones, with floral patterns on bedspreads and curtains, cherry furniture, and moss-green carpeting. The bathrooms are standard-size (larger with whirlpool baths for the more luxurious units). All rooms have pay-per-view movies and toiletries that include duck-shaped soaps. Parking and breakfast are extra, and it's $30 to $35 for an extra adult staying in the room. The concierge floor, which requires a special key for entry, has its own concierge desk, a comfortable lounge, and a separate room for smokers. Guests on this floor get free continental breakfast, happy-hour hors d'oeuvres, and

sweets in the evenings as well as such extras as terry-cloth robes.

With its 80,000 square feet of meeting and function space, the hotel is a popular site for conferences and social functions. Its largest ballroom can seat as many as 1,200 for dinner and up to 1,600 for a reception or other function.

One practical note: Though its main pedestrian entrance still faces Union Avenue, the motor entrance and parking facilities are farther down Second Street. Valet parking is $21 per day, and self-parking is $16 per day. Ask about special weekend packages.

Radisson Hotel Memphis $$$$
185 Union Avenue
(901) 528–1800, (800) 333–3333
www.radisson.com

Located just across Union Avenue from AutoZone Park and close to Beale Street and Peabody Place Entertainment Center, the Radisson Hotel Memphis has TGI Fridays restaurant downstairs and 272 rooms upstairs. It opened in 1996, after its owners invested $24 million to convert the old Tennessee Hotel (built in 1929) and other buildings into a modern hotel. The brick arched wall that separates Fridays from the main lobby is the facade from one of those buildings. The dimly lit lobby is outfitted with comfortable chairs and sofas as well as tables and a fountain. All three meals, including breakfast, are available at Fridays, part of the chain famous for its festive atmosphere and frozen drinks.

Hotel rooms are larger than in most downtown hotels, and many include good-size bathrooms, with a separate shower stall and tub, as well as the usual amenities. An outdoor swimming pool and a small fitness center are on the third floor. Ask about the special Redbirds package and other deals. Because parking is so tight in the area, valet parking is advisable ($10 a day). You'll probably want to steer clear of the Greyhound Bus station next to the Radisson.

The Peabody Ducks

Celebrities may stay there from time to time, but the most famous inhabitants of The Peabody hotel aren't people at all. They're the mallard ducks you see swimming in the elegant fountain in the hotel's grand lobby.

Every day at 11:00 A.M., a red carpet is unrolled in the lobby, and the ducks, after taking the elevator down from their penthouse suite, march down the red carpet to John Philip Sousa music. They go up a small ramp and plop into the fountain for the day. At 5:00 P.M. they leave the fountain for their rooftop home, with similar pomp and circumstance.

The tradition began in the 1930s, when it was legal for duck hunters to use live ducks as decoys instead of the plastic ones now used. Hotel general manager Frank Schutt and a friend returned to the hotel after a weekend hunting trip, and, as a joke, they put some of their decoys in the elegant fountain to swim around. The guests loved it, so the practice continued. Edward Pembroke, a bellman who had worked as a circus animal trainer, took charge, and created the ritual of the daily musical march to and from the fountain. (He was Duckmaster until 1991.)

At present the five ducks that grace the fountain are raised by a local farmer. They live at The Peabody until fully grown; they are returned to the wild upon their retirement.

It seems, though, that the spectators are a very important part of the march. When the Peabody ducks first went on

The famous ducks in The Peabody's lobby make their way home after a day's swim in the lobby fountain. THE PEABODY MEMPHIS

tour to other cities, their march down the red carpet was a disaster—the spectators kept at a distance, and the birds scattered. It was found that they rely on the rows of toes on either side of the carpet created as everyone crowds in for a closer look.

Residence Inn by Marriott Memphis
Downtown $$$-$$$$
110 Monroe Avenue
(901) 578-3700
www.marriott.com/memri

This brand-new Residence Inn, housed in a 13-story historic art nouveau building, provides the amenities of extended-stay suites in a Main Street location that's within easy walking or trolley-riding distance of the downtown attractions, restaurants, and other places of interest. The historic Wm. Len apartment building has been renovated, resulting in an attractive lobby that incorporates the building's art nouveau architectural elements as well as 90 suites ranging in size from efficiencies to two-bedrooms. If money is no object, ask about the luxury penthouse suites. The hotel has most of the usual Residence Inn amenities, including a free hot full-breakfast buffet and weekday happy hour with heavy appetizers as well as a fitness center and self-service laundry. Pets are allowed for a $100 nonrefundable fee. No on-site parking is available, but there's valet parking for $10 a day.

Sleep Inn & Suites at Court Square $-$$
40 North Front Street
(901) 522-9700, (800) SLEEPINN
www.sleepinn.com

A central downtown location and simple, well-maintained rooms have made this 124-room hotel a popular option for leisure and business travelers since it first opened in 1996. The hotel's motor entrance is on Front Street, with its other side facing the pedestrian Main Street, allowing guests to walk right out the door and a few blocks to restaurants, bars, and attractions. A trolley stop is just in front as well. The small but cheerful lobby of teal and burgundy offers a dining room where guests enjoy a complimentary continental breakfast, as well as a modest fitness center. Parking is free for guests. Each room has pay-per-view movies and free high-speed Internet.

SpringHill Suites by Marriott $$$-$$$$
21 North Main Street
(901) 522-2100, (888) 287-9400
www.springhillsuites.com

This newly built suites hotel has the best of both worlds: a convenient downtown location right on the trolley line and a suite layout more in keeping with what you find in the suburbs. The seven-story hotel has 102 smallish suites, each with separate areas for work, relaxing, sleeping, and eating as well as a pull-out sofa, a small refrigerator, a microwave, and the usual lineup of amenities plus free high-speed Internet. The rooms are outfitted with dark muted tones and dark wood furniture. You'll find an outdoor swimming pool as well as an exercise room, a business center, and guest laundry facilities. The room rates include a free continental breakfast, and although there's no restaurant, many dining options are available within walking distance of the hotel. SpringHill Suites, which operates next to the Sleep Inn & Suites at Court Square, is owned and managed by the same group. Parking is available for $5.00 a day.

Talbot Heirs Guesthouse $$$$
99 South Second Street
(901) 527-9772, (800) 955-3956
www.talbothouse.com

Just across Second Street from The Peabody stands Talbot Heirs, a discreet, quiet, homey hotel that feels miles away from the social hubbub of The Peabody's grand lobby. That's by design: Owners Jamie and Phil Baker, former road warriors who grew weary of hotels, converted this Gayoso Historic District apartment building into a guesthouse in 1995 specifically for people who hate hotels. It has attracted such luminaries as filmmaker Francis Ford Coppola and model Claudia Schiffer. Jamie decorated the nine units herself with an eye to making it feel as though you're staying in a friend's apartment, including original artwork in many rooms. Each has an apartment-size kitchen equipped with basic cooking and eating utensils, and the full-size refrigerator is stocked with milk, yogurt, cereal, juice, soft drinks, and snacks. Each unit is different, ranging from a funky yellow studio with black-and-white linoleum floors to a spacious apartment with deep-peach walls, a four-poster bed, and a private deck. The staff prides itself on taking care of its guests, whether it's recommending restaurants, engaging a personal chef to cook a meal, or arranging transportation. Some guests fax a grocery list ahead of their arrival so that their cupboard is pre-stocked to their liking. Other amenities include free high-speed Internet access and, upon request, a VCR, a treadmill, or a fax machine at no extra charge.

Wyndham Garden Hotel $$$
300 North Second Street
(901) 525-1800, (800) WYNDHAM
www.wyndham.com

This 230-room hotel, 9 blocks from The Peabody, is a bit off the beaten path for tourists but convenient to the Memphis Cook Convention Center and the Pyramid Arena. (If you cross Second and go through the Memphis Marriott Downtown, you'll find the convention center and a trolley stop.) This hotel was gutted and renovated in 1999, when Wyndham purchased the property. The airy lobby features marble floors and a round table at the center, where you'll find complimentary newspapers. Relax in the small library just off the lobby, where you can order drinks from the adjacent restaurant/bar. The restaurant features basic American fare including sandwiches, salads, and pastas and is available for room service at dinner only. A breakfast buffet is served in the restaurant. There's also a small fitness center, and there's a pool across the driveway from the entrance. The rooms feature handsome striped curtains, cocoa carpeting, furniture with a walnut finish, and a standard-size bathroom. In-room video games and movies are available for an extra charge, but Internet access is free. Parking is $5.00 a day.

Medical Center/ Midtown

Hampton Inn—Medical Center Midtown $
1180 Union Avenue
(901) 276-1175, (800) HAMPTON
www.hampton-inn.com

This modest hotel, just a mile from downtown next to the I-240 exit, is favored by families of patients being treated at nearby hospitals and clinics. It has a swimming pool and offers free continental breakfast. The small lobby has a sunken sitting area with a TV and breakfast tables. The rooms, decorated in dark colors with oak furniture and chintz bedspreads, have either a king-size bed or two double beds. The hotel offers special rates if you or a relative are being treated at an area hospital. Parking is free.

Holiday Inn, University of Memphis $$
3700 Central Avenue
(901) 678-8200, (888) 300-5491
www.holiday-inn.com

This gorgeous new hotel is easily the best place to stay in the area between downtown and East Memphis. Situated actually a bit east of midtown across from the University of Memphis campus, it blends in so well with other university buildings you might drive right past it the first time. The 82-unit hotel is part of the U of M's Kemmons Wilson School of Hospitality, yet it's as professionally run as any hotel. It's entirely composed of well-appointed two-room suites, each with kitchenette, high-speed Internet access, and the usual amenities. The cavernous atrium lobby features comfortable seating areas as well as an exhibit detailing the career of Kemmons Wilson, the Memphis businessman who founded Holiday Inns and is credited with inventing the modern lodging business. There are also two on-site restaurants, a fitness center, gift shop, and newsstand. Pets are accepted with a non-refundable $50 fee.

Red Roof Inn   **$**
42 South Camilla Street
(901) 526-1050, (800) RED-ROOF
www.redroof.com

This former La Quinta Inn reopened in 2003 as a Red Roof Inn. Its location near the medical center between downtown and midtown enables guests to easily reach a variety of attractions in those parts of the city, and it's right at I-240, which puts the rest of the city within convenient driving distance. The hotel offers 130 units, including two suites, all of which come equipped with HBO and Internet access. There's a free continental breakfast and a *USA Today,* and an outdoor pool for guests' enjoyment. Like other Red Roof Inns, this property may not be luxurious, but it's a good value. Parking (even for big trucks) is free.

East Memphis

AmeriSuites   **$$**
1220 Primacy Parkway
(901) 680-9700, (800) 833-1515
www.amerisuites.com

One of a trio of hotels across the street from St. Francis Hospital, this all-suites property is a good value, especially on weekends. The 128-unit hotel, built in 1997, has a small tiled lobby that opens onto a breakfast room, with plenty of tables and chairs, where guests get a free deluxe continental breakfast. Nestled in next to the front desk is a small, modern business center. Other amenities include a small but cheerful fitness center, a good-size outdoor pool, and guest laundry facilities. All rooms have tiny kitchens, complete with minifridge stocked with snacks, microwave, and dishes; a 25-inch TV with VCR; sleeper sofa; and the usual amenities. The hotel allows pets weighing less than 10 pounds. Park Place Centre shopping center is just to the east, and Poplar Avenue is just a block or so north.

Courtyard by Marriott   **$$-$$$**
6015 Park Avenue
(901) 761-0330, (800) 321-2211
www.courtyard.com

This 146-room hotel caters to a corporate clientele during the week and to soccer teams, groups, and families on the weekends, when rates drop by as much as $30. Attractive even before being redone in 2002, the lobby has plenty of private sitting areas, a small bar, and the Courtyard Café, where a breakfast buffet is served. Just beyond and accessible from the lobby is the chain's signature courtyard, with a small swimming pool and a gazebo. There's also a whirlpool spa, guest laundry facilities, and a small fitness center. The spacious guest rooms face either the courtyard or outside. You'll find the hotel on the corner of Park, just across Primacy from St. Francis Hospital, and just a block from Park Place Centre shopping center and its restaurants and shops.

Doubletree East Memphis   **$$$-$$$$**
5069 Sanderlin Avenue
(901) 767-6666, (800) DOUBLETREE
www.doubletreememphis.com

This 264-room hotel, formerly the Hilton East Memphis, is the closest of the East Memphis hotels to downtown (about 10 miles), situated near good shopping centers as well as the Memphis Racquet Club. The sunny, sleek lobby features cream-and-black tiled floors and terrarium-style windows that rise five stories, and both the lobby and guest rooms have an art deco feel to them. Just off the lobby is Cal's Champion Steakhouse, named for University of Memphis basketball coach John Calipari, where they serve steaks and casual American cuisine and a breakfast buffet in the mornings. There's also an indoor-outdoor pool, fitness room, and airport shuttle service (sometimes available for other trips within 3 miles). Doubletree is a great choice for tennis and racquetball players, since hotel guests get passes to the racquet club and a local health club. During the Kroger St. Jude and the Cellular South Cup indoor tennis championship at the club, you can walk to the matches from the hotel. The Doubletree's executive floor offers extra amenities, including larger rooms, a business center, concierge staff, and a lounge with free continental breakfast and happy hour with hors d'oeuvres.

Embassy Suites $$$$
1022 South Shady Grove Road
(901) 684-1777, (800) EMBASSY
www.embassy-suites.com
This exceptional all-suites hotel has a beautiful atrium with hundreds of plants and one of the city's best Italian restaurants. They do not scrimp on the amenities for families and business travelers alike. All 220 suites open onto the five-story, skylighted lobby. You'll find plenty of comfortable sitting areas, among a series of ponds and waterfalls that run through the middle of the lobby, complete with fish and even some small ducks. In the back of the lobby is an enormous dining room and two buffets, where cooked-to-order breakfast is served every morning and a social hour with drinks and hors d'oeuvres every evening. Both are included in the cost of your room. In addition, Frank Grisanti's restaurant, a popular East Memphis Italian restaurant near the front of the lobby, serves lunch and dinner and provides room service. There's also a business center, a gift shop, a well-furnished fitness center, an indoor pool, a whirlpool bath, and a sauna—all grouped together just off the lobby. Families will appreciate the video arcade, with all kinds of games, and guest laundry facilities.

The suites are spacious and plush, with a sleeper sofa and a granite-topped wet bar with minifridge and microwave in the living room. The bathrooms have standard tubs and good counter space, and with an extra sink and vanity in the bedroom, two people can get ready at the same time. Other amenities include video games, movies, and Internet access, all available on the room TV for an extra charge. Be sure to ask about family weekend packages, a

hotel specialty. This hotel is right next to Regalia, an upscale shopping center.

Hampton Inn—Poplar $$
5320 Poplar Avenue
(901) 683-8500, (800) HAMPTON
www.hampton-inn.com
Located in East Memphis across the street from Corky's, one of the city's most famous barbecue restaurants, and 1.5 miles from Oak Court Mall and other shopping, this 125-room hotel offers free continental breakfast and an outdoor swimming pool. The small lobby opens onto a sitting area/dining room with upholstered furniture, TV, and tables for breakfast. Much of the clientele is short-term—families in town for a soccer game or event or business travelers in town for just a night or two. The hotel doesn't have a fitness center, but it provides guests with free passes to a health club. The entrance is just east of the hotel on Estate Place.

Hampton Inn & Suites Shady Grove $$
962 South Shady Grove Road
(901) 762-0056, (800) HAMPTON
www.hampton-inn.com
This 133-unit property offers suites as well as rooms. With a lofty two-story ceiling and attractive fireplace, the large, handsomely decorated lobby includes an extensive kitchen-style buffet area, where a free continental breakfast is served to guests. Outside is a patio with barbecue grills and a swimming pool. Other hotel amenities include a small fitness center, a guest laundry facility, a tiny convenience store, and free shuttle both to the airport and (depending on availability) to destinations within a 5-mile radius. Dining and room service are available from Frank Grisanti's, the Italian restaurant at the Embassy Suites Hotel next door. The suites feature a small kitchen, and the living area has a TV with movies and video games available for a fee, as well as a sleeper sofa; the bedrooms have an extra vanity and sink. You can walk across a parking lot to visit the shops and restaurants of the Regalia shopping center.

Hawthorn Suites $$
1090 Ridge Lake Boulevard
(901) 682-1722, (800) 527-1133
www.hawthorn.com

This 113-unit hotel, in a quiet area just a few blocks off busy Poplar Avenue, offers many of the comforts of home. The suites, cheerfully decorated in peach and teal, have small bedrooms, each with either a king-size bed or two double beds, a living room with tables and four chairs, and a full kitchen complete with full-size refrigerator, microwave, dishwasher, and the basics for preparing and serving a simple meal. There's a VCR, too. Cinema buffs will find a movie theater (Ridgeway Malco) just across the street, and there are several nearby restaurant choices. The Hawthorn also has other entertainments, including a swimming pool, a basketball court, and a fitness center. It serves a full hot breakfast in the mornings, and during the week there's a happy hour featuring a keg of beer and appetizers. Other amenities include a restaurant with dinner buffet, coin-operated laundry facilities, and whirlpool spa.

Hilton Memphis $$$$
939 Ridge Lake Boulevard
(901) 684-6664, (800) 444-2326
www.parkvistamemphis.com

This splendid 27-story cylindrical glass hotel, an East Memphis landmark, offers upscale accommodations with wonderful views in all directions from its location off Poplar near I-240. Built in 1975 in a late modernist style, the hotel has since changed ownership several times, finally becoming the Hilton Memphis in 2004. At that time the hotel underwent a $12 million redesign, and as a result, the 405 rooms have a "residential retro" look—a mixture of bright colors and eclectic art. All of the public spaces and meeting areas have been reworked, too, so that the lobby retains its two-story floor-to-ceiling windows but now has a nontraditional front desk, with individual check-in pods that are more personalized for the guest. Other amenities include a health and fit-

ness center, a heated outdoor pool, and a restaurant called the Rooks Corner. The hotel has traditionally been a popular site for special events, and it's here that local politicians gather on election night with their supporters. Amenities include room service, a business center with Internet access, and free transportation to and from the airport. There are also a few suites (where Lisa Marie Presley stays when she's in town).

Holiday Inn Select Memphis East $$$
5795 Poplar Avenue
(901) 682-7881, (800) 300-5491
www.holiday-inn.com

This 10-story Holiday Inn, built in 1986, was recently upgraded to Holiday Inn Select after a $5-million renovation of its guest rooms, meeting facilities, and common areas. Its lobby area, with a sunken living room that offers views of a pretty blue-tiled fountain through terrarium-style windows, connects to Monterrey Grill, a restaurant serving American food for all three meals, complete with a spiffy new lounge. You'll find the large indoor pool, with a nice-size whirlpool spa nearby, on the other side of the restaurant. Holiday Inn Select has 243 rooms, including a concierge floor with rooms and luxury suites on the 10th floor. The traditional-style suites (which cost extra) are spacious, with the largest, nicest bathrooms of just about any hotel in the city. Guests staying in the suites or other 10th-floor rooms have access to a small but elegant concierge lounge, where there's free continental breakfast and happy hour in the evenings. The standard rooms are generous in size, with either two queen beds or a king bed plus sleeper sofa (no charge for extra guests). These rooms also have fresh new bathrooms. Other amenities include room service, passes to a nearby health club, and a free airport shuttle, which, depending on availability, can also take guests to destinations within 3 miles. The hotel does accept pets but requires a $25 fee.

Homestead Studio Suites $
6500 Poplar Avenue
(901) 767– 5522, (888) STAY HSD
www.homesteadhotels.com

Opened in 1999 just west of Germantown, this sparkling-clean, few-frills hotel may cater mostly to business travelers, but at $59 to $74 a night, it's a great value for vacationers, too. The small lobby has a tiny front desk, a convenience store, and a small sitting area with a TV and a few tables and chairs; on the second floor there's a modern coin-laundry facility equipped with six washers and six dryers. There's a fitness center, too. The 134 guest rooms are bedroom–living room–kitchen combos with a king or queen bed, a work desk, and a breakfast bar with two barstools that separates the tiny kitchen area from the rest of the room. The kitchen has a full-size refrigerator, a stovetop with two burners, a small microwave, and enough cooking and dining utensils for a simple meal. Given the small-but-not-claustrophobic size of the rooms, three or four could definitely be a crowd. Pets are allowed for a $25 to $75 fee. The price drops if you stay at least seven nights.

Homewood Suites by Hilton $$$
5811 Poplar Avenue
(901) 763–0500, (800) CALL HOME
www.homewood-suites.com

Staying at Homewood Suites is more like living in an apartment complex with generous amenities than staying at a hotel. When you arrive to check in, you enter a spacious "lodge" decorated with pine paneling and furniture, brick flooring, and homey fabrics. There's plenty of room for watching TV, reading in front of the fireplace, and holding impromptu meetings. The large kitchen-style buffet is where the staff serves a lavish free continental breakfast daily. Also, in the early evening there's beer, soft drinks, and a light supper (burgers, nachos, etc.) Monday through Thursday. Just off the main lodge area is a small convenience store, a modest fitness center, five meeting rooms, and a business center. Go out the back and you'll find a heated pool,

a whirlpool spa, and a tiny basketball court amid attractive landscaping. Grills are available to guests who want to cook out, and nearby is a small but cheerful guest laundry facility with three washers, three dryers, and a folding area. From the lodge you can drive or walk to the 143 suites, divvied up among seven buildings. The smallest suite is a one-bedroom with a king-size bed plus a sleeper sofa in the living room; the largest suite has two bedrooms and two bathrooms plus a separate kitchen area—ideal for large families or groups. All have full kitchens. Each room has a TV, one with VCR, and both movies and video games are available for a fee. A shuttle offers rides to or from the airport or (depending on availability) destinations within 5 miles of the hotel. Those who hate to grocery shop will be happy to know there's a free shopping service: Just leave the staff your grocery list in the morning, and the food will be in your fridge that afternoon. Pets (except for cats) are allowed, but the fee is $50 for a short stay. *Note:* Rates drop if you stay five days or longer.

LaQuinta Inn & Suites $-$$
1236 Primacy Parkway
(901) 374-0330, (800) 687-6667
www.lq.com

This attractive, pale-peach hotel is across from St. Francis Hospital, just a few blocks off Poplar and close to I–240. Built in 1998, it won a local beautification award for its well-tended grounds, but its good looks don't stop there. The inviting lobby has high ceilings, a fountain, and Spanish-style architectural elements. It features a small fitness center, a guest laundry facility, a swimming pool, and a whirlpool spa. It offers free shuttle to the airport and nearby destinations as well as free continental breakfast and morning newspaper. The rooms and suites are done up in deep plum, teal, and green and feature movies and video games for an extra charge. The suites also have refrigerators and microwave ovens but no utensils for meals. French doors divide the living area from the bedroom. Pets are allowed at no extra charge.

Marriott Residence Inn $$$-$$$$
6141 Old Poplar Pike
(901) 685-9595, (800) 331-3131
www.residenceinn.com

Discreetly tucked next to a clinic a block off Poplar Avenue, this 105-suite property provides apartment-style living with plenty of hotel-style amenities, including daily housekeeping, free breakfast, and shuttle service to and from the airport or destinations within 5 miles. The large, modern lobby has marble floors that lead to a dining area and meeting rooms in the back and, to the side, a large carpeted sitting area with lots of magazines, a phone, and TV. You'll find a whirlpool bath and a small fitness center indoors, and outdoors, a medium-size outdoor pool and a sports court. The one-bedroom suites are a good 600 square feet, with queen-size beds in the bedrooms and sleep sofas in the living rooms. You'll find a kitchen with full-size appliances, as well as the necessary utensils for cooking and serving simple meals. The living-room area and bedrooms are traditionally decorated with teal, plum, and light-mauve fabrics.

The two-bedroom suite can accommodate five people, since the living-room sofa pulls out into a bed, and features two full bathrooms. Curiously, the bedrooms in the suites aren't that private, as only a curtain separates them from the living room and the loft bedroom is open to the living room below. All rooms have pay-per-view movies and free Internet access, and some have working fireplaces. Other amenities include a guest laundry facility, grocery-shopping service, and a social hour during the week that includes free appetizers, wine, beer, and soft drinks. Pets are allowed for a $100 fee. The property is next to the railroad tracks, so if you're a light sleeper, ask for a room on the other side. *Note:* The entrance is on Poplar. Watch for the sign just east of Ridgeway and cut through a small shopping-center parking lot to reach the hotel. Rates vary according to length of stay.

Park Place Hotel $
5877 Poplar Avenue
(901) 767-6300

Sandwiched in between the Ridgeway Inn and Holiday Inn Select Memphis East, this former Comfort Inn was refurbished and reopened as Park Place Hotel in May 2004. The hotel has 126 rooms, all with free continental breakfast, and there's an outdoor pool, too. As with other hotels in this location, you have easy access to I-240, allowing you to reach other areas of the city fairly quickly.

Southeast Memphis

Best Suites $$
2575 Thousand Oaks Boulevard
(901) 365-2575, (800) BESTINN
www.bestinn.com

Built in 1999, this all-suites hotel operates next to I-240 behind Memphis Marriott East. To get there you take a circuitous route after turning off Perkins near American Way, a factor that effectively buffers the property from the surrounding neighborhood. Best Suites has a bright lobby and offers a number of amenities, including free hot-breakfast buffet, free drinks and snacks in the evenings, convenience store, and guest laundry. The indoor pool and whirlpool spa are in a greenhouse-type structure on one side of the hotel. The 111 suites range in price depending on the features, which can include in-room whirlpool baths. Some of the units are the company's Evergreen suites, featuring a premium air-purification system, a separate water supply comparable to bottled water, and soft-water showers. The property is designed for long stays, and the price drops if you're there for at least a week.

Fairfield Inn $
4760 Showcase Boulevard
(901) 795-1900, (800) 228-2800
www.fairfieldinn.com

Fairfield Inn, built in 1998, offers clean rooms decorated in calm mauve tones. Although less buffered from the surrounding area than neighboring Memphis Marriott East, Hampton Inn, and Best Suites, it's still a good bet. Guests are offered standard amenities plus free continental breakfast and access to an outdoor pool, a whirlpool, a small fitness center, and a guest laundry. The property has a small lobby with separate breakfast room and 89 rooms with either two double beds or a king-size bed plus sleeper sofa.

Hampton Inn—Perkins Road $
2700 Perkins Road
(901) 367-1234, (800) HAMPTON
www.hampton-inn.com

This 132-room hotel, next to the Memphis Marriott East, has a modest lobby with a big dining-room area, where a free deluxe continental breakfast is served. The rooms, which have either two double beds or one king-size bed, are decorated in a traditional style and offer pay-per-view movies and free Internet access. There's an outdoor pool. Guests get free passes to a nearby health club. Children 12 years of age and younger stay for free.

Holiday Inn–Mt. Moriah $–$$
2490 Mt. Moriah Road
(901) 362-8010, (800) 477-5519
www.holiday-inn.com

Located just off the Mt. Moriah exit of I-240, this 197-room property was converted to a Holiday Inn in 1993 and has since had a $2.5-million interior renovation. The hotel has a small lobby with a tiny sitting area and a restaurant that provides three meals a day and room service. There's also a small lounge with a full bar and a small jukebox. The attractive swimming-pool area, in a large courtyard that's protected from the street noise, is surrounded by flower beds. The pool is large and has bright blue umbrellas over the tables; indoors there's a small but very clean fitness center. The rooms are traditional, with dark wood furniture that includes an oversize work desk, and the usual amenities. A free shuttle is available both to and from the airport and destinations within 5 miles. The hotel sits right at

the beginning of a string of car dealerships, so if you want to buy a new car or get yours fixed, you're in the right place.

Memphis Marriott East $$$
2625 Thousand Oaks Boulevard
(901) 362-6200, (800) 627-3587
www.marriotthotels.com/memtn

Opened in 1986 and renovated to the tune of $5 million in 1999, this upscale, full-service hotel is just off I-240 at Perkins Road. With 14 stories and 320 rooms, the Marriott is one of the city's largest hotels. The bright, spacious lobby, with beige and maroon marble on the floors and touches of rich wood paneling on the walls, has plenty of small sitting areas with red-and-gold striped armchairs, tables, and brocade sofas. To the rear the Blue Shoe Bar & Grill serves American and Southern specialties for all three meals amid lively decor that features Cubist-style paintings, upholstered booths, and art deco light fixtures. The guest rooms, though, are traditional, with floral bedspreads, kelly-green carpeting, and cream-color brocade draperies. The rooms have either two double beds or one king bed plus a pullout sofa. The bathrooms are bigger than most, with the sink and vanity in a separate dressing room. Amenities include Internet, movies, and video games available on room TVs for an extra fee. The hotel also has an outdoor pool (on the ground floor but buffered from the outside world), and a fitness area with workout room, sauna, indoor pool, and whirlpool spa. The 12th and 14th floors are concierge floors, featuring a staffed lounge, free continental breakfast, drinks and appetizers in the evenings, and some in-room extras such as terry-cloth robes.

South Memphis/Airport

Clarion Hotel Airport $
1471 East Brooks Road
(901) 332-3500
www.choicehotels.com

This hotel, a former Ramada Inn, was recently renovated and upgraded to a

Clarion property that features business-class rooms, an attractive lobby, a fitness center and swimming pool, free breakfast, and high-speed Internet. Situated close to the airport as well as to Graceland, the Clarion offers free shuttle to those places as well as to area rental-car offices. Pets (15 pounds or lighter, two per room) are allowed for $10 a night per pet. While the hotel is nice and well secured, the surrounding neighborhood isn't so nice. So exercise caution as you go to and from the property.

Days Inn at Graceland $
3839 Elvis Presley Boulevard
(901) 346–5500, (800) DAYS INN
This modest 61-room hotel, just a stone's throw from Graceland and other Elvis attractions, features free nonstop Elvis movies in your room, a guitar-shape swimming pool, free continental breakfast, and airport shuttle. It's a favorite during Elvis International Tribute Week, when it is filled with regulars, some of whom have stayed at the hotel every year since Graceland opened. The rooms are standard, with in-room safes and well-worn bathrooms, but the lobby and exterior of the hotel are festooned with Elvis memorabilia and artwork.

If you're nervous about catching an early morning flight, or if you experience a long flight delay, remember the Radisson Inn Memphis Airport is right at the airport. Other hotels in the south Memphis airport area are quite accustomed to serving guests who need to get to the airport quickly.

Elvis Presley's Heartbreak Hotel $–$$
3677 Elvis Presley Boulevard
(901) 332–1000, (877) 777–0606
www.heartbreakhotel.net
This hotel was purchased by Elvis Presley Enterprises and was lavishly renovated into a stylish 128-room hotel that takes you back to the 1950s. It's a great choice for Elvis fans, because it's across the

street from Graceland and a few blocks from the other Elvis attractions and related restaurants and shops. It's set back from seedy Elvis Presley Boulevard, with a guarded gate for security. The lobby features plush retro furniture, and a 1950s-style TV that plays Elvis movies. The theme continues in the lounge and restaurant, with animal prints and bright colors—and in the patio, where you'll find a heart-shape swimming pool. The rooms have most of the usual amenities, plus a free in-house TV channel of around-the-clock Elvis videos, a minifridge, and a microwave.

The rooms, although brightened up with blue-and-gold harlequin bedspreads, are pretty standard, but the real dazzlers are the hotel's four themed suites, including the Burning Love suite (use your imagination) and the Graceland Suite, complete with "jungle room" den. Each of them is almost 1,100 square feet, with two sitting areas, two bedrooms, and two baths. Other hotel amenities include free deluxe continental breakfast, a fitness center, and a free shuttle both to the airport and to downtown attractions, including Beale Street and Sun Studio. Ask about packages that might include Graceland-tour reservations.

Holiday Inn Select Memphis Airport $$
2240 Democrat Road
(901) 332–1130, (800) 300–5491
www.holiday-inn.com
A $7-million renovation in 2000 transformed the former Four Points Sheraton ITT into this sleek, handsome hotel. Its 374 rooms, 33,000 square feet of meeting space, and its proximity to the airport make it very popular for conferences, meetings, and other functions. The lobby is a huge lofty atrium with sand-color tiles, with a few islands of navy-blue carpet with tables and chairs, a lobby bar, and a Java Coast coffee kiosk that's always humming in the mornings. The registration desk is to the right, with a gift shop on one side and a business center on the other. Down one level from the lobby, a

restaurant serves all three meals and provides room service. The hotel actually consists of two buildings with a hallway connector. The smaller, quieter building is called the executive center, and it features a little house within its atrium that's home to a large fitness center with separate saunas for men and women. The guest rooms are decorated traditionally, with ergonomically correct chairs, and the TVs feature Internet access, movies, and video games for extra fees. Other amenities include guest laundry facilities and free airport shuttle.

Radisson Inn Memphis Airport $$
2411 Winchester Road
(901) 332-2370, (800) 333-3333
www.radisson.com

This 210-room hotel is literally at Memphis International Airport—you turn into the parking lot just a few blocks before you reach the terminal's arrivals and departures ramps. The hotel's two tennis courts are so close to one of the taxiways that you could make eye contact with passengers as their planes roll past. The smallish pink lobby has a business center near the front desk and 5,500 square feet of meeting space in the back. There's also a restaurant, which serves three meals a day (buffets for breakfast and lunch) and provides room service. A separate lounge/bar and a small fitness center with shower are also available. The swimming pool, on the lower level, is surrounded by the hotel on three sides and enough shrubbery on the fourth side to buffer it from all the airport noise, although you can't get away from the sound of aircraft arriving and departing. The traditional rooms offer standard amenities including pay-per-view movies, free Internet access, and video games in the rooms. A free airport shuttle is available.

BED-AND-BREAKFASTS AND COUNTRY INNS

Bonne Terre Country Inn and Café $$$$
4715 Church Road West
Nesbit, Mississippi
(662) 781-5100
www.bonneterre.com

Situated on 100 acres of Mississippi countryside, Bonne Terre is such a quiet, perfect place to get away from it all you might forget you're 15 miles from Memphis. The colorful rooms have pretty chintz curtains, antiques, and other decorations that make them feel quaint, even though the buildings were constructed fairly recently. All the guest rooms have a private bath, fresh flowers, down comforters, and other amenities that might include a fireplace, balcony, or whirlpool bath. Some of the rooms are a bit small, however, so you might want to ask about that when making your reservations.

One of the best parts about staying at Bonne Terre is eating at its cafe, which serves an eclectic menu in pretty, relaxed dining rooms. (See the Restaurants chapter for details.) Breakfast is included with the room, but you will probably want to eat at least one other meal there during your stay.

Bonne Terre is a great spot for relaxing or strolling, with its woodsy location and small lakes; there's also swimming in summer and horseback riding (which can be arranged by management). Don't be surprised if you see a wedding party during your stay: With its event rooms, newly built reception hall, and chapel, Bonne Terre has become a very popular place for weddings, corporate events, and other gatherings.

Although children are allowed, Bonne Terre is more oriented toward adult guests.

The Bridgewater House $$
7015 Raleigh LaGrange Road
(901) 384-0080
www.bbonline.com/tn/bridgewater

Formerly a schoolhouse, the Bridgewater House has been restored into a Greek Revival home with high ceilings, original hardwood floors, leaded-glass windows, and a 250-year-old Adams mantel in the living room.

Owners Steve and Katherine Mistilis take good care of their guests, offering snacks upon arrival and cooking breakfast that might include Belgian waffles or their personal version of eggs Benedict (eggs Bridgewater). There are two large guest rooms, each with private bath, antiques, down comforters, and robes. The Bridgewater is about a mile from Shelby Farms, a large city park where horseback riding, hiking, and other activities are available. The inn is a good 20-minute drive from Memphis and the attractions there.

Children are allowed only on occasion, and smoking is allowed only on the porch or patio.

Dockery House Bed and Breakfast $$–$$$
3831 Robertson Gin Road
Hernando, Mississippi
(662) 449-5427
www.bbonline.com/ms/dockery

Owned and operated by Martha and John Garner, the Dockery House bed-and-breakfast inn is situated on three acres amid pecan trees, meadows, and a pond. Not too far from downtown Memphis but well away from the hustle and bustle, the Dockery House has two rooms and one suite in a restored 1876 farmhouse, all of them nicely appointed with luxury baths, hand silk-screened wallpaper, and a TV and VCR. The loft room also offers a washer and dryer along with a full kitchen. Dockery House serves a full country breakfast, too. A deposit is required on all reservations, and a 72-hour notice is required to receive a full deposit refund. Children and pets are welcome.

Magnolia Grove Bed and Breakfast $–$$
140 East Commerce Street
Hernando, Mississippi
(662) 429-2626, (866) 404-2626
www.magnoliagrove.com

The Magnolia Grove, only a 30-minute drive from Memphis, provides guests with

an escape from modern city life to the early 20th century. This bed-and-breakfast inn, housed in a turn-of-the-century plantation home, is beautifully appointed, complete with antiques, chandeliers, and stained-glass windows. Upon arrival guests are treated to homemade desserts; a full breakfast is served each morning. Three guest rooms are individually decorated with period antiques and a queen-size bed, and all of them have a private bath. Keep in mind there's a 72-hour cancellation policy, so if you cancel after that point, you will be responsible for the cost of one night's stay.

Santi Lodge Bed and Breakfast $$
85 Willow Bend Drive
Arlington, Tennessee
(901) 867-2274
www.santilodge.com

Santi Lodge may be situated only minutes from I-40 and the traffic around Wolfchase Galleria shopping mall, but it feels as if you are miles away from an urban area. The log-cabin lodge is set on 100 acres and offers five rooms, each with air-conditioning in summer, private bath, and satellite TV. Some rooms include such extra amenities as fireplaces, walk-in closets, and private patios. A continental breakfast is served to guests, and you also have access to a fax machine, a copier, washer and dryer, and other amenities. The lodge hosts a number of large groups for business meetings, weddings, and the like, and at times a minimum two-night stay is required.

Sassafras Inn $$
785 Highway 51
Hernando, Mississippi
(800) 882-1897
www.memphis.to

The Sassafras Inn promises a romantic getaway for couples, complete with prettily decorated rooms, a heart-shape swimming pool, and a hot tub. It's a getaway from the city as well, situated south of Memphis in Hernando, Mississippi. Each room has a queen-size bed, a private bath, and a TV with VCR. Ask about the Heart's Content Cottage, too. Guests get a full breakfast, which they can opt to enjoy in their rooms, in the dining room, or by the pool. No children or pets are permitted, and smoking is allowed only in a designated area. Be aware the Sassafras has the following policy: "In keeping with the high standards of a Christian Bed and Breakfast, no unmarried couples or public drinking." It also has a seven-day cancellation policy.

Shellcrest $$$$
669 Jefferson Avenue
(901) 523-0226
www.shellcrest.com
The Shellcrest is a beautifully restored Victorian Italianate town house, located just east of downtown Memphis. The house is furnished with antiques and has two large one-bedroom apartments, each with a parlor, morning room, and full kitchen. Guests have access to a private garden, covered porches, and washer and dryer, and they can take advantage of free grocery delivery and a private-car service. Shellcrest, so named for the shell motif incorporated into the design, caters primarily to long-term visits but, depending on availability, is open to bed-and-breakfast guests for short visits. Breakfast is included for short-term guests only. No children are allowed, and smoking is allowed only on the veranda or covered porches.

RV PARKS

Note: T. O. Fuller and Meeman–Shelby Forest State Parks also have RV access. See the Parks and Recreation chapter for contact information.

Agricenter International
7777 Walnut Grove Road
(901) 355-1977
Set well off busy Walnut Grove Road on the Agricenter's extensive grounds, this RV park has 500 sites for RVs and campers only. Each site has water and electricity hookups, but no sewer hookups, although a dump station is available. When you arrive, go to the Agricenter main building or the farmers' market, which operates in a bright-red barn. If neither is open when you arrive, you can pay at the self-pay box on the south side of the farmers' market building. The cost is $18 a night, $15 a night for seniors. The RV park doesn't take reservations except during the busy periods of May and June, so be sure to call ahead if you want to stay there at that time of year.

Memphis Graceland KOA
3691 Elvis Presley Boulevard
(901) 396-7125, (800) 562-9386
www.koa.com
Tucked behind Heartbreak Hotel and a two-minute walk to Graceland, this RV park has sites for RVs and tents. The biggest attraction is that it's within walking distance of the mansion and other Elvis-themed restaurants and shops. The KOA has 72 sites with full hookups (water, electricity, and sewer) at $33.95 a night, 19 sites with water and electricity for $30.95 a night, and tent sites for $21.95 ($26.95 with water and electricity). After you stay six nights, the seventh night is free. The owners take major credit cards except for American Express and have a rule limiting guests' Internet time in the evenings. Amenities include laundry facility, bathhouse with showers, small convenience store, and swimming pool. Pets are allowed, but they must be leashed and cleaned up after. Owners Mary and Jim Parks live on the premises, maintain a secure facility, and are into the spirit of things. In front of their trailer is a sign that reads: ELVIS FANS ONLY/VIOLATORS WILL BE ALL SHOOK UP. Open year-round.

Mississippi River RV Park
870 Cotton Gin Place
(901) 946-1993
Tucked away near the National Ornamental Metal Museum and just a few minutes from downtown Memphis, this RV park is owned

and operated by French-born Huguette Buford, who runs a tight ship. There are sites for 32 RVs, costing $22 to $24 for each concrete pad with electricity, water, and sewer hookups. The rates are for two adults. Children younger than age 10 are free, but it's $2.00 a night for each extra person. Amenities include a laundry facility and a bathhouse with showers. Sites are available for tents, too, and it's a popular camping spot during the Memphis in May music fest. It's open year-round. Ask directions before you come, as it's tricky to find the place. Dogs are allowed, but only if you clean up after them.

Tom Sawyer's Mississippi River RV Park
1286 South Eighth
West Memphis, Arkansas
(870) 735-9770

This lush, green, spacious RV park is on the Arkansas side of the Mississippi, with views of the river from some sites. To get there from Memphis, follow I-55 into Arkansas and take exit 278. Follow the signs, and don't be alarmed as you zigzag through industrial areas. When you cross the levee, you leave all that behind and go down a country road lined with huge trees. The park has 55 pull-through sites with full hookups (water, electricity, and sewer) for $20 to $22 a night, plus plenty of room for tents. Amenities include a free laundry facility, a bathhouse with showers, fishing in the river or pond, walking trails, and a large field for sports. If you stay six nights, the seventh night is free. Pets are allowed, on leash only. The management is curmudgeonly and strict about the rules.

RESTAURANTS

Memphis is famous for its ribs and other pork barbecue, and although you'll find dozens of 'cue restaurants, they're not the only culinary show in town.

The city boasts some outstanding restaurants with national reputations, including Chez Philippe at The Peabody, where French-born José Gutierrez works his magic, and Erling Jensen, where the Danish-born chef of the same name turns out remarkable dishes. Many of the city's top chefs are native Memphians, and Wally Joe and Cielo are examples of dazzling, sophisticated restaurants that just happen to be in Memphis.

In short, you'll find a remarkable number of good restaurants for a city this size, and new ones are opening every year. You'll find that Memphians are doggedly devoted to Southern home cooking, particularly at midday. Plate lunches and meat-and-threes are the names you'll hear, as lunch restaurants all over the city serve up fried chicken, sweet tea, corn bread, and every kind of vegetable (and even things that aren't vegetables, since in the South macaroni and cheese, cottage cheese, and congealed salad are included on the veggie menu). Every restaurant seems to have some variation on the meat-and-threes at lunch, even if the place isn't really known for home cooking. (And yes, some do serve this fare for dinner.) Memphis, like other cities, also is rich in ethnic restaurants, from authentic Mexican and Indian to Thai and Vietnamese. You'll find lots of Italian restaurants, too, some of them well-loved institutions that have been operated 20 years or more by local families of Italian descent.

We would be remiss, however, if we didn't say a little more about barbecue. Memphis has evolved into the pork barbecue capital of the world, and if you don't believe it, check out the World Champi-

onship Barbecue Cooking Contest that takes place here every May (see the Annual Events chapter for more details). During barbecue-fest weekend, some 300 cooking teams set up operations at Tom Lee Park as they compete for prizes on barbecued pork ribs, whole hog, and pork shoulder. The city has great barbecue restaurants, so be sure to sample some barbecue ribs (wet or dry) and a savory pork-shoulder sandwich during your stay. (See the Close-up on barbecue in this chapter for more information.)

Finally, if you prefer the familiar, you'll find every kind of chain restaurant in Memphis. Fast-food options include Wendy's, Papa John's Pizza, and many, many more. Other chain restaurants include Outback Steakhouse, Olive Garden, Bahama Breeze, and Applebee's. On the more upscale end, there's Ruth's Chris Steak House and Benihana. By the way, Memphis restaurants are quite used to accommodating low-carb dieters, so speak up if you need to substitute vegetables or other foods for starchy and sugary dishes.

The listings in this chapter focus mainly on locally owned restaurants and are organized according to type of cuisine. Within each section we list the restaurants in alphabetical order. Within each type of cuisine, you'll generally find lots of variety in the decor, location, and size of the restaurants. The ambience, too, can vary quite a bit, ranging from elegant to casual, so you'll find beautiful showplaces as well as places that might be described as holes in the wall.

Most restaurants accept major credit cards and are wheelchair accessible. We note the exceptions in individual write-ups. Most places accommodate both smokers and nonsmokers, although some ban smoking entirely. Unless otherwise noted, smoking is allowed, and all restaurants by law are required to have nonsmoking sections. Most restaurants have parking lots or reasonably ample street parking, with the exception of those in the downtown central business district. Here, you can park in a nearby garage or on the street.

Restaurants in Memphis tend to have full bars, so unless we specify no alcohol, beer only, or just beer and wine, you can expect to find a well-stocked bar with wine and beer as well. In restaurants where there's no liquor or just beer, it's standard procedure to bring your own wine if you like, but you may pay a modest "corkage" fee.

If you have specific questions or concerns, such as whether the kitchen can accommodate vegetarians or special diets, feel free to call the restaurant. It's never a bad idea to call ahead anyway, because restaurants can sometimes close, change their hours of operation, or change the menu.

PRICE CODE

The price code in this chapter is based on the cost of dinner for two, without appetizers, desserts, drinks, tax, or tip. Your bill may vary, depending on what you order and fluctuating restaurant prices. Prices are for dinner, so keep in mind that lunch at the same restaurant usually costs less.

$	Less than $20
$$	$21 to $40
$$$	$41 to $60
$$$$	$61 and up

AMERICAN

Brontë $
387 Perkins Road Extended
(901) 374-0881
www.daviskidd.com
This bistro is frequented by book lovers as well as people who have never heard of the Brontë sisters. Although most bookstore cafes in Memphis offer mainly coffee, sweets, and sandwiches, Brontë, situated inside Davis-Kidd Booksellers in Laurelwood shopping center, has a large

menu with all kinds of entrees, salads, and other fare. The walnut-spinach and roasted-garlic linguine is a big seller, as is the chicken-wonton salad, served on greens with crisp wontons. This is a great place for dessert, especially the blueberry pie, an entire quarter pie, served with ice cream if you like. It's open for lunch and supper and serves light brunch fare most days. It's also a popular place for moms and young kids, especially after story hours. Open seven days a week, closing early on Sundays. Beer and wine are available, but smoking is not allowed.

Equestria $$–$$$
3165 Forest Hill-Irene Road, Germantown
(901) 869-2663
www.equestriacuisine.com
Locals love the decor of this equestrian-theme restaurant, with its beautiful wood finishes, subtle lighting, and other touches creating an elegant yet casual atmosphere. As far as the menu goes, the restaurant once served mainly steaks but now has a diverse menu that includes such dishes as porcini-dusted tilapia with spinach risotto, pork tenderloin with poached Granny Smith apples, and crab cakes with green onion tasso sauce. There's also a sizable wine list. Open for dinner Tuesday through Saturday.

Felicia Suzanne's $$$
80 Monroe Street
(901) 523-0877
www.feliciasuzannes.com
This fine-dining restaurant is the creation of Felicia Willett, a Mid-Southerner who worked closely with New Orleans culinary superstar Emeril Lagasse for many years. The menu features dishes with a Southern accent, such as fresh crab salad with fried green tomatoes and crispy fried oysters with New Orleans barbecue sauce over grits. The dining room features lavender hues and 25-foot ceilings, and during nice weather its courtyard features special hors d'oeuvres as well as the dinner menu. Some find the restaurant's management to be overly finicky about things such as dress

(men are required to wear jackets in the dining room) and the need for reservations (it's best to make them). The restaurant can be found in the lobby of the Brinkley Plaza office building at Main Street. Open Tuesday through Saturday for dinner.

Five Spot $$
84 G. E. Patterson Boulevard
(901) 523-9754

This funky little restaurant, situated downtown just off South Main Street, really is teeny tiny: Three tables and some seats at the bar. But locals love this eccentric place that's short on amenities but serves great food, such as grilled lamb chops, skillet shrimp, and beef tenderloin with bordelaise sauce. Be sure to try the excellent cheese grits, but bring your own bottle unless you want to drink beer. This is very much a fly-by-the-seat-of-your-pants operation, so you never know what you will get. The restaurant is in the back of Earnestine & Hazel's Bar and Grill, with its entrance across Patterson from Central Station. Beer only. Open Tuesday through Saturday for dinner; reservations on the weekends only.

Grill 83 $$$-$$$$
83 Madison Avenue
(901) 333-1224
www.madisonhotelmemphis.com

Grill 83 is arguably the best-looking eatery in Memphis. Situated downtown in the luxurious Madison Hotel, this modern restaurant is beautifully lighted and decorated with warm wood veneers, colorful finishes, and offbeat light fixtures that create an intimate, big-city feel. Cocktails here are elegant, served with a flourish and pricey, and the handsome bar is a favorite see-and-be-seen spot. The lunch features upscale versions of classics, including a sirloin burger, but dinner is the best time to dine here. The menu at Grill 83 changes seasonally but always features its fabulous signature steak, a 16-ounce bone-in prime Kansas City filet that's worth a splurge. Open for breakfast, lunch, and dinner every day. Reservations recommended for dinner.

The Grove Grill $$-$$$
4550 Poplar Avenue
(901) 818-9951
www.thegrovegrill.com

This lively and hopping East Memphis restaurant, tucked away in the back of Laurelwood shopping center, attracts big crowds of East Memphis residents. They love the warm atmosphere, the fresh oysters, and Southern-accented menu with dishes including seafood pasta jambalaya, wood-grilled black Angus New York strip steak with béarnaise, and low-country-style shrimp and grits. Open every day for lunch and dinner. Reservations recommended.

Houston's $-$$$
5000 Poplar Avenue
(901) 683-0915
www.houstons.com

The restaurant may be part of a chain, but the friendly, attentive service and dependably good food make it a local award winner year after year. The restaurant stays busy with patrons who come for both the royal treatment and for prime rib, grilled fish, hearty salads, and sandwiches. The dark wood helps to create an intimate ambience. The restaurant is situated back from Poplar, west of Wild Oats food market. Expect to wait for a table during the most popular mealtimes, particularly on weekends, when it can take as long as 45 minutes to get seated. Open every day for lunch and dinner.

ASIAN

Asian Palace $-$$
2920 Covington Pike
(901) 388-3883

Asian Palace Express
4970 Park Avenue
(901) 761-7888

You can get fried rice and egg rolls at many places around town, but Asian Palace is generally considered the best Chinese restaurant in town, given its huge menu and consistent quality. Situated off the beaten path near Covington Pike's

Auto Row, this large restaurant has everything from cold jellyfish and potstickers to scallops, Peking duck, and shrimp with walnuts and oysters, with a good selection of seafood dishes amid predictable Chinese restaurant decor. Their wonton soup is a standout version of this old standard. Don't miss the amazing, multicourse dinner Asian Palace prepares each winter to celebrate the Chinese New Year. A take-out-only branch of the restaurant can be found in East Memphis, a more convenient location for many of the restaurant's fans. The restaurant serves beer and wine. Open for lunch and dinner.

Bangkok Alley $-$$
830 North Germantown Parkway
Cordova
(901) 753-7250

This super-friendly Thai restaurant, situated amid the many shopping centers and chain restaurants along Germantown Parkway, is an oasis for lovers of this spicy Asian cuisine or anyone who wants an alternative to the usual suburban fare. You'll find a menu that combines familiar dishes such as red and green curries, pad thai, and spring rolls with chef's specials, among them, seafood keow whan, with scallops and a curry coconut sauce. Be sure to check out the whimsical wall decorations, created by Memphis artist/puppeteer Jim Crosthwait. Open for lunch Monday through Friday and for dinner Monday through Saturday. Beer and wine only. No smoking allowed.

Bhan Thai $-$$
1324 Peabody Avenue
(901) 272-1538
www.bhanthairestaurant.com

This midtown favorite serves up great ambience with its Thai cooking. Housed in a pretty turn-of-the-century house jazzed up with curry-yellow walls and funky light fixtures, Bhan Thai also has a pleasant back deck area, which is open during nice weather and often features live music. The menu features the basics such as pad thai and satays as well as some unusual dishes.

Don't miss the salmon with green curry or the Paradise Island salad—shrimp, scallops, and other seafood served cold in a spicy lemongrass sauce with lime. Lunch features a limited menu, with choices such as ginger teriyaki chicken and Bhan Thai spicy fried rice. The seasoning tends to be mild, so speak up if you like yours on the fiery side. Open Tuesday through Saturday for lunch and dinner.

Chao Praya $-$$
3588 Ridgeway Road
(901) 366-7827

Although it's off the beaten path, this Thai restaurant is worth a detour for some of the best Thai cooking in the city. The kitchen is the domain of a Thai couple that operated restaurants in their homeland and once cooked for the Thai royal family. Even standards like chicken satay and fresh spring rolls have a lively new personality under their culinary command. Don't miss the kra pow, a refreshing chopped chicken dish with fresh basil, or the sweet-and-sour Chao Praya duck. Housed in a shopping center near Hickory Ridge Mall, the restaurant (which used to be Shu's) is pleasant enough, with comfortable banquettes and tones of rust, beige, and black. Open every night for dinner and Monday through Friday for lunch.

The Emerald $
5699 Mt. Moriah Road Extended
(901) 367-2827

This family-run restaurant is the city's original Thai restaurant, serving an authentic menu of pad thai, red-curry dishes, and traditional soups and more. The servings are generous, and at lunch you can order from the menu or sample the all-you-can-eat lunch buffet that's enjoyed by those who work in the area. The Emerald serves lunch Monday through Saturday and dinner every night.

Ja Ja's Cuisine of Thailand $
192 Washington Avenue
(901) 850-5222

Situated a block east of the historic town square of suburban Collierville, this is an unlikely spot for such a gem of an ethnic restaurant. Ja Ja is the nickname of Thailand native Pen Fryer, who moved here with her American husband in 1979. Ja Ja runs the kitchen with delectable results, turning out first-rate Thai spring rolls, sticky rice, and pad thai and spicier dishes, such as curries, goy, and lemongrass chicken, which can be as hot (or mild) as you like. The servers know the menu and can give you as much or as little information as you like. It's family friendly, with a kid's menu that features corn dogs and chicken nuggets, and a gift shop with Thai foods and imported gifts. Open Tuesday through Saturday for lunch and dinner. Beer and wine only; no smoking.

Jasmine Thai and Vegetarian Restaurant   **$–$$**
916 South Cooper Street
(901) 725-0223
Tucked into a quaint little frame house in midtown's Cooper-Young neighborhood, Jasmine moved here in 2003 after several years of operating on Covington Pike. It serves an extensive menu of Thai and Chinese dishes, with plenty of vegetarian choices and a bit more heat than most Thai restaurants around town. You'll find the usual suspects, such as spring rolls, spicy Thai soups, and curries, as well as popular favorites including Three Flavor Fish and crispy bean curd and fried vegetables with garlic sauce. Open for lunch and dinner every day. Beer and wine only; no smoking.

Mikasa Japan   **$$–$$$**
6150 Poplar Avenue
(901) 683-0000
Tucked in the Regalia shopping center, Mikasa is a favorite among many local aficionados of Japanese cuisine. It features traditional dishes with an emphasis on seafood, with shrimp tempura, chicken teriyaki, and sushi. Open for dinner every day; lunch Monday through Friday.

P. F. Chang's China Bistro   **$–$$**
1181 Ridgeway Road
(901) 818-3889
www.pfchangs.com
Located at Park Place Centre shopping center in East Memphis, P. F. Chang's may be a chain restaurant, but for many Memphians, it's their favorite Chinese restaurant for lunch or dinner. They flock here for its urbane atmosphere, its knowledgeable and professional service, and its jazzy take on the traditional Chinese restaurant. The menu includes Cantonese, Sichuan, and other styles of Chinese food and wines that are chosen to go well with the dishes. Favorites include the chicken and vegetable lettuce wraps, dumplings, Beef a la Sichuan, and Cantonese roasted duck. Diners, though, are encouraged to create their own combinations using the menu as inspiration. The ultramodern bar, high ceilings, and harvest-moon lights make for a festive, big-city feel. Reservations recommended.

Pho Hoa Binh   **$**
1615 Madison Avenue
(901) 276-0006
Pho Hoa Binh, situated near a laundromat in a dowdy midtown shopping center, doesn't look like much from the outside. But don't be fooled by its dingy exterior or its uninspired interior design. This friendly, family-run place serves up some of the freshest and tastiest Vietnamese cooking in the city at bargain prices. Standouts include the special green mussels, zesty lemongrass garlic chicken, and savory Vietnamese soups (*pho*). The restaurant serves a menu of some 200 Vietnamese and Chinese dishes, so there is truly something for everyone. Pho Hoa Binh serves an all-you-can-eat lunch that is a favorite midtown bargain. Open daily for lunch and dinner; beer only.

Saigon Le   **$–$$**
51 North Cleveland Street
(901) 276-5326
The food at this family-run Vietnamese restaurant is bright, fresh, and so flavorful

Memphis Barbecue Primer

Memphis doesn't fancy itself the capital of pork barbecue for nothing. Dozens of restaurants of all sizes practice the art and science of cooking smoky, flavorful pork ribs and shoulder, as well as other barbecued meats such as beef, poultry, and shrimp.

Here's a quick primer on Memphis barbecue:

Memphis-style barbecue differs from its counterparts in Texas and elsewhere in that it's mostly pork (unlike Texas barbecue, which is usually beef). The sauce is a tomato-based sauce with varying degrees of heat (unlike that in the Carolinas, where the sauce is vinegar-based).

In Memphis ribs are served in two styles, dry and wet. Dry ribs are cooked without sauce; instead they are rubbed with a mixture of dried spices and herbs before cooking for flavoring. Some restaurants sprinkle on more of the seasoning on ribs before serving. Wet ribs are cooked in sauce and arrive at the table generously doused with sauce. You eat them with your hands, so don't even try to be neat about it.

Pork shoulder is served on a plate or on a bun, usually with sauce and always with a mustardy coleslaw as its only dressing. The pork is usually pulled (that is, pieces of meat are pulled off the bone by hand) but can be ordered sliced or chopped as well.

Barbecue is usually served with coleslaw and beans, although other options include potato salad or barbecue spaghetti, a peculiarly Memphis concoction consisting of spaghetti tossed with bits of meat and barbecue sauce. If you aren't ordering a sandwich, you'll find that at many places your order will arrive with "edible napkins," aka slices of white bread.

Proprietors of Memphis barbecue restaurants are happy for you to purchase some of their sauce or seasoning (and these make great gifts for the folks back home), but don't count on being able to pry loose any secret recipes.

Look for the listing of top Memphis 'cue restaurants in this chapter.

If you want to really see people go crazy over perfecting pork barbecue, don't miss the World Championship Barbecue Cooking Contest that takes place in Memphis each May. (See the Annual Events chapter for more information.)

you'll want to try everything. Try the fresh spring rolls, deep-fried Saigon egg rolls, noodle dishes, and soups of all kinds. Start with an order of the delicious green-shell mussels with French butter sauce. The decor is nothing special, but it's comfortable and clean. This restaurant has a loyal following of Memphis regulars, including families. Saigon Le is situated on Cleveland between Madison and Poplar. Unless you're drinking beer or nonalcoholic beverages, bring your own bottle. Open for lunch and dinner Monday through Saturday; closes at 9:00 P.M. sharp. The restaurant is wheelchair accessible but the restrooms are not.

Sawaddii $-$$
121 Union Avenue
(901) 529-1818

This stylish downtown restaurant delivers lively Thai specialties such as satays, spicy beef noodles, and red-curry dishes at reasonable prices. It can fill up fast, so reservations are a good idea. Check out the large photograph over the bar of a young Elvis Presley (during his army days) hanging out with Siamese royalty. Sawaddii (a variation on the Thai word for "how are you," incidentally) is open for lunch Monday through Saturday and for dinner every evening. No smoking except in the bar/lobby area. Beer and wine only.

Sekisui $-$$
50 Humphreys Boulevard
(901) 747-0001

160 Union Avenue (downtown)
(901) 523-0001

25 South Belvedere (midtown)
(901) 725-0005

1884 North Germantown Parkway
Cordova
(901) 309-8800

Memphis is lucky to have a group of outstanding sushi restaurants despite its inland location, thanks to Japanese-born restaurateur Jimmy Ishii. Sekisui serves great sushi as well as a complete menu of other Japanese dishes, including tempura, kushiyaki dinners, and teriyaki. The Humphreys Boulevard location is the best looking, with its East-meets-California feng-shui ambience, rice-paper panels, and tiny indoor brook. It features a *robata* menu and a weekend brunch. Open seven days a week.

Sekisui downtown is situated at the Holiday Inn Select with an American restaurant, Union Café, so diners can order from both menus. Its sushi bar has big windows, perfect for people watching. The midtown Sekisui features a popular sushi happy hour, with little boats floating plates of freshly made sushi throughout the restaurant.

Sekisui Pacific Rim & Sushi Bistro $$-$$$
4724 Poplar Avenue
(901) 767-7770

This hip restaurant is a treat for those who like imaginative East-West flavor combinations. As the Pan Asian restaurant in Japanese-born entrepreneur Jimmy Ishii's portfolio, Pacific Rim serves up dishes such as soba noodles with seafood in soy broth, kiwi-glazed duck breast with red-curry reduction, various fish tartars, tataki (seared fish or beef), and salads. The menu is heavy on appetizers, so this is a good place to order lots of small dishes to taste. There's also a full sushi menu and a good-looking sushi bar. The restaurant has a good selection of sake (Japanese rice wine), and the traditional wine list includes a generous selection by the glass. Open for lunch Monday through Friday and for dinner every night.

BARBECUE

Here are some choice places to try Memphis barbecue, and you can decide for yourself if dry ribs are better than wet ribs (an ongoing debate among barbecue lovers). You won't break the bank at these places. A pulled-pork sandwich is usually $4.00 or less, a large order of ribs $10.00 to $15.00. Be sure to read the Memphis Barbecue Primer Close-up in this chapter so you can talk the talk when you place your order.

The Bar-B-Q Shop $-$$
1782 Madison Avenue
(901) 272-1277
www.dancingpigs.com

This friendly barbecue restaurant has been a midtown favorite ever since veteran smoke-master Frank Vernon and his wife, Hazel, opened the shop some 25 years ago. Bar-B-Que Shop has all the usual favorites, including ribs and barbecue spaghetti, served with Texas toast. Try the Bar-B-Q Shop Special if you want to sample some of everything. The Vernons'

Dancing Pigs brand of sauce and rub is available for purchase, too.

Central B B Q $–$$
2249 Central Avenue
(901) 272–9377
www.centralbbq.net

This rowdy midtown barbecue joint is the newest kid on the block, and it's made a splash with its smoked hot (make that really hot) wings, great fresh coleslaw laced with red bell pepper, homemade potato chips, and, of course, plenty of barbecue pork. Central B B Q addresses the wet-ribs-or-dry-ribs conundrum by serving a slab that's half wet, half dry. You can eat on the deck or in the dining room, rubbing elbows with college students, families, and other locals. Beer only.

Corky's Ribs & BBQ $–$$
5259 Poplar Avenue
(901) 685–9744

1740 North Germantown Parkway
Cordova
(901) 737–1988

743 West Poplar Avenue, Collierville
(901) 405–4999
www.corkysbbq.com

Corky's serves up some of the most popular ribs and pork shoulder in town at its three suburban restaurants. The meats are slow-cooked over hickory wood and charcoal, and you can order the ribs in both dry and wet styles. The restaurants are casual, rustic-style places, where you can expect to wait for a table during peak dinner hours, because they don't take reservations. All three have a drive-through window, so you can get your barbecue to go. Corky's also does a huge mail-order business (see the Web site for more information) and sells its meats (frozen), sauce, and seasoning at supermarkets. It has been voted the best ribs restaurant in Memphis for more than 15 years by readers of *Memphis* magazine. The Cordova and Poplar Avenue restaurants serve beer, but no liquor or wine. Open every day. *Note:* You will see Corky's franchises in

other parts of the South, but the Memphis locations are operated hands-on by the Pelts family, the original owners.

Cozy Corner Restaurant $
745 North Parkway
(901) 527–9158

Situated east of downtown at Parkway and Manassas, this modest family operation has been cooking up fabulous barbecue since 1977, including some of Memphis's finest ribs, sliced pork or beef sandwiches with slaw, and delectable barbecued baloney sandwiches (no kidding). But the pièce de résistance is the barbecued Cornish hen, pink with smoked flavor and just the right size for one person, which even impressed Julia Child during a visit in the 1980s. Everything can be ordered either hot or mild (and mind you, mild still packs plenty of flavor). You line up at the counter to place your order, then settle in at a formica-topped table to wait for your number to be called. Open for lunch Tuesday through Saturday, but if your heart is set on sampling the Cornish hens, get there early, because they often sell out before the 5:00 P.M. closing time. No beer or alcoholic beverages.

The Germantown Commissary $–$$
2290 South Germantown Road
Germantown
(901) 754–5540
www.gtownbbq.com

This rustic barbecue shack, steeped with hickory smoke and situated near the railroad tracks, certainly looks the part. It has operated for more than 20 years and has many regular customers and fans. The Commissary serves up excellent ribs (sort of in between wet and dry), barbecue shrimp, and sandwiches as well as variations on the traditional such as barbecue nachos and a barbecue salad. Beer is available. Don't forget the homemade lemon, coconut, and chocolate pies, that is, if you have any room left. Open every day for lunch and dinner; reservations for groups of 12 or more only.

Interstate Bar-B-Q & Restaurant $-$$
2265 South Third Street
(901) 775-2304

150 Stateline Road
Southhaven, Mississippi
(662) 393-5699
www.jimneelysinterstatebarbecue.com
So named because the original is near
where the interstate crosses Third Street,
Interstate is operated by Jim Neely, widely
considered the godfather of Memphis barbecue. This casual, bustling restaurant
serves up great pulled-pork sandwiches
and generously cut ribs, but the sauce is a
real standout: dark, thick, rich, smoky, and
sweet but not too sweet. This is a good
place to try that Memphis concoction,
barbecue spaghetti. Interstate has a drive-
through as well. Open Monday through
Saturday for lunch and dinner.

Neely's Bar-B-Q $-$$
670 Jefferson Avenue
(901) 521-9798, (888) 780-7427

5700 Mt. Moriah
(901) 795-4177
www.memphisbarbecue.com
Neely's Bar-B-Q is owned and operated by
the four Neely brothers, who as nephews
of Jim Neely spent many years working
closely with their uncle at Interstate Bar-
B-Q. They learned their lessons well:
Neely's does great pork shoulder and both
wet and dry pork ribs as well as beef
brisket and ribs, unusual for a non-Texan
barbecue place. The sandwich menu
includes not just pork shoulder but also
sliced smoked turkey, smoked sausage,
BBQ nachos, and chopped or sliced barbecue beef, and Neely's barbecue spaghetti
is also popular. The atmosphere is homey
and casual, but calmer and a bit nicer than
most Memphis barbecue joints. Take-out
orders are available, too. The Jefferson
location is just a few blocks from downtown, once you cross the overpass. Draft
beer is available. Open Monday through
Saturday for lunch and dinner.

Payne's Bar-B-Q $
1762 Lamar Avenue
(901) 272-1523

1393 Elvis Presley Boulevard
(901) 942-7433
You'll find one of the best lunch deals in
town at Payne's, where you can get a
first-rate sliced or chopped barbecue
sandwich with homemade slaw. The
Lamar Avenue location is housed in a former gas station, with tables lining the area
where the bays used to be. You place your
order at the counter from Payne's all-pig
menu (not for vegetarians), where you
can hear them chop the meat for your
sandwich. The meat is subtly smoky, with
pieces of jerkylike outside crust. No credit
cards; no beer or alcoholic beverages. It's
open Monday through Saturday for lunch
and three nights a week for supper. The
Elvis Presley location is open Monday
through Saturday for lunch and dinner.

The Rendezvous $-$$
52 South Second Street, Rear
(901) 523-2746
www.hogsfly.com
You can literally follow your nose to this
famous Memphis institution, which perme-
ates downtown with its smoky fragrance.
Make your way down the alley between
the Holiday Inn Select and Best Western
on Union, then go downstairs. A visit to
the Rendezvous, opened in 1948 by Charlie
Vergos and still operated by the family, is a
must for visitors and a favorite for locals.
Nobody can match the scene here, with its
festive crowd, red-checked tablecloths,
memorabilia on the walls, and the constant
parade of sassy waiters bearing giant trays
of barbecue ribs and other specialties.
Rendezvous is famous for its dry ribs, but
you can get them wet, or stick with lean
pork loin, chicken, Greek salad, or meatless
red beans and rice if you're sticking to a
diet. Start with a cheese-and-sausage
plate. The place gets packed on weekends,
so expect a wait. Alternatively, try to go
early, say around 5:00 P.M., or get your

order to go. Rendezvous also does a significant mail-order business (888–464–7359). Beer and wine only. Open for dinner Tuesday through Saturday and for lunch on Friday and Saturday.

BISTROS AND ECLECTIC

Automatic Slim's Tonga Club $$–$$$
83 South Second Street
(901) 525–7948

This hip downtown restaurant, the brainchild of Memphis-born chef and artist Karen Blockman Carrier, never goes out of style. Named for a character in the well-known blues tune "Wang Dang Doodle," the restaurant reflects Carrier's love for the bright cuisine and colors of the Caribbean and Southwest and always has intriguing artwork on the walls. The menu combines Asian, American, Caribbean, and Southwestern cuisines, resulting in eclectic, flavorful dishes such as coconut mango shrimp, voodoo stew (an exotic cousin to bouillabaisse), whole red snapper, and imaginative sandwiches and salads. The bar is a hangout for the smartly dressed crowd, who are particular about their martinis. Automatic Slim's frequently plays host to in-the-know film crews when there's a movie being shot in town. There's live music on Friday nights. Open for lunch Monday through Friday and for dinner Monday through Saturday. Reservations recommended.

Beauty Shop & Dō $–$$$
966 South Cooper Street
(901) 272–7111

This happening eatery is named for its location, a former beauty shop where Priscilla Presley and other Memphis glamour girls used to get their hair done. The glass-brick-enclosed styling stations are now banquettes, and the shampooing sinks are used to ice down beer. The restaurant lives up to its motto, "Look Good, Eat Good," with a bar area that positively glows, thanks to the copper leaf on the walls, and plenty of funky artwork

and light fixtures throughout the place. It's the handiwork of restaurateur Karen Blockman Carrier, who also operates Automatic Slim's Tonga Club and Cielo. The menu offers up such fare as a watermelon and jerk chicken wings appetizer and whole fried striped bass. In 2004 the restaurant added a sushi bar, called Dō (pronounced dough), which serves sushi with a twist, tempura, and other dishes such as broiled fresh oysters with spicy mayo and ponzu sauce. Beauty Shop is open for lunch every day and for dinner Monday through Saturday. Dō is open for dinner Tuesday through Saturday.

The Brushmark $–$$
1934 Poplar Avenue
(901) 544–6225
www.brooksmuseum.org

This elegant lunch spot, located inside the Memphis Brooks Museum, features a menu created by Jennifer Dickerson, one of the city's most talented young chefs. The menu changes every day, but you can expect to find treats such as shrimp and grits, pan-seared smoked duck breast with honey-wasabi drizzle, and Asian tuna salad in addition to traditional Brushmark favorites such as African peanut soup and crepes. The restaurant also serves dinner on the first Wednesday of each month (except January and July) as part of an entire evening of festivities. The Brushmark features a covered deck overlooking the park, a great place to lunch al fresco during nice weather. Lunch is served Tuesday through Sunday.

Café 61 $$
8 South Second Street
(901) 523–9351

Café 61 is a funky, bright orange little restaurant that's modeled after an old Delta juke joint. It features a spunky, wide-ranging menu of dishes such as tasso-stuffed shrimp with five-pepper jelly and its King Creole Pork Chop 61, dry-rubbed, grilled, and served with Creole cream sauce. A sister restaurant of midtown's On Teur eatery, Café 61 is situated downtown across from The Peabody on Second Street (although it's Third Street, just a block away, that literally turns into the legendary Highway 61 before continuing through the Mississippi Delta). Café 61's fish taco with fresh mango is a favorite among downtowners. Some of chef Derk Meitzler's dishes can be fiery hot, so be sure to ask about the heat level when you order. The restaurant is friendly and casual as can be. Open for lunch and dinner.

Café Samovar $$-$$$
83 Union Avenue
(901) 529-9607
The Sadetsky family emigrated from the Ukraine and somehow ended up in Memphis, which is great news for the downtown culinary scene. Café Samovar proudly presents Russian classics such as pirogi, blinis, and borscht, as well as outstanding soups and salads, including its picturesque *salade niçoise.* Lunch is very popular here among the downtown executive set, with excellent salads, blini, chicken kiev, and sandwiches. The lunch prices are half those of dinner. The more substantive dinner fare features items such as sea bass with caramelized bananas and pork tenderloin with bacon-mango sauce. As a starter at dinner, try the generous Taste of Russia appetizer platter. The interior is very cheery with its Christmas colors, and on pleasant days you can sit out on Samovar's deck to enjoy people watching with your meal. There's also belly dancing on weekends and a good vodka menu. The restaurant serves lunch and dinner Monday through Friday and dinner only on Saturday. It's a good idea to call ahead for dinner during the week.

Cielo $$$
679 Adams Avenue
(901) 524-1886
This Memphis original is a historic Victorian house on the outside and an extravaganza of gold leaf, faux finishes, funky lamps, and intriguing artwork on the inside. The result is an upscale restaurant that feels magical, romantic, and fun with food that's as dazzling as the decor. It's the creation of Karen Blockman Carrier, who also owns Automatic Slim's restaurant. The menu includes escargot braised with pernod, steak au poivre, and crispy half duck with celery root slaw. The dining rooms are intimate and inviting, and the upstairs bar is a stylish spot for a glass of wine and appetizer. The adjacent lounge is cozy, and cigar smokers are welcome. There's live piano music on weekends. Open for dinner Tuesday through Saturday. Reservations recommended.

Elfo $-$$
3092 Poplar Avenue
(901) 888-0402
This attractive midtown lunch restaurant, tucked inside a swank little enclosed shopping center, is popular among ladies who lunch as well as working folk. Its owners are members of the Grisanti family, best known for their Italian cuisine, but Elfo takes a different tack here. Its bistro-style menu includes dishes such as wild mushroom tart, Creole crab cakes, and pink peppercorn–encrusted salmon. The restaurant can fill up quickly, but if you have to wait, there are plenty of boutiques under the same roof to keep you entertained until your table is ready. The restaurant is literally inside Shops at Chickasaw Oaks center, so park and walk all the way into the building to find Elfo. Open for lunch Monday through Friday.

Erling Jensen, The Restaurant $$$-$$$$
1044 South Yates Road
(901) 763-3700
www.ejensen.com
The culinary artistry of Danish-born Erling Jensen is the centerpiece of this top-echelon East Memphis restaurant, which along with its chef has been voted the city's best by readers of *Memphis* magazine each year since 1997. The simple exterior of this pale-yellow house near busy Poplar Avenue and its mellow but elegant interior don't prepare you for the plates of food, visual works of art that are scrump-

Restaurants are particularly notorious for closing or making other changes with little or no notice. Always call ahead, or check frequently updated resources, including Memphis *magazine or www.memphisrestaurants.com. It's the Memphis Restaurant Association Web site, which includes most (but not all) of the city's eateries.*

tious beyond belief. Chilean sea bass and mussels in saffron broth, elk loin in lingonberry preserves, lobster pancakes with wild mushrooms—these are just a few examples as Erling incorporates global elements into a foundation of traditional French cooking. The portions are so generous that dessert may seem impossible, but it's worth making room for the likes of roasted caramelized pineapple, honey coconut flan, and soufflé du jour. The menu changes often but always includes some salads, black Angus steaks, and other items for less fanciful tastes. The wine list, which includes some modestly priced choices, is a worthy companion to the food. Erling Jensen is definitely one of the priciest places in town, but it's money well spent for lavish portions of sublime and beautifully presented food, for service that's professional, friendly, but not stuffy, and for the ambience. Open nightly for dinner. Reservations recommended and a jacket for men recommended but not required. Valet parking available.

Garland's $$-$$$
**712 West Brookhaven Circle
(901) 682-5202**
This fine-dining restaurant, which had been called Christopher's until its namesake chef departed, still makes its home in a quiet, elegant house just off bustling Poplar Avenue. These days Garland's features spicy eclectic cuisine, with imaginative combinations such as sautéed shrimp in habañero vanilla cream sauce and Charleston-style shrimp and grits with

sautéed spinach and lemon scampi sauce. Open for dinner Tuesday through Saturday. Reservations recommended.

Harry's Detour $-$$
**532 South Cooper Street
(901) 276-7623**

**Harry's Detour South Main
106 G. E. Patterson Boulevard
(901) 523-9070**
These ultracasual restaurants feature the imaginative cooking of Harry Nicholas, a Memphis eccentric and talented chef. Harry's features lots of pecan-smoked dishes, including its delectable mahi Redondo spread, and also serves bacon-wrapped sea bass, fiery chaurice sausage, and scallops in a rich cream sauce. Take note that spicy dishes are often fiery indeed, so ask. Don't skip dessert here, where the warm bread pudding and homemade rum cake are magnificent! The midtown restaurant also serves an imaginative Sunday brunch, and there's an outdoor deck that's nice during pleasant weather. The downtown location features a covered patio with fireplace. Harry's serves beer, but BYOB if you're drinking wine. The midtown location is open for lunch and dinner every day except Monday. The downtown location is open for lunch Tuesday through Saturday and for dinner Wednesday through Saturday.

Jarrett's $$-$$$
**5689 Quince Road
(901) 763-2254
www.jarretts.com**
Don't let the modesty of its location in an East Memphis shopping center fool you. This warm and lively bistro is where Memphis-born chef Richard Farmer works wonders in the kitchen. Readers of *Memphis* magazine voted Jarrett's (named for the Farmers' son) the most underrated restaurant in town, while voting Farmer, who has cooked at the James Beard House in New York, as one of the city's best chefs. Jarrett's serves a creative American regional menu featuring

mushroom-and-cheese strudel, smoked-trout ravioli with Arkansas caviar, horseradish-encrusted grouper, and pecan barbecue rack of lamb. Lots of pride is taken in the wine list, which features California and French vintages, and wine tastings are held almost every Monday. Open for dinner Monday through Saturday. Look for the restaurant at Yorkshire shopping center on Quince, just a few blocks west of Ridgeway.

Lulu Grille $$–$$$
565 Erin Drive
(901) 763–3677
www.lulugrille.com
Every neighborhood should have a place like this around the corner. This bistro has a loyal East Memphis following, as regulars have been swarming here for more than a decade for such favorites as shrimp and lump crabmeat with bow-tie pasta, grilled lamb loin, and grilled ruby-red trout. The desserts are to die for here, and you certainly wouldn't want to pass up the coconut cake or other homemade specialties. The ambience is cozy and romantic, and the food is consistently wonderful. You may have to hunt for the restaurant, which is tucked in the back of White Station Plaza shopping center. Open daily for lunch and dinner. Reservations recommended.

McEwen's On Monroe $$–$$$
122 Monroe
(901) 527–7085
www.mcewensonmonroe.com
This urbane downtown bistro is wildly popular with food lovers, who flood this place for McEwen's consistently outstanding food, great wine list, and the hospitality of owner Mac Edwards. The kitchen turns out such delectable dishes as tuna seared to perfection, shrimp with roasted sweet pepper grits, and mushroom-encrusted rack of lamb. The banana cream pie is a favorite Memphis dessert. The bar, with its exposed-brick walls and uptown ambience, is a great spot for a martini or, better yet, a glass of wine, since as a knowledgeable former wine rep, Edwards

maintains one of the best selections around. A menu of small plates is available in the early evening as well. The dining room, with its warm green colors and bright paintings, is inviting and comfortable. Reservations are a must for dinner. Open for lunch Monday through Friday and for dinner Tuesday through Saturday.

Mantia's $–$$
4856 Poplar Avenue
(901) 762–8560
www.mantias.com
Mantia's, a bustling East Memphis gourmet shop, is also a restaurant, serving up sandwiches, salads, and pastas for lunch and a smaller menu of somewhat more substantial fare for dinner. Among sandwiches the homemade chicken salad, pimento cheese, and panini caprese are always smart picks; salad choices include an Oriental chicken salad with mandarin oranges and a club salad. The evening menu is heavy on pastas and specials that might include peach-glazed pork or hazelnut-crusted fish. Wine and beer are available. Open for lunch Monday through Saturday and for dinner Tuesday through Friday. You can't see Mantia's from Poplar, because it's hidden behind the liquor store on the north side of the street, but it's back there. (See the Shopping chapter for details on the gourmet shop.)

Melange $$–$$$
948 South Cooper Street
(901) 276–0002
www.melangememphis.com
This stylish Cooper-Young restaurant garners rave reviews for its fresh, well-prepared American-European cuisine. Melange is actually two places: the swank, quiet dining room with no smoking, and a bar with a menu of tapas (plates of "little bites," served with cocktails in the Spanish tradition), with late hours and smoking. Pass through the double doors into "The Dining Room at Melange," and it's a different world, with bleached wood, green plants, and fresh flowers. Among its signature dishes is duck prepared three ways

(*pas de trois*), caramelized fillet of escolar, and hot Grand Marnier soufflé, although the menu changes seasonally. The service is professional, and the wine list, which won kudos from *Wine Spectator* in 2001, is one of the best in the city. Melange is open for dinner seven nights. Even after the dining room closes, you can order from the tapas menu until the wee hours.

Napa Café $$–$$$
5101 Sanderlin Avenue
(901) 683–0441
www.napacafe.com
This attractive East Memphis restaurant serves imaginative bistro fare with dishes such as pan-roasted wild salmon with sweet carrot confit and rack of lamb with fig-onion marmalade. It also has a wine list with more than 160 wines, including some from boutique vineyards, and offers at least 20 of them by the glass and nearly 30 as half bottles. The restaurant is decorated with a plum-red finish on the walls and a whimsical handpainted mural in the back. It's situated inside Sanderlin Center shopping center, located just east of the Doubletree Hotel. Open for lunch weekdays and dinner Monday through Saturday. Closed Sunday.

On Teur $–$$
2015 Madison Avenue
(901) 725–6059
This breezy, hip eatery near Overton Square in midtown has gained a huge following of Memphians and Rhodes College students for scallops Henri, steak Saigon, and other delicious, flavorfully sauced dishes. There's the tiny dining room, where you can watch the chefs at work, or the tented deck area strewn with pinlights. (It's enclosed and climate controlled, except during nice weather, when the sides are removed.) On Teur is a midtown institution, and the food speaks for itself. *Note:* Pay attention if a dish is described as hot, because they aren't kidding. Your server can give you the skinny about the heat. On Teur serves beer but not wine or liquor. Bring your own, or get directions to the liquor store just down the street. Open daily for lunch and dinner.

Seasons at the White Church $–$$
196 North Main Street
(901) 854–6433
www.seasonsatthewhitechurch.com
Formerly a 19th-century church, with its colorful stained-glass windows, the building provides an inspiring atmosphere for enjoying such specialties as roast pork with jalapeño lime brown butter, and fresh fish preparations that might include roasted mahimahi with ginger shallot butter. The restaurant has a country French feeling and features a wine list of more than 175 bottles. The old church is at the corner of West Poplar and North Main near the Collierville town square. Open for lunch Tuesday through Saturday and for dinner Thursday through Saturday.

Stella $$$
39 South Main Street
(901) 526–4950
www.stellamemphis.com
This stylish downtown restaurant showcases the cooking of John Kirk, a young chef who creates Southern-accented dishes that include jerked grilled catfish, smoked chicken fricassee with cheese grits, and buttermilk-fried oysters. Stella makes its home in a former jewelry store at the corner of Monroe Avenue, where rich wood finishes on the interior walls and original tile floors add character to the restaurant, and large two-story windows lend an airy feeling. There's a balcony with extra tables, and tables are set up along the sidewalk where you can sit during nice weather. The restaurant opened in spring 2004 but already has the polish of a longtime classic. Open Monday through Friday for lunch and every night for dinner. Reservations are recommended.

Tsunami $$–$$$
928 South Cooper
(901) 274–2556
www.tsunamimemphis.com

This hip eatery, which operates in midtown's Cooper-Young neighborhood, serves up wonderfully prepared fish and seafood dishes as well as soups and salads with an Asian flair. The sake-steamed mussels and crispy calamari are standouts among the appetizers, and any entree that's served with black Thai rice is a must. Roast sea bass with soy beurre blanc is Tsunami's signature dish, but you won't go wrong with other options, which might include spice-crusted tuna and hot and pungent shrimp with coconut milk. Its crème brûlée may be the best in the city. Open Monday through Saturday for dinner.

Wally Joe $$–$$$
5040 Sanderlin Avenue
(901) 818-0821
www.wallyjoememphis.com
Wally Joe is one of the most gorgeous restaurants in the city. Its dining room is decorated with handsome wood finishes, a windowed wine cellar, backlit displays of wineglasses, and, last but not least, a wide-open view into its sparkling kitchen, where you can watch the chefs at work. But the food, in the hands of its affable namesake chef, is the star. The menu of American cuisine with subtle Asian undertones lists spiced quail satay, the restaurant's signature Pork in Four Movements that includes Joe's take on barbecue, and its duo of lamb, a combination of grilled rack and lamb confit. Joe got his start creating the award-winning KC's Restaurant in Mississippi, where the wine list won recognition from *Wine Spectator*. Already large enough to include many splurge-worthy bottles as well as more moderately priced choices, the list is expected to grow even grander throughout the years. Joe himself has been doing a star turn recently, appearing as host with three other Southern chefs in the Turner South cable program *Off the Menu*. Open for lunch Wednesday through Friday and for dinner Monday through Saturday.

Washington Street Bistro $$–$$$
170 Washington Street, Collierville
(901) 850-1470

This sunny suburban bistro is a favorite among Collierville residents, with its bright yellow walls and cheerful ambience. Situated just off the historic town square, Washington Street Bistro serves a wideranging menu that includes dishes such as crab cakes with Louis sauce, oven-roasted pork tenderloin, and filet mignon with Madeira sauce. For dessert, don't miss the sumptuous gooey butter bars or the chocolate cashew brownie that's actually a deeply chocolate layer cake. It's definitely a neighborhood restaurant, where owner/chef Walt Norwood likes to take a break from the kitchen to visit with customers. Wine and beer only; no smoking. Open Monday through Saturday.

YiaYia's Eurocafe $$–$$$
7615 West Farmington Boulevard
Germantown
(901) 756-4004
This trendy eatery, with its lodgelike warm wood and stone interior, offers a menu of what it calls "homestyle Mediterranean" cuisine, including such dishes as crab risotto cakes, wood-roasted salmon salad, oak-fired pizzas, and whole oven-roasted fish. There's also an all-you-can-eat brunch buffet on Sundays, where you can sample some of everything. Open for lunch and dinner every day. YiaYia's bar is also an alluring nightspot for area yuppies, especially on Wednesday and Friday nights, both for happy hour and later.

CAJUN/NEW ORLEANS COOKING

Cayenne Moon $$–$$$
94 South Front Street
(901) 522-1475
www.cayennemoon.com
This is one of the best places in downtown Memphis for New Orleans–style fare, with an extended menu that includes zesty, seafood-filled jambalaya and gumbo as well as lump crab–stuffed mushrooms and ravioli stuffed with crawfish and andouille sausage. The buttery fresh rolls

and sweet-potato fritters are a delectable addition to meals at Cayenne Moon, and be sure to try the maple bread pudding with praline sauce. This former cotton warehouse, with its exposed brick walls and wrought-iron details, even looks the part of a French Quarter oyster bar. The restaurant serves beer only, and smoking is not allowed. Open for dinner Tuesday through Saturday.

Mister B's $$–$$$
6655 Poplar Avenue, Germantown
(901) 751-5262

Tucked away in the Carrefour shopping center, this New Orleans–style seafood kitchen is well liked by Memphis suburbanites, who come here for fried oysters, shrimp Creole, and po'boys as well as for steaks. That's the dinner menu; for lunch Mister B's serves hearty plate lunches featuring country-fried steak, meat loaf, and the like. Even though the address is Poplar Avenue, to find Mister B's, drive to the back of the shopping center, where you'll find it just west of Borders bookstore. Open for lunch Monday through Friday and for dinner Monday through Saturday.

Owen Brennan's $$
6150 Poplar Avenue
(901) 761-0990
www.brennansmemphis.com

This festive restaurant brings a taste of New Orleans to Memphis with its Big Easy ambience, authentic Creole specialties, and live jazz on weekends. Although not run by the Brennan family of restaurants in New Orleans, Owen Brennan's serves up very authentic po'boys, shrimp Creole, jambalaya, and other specialties. For a festive occasion order the bananas Foster, which will be flambéed and served at your table. The main dining room, with its ultrahigh ceilings, is festooned with Mardi Gras decor, and there are smaller, more intimate rooms available as well as an enclosed patio area. The brunch is extremely popular here, featuring eggs Sardou and other dishes off the menu as well as a lavish buffet. Open

for lunch and dinner Monday through Saturday and for brunch on Sunday.

Timbeaux's on the Square $$–$$$
333 Losher Street
Hernando, Mississippi
(662) 429-0500
www.timbeauxs.com

This friendly small-town restaurant calls itself a Cajun steak house. Here, you'll find a diverse crowd of diners ranging from families with children to high-rollers on their way to the casinos. It's a pleasant restaurant with exposed brick walls and plantation shutters, but more important, the food is great. Barbecue shrimp, Black n' Bleu filet with blue-cheese mashed potatoes, and fresh local striped bass are standouts at dinner. Lunch consists of po'boys and other sandwiches and plate lunches that feature local produce. There's a wine list, and the bar often features special cocktails made from watermelon or other fresh fruits. Timbeaux's is usually packed on the weekends but doesn't take reservations, so it's a good idea to call ahead to get on the waiting list. Open for lunch Monday through Friday and for dinner Monday through Saturday.

DELIS

Bogie's Delicatessen $
715 South Mendenhall Road
(901) 761-5846

Bogie's Downtown Deli
80 Monroe Avenue
(901) 525-6764

Bogie's Delicatessen Midtown
2098 La Salle Place
(901) 272-0022

This unpretentious deli makes great sandwiches, which feature Boar's Head deli meats and cheeses, as well as salads and soups. The homemade prepared salads are outstanding, particularly the potato salad and the fresh shrimp salad, available only on Fridays. Order the salad-sampler platter if you want to try them all. For some reason Bogie's has red, ripe tomatoes all year-round, a nice touch on both salads and sandwiches. You order at the counter, and they'll bring your food to your table. The midtown Bogie's has a pleasant covered deck. Open for lunch Monday through Saturday; hours vary by location.

Fino's from the Hill $
1853 Madison Avenue
(901) 272-3466

Midtowners inundate this little Italian deli to get the crusty, oversize sandwiches and hearty pasta specials. The owners bring in authentic Italian meats, cheeses, olives, and other goodies from the Hill, St. Louis's Little Italy, which they pile onto fresh-baked French bread for the sandwiches. Meat and cheese platters are available for low-carb dieters. These ingredients also find their way into saucy pasta dishes and salads. You can also get Italian desserts, or buy olives, meats, and Italian grocery items to take home. It's extremely casual, down to the paper plates and bus-your-own-table policy. Order at the counter, find a table, and wait for your name to be called, which is when you pick up your food and pay. You can get your order to go and take it to nearby Overton Park for a picnic on a nice day. Fino's is on the bottom floor of an apartment building called The Gilmore, where there's a parking lot in the back. Open for lunch and early dinner Tuesday through Saturday. No liquor. No credit cards.

Fat City $
175 Peabody Place
(901) 526-9775

This New Orleans–style cafe specializes in cafe au lait and beignets, but the real reason to visit this friendly small place is its shrimp po'boys, muffalettas, and other Big Easy sandwich concoctions. Fat City, situated on the street level of the Hampton Inn & Suites near Beale Street, also serves panini (more like po'boys flattened in a press than the authentic Italian sandwich)

as well as fried catfish nuggets and fries. The big round muffalettas are large enough to feed a family of four. Beignets, the French Market–style donuts rolled in powdered sugar, are messy to eat but sure to satisfy any sweet tooth.

Front Street Delicatessen $
77 South Front Street
(901) 522-8943

This friendly, small take-out place serves breakfasts featuring country ham and homemade biscuits as well as sandwiches and a few plate-lunch choices every day. Tom Cruise hung out here while filming the movie of the John Grisham book *The Firm*. There are a few seats inside, and a few tables set up outside during good weather. Open for breakfast and lunch Monday through Friday, and on weekends during Memphis in May or other major downtown events. Beer only.

Jason's Deli $
1199 Ridgeway Road
(901) 685-3333

1585 Chickering Lane, Cordova
(901) 844-1840
www.jasonsdeli.com

This large, cheerful deli with red-leatherette booths may be another chain restaurant, but it has definitely won over the hearts of Memphians, who love the extensive salad bar (perhaps the best in town), muffalettas, and other hot sandwiches. You place your order at the counter and pay, and servers bring you your food. The menu, which is quite long, includes healthy-heart selections, fine soups, and stuffed baked potatoes. The free soft ice cream is a nice, friendly touch. Jason's is packed at lunchtime, so expect a line during the busiest times. Open every day for lunch and dinner.

Kwik Check Food Store $
2013 Madison Avenue
(901) 274-9293

This is not a restaurant at all, but a mid-town convenience store that happens to have some of the most inventive, scrumptious sandwiches in town. You order at the back counter, choosing from muffalettas, vegetarian, falafel, roast beef, and turkey sandwiches, or Kwik Check's own concoctions. Among them: the Hey Zeus, made from roast beef, turkey, feta, and lemon-herb dressing wrapped in pita bread. You probably want to get your order to go, but there is a small counter at the front of the store if you want to eat your sandwich there. Open every day for lunch and dinner.

DINERS AND BREAKFAST PLACES

The Arcade $
540 South Main Street
(901) 526-5757

This casual restaurant, arguably the oldest eatery in the city (it dates from 1919), is a step back in time since the proprietors—the grandson of the founder and his wife—have kept the original diner decor intact. Because of its vintage look, the Arcade has been featured in movies, including 2003's *21 Grams* and the cult film *Mystery Train*. The Arcade serves breakfast all day as well as pizzas, sandwiches, salads, and plate-lunch specials during the week. It's a favorite hangout both for neighborhood residents and visitors in the popular South Main district. Also open for lunch and dinner on the weekends.

Blue Plate Café $
5469 Poplar Avenue
(901) 761-9696

2921 Kirby-Whitten Parkway, Bartlett
(901) 213-1066

Just off the I-240 exit and convenient to many East Memphis hotels, this bright yellow house is one of the few places in Memphis where you can get a big old-fashioned breakfast, complete with pancakes. It's packed on the weekends, and in addition to serving breakfast all day, Blue Plate also serves plate lunches. There's a second loca-

tion in Bartlett, with the same menu. Open every day for all meals, except the Poplar location closes for Sunday dinner.

Brother Juniper's College Inn $
3519 Walker Avenue
(901) 324-0144

Brother Juniper's, a popular restaurant near University of Memphis, is one of the best places in the city for breakfast. Expect a wait on Saturdays, when people flock there for omelets, homemade breads and biscuits, and other breakfast favorites. The lunch menu consists mainly of sandwiches, homemade soups, and potato casseroles as well as items from the breakfast menu. The service is friendly and down to earth at this casual cafe, which feels like a bit of a throwback to U of M's hippy days. Closed on Mondays and Sundays. No credit cards. Smoking is not allowed inside the restaurant. Although the dining room is wheelchair accessible, the restrooms are not. There's a second location at the Pink Palace Museum at 3050 Central Avenue (901-320-6320), which also serves dinner.

Denny's $
166 Union Avenue
(901) 522-9938

This downtown unit of the well-known breakfast chain is noteworthy because it's the only place in that area where you can get breakfast, lunch, or dinner 24 hours a day. Here you'll find Denny's Original Grand Slam and other familiar breakfast combos in addition to sandwiches and other fare. The restaurant is situated inside the Benchmark Hotel. No alcohol served.

Silver Caboose Restaurant & Soda Fountain $-$$
132 East Mulberry Street
(901) 853-0010

The Silver Caboose has been a fixture on the picturesque Collierville town square for generations. This homey restaurant calls itself a steak house (and does serve steak), but it's actually a wonderful old-fashioned diner complete with a classic soda fountain. Silver Caboose has friendly staff and comfort-food favorites, including a fabulous grilled bacon and cheese sandwich. This is a good place to try classic Southern cuisine, including chocolate chess pie as well as tomato aspic, the quintessential Southern ladies' luncheon salad. Open every day for lunch.

FRENCH

Bonne Terre Café $$$
4715 Church Road West
Nesbit, Mississippi
(662) 781-5100
www.bonneterre.com
This gem of a restaurant is worth an excursion into Mississippi to enjoy the warm country French ambience and outstanding cuisine. Be prepared to splurge, as the restaurant serves only three- and four-course dinners. The menu includes such delectables as spice-rubbed rack of lamb, housemade pasta with lobster, and pan-seared halibut with braised artichokes. Open Monday through Saturday for dinner, lunch on Thursday, and for its terrific jazz brunch on the first Sunday of each month. Beer and wine are served, but smoking is not allowed. Ask about limousine service, or expect about a 20- to 30-minute drive from Memphis. To get there take I-55 to Nesbit, then the Church Road exit, and go 4.4 miles on Church. Reservations are recommended. (For more information about Bonne Terre Country Inn, see the Accommodations chapter.)

Café 1912 $$
243 South Cooper Street
(901) 722-2700
This lively little bistro, situated just south of Overton Square, is the casual, less pricey sister of La Tourelle, the fine-dining restaurant around the corner. Café 1912 has a fun feel to it, with bright colors on the walls, an open kitchen, and young hip waitstaff. The menu consists of bistro fare such as strip steak with béarnaise sauce

and steamed mussels in white wine. The restaurant serves beer and a small, thoughtful wine list priced at $5.00 a glass, $20.00 a bottle. Dinner is served every night, and lunch is served on the weekends.

Café Society $$-$$$
212 North Evergreen
(901) 722-2177
This is the classic little French restaurant around the corner for many Memphians, some of whom have been dining here for years. Café Society skillfully prepares a French continental menu that includes French onion soup, bacon-wrapped shrimp, sautéed veal tenderloin, and seafood bisque served in a bowl that's actually a scooped-out round French loaf. The restaurant has a warm ambience and reliable service, and the bar is a great place for a glass of wine and an appetizer. In summer you can sit outside at a sidewalk table. Open for lunch Monday through Friday and for dinner Monday through Saturday. Reservations recommended.

Chez Philippe $$$-$$$$
149 Union Avenue
(901) 529-4188
www.peabodymemphis.com
One of the most elegant dining experiences in Memphis can be had at Chez Philippe, The Peabody hotel's flagship restaurant. It always receives high marks from readers of *Memphis* magazine for its romantic ambience and its gifted chef, and it's the only restaurant in Memphis to be awarded four stars by *Mobil Travel Guide*. You enter the restaurant from the grand lobby through gilded wrought-iron gates into an opulent dining room. The lavish decor, with velvet draperies, crystal chandeliers, and gilded finishes, makes you feel like royalty, as does the white-gloved service. The dining room is arranged as three levels, which helps to create an intimate feeling. José Gutierrez, an acclaimed Master Chef born and trained in France, dazzles diners with a menu of contemporary French cuisine with Southern elements. The menu

changes seasonally, and it might include smoked lobster bouillabaisse and smoked pork tenderloin brushed with mustard and sage. You can order a fixed menu or a la carte. Ask about the monthly chef's tables, which allow you to sample food and wine in José's kitchen. Open for dinner Tuesday through Saturday. Reservations are recommended. No smoking is allowed. Parking is free if you valet-park at The Peabody and bring your ticket in for validation.

La Tourelle   **$$$**
2146 Monroe Avenue
(901) 726-5771
www.latourellememphis.com
La Tourelle, which opened in 1977 as one of the city's first fine-dining establishments, is still among the best, cherished among romantics and gourmands alike. With creamy apricot walls, lace curtains, and colorful French posters, it's one of the city's most romantic restaurants. What's more, the food shines under the direction of chef de cuisine Justin Young, the latest in a long line of gifted chefs that has included Erling Jensen. The dishes are simply prepared, with flavorful demi-glace and reduction sauces, incorporating foie gras, fish, and meat, served with interesting vegetable combinations. Its wine list has won kudos from *Wine Spectator.* Ask about The Tower menu, which allows you to enjoy the same great food for less. Open Tuesday through Sunday for dinner and for brunch on Sunday. Reservations recommended.

Paulette's   **$$-$$$**
2110 Madison Avenue
(901) 726-5128
This pretty, charming restaurant in Overton Square is a tried-and-true Memphis "cornerstone" restaurant for an elegant lunch or Sunday brunch, not to mention a romantic dinner for two. It's decorated like a quaint French country inn, with stucco walls and dark, exposed beams, and has live piano music on weekends. As for the food, Paulette's serves up its traditional standards, such as fillet Paulette and

Louisiana shrimp crepes, and is famous for the hot, freshly made popovers served at every meal. You'll find plenty of crepes, salads, and other choices, including elegant variations on eggs Benedict for brunch, as well as luscious desserts. There's piano music on weekends. Open for lunch Monday through Saturday, dinner every day, and for Sunday brunch. Reservations recommended.

Three Oaks Grill   **$$-$$$**
2285 Germantown Road South
Germantown
(901) 757-8225
Three Oaks Grill, owned and operated by the owner of Paulette's, is a fine-dining venue convenient to persons who live and work in Germantown. Like its midtown sister this restaurant delivers great atmosphere, service, and delectable continental cuisine with a French accent. Among the favorites on the menu are ginger-roasted salmon, rack of lamb, and filet mignon. Situated in the town's historic district across from the old train depot, the restaurant has a clubby main dining room complete with fireplace as well as a second Southwestern-style room with tile and white stucco. Open for lunch Monday through Friday, for dinner every night, and for brunch on Sunday.

GERMAN

Erika's   **$-$$**
52 Second Street
(901) 526-5522
If you were to get caught in the pouring rain, you could find no better refuge than Erika's. Comfort food with a German accent, featuring specialties such as wiener schnitzel, bratwurst, and flavorful sauerkraut, is cooked up by Erika Seipel, who has operated this restaurant since 1977. Don't miss the substantial yeast rolls, but be forewarned that eating more than one may mean no room for dinner. The decor has changed little throughout the years at this homey eatery, which contin-

ues to be a popular lunch spot for down-town power brokers. Erika's serves beer, but you can bring your own wine. Open for lunch Tuesday through Friday and for dinner on Friday and Saturday.

GREEK

Jim's Place   **$$-$$$**
5560 Shelby Oaks Drive
(901) 388-7200
Jim's Place, family owned and operated here since 1921, is one of the city's oldest restaurants, having moved from down-town Memphis to its current location in the 1970s. It's situated off the beaten path on a woodsy lot amid warehouses and other commercial businesses off Summer Avenue. This large and beloved Memphis establishment is chopped up into smaller, cozy dining rooms nicely decorated in dif-ferent styles, with views of the grounds particularly attractive in spring and sum-mer. Greek specialties such as pork ten-derloin or beef kabobs grace the menu, but there's also shrimp stuffed with lump crabmeat, grouper Pontchartrain, and excellent steaks. Jim's Place is a wonderful setting in which to celebrate a birthday or other special occasion. Open for lunch Monday through Friday and for dinner Monday through Saturday. Reservations accepted during the week and on week-ends only for large parties.

Melos Taverna   **$-$$**
2021 Madison Avenue
(901) 725-1863
Quietly busy for many years, this intimate restaurant serves a menu of traditional Greek specialties including dolmades, moussaka, roasted lamb, and souvlaki, brought to your table with loving care by Melos's longtime servers. The generous Grecian-feast platters in the back of the menu are the best deal, because you can try lots of different items in one meal. If earlier diners haven't already snapped all of it up, be sure to try the marinated-octopus appetizer. Most dinner portions

are quite generous, so ask your server what's reasonable for your party. Often one dinner plus appetizers is plenty for two people, and the platters are big enough to feed a herd. The restaurant is cozy and dark, with candles in wine bot-tles and checked tablecloths. The short and modest wine list includes a number of Greek wines. Open for dinner Tuesday through Saturday.

Mojo's Greek and Mediterranean   **$-$$**
775 South Highland Street
(901) 458-0030
This nondescript student hangout near the University of Memphis serves good Middle Eastern fare, including roast lamb and hen stuffed with rice and ground beef. Lighter fare includes falafel, hummus, and sandwiches that are easy on the wal-let. Mojo's serves beer only. The restaurant is wheelchair accessible, but the rest-rooms are not. Open for lunch and dinner Monday through Saturday.

INDIAN

Amber Palace   **$-$$**
97 South Second Street
(901) 578-9800
This Indian restaurant in downtown Mem-phis is operated by the same efficient management as India Palace in midtown and serves a very similar menu as well as a popular all-you-can-eat buffet for lunch. If you're new to Indian cuisine, try the ten-der tandoori chicken and warm flat-bread. Beer only.

India Palace   **$-$$**
1720 Poplar Avenue
(901) 278-1199
With its colorful jungle murals, polite ser-vice, and daily lunch buffet, local fans of Indian cooking fill this spot up, particularly on tight lunch hours. The menu is easy to understand and has all the usual suspects, such as tandoori chicken, biryani, curries, masalas, and 11 types of Indian bread. Try one of the complete dinners, such as the

vegetarian dinner, if want to sample lots of different dishes. The kitchen is usually very careful about keeping the hot spices in check, so have a chat with your server if you want a full allotment of heat. The restaurant also has comfortable booths, and even though there are white table-cloths, it's pretty casual. India Palace is open for lunch, when you can choose from the menu or the all-you-can-eat buffet, and for dinner daily. Beer only.

Mayuri Indian Cuisine $-$$
6524 Quince Road
(901) 753-5979
www.mayuriindiancuisine.com
Mayuri is the place to go for authentic Indian cooking, so don't be surprised if the crowd is mostly Indian. The restaurant prides itself on being able to offer both north and south Indian dishes and boasts a team of chefs recruited from various areas of India. You'll find the usual biryanis, tandoori dishes, curries, and samosas, but also an offering of south Indian dishes that include rice crepe stuffed with potato curry, and lentil cakes. The atmosphere is spare and clean, with a few Indian-theme pictures and decorations to liven things up. The all-you-can-eat lunch buffet features spicier seasoning than the buffet fare at most of the other Indian restaurants around town. Open for lunch and dinner every day. Beer only; no smoking.

ITALIAN

Bari $$-$$$
22 South Cooper Street
(901) 722-2244
This small midtown restaurant, named for the famous port town in southeast Italy, features the cuisine of that area. Operated by Jason and Rebecca Severs, Bari features small portions of seafood, pasta, salads, and other items, so you can try lots of different things. Jason Sever's focus is on simple preparations that allow the fresh ingredients to shine. So the dishes have simple dressings but not a lot of heavy sauces or elaborate flourishes. You can't miss the bright yellow exterior of Bari, situated just off of Overton Square, although the simple white-washed interior is reminiscent of Mediterranean fishing villages. If you're headed to a play at nearby Playhouse on the Square, Bari is a great spot for a pre-theater or post-theater dinner or light supper. No smoking. Open for lunch Tuesday through Friday and for dinner Tuesday through Sunday.

Bol a Pasta $-$$
2200 North Germantown Parkway
Cordova
(901) 384-7988

3160 Village Shops Drive, Germantown
(901) 757-5609
This family-friendly restaurant, another one operated by the Grisanti family, serves all kinds of pasta as well as other specialties such as steaks, shrimp scampi, and seafood entrees. An often-requested dish is the sirloin steak carbonara with pasta alfredo. Parents and kids alike are at home at these casual restaurants, decorated with colorful original murals. Open every day for lunch and dinner.

Brooklyn Bridge Italian Restaurant $$
1779 Kirby Parkway
(901) 755-7413
This family-owned Italian restaurant features lasagne Amalfitano, manicotti, and other pastas as well as such entrees as veal and shrimp scampi. The Correale family's homemade sauce goes on the specialty of the house: Brooklyn Bridge's well-known pizza. This is New York–style Italian food served in an attractive place with friendly service. What could be better? Open for dinner Monday through Saturday.

Capriccio Grill $$-$$$
149 Union Avenue
(901) 529-4000
www.peabodymemphis.com
One of two restaurants at The Peabody, Capriccio Grill serves a northern Italian menu in a sleek, modern dining room. Its

companion is the Capriccio Café, which serves sandwiches and delectable cakes, pies, and other sweets. The pastas, pizzas, and some other dishes at the restaurant are reasonably priced. However, since Capriccio Grill charges Chez Philippe prices for much of its menu, you might as well have a more memorable dining experience at Chez Philippe. Open seven days a week for lunch and dinner.

Ciao Bella da Guglielmo $-$$
522 South Mendenhall Road, Suite 300
(901) 205-2500

This tiny neighborhood restaurant features handmade pizzas, pastas, and other Italian specialties served in a bustling, casual atmosphere. Situated next to a Kroger supermarket (oddly enough), it's a great favorite among Memphians for its fresh, well-prepared dishes. Open for dinner every night.

Coletta's $
1063 South Parkway East
(901) 948-7652

2840 Appling Road
(901) 383-1122
www.colettasrestaurant.com

This longtime Memphis institution is famous for inventing barbecue pizza, a local favorite that's still on the menu. This Italian restaurant is a good place for old-fashioned favorites such as spaghetti and meatballs, ravioli, and homemade Italian sausage. Memphians love their pizza, an old-style pie that's been made the same way for years. You'll find the original Coletta's in an offbeat location in south Memphis (call or go online for directions), or you can visit its newer suburban place on Appling Road near Bartlett. It's open every day for dinner and Monday through Saturday for lunch.

Dino's $
645 North McLean Boulevard
(901) 278-9127

The decor is nothing fancy, but for some 30 years midtowners have come here for the old-fashioned Italian cooking and down-home warmth of Dino's. The friendly family restaurant serves up great homemade Italian specialties and southern-style meats and vegetables, both for lunch and dinner. This is a great place to get spaghetti and meatballs, lasagne, Italian salad, or homemade comfort food such as turkey and dressing or fried-chicken dinners. The restaurant recently starting adding more upscale entrees such as osso bucco and seafood lasagna to the menu on weekends, priced in the $15 to $20 range, but most regulars prefer the home cooking. Breakfast, served beginning at 7:00 A.M., includes eggs, bacon, pancakes, waffles, and other breakfast basics. Beer is served here, and you can bring your own wine.

Frank Grisanti's Italian Restaurant $$-$$$
1022 Shady Grove Road
(901) 761-9462
www.frankgrisanti-embassy.com

This handsome Italian restaurant is owned and operated by Frank Grisanti, who's part of the third generation of this renowned local restaurant family. It's inside the Embassy Suites Hotel next to Regalia shopping center, and hotel guests there or at the neighboring Hampton Inn can get room service from the restaurant. Some of the many Italian specialties are seafood fra Diavolo, manicotti, ravioli, sweet sausage ragu, and a family tradition, Elfo Special, a buttery shrimp and spaghetti dish. Frank Grisanti's also serves steaks, including its 16-ounce New York strip and rib-eye Toscano, and several veal and fish entrees. You can eat in the wood-paneled dining rooms or at one of the tables outside the restaurant in the lofty atrium of the Embassy Suites Hotel. Open Monday through Saturday for lunch and every day for dinner.

Marena's Gerani $$-$$$
1545 Overton Park
(901) 278-9774

This colorful neighborhood restaurant in midtown is tailor-made for special nights, with its romantic atmosphere. Marena's focuses its menu on specialties from northern Italy and the Mediterranean, with dishes such as Greek beef tenderloin and salmon and scallops on pasta with dill sauce. Dessert lovers will be very happy with Marena's signature crème caramel, poached pear in marsala wine sauce, and homemade sorbets. Open for dinner Tuesday through Sunday. The restaurant serves wine only, and smoking is not allowed.

Memphis Pizza Cafe $
2087 Madison Avenue
(901) 726-5343

5061 Park Avenue
(901) 684-1306

7604 West Farmington, Germantown
(901) 753-2218

8385 Highway 64, Cordova
(901) 380-3888

With its cracker-crisp thin crust and fresh toppings, the pizza at these ultracasual restaurants has been embraced by locals since the first cafe opened in 1994. Pizzas of note are the Café Supreme with seven meat and veggie toppings, Veggie Supreme with eight toppings, and the Alternative, a white pizza with no sauce but plenty of mozzarella and garlic. The menu also includes calzone, a few salads, and sandwiches, and there's beer and a few wines by the glass. During the nice weather, check out the back deck of the Madison Avenue location. Open every day for lunch and dinner.

Pete and Sam's $$
3886 Park Avenue
(901) 458-0694

1725 Appling Road, Cordova
(901) 380-5771

This family-owned and operated Italian restaurant is a true Memphis institution and one of the city's most loved restaurants. Here they serve up an array of Italian specialties, including homemade lasagne, spaghetti and meatballs, and Italian spinach. Believe it or not, the steaks are awesome, too! The standout for many

diners is the handmade pizzas, which feature such toppings as roasted peppers and barbecue chicken. At the original Pete and Sam's, it looks like the decor hasn't changed a bit in 50 years, although it was completely remodeled a few years ago. In 2003 a suburban satellite opened with the same menu. Beer is available at the Park location, full bar at the Appling restaurant. Reservations are recommended on weekends. Open for dinner only, seven nights a week. The dining room is wheelchair accessible, but not the restrooms.

Ronnie Grisanti & Sons $$-$$$
2855 Poplar Avenue
(901) 323-0007

This is one of the city's outstanding restaurants, featuring the cuisine of Tuscany as well as traditional Italian dishes such as handmade ravioli and manicotti, for which the Grisanti family is known. The kitchen is in the hands of fourth-generation sons Alex and Judd Grisanti, who learned their trade both inside and outside the family and who travel to Tuscany each year to gather new ideas. The result is a menu that's sophisticated, varied, and dazzling enough to be featured in *Food Arts* magazine. Nightly specials are always worth a try, particularly the fish. Always tasty dishes such as steak stuffed with Gorgonzola, veal chops, and pumpkin ravioli are pleasers. As tempting as these options may be, you'll be glad you saved room for the restaurant's grand desserts, naturally all made on the premises. Ronnie's, as locals call the restaurant, is wildly popular, and because it doesn't take reservations except for groups of six or more, expect to wait for a table, especially on the weekends. Open for dinner Monday through Saturday.

MEXICAN

Café Ole $-$$
959 South Cooper Street
(901) 274-1504

This casual, hip restaurant/bar in the

Cooper-Young neighborhood is a fun place to have a meal or drink margaritas at the bar, and its outdoor patio is very popular during nice weather. It's long on atmosphere, and its Mexican food such as quesadillas, fajitas, vegetable burritos, and other fare are filling and savory. Monday evenings, when there are $1.50 margaritas, are particularly lively. Open for lunch and dinner seven days a week.

La Playita Mexicana $-$$
6194 Macon Road
(901) 377-0181
Lovers of fresh seafood and Mexican food will be in heaven at this modest eatery, situated down from Bass Pro Shop in a shopping center near Bartlett and just off of Sam Cooper Boulevard. You'll find deliciously authentic versions of Mexican favorites such as enchiladas, fajitas, and huevos rancheros. Not to be missed, though, is Playita Mexicana's fried red snapper, served hot, golden brown, and perched on your plate as if still swimming. The restaurant also serves fabulous ceviche and seafood "cocteles," which are large servings of fresh chilled shrimp, octopus, or other seafood served with fresh salsa and lime. There's a bar, which is stocked with an array of tequilas. The atmosphere is a bit more polished than most of the authentic Mexican restaurants in the area, with the green and red decor from the Chinese restaurant that previously operated there. Open for lunch and dinner every day.

Las Tortugas Deli Mexicana $
1215 South Germantown Road
(901) 751-1200
www.lastortugasdelimex.com
This friendly little sandwich shop specializes in *tortugas* (turtle in Spanish), sandwiches named for the fresh-baked buns (with a subtle tortoise-shell design) from which they're made. The most popular are the fried snapper and the egg-and-chorizo *tortugas* as well as the "elephant ear," made with an oversize slice of beef steak. You can choose from an array of other

specialties such as Mexican pork barbecue tacos, quesadillas, and flautas. Owner Jose Megallanes will happily answer any question or help you choose from the menu. Open for lunch and dinner Monday through Saturday. Beer only.

Molly's La Casita $-$$
2006 Madison Avenue
(901) 726-1873
www.mollyslacasita.com
Housed in a peachy, bright building near Overton Square, this longtime midtown business serves up a great Tex-Mex menu that includes all the usual suspects, such as fajitas, chiles rellenos, quesadillas, and burritos. One of the oldest restaurants in midtown, Molly's is something of a shrine to the late Molly Gonzales, the senora whose recipes are served at the restaurant. It's a very popular spot and has tons of regulars, who are often on a first-name basis with the servers. Open seven days a week for lunch and dinner. There's a parking lot behind the restaurant.

Salsa $-$$
6150 Poplar Avenue
(901) 683-6325
Tucked away in the corner of Regalia, an upscale shopping center, you'll find Salsa, a restaurant that serves Mexican with a California flair in a lively, festive atmosphere. Specialties include fajitas, pollo chipotle, and other straightforward, flavorful dishes. Salsa also has wine tastings, which are very popular among locals, and a guitarist plays on Wednesday and Saturday. Open for lunch and dinner Monday through Saturday.

Taqueria Guadalupana $-$$
4818 Summer Avenue
(901) 685-6857

5848 Winchester Road
(901) 365-4942
The friendly management, truly authentic Mexican cooking, and low prices make this modest-looking restaurant a big hit with gringos and Hispanics alike. Enchiladas,

burritos, refried beans, and other Mexican standards are outstanding here, but the Cornish hen—cut up, deep fried, and served with tortillas, beans, and rice—is to die for. Also sublime is the shrimp cocktail: 10 or 12 big fresh shrimp served in a tall glass with fresh salsa and avocado. The atmosphere is clean and austere and decidedly casual except on Sundays, when T-shirts mix with Sunday best. There's no liquor license, so bring your own bottle. Open for lunch and dinner every day. No credit cards; cash only.

PUB GRUB AND BURGERS

If you want more options for pub grub, be sure to check out the Nightlife chapter as well. Every bar and nightspot in town is required to serve some kind of food, and many serve extensive menus of appetizers, burgers, and sandwiches, and sometimes heartier fare. Here, we list the top local favorites.

Boscos Squared   **$-$$$**
2120 Madison Avenue
(901) 432-2222
www.boscosbeer.com
This locally owned midtown brewpub is a favorite restaurant and watering hole and also brews its own award-winning beers. The menu includes handmade pizzas baked in a wood-burning oven, artichoke and spinach dip, and wood-oven shrimp appetizer, as well as more substantial fare, including its smoked double-cut pork chop and black bean and goat cheese tamale. Its Sunday brunch features Memphis chanteuse Joyce Cobb. Boscos's new outdoor deck is popular during good weather, and its bar is popular all the time. Reservations recommended. Open every day for lunch and dinner.

Dyers Cafe   **$**
4774 Summer Avenue
(901) 680-9887

Dyers Burgers
205 Beale Street
(901) 527-3937

Dyers Bartlett
7185 Highway 64, Bartlett
(901) 383-1270
Dyers has the most famous grease in town. When the restaurant moved to Beale in 1998, the cooking grease was carefully loaded onto a flatbed truck and whisked to its new home under police escort. Legend has it that it's the original grease Elmer Dyer first used in 1912. (Actually, the grease recycles itself, as the cooking burgers add new grease to the pot.) Don't be put off by this tale of grease, because the Dyer burger (which is deep-fried, not grilled) is actually one of the best you'll ever have, thin and delicious. The decor is nouveau-retro diner with booths, neon, and a stainless-steel eat-at counter. Dyers on Beale is open all day for lunch and dinner, and into the wee hours as long as there's a crowd on the street. The Bartlett location and Dyers Cafe are open for lunch and early supper every day.

Glass Onion   **$-$$**
903 South Cooper Street
(901) 274-5151
The Glass Onion actually has a lot better food than your usual bar and grill. Housed in a bungalow in the hip Cooper-Young neighborhood, it feels like a bar on the inside, and while you can order typical pub fare, there are many more choices: Thai shrimp salad, Caribbean jerk chicken, tasso-stuffed shrimp with Gouda grits and herb-garlic cream sauce, beef tenderloin medallions with a crawfish bordelaise, and yellow-curried Thai sticks (a variation on crispy egg rolls). The Glass Onion has attractive hardwood floors, which warm up the rather spare interior. Tables are available on the front deck during nice weather. Open for lunch and dinner, with live music some nights.

Gordon Biersch Brewery $-$$
145 South Main Street
(901) 543-3330
www.gordonbiersch.com

This downtown brewpub has a great atmosphere, with dramatic-looking stainless-steel brewing equipment as a backdrop to its warm dining room. But its sidewalk patio, overlooking a pedestrian area of Main Street, is what makes this West Coast chain noteworthy: There are few better spots for people watching and taking in the downtown scene. Gordon Biersch has a varied menu, which includes hazelnut-crusted chicken, key-lime shrimp and lobster, and its popular handmade pizzas. There are always five handmade beers (one of them seasonal) on tap, as well as a full bar and wine. Open daily for lunch and dinner.

The Half Shell $-$$
688 South Mendenhall Road
(901) 682-3966

7825 Winchester Road
(901) 737-6755
www.halfshellmemphis.com

This unpretentious East Memphis watering hole looks as if it could be on the beach somewhere, with its cypress wood and lanai feel. Specialties of the house are whatever fresh fish has been flown into Memphis that day, along with seafood gumbo, shrimp and lobster brochette, and steaks. The original qualifies as a local landmark, having been in business at the same corner on Mendenhall for many years. The new location is in the Southwind area of southeast Memphis. Later in the evening a cocktail crowd of regulars congregates at the bar, mostly the 30-something and 40-something set. The Half Shell is open from lunch through late-night dinner seven days a week.

Huey's $
1927 Madison Avenue
(901) 726-4372

Huey's Downtown
77 South Second Street
(901) 527-2700
www.hueys.cc

Huey's, with its hefty burgers and Sunday evenings of free live music, has become a Memphis institution since it was first started by a member of the Box Tops, a local 1960s garage band who had a hit called "The Letter." Memphians from all walks of life seek out the comfort-food familiarity of Huey burgers, thick hot fries, and potato soup. Kids love the baskets of chicken fingers and the traditions of writing on the walls (so bring a permanent marker) and blowing frill picks into the soft ceiling through drinking straws. The kitchen makes a delightful grilled-fish sandwich and salads, and there's a full bar. The midtown Huey's on Madison Avenue is the original and by far the favorite, although now it's a small chain, with each location almost exactly the same inside. Huey's is also, perhaps surprisingly, one of the city's best bets for live blues and jazz. (See the Nightlife chapter for more details about the music.) Open for lunch and dinner seven days a week. Huey's also operates several suburban locations. Check the Web site for details.

Le Chardonnay $-$$
2100-5 Overton Square Lane
(901) 725-1375
www.lechardonnay.com

Le Chardonnay is Memphis's original wine bar. Many people love the dark ambience (you practically need a flashlight to see the menu), the great wine list, and accompaniments such as the handmade pizzas and baked Brie at this longtime midtown hideout. Le Chardonnay, however, is an excellent choice for a full meal, with its fancy lunchtime sandwiches, outstanding fresh salads, and scallops carbonara. In the evenings its wood-burning oven is fired up, producing some of the best gourmet pizzas in town. It's a great spot for a romantic glass of wine or dinner. In addition to the tables, there are couches and overstuffed chairs that get snapped up quickly. Open for lunch Monday through Friday and for dinner every night.

Marlowe's Ribs and Restaurant $-$$
4381 Elvis Presley Boulevard
(901) 332-4159

You'll get a warm welcome at this super-friendly, family-run restaurant just a mile and a half from Graceland. In business since 1974, it's the kind of place that opens on Christmas to take care of its regulars and delights in greeting newcomers as well. The wide-ranging casual menu includes barbecue, which you can order as ribs, a sandwich, on a pizza, on nachos, or in a salad. Other choices include steaks, burgers, catfish, and homemade lasagne. If you're staying in an area hotel, Marlowe's will deliver food to your hotel or give you a ride to and from the restaurant in its shuttle bus. Open Monday through Saturday for lunch and dinner.

SEAFOOD

These are the restaurants that call themselves seafood restaurants. But if you were to ask gourmand Memphians where to find the best fish and shellfish, they would likely steer you to places that don't define themselves as "seafood restaurants" per se. These include Jarrett's, Tsunami, Bari, Sekisui, and in Collierville, Seasons at the White Church.

Anderton's $$
1901 Madison Avenue
(901) 726-4010
This old-fashioned seafood restaurant has been a Memphis institution since 1945, back when this midtown location was considered East Memphis. The exterior facade is the original, done in sea-green ceramic tile with a nautical theme that continues inside the restaurant. Be sure to check out the bar, which is an actual ship, surrounded by a nautical-themed mural that includes a likeness of the restaurant's longtime owner. The restaurant serves all kinds of seafood, including its famous stuffed pompano en papillote and its baby lobster dainties (small lobster tails imported from Denmark). Anderton's also has seafood platters, and many regulars swear by the hand-cut steaks, the most popular of which is the tenderloin. Open

for dinner Monday through Saturday, call ahead about lunch.

Olive Branch Catfish Company $
9659 Old Highway 78
Olive Branch, Mississippi
(662) 895-9494
This homey catfish restaurant has been here for years, long before Olive Branch became as suburban as it is today. The decor is nothing special, but the excellent fried catfish certainly is and keeps the customers coming back for more. You can also get catfish grilled or blackened, or if you're really hungry, a platter that includes all three. Steaks, chicken, shrimp, and sandwiches are also served here. The restaurant serves beer. Open for lunch and dinner seven days a week.

SOUTHERN HOME COOKING

This type of restaurant serves up basic meat-and-vegetables fare that might be called family dining in some parts of the country. Around here you'll hear these meals called meat-and-threes, or, more likely, plate lunches. They're most popular at lunch, and in fact many of these places don't even open for dinner. Don't be surprised to see such things as macaroni and cheese or Jello salad classified as vegetables. This cuisine is so popular with Mid-Southerners for lunch that you'll find some form or variation at just about every restaurant in town.

Alcenia's Desserts & Preserves Shop $
317 North Main Street
(901) 523-0200
This cheery eatery, with its bright tablecloths, pink walls, and black-and-white linoleum, serves soul-food favorites such as catfish, fried chicken, turnip greens, and fried green tomatoes. You'll receive a warm welcome from owner BJ Chester-Tamayo, who uses her mother's recipes and knows many of her customers by name. All the meats are cooked to order,

so that's about a 20-minute extra wait for the fried chicken or other entree that arrives at your table piping hot. The desserts are sumptuous: Don't miss the buttery, pecan-encrusted bread pudding or the sweet potato cake. Alcenia's also serves breakfast on Saturday mornings, with specialties that include salmon croquettes, fried green tomatoes, pancakes, and omelets. Open for lunch Tuesday through Friday and for breakfast on Saturday. Sometimes open for early dinner.

Buntyn Café $
4972 Park
(901) 844–2233

The Wiggins family has been serving up home-cooked meals since 1946, including homemade yeast rolls the size of Big Macs. Pricier than most lunch places, the Buntyn serves huge portions in an atmosphere that's more dressed up than most. Favorites include its signature vegetable-beef soup (with or without a grilled-cheese sandwich), batter-fried chicken, cobbler of the day, and homemade icebox pie. Until 1998 Buntyn operated in midtown across the street from the railroad, where at one time passengers and railroad workers were frequent customers, but its loyal clientele has followed to East Memphis. Open for lunch and dinner Monday through Friday, for Saturday dinner, and Sunday lunch. Smoking is not allowed.

Cupboard Restaurant $
1400 Union Avenue
(901) 276–8015

149 Madison Avenue
(901) 527–9111
www.cupboardrestaurant.com

At their hugely popular downtown and midtown restaurants, the Cavallo family serves huge portions of fresh vegetables and casseroles, including turnip greens, corn pudding, fried green tomatoes, and spiced beets, meat (including meat loaf and fried chicken on various days) optional. You could easily make a meal on one or two of the vegetables. In summer Cup-

board gets plentiful supplies of flavorful Ripley, Tennessee, homegrown tomatoes. If you still have room, the desserts include lemon and chocolate icebox pies as well as fruit cobblers. The downtown location is a block east of Main Street and opens for weekday lunch only. The midtown location, which has plenty of parking in the back lot, opens for lunch and dinner during the week and lunch only on Sunday.

Ellen's Soul Food $
601 South Parkway East
(901) 942–4888

This south Memphis family restaurant is as basic as it gets, with its bare-bones decor and handwritten menus, but you can't beat the fried chicken, meat loaf, and baked chicken that come out of the kitchen. With your meat entree you'll get a choice of two vegetables (be sure to try the greens if they're on the menu that day) and a plate of piping-hot johnny-cakes (thick cornmeal pancakes), which by themselves are worth the price of admission. Ellen's serves a traditional breakfast and, for lunch and early dinner, its soul food menu, Tuesday through Sunday. No credit cards.

Four Way Restaurant $
998 Mississippi Boulevard
(901) 507–1519

This is the latest incarnation of Four-Way Grill, a longtime soul-food restaurant with a fiercely loyal Memphis following. The new owners continue the Four Way tradition of serving plate lunches with fried catfish, meat loaf, and plenty of Southern-style vegetables. This south Memphis restaurant is more visible to tourists these days, since it is situated just around the corner from the Stax Museum of American Soul Music at Walker and Mississippi Boulevards. Open for lunch and early dinner Tuesday through Sunday; no alcohol.

Gus's Fried Chicken World Famous $
510 South Front Street
(901) 527–4877

A pair of Memphis entrepreneurs has brought Gus's legendary fried chicken to Memphis from Mason, Tennessee, where it has been winning kudos from *GQ* magazine and elsewhere. The Front Street restaurant, a franchise of the original, retains a casual atmosphere and menu, which includes 40-ounce bottles of beer, slaw, french fries, and last but not least, some of the best fried chicken on the planet. With its mahogany crust and tender meat, Southern-fried chicken doesn't get better than this. Gus's serves beer only, so BYOB if you're drinking something else. Open seven days a week for lunch and dinner. For the full Gus's experience, visit Mason, Tennessee, the shotgun home of the original establishment (901-294-2028). (See the Day Trips chapter for more details.) This is the rare downtown restaurant where you'll find plenty of street parking.

Little Tea Shop   **$**
69 Monroe Avenue
(901) 525-6000
This friendly plate-lunch restaurant has been serving up homemade favorites since 1918. Under the careful management of Suhair Lauck, the Tea Shop attracts a who's who of downtown Memphis business executives and lawyers. Once at your table, you mark your choices on a long menu sheet that serves as your bill. The menu changes every day, with rotating favorites such as fried chicken, corn beef, and chicken pot pie. Don't miss the buttery corn-bread sticks here, and this is a great place to try turnip greens cooked Southern style. If you're not in the mood for meat and vegetables, try the chicken or tuna salad, which arrive on a pretty plateful of fruit. Believe it or not, the restaurant uses no pork in its preparations. Open for lunch only Monday through Friday. Despite its name it's not open for afternoon tea.

Woman's Exchange   **$**
88 Racine Street
(901) 327-5681
Established in 1885 and tucked away in a small midtown house off Poplar, Woman's Exchange volunteers operate a tearoom where you can get an old-fashioned Southern ladies' luncheon, complete with homemade rolls and congealed salad. The menu is limited to a few selections, which change every day, and sometimes include seafood gumbo, chicken salad, and beef tenderloin. While you're there, browse through the gift shop, where you'll find pricey, exquisite handmade children's clothing and other gifts. Open for lunch only Monday through Friday and occasionally for afternoon tea. No smoking.

STEAK HOUSES

Anna's Steak House   **$$**
6963 Highway 70 (Summer Avenue)
Bartlett
(901) 383-9989
www.elvistyle.com/anna's/annas.htm
Anna's is definitely a Memphis thing, known as much for its steaks as for the owner's collection of Humes High School memorabilia. The latter may interest you more than you think, since Humes is where Elvis went to high school. Anna Hamilton serves up plenty of hospitality and Elvis stories, as well as filet, prime rib, Cajun shrimp, homemade potato rolls, and freshly baked pies. A Humes High School reunion takes place on the fourth Friday of the month, and on Elvis's birthday, Anna serves birthday cake (with icing in the Humes school color, of course) to all of her customers. Open for dinner every night.

The Butcher Shop Steak House $$–$$$
101 South Front Street
(901) 521-0856

107 South Germantown Parkway
(901) 757-4244
The Butcher Shop has been a fixture in downtown Memphis for more than 20 years. The big attraction at this casual steak restaurant, situated amid the lofty cotton companies on Cotton Row, is that

you can pick out your own steak and even cook it yourself if you like. You can order salmon or marinated chicken if you don't want steak. Open seven days a week for dinner. The Germantown Parkway location lacks the charm of Front Street, but you can still choose and cook your own steak here, too.

Folk's Folly $$-$$$$
551 South Mendenhall Road
(901) 762-8200
www.folksfolly.com

This pricey steak house packs in the expense-account crowd and plenty of loyal regulars, who return here for hand-cut aged steaks, Maine lobster, grilled Scottish salmon, and other delectables. Started by businessman Humphrey Folk in 1977, it continues to please lots of diners. The wine list here is one of the city's most extensive and has earned the *Wine Spectator* Award of Excellence. Many Memphians swear by the restaurant's butcher shop, where you can buy the same steaks and seafood served at the restaurant to take home and cook yourself. There's also a lounge and piano bar called the Cellar. Open every day for dinner; free valet parking is available. Reservations recommended.

Texas de Brazil $$$$
150 Peabody Place
(901) 526-7600
www.texasdebrazil.com

This downtown restaurant, part of a small Texas-based chain, is nirvana for the Atkins crowd. While not a typical steak house, it features Angus beef as one of the 14 flamed-grilled meats you can choose from as part of the $33.50 fixed all-you-can-eat menu. The meats are brought to your table on swords by carvers who will give you as much as you want. The price includes as many trips as you like to Texas de Brazil's lavish salad and sides bar, which features everything from sushi and marinated portobello mushrooms to a dreamy cream of asparagus soup—and, of course, salad. Those who don't eat meat can order lobster tails and shrimp instead or graze happily on the salad bar. It's very popular on the weekends, so reservations are a must. Open for dinner every night, for Sunday brunch, and for lunch during the week with an abbreviated menu.

NIGHTLIFE ⓨ

Memphis nightlife is centered on historic Beale Street, a 3-block stretch of clubs where music can be heard well into the wee hours seven days a week. The west end of Beale is one of the most lively blues centers you'll find anywhere in the country, although there are also some chains such as Hard Rock Café.

Anchoring the street is B. B. King's Blues Club, which consistently brings in first-rate and high-profile national blues and roots acts, in addition to having the strip's best house acts, including diva Ruby Wilson. Other choice Beale venues are Rum Boogie Café, which boasts regular performances from Beale stalwarts James Govan and the Boogie Blues Band, and King's Palace Café, where you can find dynamic jazz singer/pianist Charlie Wood most nights.

On Beale between Second and Fourth Streets, the clubs have sidewalk bars, and you can buy drinks there and carry them around with you. The bars can serve until 5:00 A.M. on weekends, although they rarely do. On Fridays and other nights, you can buy a wristband for $15 (or more on special nights), which gets you into many of the clubs. Things change regularly on Beale Street, so you might want to check local newspapers or log onto www.bealestreet .com for the latest information on the street.

The local blues scene, however, isn't restricted to Beale Street. The finest venue for Memphis roots music may be the Center for Southern Folklore, an intimate club and folk-art gallery located in the Pembroke Square Building just north of Beale Street. (See the Attractions chapter for more information about CSF.) Inside the Gibson Guitar plant directly south of Beale, you'll find The Lounge, which offers a good lineup of live music amid sophisticated uptown decor. Then, for the brave of heart, there are the juke joints, Delta remnants that still litter the city. Wild Bill's in north Memphis has become a hip spot in

recent years and boasts a house band, the Hollywood Allstars, which might be the city's most authentic blues band.

The local rock scene is anchored by a handful of clubs in the midtown and downtown areas. The New Daisy Theatre on Beale Street books prominent national club acts as well as lots of local hard rock.

In midtown, the Hi-Tone Café specializes in roots-rock and Americana acts and books a more consistently interesting lineup of national acts than any other small club in town. The Hi-Tone is also a favorite spot for local punk, garage, and roots bands. The Young Avenue Deli, also in midtown, books many of the same local bands as the Hi-Tone, as well as an uneven, if often impressive, lineup of national acts that tend more toward college-oriented jam bands and alternative rock. The Blue Monkey near Overton Square features a diverse lineup of local acts and occasional national ones that appeal to a more upscale, and more adult, crowd. The other major rock club in Memphis is Newby's, the cornerstone of the University of Memphis–based Highland Strip, where the club books rock, roots, and blues acts.

For something a little different, visitors can look to a couple of coffeehouses: Precious Cargo Exchange downtown for jazz, reggae, and hip-hop and Otherlands in midtown for acoustic music.

Memphis also has its share of the usual nightlife suspects, including sports bars, gay bars, and dance clubs. There are a few country-and-western bars as well, not surprising for a city that sits between Nashville and Texas.

A glitzy alternative to the Memphis nightlife scene lies 30 miles south in Tunica County, Mississippi, where you'll find the biggest gaming resort in the South. There, the action goes 24 hours a day at nine world-class Las Vegas–style casinos, each with hundreds of slot machines as well as dozens of game tables featuring black jack, craps, and other gaming staples. All of them have good quality restaurants and their own hotels, and many feature big-name live entertainment. (For more details, check out the Casinos chapter.)

In terms of concerts Memphis gets major acts each year that have included the Rolling Stones, Kid Rock, and Justin Timberlake. The city's prime concert venue is the downtown Pyramid Arena, but when FedExForum opens in fall 2004, it's expected to get many of the concerts. There are also shows at the Mid-South Coliseum, the Orpheum Theater, and Mud Island Amphitheater. For country and blue-grass the Lucy Opry at Bartlett Performing Arts Center in the suburbs is the prime venue, although the suburban German-town Performing Arts Center also books bluegrass and New Age acts in addition to a first-rate cast of classical performances.

The city's concert scene is augmented by a great collection of music festivals, including the Beale Street Music Festival, a three-day May event packed with national and local music acts that has grown into one of the nation's leading music events. On a much smaller scale is the Memphis Music and Heritage Festival, a definitive celebration of local and regional artists held downtown each Labor Day weekend. See the Annual Events chapter for more details on these and other festivals, and check local newspapers for smaller events that might be taking place during your visit.

As de facto capital of the Mississippi Delta, Memphis is also close to a legion of small-town blues festivals, the best of which is likely the King Biscuit Blues Festival in nearby Helena, Arkansas. Others include the Delta Blues Festival in Greenville, Mississippi, and the Sunflower River Blues and Gospel Festival in Clarksdale, Mississippi. (For more information see the Day Trips chapter.)

If you party in Memphis, you should be aware of the drunk-driving laws, which are severe. You are considered to be driving under the influence if your blood-alcohol level reaches .08, and carrying open containers of alcoholic beverages in cars is illegal. It's best to have a designated driver in your party (the bartender may well give them their soft drinks for free) or to stay within walking distance of Beale or wherever you plan to drink. Bars in Memphis can stay open until 3:00 A.M., and in the Beale Street Entertainment District they can go until 5:00 A.M. Some do stay open that late, either every night or on the weekends. We note closing times in individual write-ups. Bear in mind that many bars will stay open later than usual as long as there's a crowd, or conversely, close early if there's not much going on. All Memphis bars are required to serve food, even if it's only a microwave burrito. Most places do a lot better than that, however, offering a decent selection of pub grub. Most clubs charge a cover of $5.00 or less when there's live music, but no cover the rest of the time. We note the exceptions in individual write-ups.

BARS AND CLUBS

Beale Street

Alfred's
197 Beale Street
(901) 525-3711
www.alfreds-on-beale.com

With its prime location at the corner of Beale and Third Streets and a huge, two-story outdoor patio, Alfred's is the prime people-watching spot on Beale. The night-time crowds tend toward the young and the yuppie, and you won't hear any of the street's trademark blues among the club's regular musical stable, which ranges from pop to salsa to "classic-rock" covers. There's also a dance floor. Open until 3:00 A.M. weekdays, 5:00 A.M. weekends.

B. B. King's Blues Club
143 Beale Street
(901) 524-5464
www.bbkingclubs.com

Blues legend B. B. King doesn't actually own this club—Beale's cornerstone venue, both literally and figuratively—but he does play here at least once a year. The club's regular stable of performers—most recently including Beale diva Ruby Wilson—may be the street's best. But what makes B. B.'s special is that it may be the only club on the street that regularly draws A-list touring-blues talent. Open until midnight during the week, 1:00 A.M. on weekends. Weekend cover is usually $7.00 to $10.00.

Blues City Café
138 Beale Street
(901) 526–3637

With a large kitchen and dining area connected to the music side, the ultracasual Blues City Café is the best spot on Beale for late-night dining, with steaks, ribs, shrimp, and catfish available into the wee hours. The musical lineup is mostly local. Sunday nights feature FreeWorld, a local jazz and jam band that has been together longer than just about any other local act. Sometimes well-known musicians or Beale Street regulars will sit in for a set. Open until 3:00 A.M. on weekends.

Hard Rock Café
315 Beale Street
(901) 529–0007
www.hardrock.com

You probably already know what to expect from this celebrated chain—loads of choice rock memorabilia, overpriced burgers, and plenty of T-shirts in the souvenir shop. The Hard Rock's music bookings are mostly local bands and, befitting the name, mostly hard rock. Open until around 11:30 P.M. during the week, until the wee hours on weekends. Cover is sometimes more than $5.00.

King's Palace Café
162 Beale Street
(901) 521–1851

One of the older clubs on Beale, King's Palace features a New Orleans–oriented menu that's considered one of the strip's most reliable dining options. As for music, local jazz keyboard player and vocalist Charlie Wood plays at King's Palace almost every night. Often compared to

Mose Allison, Wood is one of the city's finest acts. Open until midnight, and often, there's no cover for live music.

Pat O'Brien's
310 Beale Street
(901) 529–0900
www.patobriens.com

Pat O'Brien's brings a piece of New Orleans to Beale Street. This is a replica of the famous New Orleans French Quarter bar, and it is one of the newest hot spots on the street. Depending on your mood, you can relax inside in Pat O's piano bar or hang out on the back patio (covered and heated during winter), which features a flaming fountain. New Orleans–style cuisine, steaks, and seafood are the more popular items on the menu, and they also serve brunch on Sundays. Be sure to try a Hurricane, Pat O'Brien's famous ruby-red cocktail.

Rum Boogie Café
182 Beale Street
(901) 528–0150
www.rumboogie.com

Rum Boogie is the longest-running bar on Beale, which began serving up blues to appreciative crowds way before urban renewal transformed the rest of the strip. Now the Boogie is a well-worn respite on a street marked by neon newness. James Govan and the Blues Boogie Band can be heard here most nights and may be the best house band on Beale. Govan is more soul than blues and is equally talented at pleasing tourists with such sing-alongs as "Mustang Sally" and showing off his deep-soul vocal chops with strong renditions of classics such as Sam Cooke's "Bring It on Home to Me." Open until midnight during the week, around 2:00 A.M. on weekends.

Silky O'Sullivan's
181 Beale Street
(901) 522–9596
www.silkyosullivan.com

A standard rite of passage for area fraternity and sorority types is the "Diver" at Silky's. Billed as "a gallon of Southern fun," the Diver is a big yellow plastic bucket filled with some type of alcoholic concoction and multiple straws. You can see tipsy young things lugging Divers up and down Beale on most nights. Inside, Silky's is more a social hangout than a serious blues club. The human jukebox act by local chanteuse Barbara Blue and a crowd-participation-friendly dueling pianos act is the most common entertainment. Silky's also has a huge outdoor patio where you can party with the bar's pet goat. Open until 3:00 A.M.

Downtown

Automatic Slim's Tonga Club
83 South Second Street
(901) 525-7948
With a great location right across the street from The Peabody hotel, chic decor, and a polished, adventurous menu, Slim's is one of downtown's finest restaurants. Its bar is also one of downtown's prime "see-and-be-seen" locales, where dress is a step above casual and the drinks of choice tend toward martinis and cosmopolitans. There's often live music on Friday nights, and sometimes on Saturday nights. Bar usually open at least until midnight.

The Blue Monkey
529 South Front Street
(901) 527-6665
www.thebluemonkey.com
Situated at Front Street and G. E. Patterson Boulevard, the Blue Monkey in downtown is a neighborhood bar that's popular among the young professionals who live in South Bluffs and the residential buildings on and around South Main Street. With its lofty ceiling and decor that includes wine labels on the tabletops and cork panels, this Monkey has an easygoing atmosphere, but no live music. In that respect, it's a different animal from the original Blue Monkey in midtown, which prides itself on live entertainment and a more hard-driving party atmosphere. The downtown bar serves a menu of hamburgers, sandwiches, and other casual fare. Open every night until 3:00 A.M. and during the day for lunch.

Café Soul
492 South Main Street
(901) 521-4677
Café Soul offers a jazz alternative to the many blues clubs on Beale Street and elsewhere in downtown Memphis. Featuring local artists, including Memphis-based trumpet player Nokie Taylor, the club also features big names such as pianist Donald Brown. This narrow club has exposed brick walls and an intriguing painting over the stage, a colorful collage of musicians playing their instruments. The cover can be quite steep, and it's advisable to reserve a table ahead of time when a big act is playing. Café Soul has a full bar and a menu of chicken wings and other bar fare. Open Tuesday through Sunday, serving plate lunches Tuesday through Friday and dinner Wednesday through Saturday.

Center for Southern Folklore
119 and 125 South Main Street
(901) 525-3655
www.southernfolklore.com
This large, brightly painted venue lives up to its name—promoting Southern culture from music to folk art to food. The music, which focuses on but isn't at all relegated to blues, is a cut above Beale in terms of authenticity. This funky space features live music most nights, including regular performances by the Daddy Mack Blues Band. The nonprofit center is a nightclub, tourist attraction, cafe, and unofficial welcome center. Most weekdays the center serves lunch alongside performances from a fine batch of local musicians. But the center also has night performances on a less regular basis, with acts such as folksinger Kate Campbell and the Holmes Brothers. Check out the artwork, too, especially the great folk art in the center's "Sofo" gallery. There's a cover charge for live music. The music hall is at the back on the lower level of the Pembroke Building, and the cafe/gift shop is in front. Look for the sign on Main Street.

Dan McGuinness Irish Pub
150 Peabody Place
(901) 527-8500
www.danmcguinnesspub.com
The best meet-and-drink spot in the
downtown Peabody Place entertainment
complex, Dan McGuinness boasts a full
Irish menu and first-rate service. The bar
also features a popular pub quiz every Friday night. Despite the Peabody Place
address, the pub faces Second Street.
Open until 1:00 A.M. during the week, 3:00
A.M. on weekends.

Earnestine & Hazel's
531 South Main Street
(901) 523-9754
This one-time brothel is one of the hot
spots in downtown's recently resurgent
South Main neighborhood. A funky two-
story bar with loads of character, Earnestine & Hazel's is a favorite spot for young,
hip Memphians to wind up a night of partying, dancing to tunes on the bar's first-rate
jukebox and downing a "soulburger," one of
the city's most heralded late-night snacks.
The bar occasionally has live music. Open
until 3:00 A.M. or later on weekends.

Felicia Suzanne's
80 Monroe Avenue
(901) 523-0877
www.feliciasuzannes.com
The bar and patio of this New Orleans–
wannabe restaurant have become a popular
spot among Memphians to splurge on
pricey cocktails and bar fare that's better
than the norm. The bar menu includes white
cheddar and fried green tomato grilled
cheese, crab cakes, and desserts. Popular
cocktails include Jack Daniels mint juleps
and sazeracs, the rye whiskey drink made
famous by Tennessee Williams. The patio is
particularly pleasant during nice weather.
The bar is open until 11:00 P.M. during the
week and until midnight on weekends.

Flying Saucer Draught Emporium
130 Peabody Place
(901) 523-8536
www.beerknurd.com
Located just a block off Beale, this beer
palace is prime real estate and a popular
place for downtown professionals to grab
a postwork drink. During the warm
months, which is most of them, the large
bar's open windows let a breeze in and the
music out. The music is mostly local and
usually not too exciting, but the Saucer has
probably the largest beer menu in the city,
75 on tap and 130 in bottles. Monday is
$2.50 pint night. It's a yuppie mob scene
on Friday and Saturday nights. Open until
2:00 A.M. on weekends.

Huey's
77 South Second Street
(901) 527-2700
www.hueys.cc
The downtown location of the popular
local burger chain offers live blues and
jazz on Sunday afternoons and evenings.
No cover. (See the midtown listing in this
chapter for more details on music and the
Restaurants chapter for more details on
food.) Open until 3:00 A.M.

Isaac Hayes
150 Peabody Place
(901) 529-9222
www.clubisaachayes.com
This swanky restaurant and nightclub nestled in the corner of Peabody Place prides
itself on presenting a wide variety of
musical entertainment. Live music of
many kinds, including blues, R&B, and
rock, can be found at Isaac Hayes on just
about any day of the week. This glam-
orous club attracts a well-dressed eclectic
crowd. The restaurant serves lunch and
dinner and offers a late-night menu as
well, and despite the name on the door,
Hayes performs here only rarely. The club
is situated on the third floor of Peabody
Place entertainment complex.

Jillian's
150 Peabody Place
(901) 543-8800
ww.jillians.com
This massive chain-entertainment complex
is a three-story fun house for adults

located within downtown's Peabody Place mall. Jillian's has a full bowling alley, a state-of-the-art arcade, several pool tables, and huge banks of big-screen TVs for sports viewing. It has been accurately described around town as "Chuck E. Cheese for grownups." The bar/restaurant is on the ground floor. Kids are allowed until 10:00 P.M.; after that, you have to be at least age 21 to enter. Open until 2:00 A.M. on weekends. Usually no cover.

Kudzu's
603 Monroe Avenue
(901) 525-4924
www.kudzus.net
Though it may call itself "a neighborhood bar looking for a neighborhood," Kudzu's really is the place in Memphis where everybody knows your name. Located in an off-the-beaten path, slightly industrial part of downtown, Kudzu's is an intimate, no-frills bar that's a popular hangout for local reporters, midtowners, and downtowners. At night, Kudzu's offers a diverse array of entertainment, from singer-songwriter nights to the occasional touring band. The bar's Wednesday-night pub quiz is a Memphis staple. Open until 2:00 A.M. or later on weekends, 11:00 P.M. or so during the week.

The Lounge at Gibson Beale Street
Showcase
Second Street and George W. Lee
Avenue
(901) 544-7998, ext. 4
www.gibsonmemphis.com
This spacious club, with its comfortable leather chairs and sofas, feels like an urbane, updated take on Manhattan supper clubs of the 1950s. It's tucked next to the Gibson Guitar Factory and has a great menu of appetizers. The drinks can be expensive, and the cover charge for the music is sometimes well over $5.00 but worth it, since the Lounge has great acts.

The Peabody Hotel Lobby Bar
149 Union Avenue
(901) 529-4000
www.peabodymemphis.com
It's been said that the Delta begins in the lobby of this grand old hotel, and there may be no better place to spot celebrities and other high-rollers than by sipping a pricey cocktail at The Peabody's lobby bar and spending an evening people watching. The hotel's usually open rooftop is a choice spot to hang out and get a glimpse of downtown from above, and on Thursday nights during summer, it's the site of a massive party featuring live music and plenty of singles action. The Peabody's Corner Bar is worth a visit when Blind Mississippi Morris plays.

Sleep Out Louie's
88 Union Avenue
(901) 527-5337
This downtown watering hole, which makes its home in a former fire station, has one of the best happy hours in town, attracting a range of professionals who work and live in the area. It also has a great patio for sitting outdoors on nice days, with service even in December if there's an unexpected heat wave. If you're hungry, there's a full menu of pub grub, too. Sleep Out is a great place to party before sporting events or other downtown happenings. Closes early.

Swig
100 Peabody Place
(901) 522-8515
www.swigmartinibar.citysearch.com
This new 1940s-style martini bar serves some 35 versions of the classic cocktail in a contemporary, elegant atmosphere. Situated in the ground floor of the 100 Peabody Place office building, Swig has a huge selection of vodka, cognac, and other spirits, as well as a casual menu. Jazz is a key part of what Swig does, and while it's usually played on the bar's state-of-the-art sound system, there's sometimes live jazz. The martini bar, which views itself as a hip, more uptown alternative to beer joints, is a satellite of the San Antonio original. It's often packed with the suit crowd after work but becomes more of a hipster hangout later on.

Midtown

Alex's Tavern
1445 Jackson Avenue
(901) 278-9086

A favorite hangout for the students at nearby Rhodes College, Alex's is a tiny bar with a big local reputation, frequently cited as a favorite bar, late-night dive, and jukebox spot by locals of all ages. Locals swear by the hamburgers here.

The Blue Monkey
2012 Madison Avenue
(901) 272-2583
www.thebluemonkey.com

The Blue Monkey is a favorite watering hole for 20-somethings in the area and is also a popular gathering place for the local college kids during lunch and dinner. The Monkey features a wide variety of live music six days a week, and the menu offers pizzas, calzones, and sandwiches, among other things. The atmosphere is comfortable and the people are great, though the crowds can be a little overwhelming on busier nights. Open until 3:00 A.M.

Hi-Tone Café
1913 Poplar Avenue
(901) 278-8663
www.hitonememphis.com

This midtown bar, located right across the street from Overton Park, is actually one of the city's finest music venues. The sound is good, the room is cozy, and the bartenders are friendly. The city's best local rock and roots acts play here regularly, and the club boasts an uneven, if occasionally spectacular, mix of similar national acts for a small club. The Hi-Tone made local concert history in 2004 when Elvis Costello played there in a rare club appearance. The crowd is hip and very casual, with most patrons in their 20s and 30s. The club has pool tables, too. *Note to Elvis fans:* Guess who took karate lessons in this building years ago?

Huey's
1927 Madison Avenue
(901) 726-4372
www.hueys.cc

This beloved local burger chain, owned and operated by a member of local '60s garage-rock band the Box Tops, is a true Memphis staple, with Huey burgers one of the city's ultimate comfort foods. The midtown location is the original. On Sunday afternoons and evenings, it's also one of the city's best bets for live blues and jazz. All Huey's locations offer intelligently and lovingly booked live music on Sundays for no cover. The midtown and downtown locations usually offer the choicest music options, but it's rare for any Huey's to offer music that isn't authentic roots music that's easy on the ears. (See the Restaurants chapter for more details on food.)

M-Bar & Lounge at Melange
948 South Cooper Street
(901) 276-0002
www.melangememphis.com

The bar of this popular Cooper-Young neighborhood eatery has a decidedly different personality from the restaurant. M-Bar is your basic dark smoky hipster lounge, with an eclectic clientele of all ages. In addition to its cool see-and-be-seen atmosphere, the bar has an extensive tapas menu with a twist: You fill out a sushi-type menu to order exactly what you want. Sunday is probably Melange's biggest party night, when the owners and bartenders spin records from the 1970s and 1980s and attract a huge crowd that parties well into the wee hours.

Newby's
539 South Highland Street
(901) 452-8408
www.newbysmemphis.com

Newby's is the signature club on the University of Memphis–area Highland Strip and second only to the New Daisy on

Beale among local rock clubs for the size of its music hall. Newby's features a wide variety of live music from old rock to jam bands, all of which appeal to students from nearby University of Memphis. Newby's also plays host to national acts, which have included Michelle Shocked and Los Lonely Boys. Other recent musical guests include the Charlie Mars Band and Jordan Knight. Newby's back patio sometimes has live acoustic music as well.

The P&H Café
1532 Madison Avenue
(901) 726-0906
www.pandhcafe.com
The quintessential midtown bar, the P&H (aka "Poor and Hungry") seems to be everybody's most beloved watering hole, with idiosyncratic local cartoons, photos, and such lining the walls and ceilings. There's also first-rate people watching, cheap beer, and pub grub, and the bar's outrageous proprietress, local celebrity Wanda Wilson. The P&H is the favorite hangout of the local theater crowd. Lately, there has been a lot more live music by local acts. No liquor is served here; it's strictly a beer joint.

Side Street Grill
31 South Florence Street
(901) 274-8955
www.sidestreetgrill.com
This bar in midtown's Overton Square neighborhood specializes in martinis and other festive cocktails and features a nice outdoor patio with umbrellas, wrought iron, and magnolia trees. Side Street is cigar friendly and employs a powerful fan to keep the indoor air relatively clean. If you're hungry, you can get a tasty and substantial steak or salmon dinner here for less than $15. Be sure to check out its Red Bar, which has more of a cocktail-lounge feel. Open until 3:00 A.M. on weekends. No cover.

Young Avenue Deli
2119 Young Avenue
(901) 278-0034
www.youngavenuedeli.com
This large bar/restaurant/club in the bohemian Cooper-Young neighborhood rivals the Hi-Tone as midtown's best music venue. The sound isn't as good and the atmosphere not as intimate as its crosstown rival, but the bar is bigger and better stocked, the music lineup, both in terms of local and national acts, is similar, and the pool tables are more plentiful at what Memphians just refer to as "the Deli." The crowd at the Deli tends to be fairly college oriented, and the bar has a reputation as a choice, laid-back meat market even when there isn't a band playing. The Deli also serves up outstanding french fries and a menu of filling sandwiches.

Zinnie's East
1718 Madison Avenue
(901) 274-7101
Zinnie's East has been a laid-back hangout in midtown Memphis for more than 15 years. This popular bar and grill features live music in its upstairs Full Moon Club and a menu of steaks, salads, and sandwiches, including the off-beat "Zinnieloney," made with a thick hand-cut slice of blackened baloney. Zinnie's has a great front deck, where you can watch the world go by during nice weather. It's a mixed crowd, depending on when you visit, and it stays open late. The larger Zinnie's East is actually a satellite of the original Zinnie's, just a few doors west at the corner of Belvedere. Old Zinnie's, as everyone calls this basic neighborhood bar, attracts a somewhat younger crowd of 20-somethings and students. Open every day.

East Memphis and the Suburbs

Bottom Line
1817 Kirby Parkway
(901) 755-2481
This no-frills local hangout, north of Poplar, which has been around for more than 25 years, caters to a yuppie crowd in

their 20s, 30s, and 40s. There's live music Wednesday, Friday, and Saturday. Lunch and dinner are served, and a happy hour goes from 2:00 to 7:00 P.M. It's a good place to take in a University of Memphis basketball game or just hang out amid the dark wood and memorabilia.

The Grove Grill
4550 Poplar Avenue
(901) 818–9951
www.thegrovegrill.com

The bar at the Grove Grill, attracting well-dressed professionals of all ages, is one of the hippest places in East Memphis to get a martini or other cocktail. Happy hour is very popular, and you can order the usual array of cocktails and beer as well as fine single-malt scotch and wines from the restaurant's wine list. It's a good-looking cherry-wood bar, with walls painted in soothing colors. It can get crowded, though, with a combination of bar customers and people waiting for tables at the restaurant. You don't have to go to the restaurant to sample Grove Grill's well-regarded cuisine. Just order fresh oysters, appetizers, or other delectables at the bar. It's situated in the back of Laurelwood shopping center near Davis-Kidd Booksellers.

Huey's
www.hueys.cc

In recent years this popular local burger chain has opened additional locations in East Memphis, Cordova, and other suburbs, all of which feature free live music on Sunday evenings. (See the midtown listing in this chapter for more details on music and the Restaurants chapter for more details on food.)

Patrick's
4698 Spottswood Avenue
(901) 682–2853

This casual East Memphis restaurant/bar, situated in Audubon shopping center, packs them in for lunch, happy hour, and evenings. Happy hour usually attracts an older crowd of bankers, stockbrokers, and other professionals, but later the crowd is

the 30s and 40s set. There's live music on weekends and Thursday nights, too. With its dark wood and checkered tablecloths, this favorite hangout serves plate lunches at midday and until 8:00 P.M., as well as steaks, burgers, and other fare.

Sidecar Café
2194 Whitten Road, Bartlett
(901) 388–0285
www.sidecarcafe.com

This popular suburban nightspot attracts a local crowd of all ages, who come in to watch NASCAR races and other sports, hoist a few, and enjoy favorite menu items such as Sidecar Club Salads and 10-ounce Fat Boy Burgers. Sidecar has a bar, a deck, and a separate restaurant area, which morphs into a party spot once the dinner crowd has left. There's live music on Wednesday, Saturday, and Sunday nights. Sidecar Café is situated next to a Harley-Davidson dealership and welcomes motorcycle enthusiasts anytime, but especially on Biker Night (Wednesday). Open daily.

The Stage Stop
2951 Cela Street, Raleigh
(901) 382–1576
www.thestagestop.net

If you want to party way off the beaten path, this is the place. Those county-fair, long-hair-and-metal days of yore never went out of vogue at the Stage Stop, a metal-and-proud-of-it rock venue in the working-class suburb of Raleigh. Check this place out on a weekend night and see why it has inspired Memphians to lovingly refer to the neighborhood as "Rockin' Raleigh."

T. J. Mulligan's
8071 Trinity Road, Cordova
(901) 756–4480

6635 Quince Road
(901) 753–8056

Houston Levee at Highway 64, Cordova
(901) 377–9997
www.tjmulligans.com

These locally owned Irish–style pubs are very popular among the yuppie set, although the crowd can range from college age to 40s, depending on the band that's playing that night. Mulligan's is busy all evening from happy hour through the wee hours, and local bands play on Tuesdays and on weekends. Mulligan's is open from 11:00 A.M. to 3:00 A.M. daily, serving plate lunches at midday and a menu of burgers, chicken sandwiches, and other fare until 2:30 A.M. You'll also find T. J. Mulligan's downtown at 362 North Main Street (901–523–1453).

BREWPUBS

Boscos Squared
2120 Madison Avenue
(901) 432–2222
www.boscosbeer.com
Even if Boscos, the popular brewpub at Overton Square, didn't brew its own beer and serve handmade pizzas and other great food, it would still be one of midtown's most happening bars. You can order a handmade beer brewed on the premises, but if you aren't a beer drinker, there's a wine list and full bar. Boscos always has a crowd, whether it's happy hour, people waiting for a table, late-night partying, or watching the game. The beer menu includes Midtown Brown, an English-style nut-brown ale, Boscos classics such as Flaming Stone and London's Porter, and seasonal beers. Boscos also has a very popular jazz brunch. It is open for lunch and dinner every day, and the bar stays open until 2:00 or 3:00 A.M.

Gordon Biersch
145 South Main Street
(901) 543–3330
www.gordonbiersch.com
Gordon Biersch may be a chain (mostly West Coast), but it's definitely worth a visit for its brewed-on-the-premises beers, handsome decor, and good food. During nice weather Gordon Biersch's patio is probably the best place to take in the downtown street scene, for it's situated right on the pedestrian portion of Main

Street for optimal people watching. The German-style beers, which include a blond bock and pilsner as well as seasonal beers, are brewed on the premises, and you see the operation through a glass wall in the back of the restaurant. The menu has an Asian flavor and includes favorites such as fried calamari and spinach and artichoke dip. Open daily for lunch and dinner.

COFFEEHOUSES

Borders
6685 Poplar Avenue, Germantown
(901) 754–0770
www.borders.com
The cafe at Borders draws a crowd that's as diverse as the bookstore and music store clientele and includes all ages as well as families. The cafe serves all kinds of coffee drinks, other beverages, pastries, and light food items such as sandwiches. Despite being part of a national chain, the Borders cafe brings in plenty of local musical acts, including bluegrass and folk acoustic musicians, who perform on many weekends. You can pick up a Borders newsletter in the store or cafe for details about music and other in-store events. The cafe provides a nonsmoking, nonalcoholic environment and operates whenever the store is open. The cafe is open until 10:00 P.M. Monday through Thursday, 11:00 P.M. on Friday and Saturday, and 9:00 P.M. on Sunday.

Café Francisco
400 North Main
(901) 578–8002
www.cafefrancisco.com
Owned and operated by a homesick San Franciscan, this lofty coffeehouse feels as though it belongs in that urbane California city. There are booths in the front, but toward the back of the store, there's a comfortable seating area with couches and a fireplace and tables with Internet access available. The cafe roasts its own coffee and also serves beer as well as pastries, bagels, and a menu of excellent sand-

wiches and salads. Café Francisco is open every day for lunch and dinner but closes early on Sundays. Strictly nonsmoking.

Deliberate Literate
1997 Union Avenue
(901) 276-0174

The cafe at this midtown bookstore, Café Literati, is a popular hangout during the day and early evening hours. There are comfortable sofas and overstuffed chairs throughout the shop, where you can relax with a book or magazine or chat with a friend or associate, as well as cafe tables outdoors to be enjoyed during nice weather. Literati serves espresso drinks, coffee, pastries, and a light menu of sandwiches, low-carb items, and homemade soups. Open daily.

Empire Coffee Company
2 South Main Street
(901) 526-1646
www.empirecoffeecompany.com

This comfortable coffeehouse has a great location in the central downtown area, right at Madison Avenue and Main Street, and draws an eclectic clientele ranging from students to business executives. The place smells great, since Empire roasts its own coffee on the premises, and servers will even roast an order while you wait. In addition to the usual coffee drinks, Empire also serves light fare including muffins, sandwiches, and salads. Empire occasionally has a jazz band or poetry slam, but it's not really a live music venue like its predecessor, the Map Room. Open every day, Empire accommodates early birds by opening at 5:30 A.M. during the week and 7:00 A.M. on the weekends.

Java Cabana
2170 Young Avenue
(901) 272-7210
www.cooper-young.com

This homey, bohemian hangout in midtown's Cooper-Young neighborhood has been around since 1993, with live music on many evenings and a comfortable atmosphere for reading and conversation. Every Thursday night there's an open-mike poetry reading, featuring local writers and sometimes visiting poets, a Java Cabana fixture since it first opened. Sunday nights there's live jazz and, the rest of the weekend, live folk, jazz, or flamenco music. Java Cabana serves up coffee and espresso drinks as well as homemade desserts and sandwiches. Smoking is not allowed at the cafe. Closed Monday; open until 10:00 P.M. during the week and until midnight on weekends. Not wheelchair accessible.

Otherlands Coffee Bar
641 South Cooper Street
(901) 278-4994

This friendly, bohemian midtown coffee shop attracts all kinds of customers, from yuppies grabbing their morning joe on the way to work, to the students, self-employed locals, and others drifting in throughout the day, to the afterwork and afterschool crowd. Otherlands serves a big menu of coffees and coffee drinks, as well as H&H bagels, pastries, soups, quiches, sandwiches, and vegan fare. In addition to the tables, chairs, and couches indoors, there's an outdoor deck in the back. Otherlands also has an eclectic shop that features cards, jewelry, and all kinds of gifts. The coffee shop is open from early in the morning to 8:00 P.M., and occasionally later for live music. Strictly nonsmoking at all times.

The Precious Cargo Exchange
381 North Main Street
(901) 578-8446

There's something going on just about every night at this colorful, artsy north Main Street cafe, from poetry readings to reggae to its Sunday gospel brunch. The cafe's owners see this as a haven for visual and performing artists and for people who enjoy their work. Situated at the corner of Overton Avenue near the Pyramid Arena, Precious Cargo serves coffees and espresso drinks as well as a menu of salads, desserts, and its special Jamaican jerk chicken. The colorfully painted walls are hung with local artists' work, and there's a chess game going most of the time. Precious Cargo serves beer, but it's BYOB for harder stuff. Open until midnight every night, with extended hours on weekends.

Sip Coffee and Conversations
2037 Madison Avenue
(901) 726-0039

This friendly midtown coffeehouse, situated just off Overton Square, is decorated with funky painted designs on the walls and garage-sale furniture from the 1970s and 1960s. Sip shares its space with Midtown Artists Market, chock-full of handmade jewelry, ceramics, and original works of art, as well as a large used-book store, so there's plenty to keep you occupied while you sip your joe. Open every day.

Starbucks Coffee
www.starbucks.com

Memphis has not been immune to the ubiquity of Starbucks, and you can find them all over the city and at the airport. They have all the familiar coffee and tea drinks, and most have both attractive seating areas and drive-through windows for to-go orders. For the location nearest you, check the phone book. If you're looking for Starbucks downtown, it's hidden away in Peabody Place Mall at 150 Peabody Place.

CONCERT VENUES

Bartlett Performing Arts and Conference Center
3663 Appling Road, Bartlett
(901) 385-6440
www.bpacc.org

Built in 1998, this suburban venue sponsors a seasonal lineup that has featured such artists as singer/songwriter Iris DeMent, the Cashore Marionettes, and the Nashville Mandolin Ensemble. This is also home to the Lucy Opry, the area's prime venue for country and bluegrass music.

FedExForum
200 South Third Street
(901) 205-2525
www.fedexforum.com

Although it's primarily the new home for the Memphis Grizzlies NBA basketball team, FedExForum is sure to be playing host to some major concerts as well. The five-story arena, just half a block south of Beale Street, can accommodate as many as 19,000 for a concert and has plenty of amenities, including on-site parking and state-of-the-art audio and video systems.

Germantown Performing Arts Center
1801 Exeter Road, Germantown
(901) 757-7256
www.gpacweb.com

This acoustically perfect theater, which opened in 1994, provides an intimate venue for performances of all kinds, including jazz and bluegrass. "G-Pac," as locals call it, hosts a series of popular performances that have included artists such as Sophie B. Hawkins, Nitty Gritty Dirt Band, and Alison Kraus.

Mud Island Amphitheater
125 North Front Street
(901) 576-6595
www.mudisland.com

When there is a performance here, you can enjoy a river view along with the entertainment on the stage. In summer 2003 there was a popular series of $3.00 concerts, including Blues Traveler, but it's unclear if these will continue. From the entrance on Front Street, you take the tram across the river to Mud Island.

The New Daisy Theatre
330 Beale Street
(901) 525-8979
www.newdaisy.com

Anchoring the east end of Beale Street, this converted movie theater is the city's largest rock club, with a 1,000-person capacity and balcony seating above a large, open standing section. It's really a venue, though, because it's only active when there's a show. Almost all the club's local bookings and a good deal of its touring shows are hard rock and metal, but the club also books a surprising amount of jazz and other acts that are too big for small clubs, too small for the Pyramid. Recent bookings have included Gillian Welch, Fuel, and Galactic. Most shows are general admission, and you can buy tickets in advance from the box office. Credit cards are not accepted.

The Orpheum Theater
203 South Main Street
(901) 525-7800
www.orpheum-memphis.com
The lavish Orpheum Theater, built in 1928 as a venue primarily for vaudeville, holds court at the foot of Beale Street in downtown Memphis. At present, in addition to hosting touring Broadway shows and other performing-arts productions, the Orpheum gets upscale, adult-oriented concerts by performers who have included Lyle Lovett, Tom Petty and the Heartbreakers, and Natalie Merchant. The Orpheum sells tickets at the theater's box office or at a satellite box office at Davis-Kidd Booksellers.

The Pyramid Arena
1 Auction Avenue
(901) 521-7909
www.pyramidarena.com
Major touring acts, including Aerosmith, the Dixie Chicks, and Kid Rock, perform here when they're in town. This arena is a 32-story, stainless-steel pyramid, with seating capacity for 21,000 people for concerts. Its management likes to boast that this is the third-largest pyramid in the world, taller than the Statue of Liberty. The Pyramid ticket office is open Monday through Friday, or you can get tickets through Ticketmaster (901-525-1515 or www.ticketmaster.com).

COUNTRY-AND-WESTERN CLUBS/BARS

Shooters Five-Star Honky-Tonk
4293 Fayette Road, Raleigh
(901) 388-4135
If country music and line dancing are your thing, head to Shooters at the corner of Stage Road and Austin-Peay Highway in Raleigh. There are free dance lessons at Shooter's main bar and karaoke starting at 9:00 A.M. in the side bar if you aren't in the mood for dancing. Shooters has lots of specials throughout the week, so call ahead for details. Open every night.

DANCE CLUBS

Raiford's
115 Vance Avenue
(901) 525-9210
Situated a couple of blocks south of Beale Street downtown, Raiford's used to be a neighborhood dance hall but in recent years has become one of the city's trendiest hangouts as a younger, more upscale crowd has flocked here. It's definitely the place for a shot of funkiness—beer served only in 40-ounce bottles and classic soul and contemporary R&B spun deep into the night by the club's irrepressible owner, Robert Raiford. The beloved sign out front reads no discrimination—and Raiford's means that, unless you try to come in wearing sneakers, a definite no-no.

SENSES
2866 Poplar Avenue
(901) 454-4081
www.sensesthenightclub.com
SENSES is Memphis's newest dance club, a big-city club whose owners spent several million dollars to make the hottest nightspot in town. With 12,000 square feet of fun, you're sure to find something you like, whether it's one of SENSES's six bars, such as the Martini Bar or the Orange Bar, a plasma-screen TV complete with Xbox, an outdoor beer garden, or the dance floor

made of reflective vinyl. There's a $10 cover for the dance floor, and there is a dress code (which is, basically, dress up!).

GAY BARS

Backstreet Memphis
2018 Court Avenue
(901) 276-5522
www.backstreetmemphis.com
This gay bar for men is definitely a late-night place, which doesn't crank up until about midnight. Backstreet recently added Coliseum, a club on the premises that features a huge dance floor. Back-street features a show bar with cabaret performances as well as a lounge area with pool tables and a dance floor. There's also a patio. Backstreet serves beer only, so BYOB if you're drinking liquor or wine. To get to this midtown bar, take Madison and turn onto Morrison past the Blue Monkey. You'll see the club to the right across the street from the back of the milk plant. Open on weekends until late (cover for Coliseum) and some nights during the week.

Crossroads
111 North Claybrook and 1278 Jefferson Avenue
(901) 276-1882
This gay bar for men, at the corner of Jef-ferson, is actually two bars: a show bar that features a DJ, as well as cabaret shows and karaoke on various nights, and a neighborhood-style bar with a country flavor, pool tables, and a jukebox. In the back is a huge patio and yard. Crossroads is a beer bar, so BYOB if you're drinking wine or liquor. There's a modest cover charge on Friday and Saturday nights. The show bar is open at night, Thursday through Sunday, and the other bar is open seven days a week starting at noon. Both sections are open until 3:00 A.M.

J. Wag's
1268 Madison Avenue
(901) 725-1909

This gay bar for men, which has been operating for more than 20 years across Madison from the Southern College of Optometry, is a fixture on the city's gay scene. J. Wag's is open 24 hours a day, and patrons describe it as a gay bar all day and a bigger gay bar at night. There are some cabaret shows, as well as a juke-box that has everything from country to disco. The bar serves beer, as well as a menu of burgers and sandwiches, but bring your own wine or liquor. The club generally charges a cover on weekends.

The Madison Flame
1588 Madison Avenue
(901) 278-9839
The Madison Flame, a gay bar for women, makes its home at a locally famous Mem-phis club address—the punk/New Wave club The Antenna operated here for many years. The Flame is a dance bar with DJ on Fridays and Saturdays and features karaoke on Wednesdays and Sundays. It's a casual bar, with darts and other bar games, and a large variety of beers. Occa-sionally, there's live music. The Madison Flame is open only at night on Wednes-days, Fridays, Saturdays, and Sundays. Sometimes there's a cover on Saturdays.

One More
2117 Peabody Place
(901) 278-6673
This gay bar for women is situated on Peabody just off Cooper Street. Open seven days a week, One More is a neighborhood-style bar that serves beer as well as a menu of pizza, burgers, and other fare. There's a jukebox, and on Wednesdays and Sundays, live music. One More is packed on weekends. Open all day and until 3:00 A.M. every day. No cover.

The Pumping Station
1382 Poplar Avenue
(901) 272-7600
This gay bar for men, formerly the Pipeline, features a DJ on weekend nights and videos after 11:00 P.M. It's casual, with pool tables and darts, an outside patio

and deck, and a beer menu with 50 different brews. The Pumping Station has special nights, including local leather night and local bears night, as well as special events such as its Sunday beer bust and buffet and dart tournaments. No cover.

JUKE JOINTS

Wild Bill's
1580 Vollintine Avenue
(901) 726-5473
Never mind Beale Street. If you really want to hear the down-home blues upon which the city's music foundation was built, you have to go to this packed north Memphis dive. The "club" itself is one small, unadorned room, the cover is usually $5.00, the beer is served only in 40-ounce bottles (if you want any other kind of alcohol, feel free to bring it yourself; Bill's will be happy to set you up), and the house band, the Hollywood Allstars, serves up the city's finest blues—bar none—on Friday and Saturday nights from 11:00 P.M. until well into the next morning. Expect a clientele that's about 75 percent older African Americans from the bar's working-class neighborhood and 25 percent 20-something white kids, with a smattering of European tourists and slumming rich folks thrown in for good measure. This is an essential Memphis experience.

MOVIES

Paradiso
584 South Mendenhall Road
(901) 682-1754
www.malco.com
Malco's Paradiso, named after the Italian film *Cinema Paradiso,* is one of the city's largest and most comfortable movie theaters, with stadium seating and 14 screens, including an extra-wide 50-foot screen. But what sets this East Memphis theater apart is its Italian look, created with

fresco-type finishes and other Italian architectural details. That makes the lobby, with its pizza cafe/coffee bar and concessions that include chicken tenders and fried mozzarella as well as beer and wine, a comfortable place to hang out before or after the movies.

Studio on the Square
2105 Court Street
(901) 725-7151
www.malco.com
Malco's Studio on the Square, unlike the city's other movie houses, has lounge areas and tables and serves specialty coffees, beer, wine, desserts, and light appetizers. It's a great place to hang around before or after the movies. The lobby has several cozy seating areas, one with a faux fireplace, and its decor has a cinematic theme, played out with vintage movie posters and an antique movie projector. This Overton Square theater has five screens that play the latest in foreign and independent films as well as some mainstream movies.

SPORTS BARS

Fox & Hound English Tavern
5101 Sanderlin Avenue
(901) 763-2013

847 Exocet Drive, Germantown
(901) 624-9060
These popular watering holes are less like English taverns and more like large American sports bars, with plenty of pool tables and big screens, where you can catch the big games of the moment. There's a good selection of beers, servers are very attentive, and its pub fare is better than most. Fox & Hound draws a good, yuppie-ish crowd both for happy hour and later in the evening. The Sanderlin location is in Sanderlin shopping center, next to the East Memphis Hilton, whereas the Exocet location is near the intersection of Germantown Parkway and Fischer Steel Road.

WINE BARS

Le Chardonnay
5 Overton Square Lane
(901) 725–1375

The dark ambience, great wine list, and wood-burning oven make this wine bar a romantic favorite among Memphians. You can get a table, sit at the bar, or nestle into one of the overstuffed chairs or couches. The wine list, which is heavy on domestic wines from California, Washington State, and elsewhere, has more than 100 choices, about equally divided between red and white. About 40 of these are available by the glass. There are also Australian, French, and Italian wines. Le Chardonnay also has a great menu that includes handmade pizzas, excellent salads, and appetizers that include baked Brie. Le Chardonnay is on the small street that runs parallel to and just south of Madison Avenue, between Cooper and Florence Streets.

AFTER HOURS

A number of the bars and nightspots we list elsewhere in this chapter are open until the wee hours, including the Beale Street clubs and gay bars (see individual write-ups). Among the most popular are Melange's M-Bar, Glass Onion, Raiford's, and Earnestine & Hazel's. Here, we list the places where after-hours partying is their main claim to fame.

Club 152 on Beale
152 Beale Street
(901) 544-7011

This self-styled after-hours club on Beale Street consistently stays open until 5:00 A.M., although in truth, so do most other Beale Street clubs during the summer and other busy times.

Two Way Inn
752 South Cooper Street
(901) 278-9113

This tiny cinderblock bar, situated south of Cooper-Young, doesn't look like much, but in the wee hours on weekends it's the hottest hangout in midtown. The joint is literally wall-to-wall people as the party crowd packs in, usually after the show ends at nearby Young Street Deli. The grill is open all night, so you can order a burger at 5:00 A.M. (eating the burger in this sardine-like environment is something else again). Two Way Inn serves beer, no wine or hard stuff.

MEMPHIS MUSIC

For the past century Memphis has been the world's signature musical city. Cleveland may be home to the Rock and Roll Hall of Fame, and Nashville, with its country glitz and major record label offices, may be Music City USA. Other American cities—notably, New Orleans, St. Louis, Chicago, Detroit, and New York—may boast incredible music legacies. But nowhere else did music hit as hard, or mean as much, as it did in Memphis.

Of the three major music earthquakes that took place in Memphis—in blues, rock and roll, and soul—certainly the birth of rock and roll here in the 1950s ranks as one of the very few true, geographically specific music explosions during the last 100 years. Others include cultural eruptions such as Jamaican ska and reggae in the 1960s and 1970s, hip-hop's New York–based birth and development in the late 1970s and 1980s, and England's Beatles and Stones–fueled "invasion" in the mid-1960s.

In addition to giving birth to rock and roll in the 1950s, this de facto capital of the Mississippi Delta witnessed the nation's most vibrant blues scene in the first half of the 20th century, as the music moved from the cotton-field juke joints into Beale Street clubs and recording studios. In the 1960s Memphis became the mecca of Southern soul. Why Memphis, a relatively small city surrounded by farmland? The reason seems to be the city's unique mix of black and white, rural and urban, Northern and Southern, which formed the demographic catalyst for these successive musical earthquakes.

Memphis is currently enjoying the most vibrant music scene it has experienced since the late soul era of Al Green and Isaac Hayes in the 1970s, with its musicians making big contributions to the national scene in hip-hop, hard rock, and, of course, the blues. With 2003 dubbed "The Year of the Blues," the city's blues scene has received more national attention recently than it had in decades. And the death of Sam Phillips in 2003, followed by 2004's 50th Anniversary of Rock 'n' Roll, has put the spotlight on that genre as well. At the same time, two very different local soul men—Justin Timberlake and Al Green—have been riding high with new music that is both critically acclaimed and commercially successful.

The fact is, however, that most music lovers are drawn to Memphis by the mystique of its musical past, a legacy that gives credence to the city's official slogan, "The Home of the Blues and the Birthplace of Rock and Roll."

In this chapter you'll find the story of Memphis music, of how musical earthquakes and some other major rumbles changed American music forever. Then we'll bring you into the present, with a portrait of what's happening today. Who knows: When it's all said and done, maybe Memphis could write another chapter in the history of American music.

Finally, we list the Memphis attractions you can visit to see where it all happened (see the Close-up in this chapter). Don't forget to check out the Nightlife chapter, to find out where you can hear the best of Memphis music.

W. C. HANDY, BEALE STREET, AND THE "BIRTH" OF THE BLUES

Memphis's first real claim on music history came early in the 20th century, when Beale Street had become the center of black culture and commerce under the guidance of Robert Church, the South's first black millionaire.

Beale at that time was a wild place, with Pee Wee's Saloon as the street's signature nightspot and with ragtime piano booming from the windows of brothels on nearby Gayoso Street. Its mix of prostitution, drugs, and organized crime made Beale Street so rough that in 1918 a statistician for Prudential Insurance determined that Memphis was the murder capital of the United States, with most of the action centered on Beale.

Memphis's first contribution to the national music consciousness came through the work of William Christopher Handy, known as "the father of the blues." Handy didn't invent the music, of course, but during his years in Memphis he was the first to transcribe and arrange the existing music. Handy still has his critics in blues circles, but the fact remains that Handy's popularization of the blues form was crucial to the genre's success.

The son of a former slave, Handy was a well-traveled and well-educated musician who specialized in jazz and ragtime. In 1902 he settled in the nearby Delta town of Clarksdale, Mississippi, where he "discovered" the local music known as the blues. Handy moved his family to Memphis soon thereafter to pursue regular work in the Beale Street clubs.

In 1912 Handy put out "Memphis Blues," one of the first published blues songs (in the era before recordings, sheet music was the primary means through which music was purchased and enjoyed at home). "St. Louis Blues" followed soon after, then, in 1916, "Beale Street Blues." These songs were a huge success for Handy, who soon moved his orchestra to New York's Tin Pan Alley but never again matched the success he'd had during his Beale Street years.

Though the first recordings were introduced in 1900 and Handy's blues songs were successful a decade later, black acts weren't recorded until the 1920s. The first recorded blues stars were largely women, and Memphis had a small role in these early successes. The most prominent early blues star, Bessie Smith, performed regularly on Beale during the 1920s, and Memphian Alberta Hunter wrote one of her biggest hits with "Down Home Blues."

MEMPHIS JUG BANDS

Though more obscure now than the solo bluesmen of the era, Memphis's greatest post-Handy contribution to the blues was the jug bands. Encompassing a variety of instruments—though almost always the jug, blown across the mouth to produce bass-like sounds, and stringed instruments such as guitar, banjo, or fiddle—jug bands featured such delightful ensemble playing and drew from such a wide variety of genres (blues, jazz, ragtime, hillbilly, and novelty songs) that they are as much proto–rock and roll as any early American pop music.

The style is said to have originated in Louisville and was popular elsewhere, but Memphis was where jug bands had the most success. The most prominent was the Memphis Jug Band, formed in the mid-1920s. In 1927 the New York–based Victor label came to Memphis for a recording field trip. Its taping of the Memphis Jug Band in downtown Memphis was the first commercial recording ever made in Tennessee. The MJB had a rotating lineup that sometimes used great female blues singers Hattie Hart and Memphis Minnie. Over a seven-year recording career, the group cut 75 sides for Victor and Columbia/OKeh, but lasted as a live unit well into the 1940s.

Other local jug bands were the Beale Street Sheiks and Cannon's Jug Stompers, whose leader, Gus Cannon, composed "Walk Right In," which the Rooftop Singers would make a number-one pop hit in 1963.

EARLY MEMPHIS BLUES SINGERS

Memphis produced several prominent blues singers during the 1920s, the first decade that the music was recorded, although Beale Street decreed they were not polished enough to play inside the clubs. Products of a Delta lifestyle where sharecropping encouraged large families and then subsequent urban migrations, several of the Delta's most prominent early blues artists ended up in Memphis.

Walter "Furry" Lewis, who worked with the Memphis Jug Band and Cannon's Jug Stompers at medicine and tent shows, is probably most synonymous with the city's blues heritage to native Memphians. Lewis first recorded in 1927 in Chicago for Vocalion and ended up cutting 20 sides in all from 1927 through 1929. Lewis then disappeared from the public eye until he resurfaced in 1959 during the blues/folk revival and returned to active recording until his death in 1981.

Victor, the record label that had recorded the Memphis Jug Band, returned in 1928 for a second session. This time, Victor captured the first recordings by Delta bluesman Tommy Johnson, in addition to more jug-band music. The flamboyant Johnson is generally considered one of the three most important first-generation Delta bluesmen, along with Charley Patton and Son House, who had less direct connection to Memphis.

The same year the OKeh label set up in Memphis for a recording trip, capturing the first recorded work of the Mississippi gentle blues giant John Hurt. He would become a major star of the 1960s blues revival, when he was rediscovered by dedicated fans. Other significant early bluesmen who were prominent on the Memphis scene included Robert Wilkins and Sleepy John Estes.

This first burst of Memphis blues activity soon ended with the onslaught of the Great Depression, drought, and the boll weevil. Record companies stopped making trips to Memphis.

CROSSROADS: ROBERT JOHNSON AND THE POST-DEPRESSION BLUES

The most important of the post-Depression blues artists was undoubtedly Robert Johnson, who spent virtually his whole life in the area around Memphis. Johnson died under mysterious circumstances in 1938 at the age of 27 and had only three recording sessions totaling just a few dozen songs. Yet despite such a small body of work and brief career span, Johnson stands as one of the most important figures in all of American music. The 1990 CD debut of his complete recordings became the first blues recordings to ever sell one million copies.

Johnson's "crossroads" legend that he sold his soul to the devil in order to acquire his otherworldly skills has become American music's most evocative myth, but the truest account of Johnson's life can probably be found in music journalist Peter Guralnick's 1988 book, *Searching for Robert Johnson.*

Presently, Johnson dwarfs his contemporaries in the public imagination, but he wasn't the only prominent blues musician this area produced during the post-Depression era. Others included pianist Peter Chatman (aka Memphis Slim), who was a Beale regular in the 1930s, as well as Washboard Sam, the original Sonny Boy Williamson, and Robert Johnson associate Johnny Shines.

Key area bluesmen who emerged in the 1940s included Howlin' Wolf and Sonny Boy Williamson II, who was becoming a star with his "King Biscuit Time" radio show in Helena, Arkansas. The Delta also produced Muddy Waters, the major star of the Chicago blues scene who was first recorded in nearby Clarksdale by the Library of Congress's Alan Lomax. More recently, the Waters story and its Memphis connection has been the focus of *Can't Be Satisfied,* a perhaps definitive biography and accompanying documentary film by Memphis-based Robert Gordon (author of *It Came from Memphis*).

RADIO AND RECORDING: THE MEMPHIS FIFTIES' EXPLOSION

Memphis's second great music explosion had its roots in radio. In 1948 the owners of downtown station WDIA gambled and made it the nation's first all-black-staffed radio station. By broadcasting black

Johnny Cash in Memphis

Johnny Cash died September 12, 2003, in Nashville. But though the country-music icon was justifiably associated with country music's capital, Cash was never a comfortable fit in that company town. Tennessee's other music city, Memphis, a town of mavericks, was perhaps truer to Cash's personality.

Cash moved to the city with wife Vivian in 1954 after four years in the Air Force, settling in East Memphis and working as an appliance salesman before he wandered into Sun Studio. And though he left four years later to go with Columbia Records, Memphis launched his career. (For that reason, much of I Walk the Line, a movie about Cash starring Joaquim Phoenix, was filmed in Memphis.)

Arkansas-native Cash was part of a generation of white Southerners who followed Elvis to Memphis in pursuit of a musical dream. Like Presley and Louisiana's Jerry Lee Lewis and Tennessee's Carl Perkins, Cash found in Sam Phillips a producer more interested in enhancing what was unique about Cash than forcing him into a proven music-industry style.

Cash would become a bigger star in the 1960s after his Nashville move, but it was in Memphis, with Sam Phillips at the controls and Memphis-born guitarist Luther Perkins at his side, that Cash developed his inimitable style and, arguably, produced his most lasting art: classics such as "I Walk the Line" and "Folsom Prison Blues." Here Cash had the freedom to develop an original sound steeped in gospel, folk, and blues, and to experiment with it. At Sun Studio tours today, fans see how Cash developed the chugging, train-engine guitar sound of "Folsom Prison Blues": by sliding a dollar bill between the strings and neck of his acoustic guitar.

Cash was surely an American-music original, but without the influence of the blues records he first heard in Memphis, the unique guitar sidekick he found there, and the lifelong guiding hand of the man he called "Mr. Phillips," Cash might never have crafted the sound that made him a legend.

music—largely the postwar blues hybrid dubbed "rhythm and blues"—in 1949 to a primarily black audience, WDIA became a massive success, tapping a previously ignored market and billing itself as the "Mother Station of the Negroes." The station also boasted Nat D. Williams and future star Rufus Thomas as part of its broadcasting team and gave Riley King, an aspiring blues musician from Indianola, Mississippi, his big break with a 15-minute slot on the station. King was dubbed the "Beale Street Blues Boy," the "blues boy"

part later giving way to the snappier "B.B."

Due to the peculiarities of the station's license, it wasn't allowed to broadcast after sunset, leaving room for another station, WHBQ, to move in and pick up WDIA's audience at night. WHBQ hired a white deejay—the brash Dewey Phillips—to spin black blues and R&B records. Phillips's show, called "Red Hot & Blue," debuted in 1949. Phillips would later become the first broadcaster to play an Elvis Presley song over the air, thus becoming a key player in the birth of rock and roll.

While WDIA and WHBQ were changing the sonic landscape of the city's airwaves, another local radio employee, WREC engineer Sam Phillips, was making moves that would forever change recording in the city. In 1950 Phillips renovated a small building just east of downtown Memphis and turned it into Memphis Recording Service. Phillips's endeavor soon became the first significant local recording since the Victor and OKeh sessions.

Phillips began to capture a new generation of postwar bluesmen. Ike Turner of Clarksdale brought his band to record and, in 1951, with sax player Jackie Brenston playing lead, Phillips cut the group's "Rocket 88," which has since been widely cited as the first rock-and-roll song. Released under the name Jackie Brenston and the Delta Cats, the song went all the way to number one. Turner soon became Phillips's session leader and talent scout, helping to bring a succession of soon-to-be-historic bluesmen into the tiny studio. Among the major blues figures who recorded with Sam Phillips in the early 1950s were B. B. King, Howlin' Wolf, Walter Horton, Little Milton, and Junior Parker.

Around this time WDIA also began recording artists, including King, Roscoe Gordon, Bobby Bland, and Johnny Ace, on program director David James Mathis's Duke label, which later relocated to Houston.

By 1952 Phillips was growing tired of recording his artists for other labels and decided to form his own record label, Sun. The label's first big hit came with WDIA deejay Rufus Thomas's "Bear Cat," an answer record to Big Mama Thornton's hit "Hound Dog."

ELVIS PRESLEY AND THE ROCKABILLY ERA

Elvis Presley may have seemed like an anomaly to most of Middle America when he burst onto television sets in the mid-1950s, but the young man with the startling voice and overactive hips didn't come out of nowhere. He came out of Memphis. With radio bringing R&B directly to white teenagers, with Beale Street making the music an around-the-corner inevitability, and Sam Phillips providing a forum, the stage was set in Memphis for someone to break out and fulfill Phillips's famous plea: "If I could find a white singer with the Negro sound and the Negro feel, I could make a million dollars."

Cultural forces—including a postwar economic and technology boom that helped turn Elvis's rock-and-roll revolution from regional subculture into teen-driven mass culture—are one big reason for the rise of Elvis Presley. No one, however, could have expected Phillips's find to be such a genius singer or to exude such overwhelming charisma. Cultural forces may be enough to explain a Carl Perkins, the great rockabilly singer who followed Elvis to Sun, but Elvis Presley is another matter entirely. (See the Close-up in this chapter and the Attractions chapter.)

A teenage Presley first entered Memphis Recording Service in 1953 to cut a souvenir disc. Phillips brought the young Presley back the next year and paired him with a couple of veteran Memphis country musicians, guitarist Scotty Moore and bassist Bill Black. Things clicked at that freewheeling and now-historic 1954 recording session, producing what would become Elvis's first single, with a silky cover of the Arthur Crudup blues song "That's All Right (Mama)" on the "A" side and a raucous version of the Bill Monroe bluegrass classic "Blue Moon of Kentucky" on the "B" side. Sam Phillips hustled an acetate of the single over to his friend Dewey Phillips at WHBQ, who debuted the song, and the new artist, on Red Hot & Blue. The response was deafening, and soon Elvis, and Sun, were on their way. Presley's first major concert followed a few weeks later at Memphis's Overton Park Shell.

Elvis rapidly spread from a local to a regional phenomenon, landing a spot on the popular country radio show "The Louisiana Hayride." Elvis's performance there drew the attention of Colonel Tom

Parker, then managing country stars Hank Snow and Eddy Arnold. He signed Elvis in August 1955. The Colonel engineered Phillips's sale of Elvis's contract to New York's RCA that November. The RCA deal and subsequent national television appearances on *The Ed Sullivan Show* and other shows turned Elvis into a national star. In January 1956 Elvis released "Heartbreak Hotel," his first million seller, and in August of that year he made his first movie, *Love Me Tender.* The rest is history.

Elvis would return to Sun Studio to record only one more time, in December of 1956 as part of an informal jam session with then-current Sun artists Jerry Lee Lewis, Johnny Cash, and Carl Perkins, which was dubbed "The Million Dollar Quartet."

It may seem crazy in retrospect for Sam Phillips to have sold Elvis's contract to RCA for $35,000, but that seemingly paltry sum was quite a hefty fee at the time, and it allowed Phillips to keep his little label solvent, thus paving the way for the extraordinary flow of artists who followed Elvis into Sun.

Jackson, Tennessee's pure rockabilly sensation, Carl Perkins, was Phillips's next discovery, and his historic "Blue Suede Shoes" would become the first record to ever top the pop, country, and rhythm-and-blues charts at the same time. Arkansas's Johnny Cash was next at Sun, with a country-heavy rockabilly that produced hits such as "I Walk the Line" and "Folsom Prison Blues." But Sun's biggest artist at that time, by far, was Jerry Lee Lewis. This wild man from Ferriday, Louisiana, and "his pounding piano" (as some early records were credited) produced major, still bone-rattling hits such as "Great Balls of Fire" and "Whole Lotta Shakin' Goin' On."

A succession of important minor artists followed at Sun, including Texas crooner Roy Orbison (who would become a major artist after leaving Sun), and second-tier rockabilly icons Billy Lee Riley, Charlie Feathers, Sonny Burgess, Malcolm Yelvington, Warren Smith, and Carl Mann. Sun's

last major star was Charlie Rich, a talented pianist from nearby Colt, Arkansas, whose first hit in 1959, "Lonely Weekends," was Sun's last. Sun Records closed soon after.

THE MEMPHIS SOUL ERA: STAX AND HI RECORDS

Though Sun's rockabilly eruption was made up entirely of white men, many of whom loved black music, the inherent racial interaction that produced Elvis would directly manifest itself in Memphis's next big thing, the Stax-based soul era.

The roots of Stax lay in banker and part-time fiddle player Jim Stewart, who founded Satellite Records in 1957 and soon upgraded his equipment with money borrowed from sister Estelle Axton. The fledgling label's first success came with " 'Cause I Love You," a duet by Rufus Thomas and his 17-year-old daughter, Carla. Carla Thomas followed the song with the sweet "Gee Whiz," becoming the label's first star.

At this time the label began a relationship with Atlantic Records and R&B-loving honcho Jerry Wexler, one that would help the label become a national player without losing its identity or autonomy. The label's first major hit came with an informal instrumental, "Last Night," recorded by a bunch of house musicians and credited to the then-fictional group the Markeys. "Last Night" was a top-five hit on both the pop and R&B charts.

Just as the label was becoming prominent nationally, legal troubles with a preexisting label forced Satellite to change its name in 1961. Combining the names of its two owners, Jim Stewart (St) and Estelle Axton (Ax), the Stax name was born. Soon William Bell's "You Don't Miss Your Water" gave the Stax label a male soul star to rival Carla Thomas.

During this time the Stax house band earned the right to be cited as one of the greatest bands ever. The legendary group coalesced into an interracial, neighborhood-bred rhythm section, consisting of Booker T. Jones on organ, Steve Cropper on guitar, Al

Elvis: The Musician behind the Legend

"I sing all kinds." That's what a shy teenager Elvis Presley said at his first Sun recording session in 1954 when asked about his repertoire, and he meant it.

In the decades since Elvis's historic rise and sad decline, the King of Rock and Roll has become such a pop-culture icon that it's easy to put aside or even underrate his actual artistic output.

So what made Elvis a great artist? The key lies in that simple statement: "I sing all kinds."

Other first-generation rockers could outdo Elvis in one way or another. Chuck Berry was both rock-and-roll's definitive instrumentalist and greatest writer. Little Richard and Jerry Lee Lewis made records that were far more viscerally powerful than those of Elvis, but no one united the various tributaries of American music with the grace, ease, or originality of Elvis Presley—and no one could sing like him. Presley's vocal gifts and love of vocal pop make him as much the last great interpretive singer—an inheritor of Bing Crosby, Billie Holiday, and Frank Sinatra—as he was the first rock-and-roller.

What Elvis accomplished at Sun was no less than an unleashing of the invisible republic that had long been at the heart of American music. He created a mass-cultural sphere in which gospel, blues, country, and pop-crooning could become part of the same thing. Elvis's music embodied black and white, city and country, urbane sophistication and proletarian vitality. Amazingly, he did all this, with varying degrees of artistic success, throughout his career.

Elvis the icon is everywhere these days, but Elvis the artist exists only in his recordings. His is among the largest, most continually repackaged bodies of work in recorded history. It is easy to get lost in all of this, but there are certain Elvis collections not to miss.

One of these is *30 #1 Hits,* the compilation that RCA released in 2002, ushering in a new period of Elvis hysteria. A 20-year-spanning survey of the King most of the public adores—from "Don't Be Cruel" to "Jailhouse Rock" to "Suspicious Minds"—*30 #1 Hits* confirms Elvis's status as a great pure pop singer, his commitment to pleasing an audience and nailing a song never wavering.

But as great as *30 #1 Hits* is, it isn't the place to start. Instead, begin with *The Sun Sessions CD,* arguably the most essential rock-and-roll recording of all. Every master take from these early recordings is now a classic, but "That's All Right" and "Blue Moon of Kentucky" can claim to be the musical definition of rock and roll. "Mystery Train," where Elvis adds a casual air of defiance to a blues dirge, might be the music's philosophical summation. *The Sun Sessions* was trumped by RCA in 1999 with *Sunrise,* a two-disc set that adds 10 tracks of early demos and live cuts to *The Sun Sessions*'s 28-song studio set. *The Sun Sessions* is tighter and more essential, but you'll want this music in whatever configuration you can find it.

And after that, start exploring, with special attention to *Elvis Presley,* Elvis's RCA debut from 1956, the first rock-and-roll album to hit number one on the Billboard pop charts; *Elvis is Back!,* his mature, bluesy, post-army comeback album; and *The Memphis Record* (or its overstuffed-but-easier-to-find substitute *Suspicious Minds*), the complete document of Elvis's 1969 sessions at Memphis American Studios (his first official recording sessions back home since leaving in the 1950s).

Jackson Jr. on drums, and Lewis Steinberg (later Duck Dunn) on bass. This ensemble, which played over virtually the entirety of the Stax catalog, also became hit makers of their own right. Under the moniker Booker T. and the MGs, they scored a massive hit with "Green Onions," which began a series of instrumental smashes.

Though most of Stax's talent was homegrown, the label's two biggest stars arrived from the outside. Macon, Georgia's Otis Redding had his first hit for Stax in 1962 with the ballad "These Arms of Mine" and quickly became the label's biggest star and most significant artist. But the label's biggest hit makers were the duo Sam and Dave, a Florida-based act sent to Stax by Wexler. Recording mainly songs written by the emerging in-house songwriting partners David Porter and Isaac Hayes, Sam and Dave scored with songs such as "Hold On, I'm Comin'" (the label's first number-one hit since "Green Onions") and "Soul Man".

The out-of-town talent kept flocking to Stax. Though he never recorded under the Stax imprint, Wilson Pickett came to Stax to write and record classics such as "In the Midnight Hour" and "634-5789." In 1965 soul singer Eddie Floyd recorded "Knock on Wood" for the label.

In 1967 a Wisconsin plane crash took the life of Redding and most of his backup band, the Barkays, bringing an end to Stax's golden age. The label would persevere into the mid-1970s, recording a new generation of soul stars, including the blues-oriented Albert King and Little Milton, the gospel-based Staples Singers, and Johnnie Taylor. The label's breakout star in the 1970s ended up being longtime studio hand Isaac Hayes, who moved in front of the microphone to become "Black Moses," recording a few classic albums and the iconic "Theme from Shaft."

Stax wasn't the only landmark soul music to come out of Memphis in the 1960s. Producer Chips Moman, who was an important part of Stax's early years, ran American studios, which came out with James Carr's soul classic, "The Dark End of

the Street." American also produced a variety of local and national acts, including Dusty Springfield and Neil Diamond.

In the 1970s, as Stax was on the way down, another Memphis soul label was on the way up. Hi Records was actually founded as a rockabilly label in the mid-1950s, but in the early 1960s, its way with instrumentals drew Willie Mitchell, a Beale Street bandleader who had had several hits on his own during the 1960s. Hi's glory years began with Mitchell's discovery of Al Green, who became the last great Southern soul singer and, arguably, Memphis's last major musical star. After a few attempts at gruff, Otis Redding–style soul singing, Green found his softer, more intimate sound with 1971's "Tired of Being Alone," a million seller. That breakthrough was followed immediately by Green's signature tune, "Let's Stay Together," which hit number one on both the pop and R&B charts and began a string of 15 top-10 singles over the next five years. Green was the dominant force for Hi, but a string of important second-tier soul stars, most notably Ann Peebles, Syl Johnson, and Otis Clay, also recorded hits there.

MEMPHIS'S FINAL ROCK-AND-ROLL GLORY YEARS

Soul may have been Memphis's major contribution to pop music in the 1960s and 1970s, but rock and roll was far from dead in the city that created it. After years of lucrative but artistically negligible film work, Elvis freed himself from Colonel Parker's grip long enough for a brief but major comeback. Clad in black leather, Elvis thrilled audiences with informal, powerhouse versions of some of his classic recordings on an NBC television special that aired in December 1968. The next month Elvis returned to Memphis for his first local recording session since leaving Sun. Elvis entered American studios as an icon with a lot to prove, and he delivered. Those Memphis sessions marked Elvis's finest music since his early RCA recordings, spawning the commanding *From Elvis in Memphis* album and the soulful classic "Suspicious Minds."

During the years Elvis had been busy in Hollywood, Memphis was part of the garage-rock "movement," producing a new generation of hit makers heavy on one-hit wonders. Among the Memphis contributions to this national, Brit-invasion-fueled craze were the Gentrys's "Keep on Dancing," the Hombres's "Let It Out (Let It All Hang Out)," and Sam the Sham's "Wooly Bully." The biggest garage band was the Box Tops, a product of American Studios fronted by teenage lead singer Alex Chilton. The Box Tops had a string of hits in the late 1960s, including "The Letter" (number one for a solid month in 1967) and "Cry Like a Baby."

Eventually, the Box Tops mutated into Big Star, a Chilton-led band whose twisted but sweet anglophiliac power pop never sold as well as the Box Tops but ended up being much more influential. Big Star recorded three records for new local label Ardent in the mid-1970s, their career petering out with limited distribution and even more limited sales. But a cult would grow up around the band, making them one of the key influences for the indie and alternative-rock movements of the 1980s and 1990s.

For the 15 years or so after Al Green found religion and bid adieu to secular music in the late 1970s, Memphis music took a turn for the mundane. The city produced an occasional notable artist (singer-songwriter Keith Sykes, indie rockers the Grifters) and brought in plenty of out-of-town acts (ZZ Top, John Prine) to record at independent studios such as Ardent. Unfortunately, though, the momentum that had driven the city's music scene for most of the century had dissipated.

It may be forlorn to expect the city to ever again witness musical eruptions as galvanic as the blues, rockabilly, and soul scenes of earlier decades, but the last few years have seen Memphis begin to make a move again, once more becoming a force on the national music scene.

THE CURRENT MUSIC SCENE

Though locals argue about how much it has to do with the city's storied musical past, everyone seems to agree that the current music scene in Memphis is the strongest it has been in more than 20 years. Memphis music is once again making major inroads into the national music scene. Most of the action is centered around rock and hip-hop, the highest profile recent local-music happenings have come from other areas.

The biggest music story perhaps has been the rise of Memphis native Justin Timberlake into one of the world's biggest pop stars. In 2003, the former *NSYNC singer made a shockingly assured move from teen-pop footnote-to-be to adult pop and R&B artist that some have seen as a blue-eyed answer to vintage Michael Jackson. Though Timberlake's professional development may have more to do with Orlando (where *NSYNC formed) than Memphis, he has nevertheless retained close ties to the Bluff City. He has referenced his Memphis heritage repeatedly on national television and in national magazine interviews and can be seen sitting courtside at Memphis Grizzlies games occasionally. Timberlake also signed on as an official spokesperson for the Memphis Convention and Visitors Bureau's 2004 "50 Years of Rock and Roll in Memphis" campaign.

And Timberlake's soul-man emergence rhymed nicely with the re-emergence of perhaps the city's greatest living soul star, Al Green. After abandoning secular music to lead his own church in the late 1970s, Green has traveled under the musical radar. But that changed in 2003 with the release of a rapturously received comeback album, *I Can't Stop*. Green recorded the album in Memphis with his old collaborator Willie Mitchell (with whom he hadn't worked since 1976) and many of the same session players that worked on his classic 1970s albums.

But Memphis is still known as a blues town, and on that front the city received a new round of attention in 2003 after the

Music Attractions

If you are a music fan, you won't want to miss these attractions. (See the Attractions chapter for more details and information on each one.)

Gibson Guitar Factory
145 Lt. George W. Lee Avenue
(901) 544-7998
www.gibsonmemphis.com
Here you can take a tour and watch guitars being made by hand.

Graceland Mansion
3734 Elvis Presley Boulevard
(901) 332-3322, (800) 238-2000
www.elvis.com
This is the home of Elvis Presley, where you can tour the house and see all of Elvis's gold records and other memorabilia.

Memphis Rock 'n' Soul Museum
200 South Third Street (FedEx Forum)
(901) 543-0800
www.memphisrocknsoul.org
This museum tells how Memphis played a key role in the development of rock and roll, soul, and other American music.

Stax Museum of American Soul Music
926 East McLemore Street
(901) 946-2535
www.soulsvilleusa.com
Built on the site of the former Stax Records studio, the museum tells the story of this famed studio, where Otis Redding, Isaac Hayes, and other Southern soul stars recorded.

Sun Studio
706 Union Avenue
(901) 521-0664, (800) 441-6249
www.sunstudio.com
This tiny studio produced musical giants, including Elvis Presley, Jerry Lee Lewis, and Johnny Cash, as well as the first rock-and-roll recording.

W. C. Handy House
352 Beale Street
(901) 527-3427 or (901) 522-1556
This modest house is where W. C. Handy lived in Memphis at the time he "discovered" the blues.

---

year was congressionally mandated as "The Year of the Blues." With the local presence of the international Blues Foundation and its signature event, the Handy Awards (which have been dubbed "the Blues Grammys"), as well as with the city's deserving if self-bestowed title "the Home of the Blues," Memphis was primed to take advantage of all the hoopla. When Martin Scorsese did the PBS documentary series *The Blues,* one of its seven independent films and companion discs focused exclusively on Memphis, while others of the films/CDs spotlighted the city, too.

And this celebration of the city's blues heritage has only helped to focus the spotlight on the central role the music continues to play on the city's music scene. The Blues Foundation and the Handys keep Memphis at the center of the national blues scene, but there's plenty of local action on that front as well. The city's most popular band in recent years might be the North Mississippi Allstars, an interracial blues rock band from nearby Coldwater, Mississippi. It has become a critical cause célèbre and commercial force, especially as a concert draw. Led by the two sons of longtime local producer and musical raconteur Jim Dickinson, the band has drawn comparisons to the Allman Brothers while selling records to jam-band aficionados and alternative-rock fans alike. Along the way they've garnered fawning press coverage in national publications such as *Rolling Stone* and the *New York Times*.

If the Allstars have crossed over, there are other notable local blues artists who are still mainly known on the blues circuit, including Alvin Youngblood Hart. His stylistically ambitious take on the blues tradition marks him as an inheritor of Taj Mahal. Richard Johnston is a young white blues player of sublime skill and surprising restraint. His one-man-band attack recently won him the grand prize at the Blues Foundation's International Blues Challenge amateur contest.

Memphis can also claim the last decade's most aesthetically influential blues scene in the form of the droning hill-country blues captured by nearby Oxford, Mississippi, label Fat Possum. Fat Possum artists such as R. L. Burnside and the late Junior Kimbrough were among the most respected blues artists to emerge in the 1990s, and their sound, with its droning, hypnotic guitar riffs and guttural vocals, is equally popular among blues, rock, and punk fans.

To catch live blues in Memphis, Beale Street is still the place to start, particularly stalwart clubs such as B. B. King's, the Blues City Café, and the Rum Boogie Café, which have continued to carry the torch as some other clubs have moved away from the blues. But the best live blues bets in town might be elsewhere: downtown's Center for Southern Folklore presents a more authentic and down-home take on the blues, usually during the lunch hour. And Wild Bill's, an old-fashioned neighborhood juke joint in north Memphis, boasts the city's best blues house band, the Hollywood Allstars, on weekend nights. Floating from club to club is Di Anne Price, a local treasure who may be as close as you can come to a Bessie Smith or Ella Fitzgerald in this day and time.

Nationally, the growth of Southern hip-hop has been a big story, and Memphis has played a role, becoming one of the music's leading markets, both in terms of consumption and production. Leading the way has been Three 6 Mafia, a "gangsta rap" collective who have released a string of gold and platinum albums—the first Memphis-based artists to have such massive and sustained success since Isaac Hayes and Al Green. The Three 6 contingent is merely at the forefront of a large local and regional scene that is likely to produce other national stars in the near future. Another promising Memphis talent is Yo Gotti, a local rapper with the major record label TVT.

Gospel music is still a force in Memphis, although its national profile has dimmed since the 1998 death of O'Landa Draper, who with his choir, the Associates, won two Grammys and was nominated for a total of six Grammys. The choir continues to perform under the name O'Landa Draper's Associates.

With hard rock and metal back in vogue in recent years, Memphis has also become a player on that scene, led by Saliva, a rap-metal band that had been at the forefront of Memphis metal for several years. Saliva signed to major label Island-Def Jam in the late 1990s, releasing two major-label albums that have garnered impressive sales and a Grammy nomination, and that has helped the band win a slot opening for hard-rock heroes Aerosmith and KISS on a national tour. Saliva is a product of a fertile local metal scene centered at the New Daisy Theatre, a large rock club on the east end of Beale Street, which should produce more stars in the future.

The city's local rock scene—outside of hard rock and metal—is a rich mix heavy on garage rock and roots-rock. Memphis has always been one of the country's biggest garage-rock cities, dating back to a 1960s heyday that produced the likes of the Box Tops, Sam the Sham, and the Gentrys. Now it's more of an underground scene, but garage bands such as the Reigning Sound, the Subteens, the Lost

Sounds, and the Porch Ghouls have made waves locally and nationally.

Equally big on the city's club scene in recent years is alternative country–oriented bands. The North Mississippi Allstars proteges Lucero are one of the city's most highly regarded acts, having turned their local success into a growing national fan base, while singer-songwriter Cory Branan—who has been featured in *Rolling Stone* and has performed on *The Late Show with David Letterman*—is widely regarded as one of the city's most important emerging talents.

Other current local acts of note are the jazzy, soulful Gamble Brothers Band and the college-rock-oriented Ingram Hill. Emerging scenes include an indie-rock scene centered around a local record label/collective called Makeshift Music (key bands: Snowglobe, the Coach & Four, and the Glass) and a hip-hop and neo-soul scene centered around a concert series called Tha Movement (key artists: FreeSol and Valencia Robinson).

As a current music-industry center, Memphis pales in comparison to its cross-state rival, Nashville. One reason is that although Nashville is the center for one genre of music—country, of course—Memphis's music heritage, much like its population, is considerably more diverse, with blues, rock and roll, jazz, soul, and gospel all sharing the city's attention. A more important reason for the industry gap may be the disparate temperaments of the two cities' most important musical entrepreneurs. Nashville—sometimes to its credit, sometimes not—is a town of company men. Those who built up the Grand Ole Opry and the city's recording infrastructure were eager to join the music establishment. Memphis, on the other hand, has always been a city of mavericks and independent record labels, with the iconoclastic Sam Phillips as a model.

That said, Memphis still boasts a stronger music-industry infrastructure than most cities. Local recording studios continue to draw national talent, particularly Ardent Studios, which has been home to mainstream rock artists such as 3 Doors Down and Sister Hazel and contemporary blues performers such as Deborah Coleman. Easley Studios is one of the most popular recording homes for indie and punk bands, such as Pavement and the White Stripes.

Memphis also boasts one of the country's most active chapters of the National Association of Recording Arts and Sciences, serving as head of a regional branch that includes St. Louis and New Orleans. And recently, the city and county government formed the Memphis and Shelby County Music Commission, a body formed to promote what the city considers its greatest natural resource.

Ready to check out some music? Turn to the Nightlife chapter for its listing of clubs and other music venues.

AFRICAN-AMERICAN HERITAGE

No book about Memphis would be complete without a description of the city's rich African-American history and culture. Many of the things Memphis prides itself on most—including the blues, rock and roll, and the Memphis sound—have their roots in the city's African-American community.

Memphis has the ninth-largest concentration of African Americans in the country, and has produced such luminaries as former NAACP chairman Benjamin Hooks and Congressman Harold Ford Jr., a rising star on Capitol Hill in Washington, D.C. The city's first black mayor, Dr. W. W. Herenton, was elected in 1992, and 10 years later attorney A C Wharton Jr. became the county's first black mayor. Basketball great Penny Hardaway hails from Memphis, as do colossal music legends Isaac Hayes, Al Green, and Aretha Franklin (she was born here). More recent Memphis musical sensations include rappers Three 6 Mafia and in the 1990s, Grammy-winning gospel powerhouse O'Landa Draper.

The city also boasts its share of black visual artists, including painter Brenda Joy Smith, blues artist George Hunt, and photographer Ernest Withers. He captured some of the country's most moving images during the 1968 garbage workers strike as well as during the riots and other events that followed the assassination in Memphis of Dr. Martin Luther King Jr. Memphis is also home to one of the South's oldest historically black colleges, LeMoyne-Owen College, which dates from 1862. Local entrepreneurs include Fred Jones, who started the Southern Heritage Classic football event that draws many thousands to Memphis each year.

Memphis also is the seat of two large African-American churches, the Church of God in Christ and the Christian Methodist Episcopal Church. Some of America's greatest gospel music came from here, with hundreds of gospel songs flowing from the pen of the late Herbert Brewster. It's also home to the Full Gospel Tabernacle, the church headed by the Rev. Al Green, the recording-artist-turned-pastor, and Mason Temple, where Martin Luther King Jr. made his famous "I've Been to the Mountaintop" speech.

Those interested in learning about the city's heritage can visit a number of African-American attractions, including Beale Street, which was the birthplace of the blues and the center of African-American culture and commerce during segregation. There's also the National Civil Rights Museum, and Slave Haven Underground Railroad Museum (Burkle Estate), a house said to have sheltered runaway slaves on their way north. The Stax Museum of American Soul Music provides a thorough education on how musical history was made here.

You can also tour the National Civil Rights Museum, and follow Martin Luther King's footsteps during his fateful trip to Memphis in 1968. You may want to take a self-guided civil rights walking tour, using the "I Am a Man" map published by Memphis Heritage, Inc. (See the Close-up on

You can book a guided tour of the sites of importance to the city's African-American heritage. One of the best ones is operated by Heritage Tours, (901) 527-3427, www.heritagetours memphis.com. It's best to call ahead for reservations.

If Beale Street Could Talk

Beale Street was the center for African-American culture and commerce in Memphis from the beginning of the 20th century until the end of segregation in the 1960s. While many Southern cities had areas where African Americans gathered, conducted business, and amused themselves, Beale Street was renowned for its music and even had a song, W. C. Handy's "Beale Street Blues," named after it.

Today, the street is an entertainment district and tourist attraction for all people, with music clubs that include B. B. King's Blues Club.

Beale Street was home to wealthy whites until the 1878 yellow-fever epidemic, when Robert Church Sr. bought up the land and built Church Park and Auditorium on Beale Street, exclusively for blacks. He built Beale into the city's center of African-American life. It continued to be segregated for the most part, and only starting in the 1940s were whites allowed to visit the street's club during designated hours. Today, in addition to the commercial businesses, you'll find several historic buildings on

Beale, including the Old Daisy Theatre at 329 Beale, a theater originally built for African Americans.

Beale Street Baptist Church at 379 Beale was the first brick-constructed, multistory church in the United States built for African Americans (today it's the First Baptist Church Beale). Church Park at Beale and Fourth Streets honors Robert Church, who first developed it many years ago.

On the street you'll also find historic markers describing luminaries including journalist/activist Ida B. Wells and WDIA radio announcer Nat D. Williams. Brass musical notes embedded in the sidewalks honor musicians, including many R&B greats.

Today the street is a tourist attraction by day and an entertainment district at night featuring live music. Beale Street has a slicker, more homogenous feel nowadays, a far cry from its glory days as the hub of Memphis's African-American culture and commerce. See the Memphis Music, Nightlife, and Kid-stuff chapters for more information about Beale Street.

Martin Luther King Jr. in this chapter for more information.)

HISTORY

African Americans first came to this area in the early to mid-1800s as slaves, brought by white plantation owners to work the fertile Delta land surrounding Memphis. The owners relied on slave labor

to produce cotton, the "white gold" that fueled the Southern economy. Slave labor built the city's first roads and buildings.

During slavery days, one of the main escape routes for slaves fleeing the South was through Memphis, and the home of Jacob Burkle (open to the public as Slave Haven; see the Attractions chapter for more information) is believed to have been a stop on what history calls the Under-

CLOSE-UP

Martin Luther King Jr. and the Memphis Black Sanitation Workers

In 1968 the city's black sanitation workers were fed up with being treated unfairly by their employer. For example, in January of that year, black sanitation workers were sent home from their jobs because of the weather, and given two hours' show-up pay, while their white counterparts remained and earned a full day's wage. In February two black workers were killed in an on-the-job accident. The black workers went on strike February 12, with immediate results: Only 34 of the city's 180 garbage trucks were able to operate the first day of the strike.

The strike also was about dignity, and to underscore that point, the strikers carried and wore placards bearing the message, "I Am a Man." The mayor refused to negotiate with the workers, saying their strike was illegal. The standoff continued, mediation was tried and failed. Marches, sit-ins, and boycotts became commonplace.

In support of the strikers, Dr. King came to Memphis on several occasions, the last of which was April 3. A few days before that, King had decided to cancel a trip to Africa in order to lead a peaceful march in Memphis.

On the evening of April 3, King addressed a crowd at Mason Temple. "Something is happening in Memphis, something is happening in our world," Dr. King told his listeners. "I've seen the promised land. I may not get there with you. But I want you to know tonight, that we, as a people, will get to the promised land."

The next day Southern Christian Leadership Conference lawyers were successful in getting an injunction against the planned march overturned. However, before the march could take

ground Railroad. Slaves were freed in 1863, and many of them migrated from the plantations to Memphis and other urban areas. In 1874 blacks were admitted to the Memphis public-school system for the first time.

In 1878 the final and worst of three yellow-fever epidemics struck Memphis, driving half of the city's 40,000 inhabitants out of the city and killing some 5,000 people. During the epidemics, blacks took on much of the burden of nursing the sick. Their survival rates were much higher than those of the whites because of an immunity to the disease passed down from African ancestors.

As whites fled the city, many sold their property to a young African American named Robert Church. Eventually, Church owned much of Beale Street, started the city's first bank for blacks, and became the South's first African-American millionaire. As a result of the fever epidemic, the city defaulted on its obligations, and in 1879 the state revoked the city charter. But when it was time to get the charter place, King was killed by an assassin's bullet on the balcony of the Lorraine Motel. Riots ensued, in Memphis and across the country, while the FBI initiated an international manhunt for the killer. A few days later, Coretta Scott King and other civil rights figures led a peaceful memorial march through downtown Memphis in memory of King and to support the strike. On April 16 the workers voted to accept an agreement that had been worked out.

This series of events had a profound impact on Memphis, creating wounds that would take years to heal. Beale Street and other areas of the city began to deteriorate as many whites moved to the suburbs and a number of businesses followed. For black Memphians, the fact that King was murdered in their city depressed morale considerably despite the positive outcome of the strike. Eventually, the city was able to parlay this chapter in its history into a celebration of how Dr. King's work specifically and the civil rights movement in general has changed the com-

plexion of America. Of course, as the National Civil Rights Museum continually reminds its visitors, there is much more to be done, both in this country and abroad.

Today, using "I Am a Man: A Civil Rights Walking Tour," a brochure published by Memphis Heritage, Inc., you can retrace the steps of the 1968 striking black sanitation workers as they attempted to march from Clayborn Temple AME Church to city hall, and see other places of importance to the civil rights movement. Look for the "I Am a Man" map on the visitor information racks found in hotel lobbies and attractions, or call Memphis Heritage (901–529–9828).

Also, visit the National Civil Rights Museum for more information about King's legacy as well as the search for his killer.

—Much of this information is excerpted from "I Am a Man: A Civil Rights Walking Tour," with permission from Memphis Heritage, Inc.

restored, Church bought the first $1,000 bond issued by the city.

The city's charter was restored in 1893, and by 1900, blacks accounted for about 50,000 of Memphis's 102,000 citizens.

A prominent black Memphis citizen during the latter part of the century was Ida B. Wells, a schoolteacher, journalist, and early civil rights activist who devoted her life to denouncing the practice of lynching and the condition of schools for African-American children. She was forced to leave Memphis, and she later moved to

Chicago, where she became a founding member of the NAACP.

BEALE STREET AND THE BIRTH OF THE BLUES

Around the turn of the century, Robert Church was actively developing Beale Street into a haven for the city's African-American population. He set about building a park, theater, and other amenities for blacks, who were denied these pleasures elsewhere in the city, and started the Solvent Bank in 1906, which by 1921 claimed to be the largest black-owned bank in the world. By night, though, Beale was a wild place, with rowdy saloons, gambling halls, and brothels.

W. C. Handy, an accomplished African-American musician who had lived all over the country, moved to Memphis in 1909, and after publishing the blues he heard on Beale, became known as the "Father of the Blues." A few decades later, the city honored Handy with a parade in appreciation for putting Memphis on the musical map, and established Handy Square (today Handy Park).

In the 1920s many early Memphis blues musicians were active on Beale, including Furry Lewis, Sleepy John Estes, and Memphis Minnie. Their music survives today, thanks to early recordings made during this era.

Since the Depression, Memphis African-American blues musicians, including Robert Johnson, Howlin' Wolf, and B. B. King, have continued to make music history. See the Memphis Music chapter for more information on the city's African-American musicians and the musical history they created, from the earliest blues to current hitmakers.

Also during the 1920s the Memphis Red Sox baseball team, part of the Negro Baseball League, threw out its first pitch, and Dr. J. E. Walker founded Universal Life Insurance, which became one of the largest African American–owned insurance

Interested in finding out what's happening in the city's African-American community? Check out www.blackmemphis .com for a frequently updated events calendar as well as a wealth of other information. As for print media, look for the Tri-State Defender (901–523–1818), a weekly newspaper with general news and information, and Grace (901– 579–9333), a bimonthly voice for Memphis African-American women.

companies in the country. In 1925 another Memphis African American emerged as a hero. In an amazing feat, Tom Lee rescued 32 people from a sinking steamship, despite the fact he couldn't swim. Today, Tom Lee Park in downtown Memphis is named in his honor.

In the 1940s WDIA became the first radio station in the United States to have an all-black format and black disc jockeys, including Nat D. Williams, B. B. King, and Rufus Thomas. In the 1950s King, Thomas, and many other African-American musicians began recording at Sun Records, an unassuming small recording studio just east of downtown Memphis. In 1960 Stax Records was started, launching the careers of Carla Thomas, Otis Redding, and Isaac Hayes before closing its doors in the late 1970s. The newly built Stax Museum of American Soul Music tells that story.

CIVIL RIGHTS AND MARTIN LUTHER KING JR.

As the civil rights movement hit its stride in the 1950s and 1960s, the Memphis African-American community was a leading participant. In 1968, the city's black sanitation workers went on strike, wearing signs that read, "I Am a Man." Dr. Martin Luther King Jr. came to the city to support the strikers, and on April 3, gave his famous "I've Been to the Mountaintop" speech at Mason Temple. The next day Dr. King was killed by an assassin's bullet on the balcony of the Lorraine Motel. (See the Close-Up in this chapter.) Riots ensued, and by the end of the month the workers had succeeded in having their demands met.

The city was profoundly affected both by King's assassination and the riots. Many families and businesses moved out of the center city, which had always been the heart of Memphis, to the suburbs that were being developed to the east. Even Beale Street, which had continued strong despite the city's ups and downs, began to deteriorate.

Historic Sites

If you're interested in Memphis's African-American heritage, you won't want to miss these attractions. The Attractions chapter has more details on most of them.

Beale Street
Downtown Memphis
www.bealestreet.com
The center of African-American cultural and commercial life for many years, and today home to thriving clubs, bars, and shops. See this chapter's Close-up, If Beale Street Could Talk, for details.

Center for Southern Folklore
119 South Main Street
(901) 525-3655
www.southernfolklore.com
Music, art, and performances here demonstrate the African-American roots of much of the South's folklore and culture.

Historic Elmwood Cemetery
824 South Dudley Street
(901) 774-3212
www.elmwoodcemetery.org
This cemetery tells the story of African-American Memphians ranging from slaves in unmarked graves to millionaire and political leader Robert Church Sr.

Mason Temple
930 Mason Street
(901) 578-3800
This is where Martin Luther King Jr. gave his famous "I've Been to the Mountaintop" speech on the eve of his assassination.

National Civil Rights Museum
450 Mulberry Street
(901) 521-9699
www.civilrightsmuseum.org
Housed in the Lorraine Motel, where Martin Luther King Jr. was assassinated, this museum tells the story of the civil rights movement. Other exhibits examine what has happened in the years since Dr. King's death, in this country and around the world.

Slave Haven Underground Railroad Museum (Burkle House)
826 North Second Street
(901) 527-3427
This home is thought to be a stop on the Underground Railroad, where runaway slaves could find refuge.

Stax Museum of American Soul Music
926 East McLemore Street
(901) 946-2535
www.soulsvilleusa.com
This museum, built on the site of the former Stax Records studio, tells the story of Otis Redding, Isaac Hayes, and other Southern soul stars and their contributions to American music.

W. C. Handy House
352 Beale Street
(901) 527-3427 or (901) 522-1556
Bandleader W. C. Handy lived in this Memphis house at the time he "discovered" the blues.

But by the 1970s things were picking up on another front, as the city's black politicians began to make some inroads. Lois DeBerry was elected as the first female African-American state representative from Memphis, and Harold Ford became the first black elected as the U.S. congressman from the ninth district, which includes Memphis. He served for 26 years, helping to pave the way for his son's success. Today, the city has an African-American mayor (W. W. Herenton), county mayor (A C Wharton Jr.), and Congressional representative (Harold Ford Jr.), as well as numerous other black officeholders, judges, and other leaders.

MEMPHIS TODAY

Visitors to Memphis these days will find that the city's rich African-American heritage is being preserved and celebrated. Beale Street—once deserted—has been converted into a thriving entertainment district. The Stax museum is not only educating people about Memphis music, but is also helping to revive the Soulsville neighborhood that surrounds the spot where the legendary recording studio once operated. The National Civil Rights Museum reminds the world of the struggle in which Memphis played such an important and tragic role.

What's more, Memphis is being talked about as a great place for African Americans to make their homes. Since the 1980s, many blacks have been moving from the North to Memphis and other Southern cities, attracted by affordable housing, a lower cost of living, and what many view as a better, less stressful quality of life. Census figures show that this movement reverses the trend in place during most of the 20th century, when blacks left the South to seek a better life up North. Memphis has been a prime beneficiary of that trend. *Black Enterprise* magazine named Memphis as one of the top 10 places in America for African Americans to live, work, and play, citing among other things church outreach and satisfaction with African-American power and influence.

SHOPPING

Memphis has always been a destination for shoppers, as people from surrounding farms and towns come in to buy the latest fashions, home furnishings, books, antiques, gourmet foods, and other merchandise. In more recent years visitors have been more interested in buying guitars, Elvis souvenirs, and hard-to-find CDs and records. You can find a good selection of all of the above in Memphis, not to mention the things you need for your home, your wardrobe, or your lifestyle.

Although there are a few pockets of retail in downtown Memphis, you'll probably have to get in the car for serious shopping, as the malls and the best shopping centers are mostly in suburban areas, whereas many antiques dealers, music stores, and gift shops are scattered around midtown.

Two major department stores operate in the Memphis area, Goldsmith's-Macy's (part of Federated Department Stores) and Dillard's (a Little Rock–based chain), both with locations in area shopping malls. Both have a good array of merchandise, but Goldsmith's, founded here in 1870, is the hometown favorite. A sister to Rich's in Atlanta, this is where generations of Memphians have been shopping for up-to-date fashions, wedding gifts, and home furnishings. Not only does Goldsmith's-Macy's tend to be a bit more fashionable, carrying designers such as Eileen Fisher and Dana Buchman, it also has frequent sales.

In Memphis you'll find plenty of the usual chain stores, including Costco, Target, Walgreen's, Sears, JC Penney, T.J. Maxx, Marshall's, Toys R Us, Gap, Ann Taylor, Victoria's Secret, and Barnes & Noble, just to name a few. Most of these are in suburban malls and shopping centers.

Memphis also has its share of antiques dealers and shops, with the largest concentration on Central Avenue between Cooper Street and East Parkway in midtown. Others are scattered throughout the city, from downtown to the far suburb of Collierville. You'll find all kinds of antique furniture, with plenty of English, French, and American pieces from the 19th and 20th centuries, as well as collectibles of all sorts. There's also a large flea market in the city, as well as a number of thrift shops for those who like to search through secondhand goods for vintage clothing and other treasures.

If you're shopping for clothes, you'll find many options. For women's clothes there's everything from the Giorgio Armani collection at James Davis to Holliday's, a locally owned discount retailer where you can try out the latest trend at bargain prices. The city's most stylish women head for East Memphis to shop at the boutiques and apparel shops clustered in Laurelwood Center and across the street at Laurelwood Collection. In recent years fashionable apparel and gift shops have been popping up on South Main Street in downtown Memphis and Chickasaw Oak Plaza shopping center at the eastern edge of midtown.

Grandparents will delight in the many children's shops, ranging from the Disney Store to Woman's Exchange, with its pricey handmade outfits. Men can choose from two locally owned clothiers, James Davis and Oak Hall, as well as chains that include Jos. A. Banks, Brooks Brothers, U.S. Male, and Eddie Bauer.

A local favorite is the Williams-Sonoma outlet store (see the Gourmet Stores of this chapter for details). The chain maintains a major warehouse in Memphis, and when the season changes or the warehouse gets too full, trucks bring the merchandise to the outlet to sell at a discount. You'll find not just Williams-Sonoma merchandise, but also items from its other stores, including Pottery Barn, Hold Everything, and Chambers. (You can go to nearby MailBoxes Etc. to ship your purchase home if it doesn't fit in your suitcase.)

Beale Street and Graceland are both hubs for souvenir shopping, although even the corner drugstore will carry a few souvenirs.

MALLS AND MAJOR SHOPPING CENTERS

Belz Factory Outlet
3536 Canada Road, Lakeland
(901) 386-3180

This factory-outlet mall is situated just off the Canada Road exit of I-40, about eight minutes from the I-240 loop. The mall has a variety of outlets and discount stores, including Bass Company Store, the Rack Room clearance store, Dress Barn and Dress Barn Woman, Van Heusen, and Nike Factory Outlet. Anyone looking to outfit a new home on a budget will want to visit Old Time Pottery, which sells dinnerware, cookware, and other items for the home. You'll also find Perfumania and Toy Liquidators. The property was recently sold, and it's expected the new owners will make some changes.

Hickory Ridge Mall
6075 Winchester Road
(901) 367-8045
www.hickoryridgemall.com

Situated in the Hickory Hill area of Memphis, this mall has more than 100 stores including Goldsmith's-Macy's, Dillard's, Gap, Bath and Body Works, Wilson Leather, and Sunco Motion Picture Company. The focal point of the mall is its famous antique Venetian-style carousel, a favorite among families. There's also a movie theater, a food court, and plentiful parking.

Laurelwood Shopping Center
Poplar Avenue at Perkins Extended
(901) 794-6022

Situated across the street from Oak Court Mall, this East Memphis upscale shopping plaza has a great collection of stores, including some of the city's most fashionable and exclusive shops. The clothier James Davis sells men's and women's apparel, much of it designer lines including Giorgio Armani. Joseph has beautiful shoes, handbags, apparel, and jewelry as well as top makeup lines; Zoe sells cosmetics, bath goodies, and other potions. David Lusk Gallery is one of the city's top art dealers, and Davis-Kidd Booksellers is a great favorite for books, magazines, and gifts. You'll also find Sears for more middlebrow needs. Across the street is Laurelwood Collection, a center that offers additional boutiques such as Bari Chase for shoes, Papel for beautiful stationery and gifts, and the Pink Door for Lilly Pulitzer apparel.

Oak Court Mall
4465 Poplar Avenue
(901) 682-8928
www.simon.com

This East Memphis favorite is the closest mall to downtown Memphis and features the area's largest Goldsmith's-Macy's and Dillard's as well as dozens of other stores. You'll find Body Shop, Origins, the usual mall suspects such as Victoria's Secret, the Disney Store, Gap, Bombay Company, American Eagle, and Starbucks. The mall is attractively designed with Italian marble, skylighting, and a fountain that features a 7,000-pound rolling marble ball. There are also a number of pushcart vendors scattered throughout the mall, especially during the holiday shopping season. There's also plenty of free parking, including covered lots near the Dillard's and Goldsmith's-Macy's entrances, a food court, and a number of other specialty shops in the immediate area.

Peabody Place
150 Peabody Place
(901) 261-7529

This downtown shopping mall, which includes Ann Taylor Loft, Victoria's Secret, Tower Records, Gap, and other shops, is noteworthy because it marks the return of retail to downtown Memphis in a big way. There's also a movie theater, entertainments such as Jillian's and Putting Edge miniature golf, Starbucks, and a number of restaurants and bars.

Raleigh Springs Mall
3384 Austin Peay Highway
(901) 388–4300
www.simon.com

This is one of the city's largest malls, and it's more than 30 years old, but lately it has taken a beating. The glitzy Wolfchase Galleria mall opened nearby in 1997, wooing away Raleigh Springs' traditional clientele and leaving it to reinvent itself as a discount shopping venue. Its other department stores gone, the mall continues to cater to bargain hunters with stores that include Sears, Payless Shoes, Simply Fashion, and City Gear.

The Shops of Saddle Creek
West Street at Poplar Avenue
Germantown
(901) 761–2571
www.shopsofsaddlecreek.com

This posh shopping center in suburban Germantown features a lot of great upscale shops, mostly chains including Williams-Sonoma Grand Cuisine, Ann Taylor, J. Jill, Banana Republic, Gap, Sharper Image, and Apple computer store. If you're hungry, there's Yia Yia's EuroCafe, while Marble Slab Creamery has good ice cream. The main shopping center is north of Poplar, but on the southwest corner of Poplar and West, you'll find Saddle Creek West, with Talbots Mens and two popular boutiques, Miguela's and Indigo. Saddle Creek South, which faces West Street, is a favorite for moms, since it has Gymboree, the Children's Place, Talbots Kids, and Gap Kids right together.

Southland Mall
1215 Southland Mall
(901) 346–1210

Situated at the corner of Elvis Presley Boulevard and Shelby Drive in south Memphis, Southland Mall was built in 1966 as the city's first mall. At that time people from Memphis and surrounding areas flocked here to shop. Now much of that crowd shops at the other malls around town, while Southland concentrates on serving its main customer base, African-American residents from the surrounding Whitehaven neighborhood and tour busses from nearby Graceland. In fact, Southland is frequently cited as an example of a mall that has changed successfully with its surrounding area. In 2004 it was bought by investors who are spending $1 million to refurbish the property. The mall is anchored by Goldsmith's-Macy's and Sears, with specialty shops that include Milano's, Holliday's, Rave, and Finish Line.

Wolfchase Galleria
2760 North Germantown Parkway
Cordova
(901) 372–9409
www.simon.com

Wolfchase Galleria is the top shopping mall in town and a good-looking one, which is embellished by the work of local artists. It's not only the newest one, built in 1997, it also features stores that you won't find anywhere else in the city, including Brooks Brothers, Abercrombie & Fitch, and Pottery Barn. You can shop at 120 stores, including state-of-the-art Goldsmith's-Macy's and Dillard's department stores, Sears, Ann Taylor, Harold's, Banana Republic, bebe, Disney Store, Gap, Laura Ashley, Inner Self, and the Coach Store. Wolfchase also has a working carousel at the entrance, as well as a food court and an eight-screen movie theater plus plenty of free parking. You'll also find lots of other stores near the mall, including Barnes & Noble bookstore, Toys R Us, and Best Buy.

ANTIQUES

Memphis has dozens and dozens of antiques and secondhand shops and malls with all sorts of furniture, collectibles, and bric-a-brac. The shops along Central Avenue between Cooper and East Parkway in midtown is where you'll find the largest concentration of antiques shops and dealers, so for an afternoon of antiquing, that's where you'll probably want to spend your time.

Central Avenue Antiques District

Consignments
2230 Central Avenue
(901) 278-5909

This consignment shop sells best-quality antiques, including 18th- and 19th-century French and English furniture as well as a good selection of silver, cut glass, and porcelain items. Consignments also gets antiques through its Westport, Connecticut, sister store, which keeps the selection lively.

For a more complete listing of Memphis antiques shops and malls, look for a small, white brochure entitled Memphis Antique Guide. *It's available at many antiques shops, or call (901) 726-5358.*

Flashback
2304 Central Avenue
(901) 272-2304

This funky retro shop, which calls itself the vintage department store, specializes in art deco as well as furnishings and collectibles from the 1950s. You can also find new upholstered furniture and chrome dinettes in retro style, as well as vintage furniture from the era, and there's plenty of 1970s merchandise as well. The shop does about half of its business in vintage clothing, which includes recycled blue jeans.

Palladio Antique Market
2169 Central Avenue
(901) 276-3808
www.PalladioAntiques.com

You can browse the antiques and decorative arts of some 45 exhibitors at this antiques marketplace, which range from investment-grade antiques to affordable coffee-table items. You can find every type of style, from 17th-century pieces to contemporary accessories. Inside the shop is an attractive cafe that serves lunch.

Second Hand Rose
2288 Central Avenue
(901) 278-3500

This shop specializes in good solid furniture, which it sells in a warehouse atmosphere. Here you'll find pieces such as pine tables, French armchairs, and chests, mostly from the late 19th century. Second Hand Rose also has a large selection of mostly antique books, oil paintings, and chandeliers. Open Wednesday through Saturday.

Toad Hall Antiques
2129 Central Avenue
(901) 726-0755
www.toadhallmemphis.com

You can't miss the bright yellow mural with the whimsical frog on the exterior of this charming antiques shop, situated at the western edge of the antiques district at Cooper. Here you'll find English, French, and continental antiques, including a lot of pottery, English china, paintings, primitive furniture, and estate jewelry. The shop prides itself on its affordable prices and constantly changing inventory. Shipping is available, too.

Outside the Central Avenue District

Jimmy Graham Interior Design
3092 Poplar Avenue
(901) 323-2322

Tucked away inside Chickasaw Oaks Plaza shopping center, Jimmy Graham has a mixture of English and continental furniture and accessories, which changes with every buying trip. The shop, which maintains a comfortable atmosphere, is also home to Graham's interior-design business. While at Chickasaw Oaks, you should also check out the other antiques shops there, too.

Wellford's Antique Collection
262 South Highland Avenue
(901) 324-1661

This shop operates out of an English cottage-style house and features 18th- and 19th-century imported English antiques. Here, you'll find drop-leaf dining-room tables, chairs, chests, and other furniture as well as china, some crystal, and a large collection of antique silver—all displayed in rooms that resemble those in an English manor house. There's also a large selection of paintings, including many landscapes. The owner, Karen Wellford, is also an interior designer.

BOOKSTORES

Barnes & Noble
Wolfchase Galleria Mall
(901) 386-2468

6385 Winchester Road
(901) 794-9394
www.bn.com

Barnes & Noble has everything you could want in a large, modern suburban chain bookstore, including a large selection of books and magazines as well as a cafe with specialty coffees, pastries, and such.

Bookstar
3402 Poplar Avenue
(901) 323-9332
www.bn.com

Housed inside a restored movie theater at Poplar Plaza shopping center at Poplar near Highland, Bookstar features a decent selection of nonfiction and fiction books. One of the biggest draws is its cafe, where you can linger over Starbucks coffee, pastries, and light fare such as soup and sandwiches amid images of great writers that are painted on the walls. It's a popular midtown meeting spot.

Borders
6685 Poplar Avenue, Germantown
(901) 754-0770
www.borders.com

Despite being part of a national chain, Borders is a Memphis bookstore and music store in that it has a large selection of books by Memphis writers and Memphis music. Local music also figures into the live music performed some weekends at its cafe. Borders prides itself on having the largest selection of books in town, as well as a selection of music and DVDs second only to Tower Records downtown.

Borders is situated in the back of the Carrefour shopping center at Poplar and Kirby near the railroad tracks.

Burke's Book Store
1719 Poplar Avenue
(901) 278-7484
www.burkesbooks.com

Burke's Book Store, a Memphis institution since 1875, specializes in used and antiquarian books as well as new books. You can find first editions, lots of works by Southern writers, as well as an array of out-of-print and used books at this cozy, family-owned shop. If you are looking for a particular hard-to-find book, Burke's will hunt a copy down for a fee. The store has a number of book signings every year, with appearances of local writers as well as best-selling authors, and it's the only place in town (and one of the few in the country) where novelist John Grisham does book signings.

Davis-Kidd Booksellers
387 Perkins Road Extended
(901) 683-9801
www.daviskidd.com

This cheerful, well-stocked book and music store features all kinds of books, magazines, CDs, and other music, not to mention a good selection of gifts, journals, stationery, and cards. Davis-Kidd has frequent in-store signings, with authors ranging from former president Jimmy Carter to local writers, as well as book clubs and musical events that have featured folksinger Kate Campbell and the

i *Don't forget that you'll find some great shopping at area museums, including the Memphis Brooks Museum, the National Ornamental Metal Museum, and Memphis Botanic Garden.*

Memphis Youth Symphony. There are also separate areas for magazine browsers to lounge and for children to play and enjoy story hours. The icing on the cake is Brontë, the only full-service bookstore restaurant in town, where you can get great salads and other fare for lunch or dinner, or pastries, specialty coffees, and other beverages at other times of the day. You'll find Davis-Kidd in the northeast corner of Laurelwood shopping center.

Deliberate Literate
1997 Union Avenue
(901) 276-0174
This locally owned book store is as much a cafe/hangout as it is a bookstore. Midtowners flock here to browse the books, gifts, and magazines or to meet with friends and business associates and enjoy coffee and espresso drinks, pastries, and light lunch fare. Deliberate Literate carries a small but eclectic inventory of books, but they'll order any book you want at a 20-percent discount. The homey atmosphere includes plenty of comfortable couches and chairs throughout the shop. Open seven days a week starting early in the morning to accommodate the many people who stop in for a coffee on the way to work.

CLOTHING AND ACCESSORIES

Kids' Apparel and Toys

Chocolate Soup
7730 Poplar Avenue, Germantown
(901) 754-7157

Tucked in the Germantown Village Square shopping center at the corner of Poplar Avenue and Germantown Road, Chocolate Soup sells moderately priced children's apparel, including girls' sizes up to 16 and boys' sizes up to 7. Chocolate Soup sells both its own designs, featuring hand-sewn appliqués, as well as other labels that include Heart Strings, Kite Strings, French Toast, and smocked dresses by Anavini. The merchandise ranges from dressy party clothes to the latest kid fashions and also includes baby gifts, elegant stuffed animals, and accessories such as pretty little purses.

Little Lambs and Ivy
1227 Ridgeway Road
(901) 767-5262
This little shop, situated in Park Place shopping center at Ridgeway and Park, sells apparel, accessories, shoes, and gifts for infants, for girls up to size 16, and for boys up to size 7. The focus is a traditional look, with brands including Anavini, Vive La Fete, Cotton Tail Originals, and Kata Mini. About half of the merchandise consists of baby clothes and gifts; shoes range from Keds to European-made brands. There's also Ivy's Closet for "big girls" apparel, painted in pink and lavender. Prices are in the moderate to better range, although the shop also carries a good selection of pricey flower-girl and other special-occasion dresses.

Village Toymaker
4615 Poplar Avenue
(901) 761-1734

7850 Poplar Avenue, Germantown
(901) 755-3309
www.thevillagetoymaker.com
This old-fashioned toy store is jam-packed with carefully selected toys for all ages and prices. However, the best thing about Village Toymaker is its staff. Tell them the age and interests of the child you're shopping for, and they'll help you find the perfect toy. Gift wrapping is free.

Woman's Exchange
88 Racine Street
(901) 327-5681

Situated in midtown just off Poplar in a modest house, Woman's Exchange is where volunteers run a children's clothing and gift shop as well as a tearoom that's a popular ladies' lunch spot. The handmade christening dresses, flower-girl dresses, baby clothes, and special-occasion dresses and boys' outfits make this shop a grandmother's dream come true. A tradition since 1885, Woman's Exchange also has beautiful linens, gifts, quilts, and handcrafted children's tables and chairs. The prices are steep, but gift wrapping is free. Open Monday through Friday.

Men's Apparel

James Davis
400 Grove Park Road
(901) 767-4640

This distinguished East Memphis shop for men and women, situated in Laurelwood shopping center, sells fine apparel in brands that include Giorgio Armani, Burberry, Oxxford, and Hickey-Freeman. It is owned and operated by the Weinberg family, longtime Memphis haberdashers, and it is staffed by knowledgeable salespeople.

Lansky's 126
149 Union Avenue
(901) 405-7625
www.lanskybros.com

The retailing Lansky family's claim to fame is outfitting Elvis, and they've parlayed that place in rock-and-roll history into a string of shops along the northern edge of The Peabody lobby. Lansky's 126 is where you'll find hipster fashions, including 7 for All Mankind jeans, B. C. Ethnic Deluxe shirts, and Johnny Cash tribute T-shirts. Its companion shop, Lansky at The Peabody, carries more traditional apparel, including Tommy Bahama shirts, Robert Talbott ties, but also rock-and-roll classics

such as its 1950s-style roll-collar pleated-back shirt. Other shops include Lucky Duck Gifts, where you can buy souvenirs of the famous Peabody waterfowl.

Oak Hall
6150 Poplar Avenue
(901) 761-3580

Generations of Memphians have been coming to Oak Hall for blazers, suits, and other high-end, traditional apparel. In business since 1859, the shop caters both to its old customers as well as their children, with suits by Hickey Freeman, Oxxford, Canale, and Ermenegildo Zegna for men. Oak Hall also carries the Burberry line as well as ties and other accessories by Hermès, and shoes. The shop is situated in Regalia shopping center at Poplar near I-240.

Women's Apparel/Boutiques

Ella
3080 Poplar Avenue
(901) 507-3597

This spacious women's apparel store at Chickasaw Oaks Plaza offers a wide range of clothes, ranging from suits and party dresses to jeans and casual tops. Ella is actually three shops, one of which is a Nicole Miller boutique that sells the designer's dressier separates, cocktail dresses, gifts, bridal gowns, and other wedding attire. A separate shop specializes in women's sportswear, with brands such as Craig Taylor, Cambio, and Ann May. Dressier apparel such as cocktail dresses, mother-of-the-bride dresses and full-length gowns, are grouped together with brands that include Tahari, Belford, and Barry Bricken. Most of the merchandise is considered to be at better price points, less expensive than designer clothes but with plenty of style. The focus is on the way Memphis women dress, so you will find clothes with color and patterns that are both appropriate and stylish.

Isabella
4615 Poplar Avenue
(901) 507-0507

This boutique, done up in purple on the walls, floors, and even the ceilings, specializes in casual fun clothes, including denim and lots of separates. Here you'll find vendors that include BCBG, Nanette Lepore, and Laundry. If you are looking for something dressier, be sure to check out Eve, its sister store just a few doors down at Laurelwood Collection shopping center. Eve carries suits, dresses, separates, and outerwear with brands that include Tahari, as well as a popular collection of unique jewelry.

James Davis
400 Grove Park Road
(901) 767-4640

This elegant women's shop, a sister to James Davis men's store, is known for its Giorgio Armani room as well as other designer apparel by Dolce & Gabbana, Burberry, and Marc Jacobs. James Davis's aim is to carry apparel that might appeal both to a mother and her teenage daughter. As a result, you'll find an area with young, casual apparel including denim for daughter that's separate from the dresses, separates, and party outfits for Mom. James Davis has an especially good selection of cocktail dresses and other party clothes during the holiday season. You'll find an attentive staff that's very knowledgeable about the merchandise.

Joseph
418 South Grove Park Road
(901) 767-1609

This chic women's shop has a great selection of shoes, bags, clothing, jewelry, and cosmetics from some of the best in the business. The apparel is mainly day-to-evening and sportswear in lines that include Armani and Michael Kors. If you love shoes and handbags, Joseph is a paradise, with shoes by Prada, Gucci, Ferragamo, Stuart Weitzman, Calvin Klein, and others. You can find beautiful handbags by Kate Spade, Prada, and Furla. The shop also carries

John Hardy, Margaret Ellis, and other lines of fine jewelry, as well as makeup by Bobbi Brown, Trish McEvoy, and others. This retail operation has been in Memphis since 1930, originally as the shoe department of Levy's Department Store.

Muse
517 South Main Street
(901) 526-8737
www.memphismuse.com

This is the place to forget about basic black and splurge on fun clothes from designers including Betsey Johnson, Ohm, Kasch Copenhagen, and Joan Vass. It's a wonderfully campy store, decorated with antique armoires, chandeliers, and red velvet, with velvet tents for dressing rooms. Muse sells a lot of brightly colored clothing its owner considers to be wearable art, as well as hats, shoes, and other accessories. You'll also find a great selection of unusual jewelry by local designers and others.

Oak Hall
6150 Poplar Avenue
(901) 761-3580

Escada, St. John's, and Rena Lange are just a few of the designers you'll find in this stylish women's apparel shop. Originally an outgrowth of Oak Hall men's store, the women's collection now has its own spacious home next door at Regalia shopping center. This open, airy store features a boutique highlighting its St. John's collection as well as comfortable seating and a huge dressing-room area. You'll find attentive service at this store, where the approach is to choose an outfit, then add pieces to make it versatile and appropriate for many occasions. The merchandise ranges from casual pieces such as Lacoste shirts and denim to dressy work and party clothes.

Tonic
431 South Main Street
(901) 578-8000
www.toniclifestyle.com

This attractive downtown shop showcases the fashions of Katrina Shelton, a young designer who worked in New York before opening her Memphis shop. Shelton designs and sells reasonably priced, simple day-to-evening pieces, including A-line skirts with discreet "credit card" pockets, in basic colors such as black and aubergine as well as seasonal colors such as bright pastels for warm weather. The store not only has a vintage look, with its 18-foot ceilings and big front windows, it also carries some vintage clothing, too.

FARMERS' MARKETS

Agricenter International Farmers' Market
7777 Walnut Grove Road
(901) 757-7790
Housed in a distinctive red barn, the farmers' market features all kinds of locally grown fruits, vegetables, flowers, herbs, and crafts in summer, as well as pumpkins in October. You won't want to miss the famous local tomatoes grown in Ripley, Tennessee, or freshly shelled butterbeans and other beans in season. The market is particularly lively on Saturdays, when you find the most vendors, the best variety of produce, and more people.

To get there turn onto the Agricenter International property from either Germantown Parkway or Walnut Grove Road, and look for the big red barn. Open all summer, but call ahead at other times of the year.

Butler Street Bazaar
11 West Butler Street
(901) 849-4325
www.butlerstreetbazaar.com
While the seasonal farmers' market is Butler Street Bazaar's claim to fame, this eclectic market near South Main Street sells everything from antiques and vintage clothing/furniture to original artwork. The Bazaar makes its home in a warehouse that was once a beer-bottling plant, then a furniture store. The hours and activity level are hit-or-miss, so call before you head over. You'll find the building at the corner of Butler and G. E. Patterson; the farmers' market is accessible around the back.

FLEA MARKETS/THRIFT SHOPS

Memphis is a good place for treasure hunting at thrift stores and flea markets. One area to try is Summer Avenue near Highland, where you'll find the Disabled American Veterans Thrift Store (3440 Summer Avenue, 901-327-4661), the Junior League of Memphis Thrift Shop (3586 Summer Avenue, 901-327-4777), and a lot of secondhand furniture shops.

The Memphis Flea Market—The Big One
955 Maxwell Early Boulevard
(901) 276-3532
This sprawling, huge flea market takes place the third weekend of every month, attracting 800 to 1,000 vendors from all over the region as well as more than 20,000 shoppers. You'll find all kinds of merchandise, used and new, including antiques, collectibles, clothes, jewelry, household goods, even computers, NASCAR items, and produce. The market takes place at the Mid-South Fairgrounds at Central and East Parkway, taking up four buildings and spilling into parking-lot areas as well. Admission is free; parking is $2.00. There's an extra flea market in December, but call ahead about the September event, because its dates change in order to accommodate the Mid-South Fair.

GARDEN SHOPS

Bayless Greenhouses
6120 Walsh Road, Millington
(901) 353-4721
It's a good drive from most parts of Memphis to Bayless, located near Shelby Forest, but well worth it for the huge selection. Bayless, which has been around for more than 30 years, grows all its own plants (except for large trees and shrubs) and is the largest grower of bedding and potted plants in the area. In spring you'll find thousands of items, including hostas, daylilies, roses, grasses, and lots of other

Gifts of Memphis barbecue sauce and dry-rub seasonings are usually well received by folks back home, and they don't take up much room in your luggage. The city's biggest barbecue joints bottle their own and sell it at area supermarkets, at their restaurants, or at airport gift shops.

perennials. Be sure to wear your walking shoes, because it's a big place.

Sam Stringer Nursery and Garden Center
2974 Poplar Avenue
(901) 458-3109

This midtown garden center sells all kinds of plants, pots, accessories, and supplies as well as Christmas trees and greenery during the holiday season. A neighborhood favorite, Stringer's has knowledgeable staffers who can make recommendations and also offers landscaping services. There's also a suburban location at 9495 Poplar Avenue in Germantown (901–754–5700).

Trees by Touliatos
2020 East Brooks Road
(901) 346-8065

This 20-acre family-owned nursery, located well off the beaten path in south Memphis, sells not only trees but also other plants and all kinds of related items. The shop specializes in water gardens and has about 14 water-garden displays. Owners Plato and Sarah Touliatos and their staff probably know more than anyone about what plants do well in this part of the country, and landscaping services are available. Ask about the shop's Saturday gardening seminars, which typically take place from March to November. Touliatos is west of the airport on Brooks near Airways. Open Monday through Saturday.

Urban Gardener
742 Mt. Moriah Road
(901) 374-9964

This shop, although it doesn't sell plants and trees, does have a great collection of fountains, bird baths and feeders, benches, planters, and other items to brighten up gardens of all sizes. The shop is in a pink building, right where Mt. Moriah curves around to meet Poplar.

GIFT SHOPS

Babcock Gifts
4626 Poplar Avenue
(901) 763-0700

This traditional gift shop is a Memphis institution, and no society bride in the city would think about walking down the aisle without first registering at Babcock. Here you'll find exquisite things, including fine porcelain by Herend, Raynaud, and Limoges; crystal by Waterford and Baccarat; and flatware by Buccellati as well as all of the traditional sterling lines. The shop also has plenty of gifts for babies, men, and women for all occasions.

Bella Notte
2172 Young Avenue
(901) 726-4131

This chic little shop next to Java Cabana in the hip Cooper-Young district has all kinds of unique gifts, ranging from exquisite baby frocks (for babies up to two years old) and old-fashioned toys to imported soaps and bath products, candles, stationery, writing papers, glassware, picture frames, and handmade jewelry.

Carabella's
99 North Second Street
(901) 525-5500

This downtown favorite has a great selection of classy and fun gifts ranging in price from several dollars to several hundred dollars. The shop has an eclectic mix of decorative accessories, candles, barware, bath products, and gifts for children and pets. Among the lines it carries is Votivo candles, Aromatique products, and the Thymes Ltd. bath line. The shop is situated on the ground floor of Talbot Heirs Guesthouse across from The Peabody.

Gestures
523 South Main Street
(901) 525-4438
www.gesturesgifts.com
This airy, pleasant shop on South Main sells beautiful and unusual fresh flowers imported from Holland and the tropics, as well as all kinds of vases and baskets to hold them. You can watch the florists build gorgeous arrangements for customers, or you can make your own arrangements right in the store. Ask about the shop's floral-design workshops. There's also a separate room with a whimsical collection of gifts for all ages and all occasions, many of them related to gardening.

Odette
48 South McLean Boulevard
(901) 725-4600
This midtown shop, situated in a turn-of-the-century house next to Starbucks, has an ethereal feel. It specializes in exquisite one-of-a-kind jewelry, hand-sewn apparel, bath products, writing paper, ceramics, and accessories for the home. Its owners pride themselves on stocking merchandise you can't get anywhere else in the city. There's free parking in the back.

GOURMET STORES

Mantia's
4856 Poplar Avenue
(901) 762-8560
www.mantias.com
This East Memphis restaurant also has a market that sells gourmet foods including pastas, oils, sauces, and sweets, as well as prepared take-out food. Its pasta with grilled chicken and Gorgonzola sauce, prepared and frozen, is a hot seller. The shop also has the most extensive selection of domestic and imported cheeses in Memphis, including its own house-made fresh mozzarella. (See the Restaurants chapter for more information.)

Viking Culinary Arts
153 South Main Street
(901) 578-5822
www.vikingrange.com
This cooking school/retail store has been the prototype for a national chain started by Viking Range Corporation, the Greenwood, Mississippi, company famous for its professional-quality stoves and other appliances. At street level is a dazzling retail space, stocked with all kinds of professional cooking tools including Viking's own brand of cookware and knives, and a demonstration kitchen in the back. There's also bakeware, kitchen gadgets, gourmet food items, and other merchandise for the kitchen except for Viking appliances (you have to go to an authorized dealer for that purchase). In the office building next door is a state-of-the-art demonstration kitchen, with multilevel theater-type seating, where you can get a single cooking lesson or a series (ask for the catalog for details). Instructors include celebrated local chefs, visitors who have included Frederic Van Coppernolle of the French Culinary Institute, and Viking Culinary Arts staff.

Williams-Sonoma Outlet
4718 Spottswood Avenue
(901) 763-1500
www.williamssonoma.com
Tucked away in Audubon Shopping Center is one of the city's great shopping spots. Here Williams-Sonoma sells merchandise from its Memphis warehouse at discounted prices. You'll find cookware, cappuccino machines and other small appliances, table linens, stemware, holiday items, and gourmet foods, not to mention merchandise from the company's other lines, most notably, Pottery Barn and Hold Everything. Over the years this has grown into a huge store, with an entire separate shop for Pottery Barn and Pottery Barn Kids furniture and other merchandise. If you're lucky, your visit will coincide with the arrival of a new truckload of merchandise, so you can get first pick.

MUSIC AND MUSICAL INSTRUMENTS

Poplar Tunes
308 Poplar Avenue
(901) 525-6348
www.catsmusic.com

This is the original Pop Tunes, opened in 1946, where Elvis used to hang out listening to records. At present it's an urban music store that focuses on rap and hip-hop, but Elvis fans can find plenty of Elvis CDs and memorabilia. Cat's Music now owns the five Pop Tunes in town, including East Memphis (4195 Summer, 901–324–3855) and Germantown (7652 Poplar Avenue, 901–255–9404).

River Records
822 South Highland Street
(901) 324-1757

This shop boasts the city's largest selection of records, with some 300,000 albums and 45s. Situated near University of Memphis, River Records has lots of pre-war blues records, 78s, and originals from the 1940s and 1950s. There's also plenty of Elvis, as well as CDs and cassettes. The shop also sells collectible comic books and baseball cards.

Shangri-La Records
1916 Madison Avenue
(901) 274-1916
www.shangri.com

This midtown record shop carries new and used albums and CDs of Memphis music, indie music, Memphis and Delta blues, funk, R&B, and more. It also has its own record label, Shangri-La Records, which has recorded The Grifters and other local bands. If you're into Memphis music, you'll definitely want to drop by. Ask about their '70s museum and live music events, which take place here from time to time. You can also order from their Web site. Shangri-La also publishes its own hipster guide to Memphis, *Kreature Comforts,* available for $2.50.

Strings and Things
1555 Madison Avenue
(901) 278-0500

Strings and Things is a shopping center for musical instruments that makes its home in a former bakery in midtown. Here you'll find that drums, electric guitars, acoustic guitars, bass guitars, keyboards, pianos, sound equipment, and recording equipment each has its own little shop, with staffers who are knowledgeable about all these instruments. All of them sell new and used instruments as well as strings and other supplies. There's also a mastering studio, and lessons are available. It's a one-stop shopping experience for anyone interested in guitars or other musical instruments.

Tower Records
150 Peabody Place
(901) 526-9210
www.towerrecords.com

Tower Records has a huge selection of CDs, magazines, and other music, including a large area devoted to Memphis music. Even though it's a chain, Tower is worth keeping an eye on as it features free, in-store performances by artists who have included Buddy Guy. Tower is on Third Street at the corner of Peabody Place.

Yarborough's Music
6122 Macon Road
(901) 761-0414
www.yarboroughsmusic.com

This locally owned music store is well known for the bluegrass jam it has put on every Tuesday night for more than 20 years. It's the place to go for acoustic instruments, including guitars as well as bluegrass instruments such as dulcimers, banjos, and mandolins. Yarborough's also has electric guitars, basses, and drums as well as lighting, audio, and recording equipment. The store is at Macon Road at Sycamore View Road.

OUTFITTERS/SPORTS STORES

Edwin Watts Golf
4625 Poplar Avenue
(901) 767-1244
www.edwinwatts.com
This chain retailer of golf equipment, apparel, and accessories for men and women is the best golf shop in town. Here you can find the most complete selection of clubs, balls, bags, and all kinds of gifts and accessories, with brands that include Calloway, Titleist, and Taylor-made. They also carry golf shoes, golf shirts, and other apparel in all the top brands. The professionals at Edwin Watts can help fit you for clubs, too, for a fee that's waived if you purchase the clubs. Club repairs also are available, usually with a 24-hour turnaround.

Outdoors Inc.
833 North Germantown Parkway
(901) 755-2271

5245 Poplar Avenue
(901) 767-6790

1710 Union Avenue
(901) 722-8988
www.outdoorsinc.com
This locally owned outfitter, which has operated here since 1974, prides itself on being the source for outdoor gear, adventure travel, training, and outdoor events. Here you'll find everything you need for mountain biking, climbing, paddling, backpacking, hiking, camping, and other outdoor activities. The staff, outdoor enthusiasts who test all the equipment themselves, are excellent resources if you're looking for the best places to enjoy canoeing, biking, or other favorite activities. The Germantown location, the largest of the stores and the one with the best selection, also has a rock wall, where you can practice your climbing skills. Brands include North Face, Gary Fisher bikes, Old Town Canoes, and Vass hiking boots. Outdoors Inc. also rents canoes and kayaks and sponsors events.

SOUVENIRS, INCLUDING ELVIS-ABILIA

A. Schwab
163 Beale Street
(901) 523-9782
This is the oldest store in the city, opened in 1876 by Abraham Schwab, whose family continues to operate the shop. This old-fashioned general store has Elvis souvenirs at reasonable prices, even though the selection is small, and loads of tourist trinkets such as key rings, backscratchers, and bumper stickers. Don't miss the voodoo corner, where you'll find all kinds of special candles, potions, and the like to help you address that big problem in your life, whether it's a wandering spouse or bad luck. Going upstairs you'll go back in time as you check out the old cash registers, signs, and other retail relics. Remember the store motto: "If you can't find it at Schwab's, you're better off without it." Open Monday through Saturday.

Graceland Plaza
3700 block of Elvis Presley Boulevard
(901) 332-3322
www.elvis.com
The most extensive selection of Elvis-abilia can be found at Graceland Plaza, across the street from Graceland Mansion. On either side of the area where you board the shuttle for the mansion tour, you'll find a number of different shops, including general souvenir shops and those with a specific focus. Gallery Elvis sells pricey objets d'art and collectibles that include a limited-edition replica of Elvis's Gibson J-200 guitar for $5,000 and a 14K gold TCB ring like the one Elvis wore for $1,600. Good Rockin' Tonight sells Elvis CDs, videos, posters, and books, and Elvis Threads sells T-shirts, hats, ties, and jackets with images of the King. You'll find more shopping at Graceland Crossing Shops, just north of the airplane museum, although it's pretty much the same merchandise: mugs, clocks, T-shirts, key chains, and more—all with images of Elvis.

Memphis Music
149 Beale Street
(901) 526-5047

This Beale Street shop has all kinds of souvenirs related to Memphis music—T-shirts, gifts, jewelry, neckties—as well as the music itself on CDs, tapes, and videos. It specializes in the blues, so you can find early blues recordings by Lead-belly, Blind Lemon, and others.

Strange Cargo
172 Beale Street
(901) 525-1516

Here you'll find unusual, more offbeat souvenirs, cards, T-shirts, and gifts as well as the more routine Memphis and Beale Street souvenirs. There are plenty of Elvis items, from posters and mugs to beach towels and salt-and-pepper shakers, plus a collection of cookie jars with images that include Elvis and Harley Davidson.

Tater Red's Lucky Mojos and Voodoo Healings
153 Beale Street
(901) 578-7234
www.taterredsluckymojos.com

This funky little shop has everything from voodoo dolls, Ex-Wife Stay Away oil, and Winning Number candles to refrigerator magnets, all kinds of T-shirts, and repro-ductions of performance posters. If your voodoo need is great and you can't shop in person, shop Tater Red's Web site. There's also Naughty Queen of Camp Betty Page posters, Elvis and Nixon key chains, iron art by Ernest, and, of course, Tater Red's Lucky T-shirts and hats.

ATTRACTIONS

Memphis is rich with interesting, fun attractions of all kinds, including Graceland Mansion, the home of the late Elvis Presley and the king of area tourist attractions. Some 700,000 people tour the mansion each year, making it one of the most visited homes in America. A visit to Memphis is not complete without venturing over to The Peabody hotel lobby to see the famous ducks, who march (to the tune of John Philip Sousa music) to their fancy marble fountain for a day of swimming. A Memphis Queen Line cruise is a relaxing way to appreciate the grandeur of the Mississippi River and to get views of the city. You'll also find a one-of-a-kind ornamental-metals museum perched on a bluff overlooking the river, the state's largest fine-arts museum, and a handful of beautifully restored Victorian homes, just to name a few possibilities.

You won't want to miss the Memphis Rock 'n' Soul Museum or Sun Studio, where Elvis made his first record. Kids of all ages will enjoy the Memphis Zoo, not to mention Pink Palace Museum, with its IMAX theater and exhibits that include a replica of the world's first supermarket (Memphis's own Piggly Wiggly). You can learn about the courageous Memphis black sanitation workers and leaders such as Dr. Martin Luther King Jr. at the National Civil Rights Museum, and see a farmhouse (Slave Haven Underground Railroad Museum) said to be a stop for slaves trying to escape up north to freedom.

We've divided the city's attractions into five categories: General Attractions, Museums, Memphis History, Memphis Music, and African-American Heritage. If you're traveling with kids, be sure to check out the Kidstuff chapter, where we've singled out the attractions that appeal most to children. You will probably also want to read the History, Memphis Music, and African-American Heritage chapters for background on many of these sites.

We list the days of operation in effect during the busy summer season, but that sometimes changes at other times of the year. It's never a bad idea to call an attraction or check its Web site in advance of your visit, to double-check hours and admission prices, which are subject to change, and to scope out information on temporary exhibitions. The Memphis Convention & Visitors Bureau at (901) 543–5300 or www.memphistravel.com also has up-to-date information on its Web site, or you can pick up a free *Memphis Travel Guide & City Map* brochure from one of the information racks you'll find all over town at hotels and attractions. It's updated every year.

Free parking is available at the attractions unless we say otherwise. However, at some, including many downtown attractions, you are on your own for finding parking, and others, including Memphis Zoo and Graceland, charge a fee.

So don't forget your sunglasses, your camera, and your adventurous spirit—it's time to see the town.

PRICE CODE

The following price code is the admission charge for one adult. Most attractions charge less for senior citizens and children ages 6 through 12, while children younger than 6 years of age usually are admitted free of charge. Some attractions are free to everyone, and we identify those in the individual write-ups.

$	Less than $5.00
$$	$5.00 to $9.50
$$$	$10.00 and up

GENERAL ATTRACTIONS

A. Schwab   Free
163 Beale Street
(901) 523-9782
A. Schwab is the oldest establishment on Beale. It was founded in 1876 by Abraham Schwab, an immigrant from Alsace, France, whose descendants still mind the store. A trip to Schwab's is like a trip back in time, when stores had wooden floors and old-fashioned cash registers.

The first floor is full of such tourist trinkets as Memphis bumper stickers, key rings, souvenir license plates, and more. The other two floors carry, well, everything. The store's motto is: "If you can't find it at Schwab's, you're better off without it." You can find straight razors, cast-iron griddles, ladies' bloomers, lye soap, and men's pants up to size 74. Upstairs are vintage signs, cash registers, and other memorabilia—on display, not for sale. Open during the day Monday through Saturday, and on some Saturday nights. You're on your own for parking.

Beale Street   Free
Downtown Memphis between Lt. George
W. Lee Avenue and Peabody Place
www.bealestreet.com
This is the most visited street in America after New Orleans's Bourbon Street and is

---

Memphis is home to a variety of specialty tour operators. Heritage Tours (901-527-3427, www.heritagetours memphis.com) focuses on local African-American heritage. Memphis Explorations (901-761-1838, www.elvistyle .com) does Memphis tours of everything Elvis. Sekisui International (901-273-0123, www.sekisuitravel.com) sets up Japanese-speaking business and other tours of Memphis. Ultimate Memphis Rock 'n' Roll Tours (901-359-3102, www.memphisrocktour.com) does Memphis music tours by the founder of Shangri-La Records and local alternative guide Kreature Comforts.

Tennessee's most visited attraction. The street has a rich history, good souvenir shopping, and plenty of places to eat and party, with most of the action between Second and Fourth Streets. Points of interest include the W. C. Handy House and Memphis Police Museum. (See additional write-ups on Beale elsewhere in this chapter.)

Center for Southern Folklore   Free
119 and 123 South Main Street
(901) 525-3655
www.southernfolklore.com
The Center for Southern Folklore for more than 30 years has devoted itself to keeping the South's music, crafts, and other traditions alive. One of the biggest draws is live music performances that feature such legends as the Fieldstones, barrel-house-musician Mose Vinson, and Blind Mississippi Morris. Contact the center for a schedule, or check the center's Web site. (Sometimes there is a cover charge for the live music.)

The center also features works by many folk artists, both in the small gallery in the back and the Folklore Store in front, and it maintains extensive archives that are available to scholars. CSF has done films about Southern folklore, which the staff will show to interested visitors.

CSF expanded in 2004, moving its Folklore Store to a separate space in the front of the Pembroke Square Building and consolidating its other activities and resources in the Folklore Performance Hall in the back of the building. Both spaces have a colorful, funky ambience created by the handpainted folk-art designs on the walls, and the back area features a Delta-style front porch that serves as the performance stage. At the Folklore Store you can browse original folk art, CDs, and other products developed by the center, listen to authentic blues and other local music, and enjoy specialty coffees, beer, sandwiches, Southern desserts, and other fare. You can find the Folklore Store right at the Peabody Place trolley stop on Main Street. For other CSF operations including the performance hall, enter through the double doors nearest to Gayoso and go to the back of the lobby. (For more information about the center, see the Nightlife chapter.) Open seven days a week. Parking is on your own.

Cordova Cellars Winery   Free
9050 Macon Road, Cordova
(901) 754-3442

This working winery offers tours of its wine-making operation as well as free samples of its wines. Don't look for any grapevines, however. Cordova Cellars originally had its own vineyard but today fruit is shipped in. In business since 1989, the winery won awards from the International Eastern Wine Competition for two of its wines. From April through October the winery has lawn concerts on Sundays featuring jazz, bluegrass, and other types of music. One of the performers in past years was cellist Joan Jenrenaud, sister of winery-owner Mary Dutcher Birks, who has appeared solo and with the group Kronos. The winery sells bottles of chilled wine at the concerts but nothing else, so remember to bring your own picnic, non-alcoholic beverages, blankets, or lawn chairs. To get to the winery, turn east onto Macon from Germantown Parkway and go about 3 miles. Macon is curvy, so stick with the twists and turns until you see the sign on the left.

The winery is open Tuesday through Sunday. Admission to the Sunday concerts is $5.00 per person.

Graceland Mansion $$$
3734 Elvis Presley Boulevard
(901) 332-3322, (800) 238-2000
www.elvis.com

If you visit only one attraction while in Memphis, Graceland Mansion should be it, even if you're not necessarily an Elvis fan. It's one of the most visited homes in America and is as American as the American dream that Elvis personifies to much of the world.

Graceland is the home that a 22-year-old Elvis Presley bought for $100,000 in 1957 for himself and his parents after his meteoric rise to superstardom and the place where he sought refuge, with family and friends, throughout his life. In those days it was situated in the best neighborhood in Memphis, and the 14-acre grounds kept the fans at bay and provided room for Elvis and his buddies to race golf carts around and indulge in other entertainments.

At present cars aren't allowed on the grounds of the mansion, but you can drive to the complex across the street, which resembles a big shopping mall, where you can park in the huge lot and follow the signs into the main building, where you buy your tickets and queue up for a bus to take you across the street to the mansion. (Plenty of souvenir shops, additional attractions, and a few restaurants are available to visit before or after you see the mansion.) You get an audiotape gizmo, with a running narration that includes Lisa Marie Presley talking about her childhood memories of Elvis in the house.

When you walk through the front door, you see the living room, dining room, and his parents' bedroom, all done up in 1970s kitsch—white shag carpeting, mirrors, bright blues and purples in the decor. Truly one of a kind are the blue and bright yellow TV room, with Elvis's stereo and record collection, as well as three TVs, and the Jungle Room, with green shag carpet on floor and ceiling and Polynesian-style furniture. The story is that Elvis himself picked out the furniture at a Memphis retailer because it reminded him of Hawaii. The kitchen looks like, well, a normal 1970s kitchen but on the large side, where old-fashioned home-cooked meals as well as Elvis's favorite, fried peanut-butter-and-banana sandwiches, were turned out at all hours.

A recent addition to the tour is the garage, converted into a gallery that features furniture and clothing that belonged to Elvis. A highlight is the round, white fake-fur bed, with a stereo and mirrors built into a headboard that curves over the bed.

Although the home tells you about the man, including the fact that he loved to

> **Elvis fans who want to pay their respects to the King and his family in the Meditation Garden at Graceland Mansion can visit in the early mornings before the tours begin. Graceland opens its gates from 7:00 to 8:30 A.M., with free admission to the grounds. Graceland is generally less crowded at that time than during the mansion tour. Call ahead (901-332-3322), as the hours sometimes vary.**

read and he collected guns, the Trophy Room, housed in a separate building, is where you learn about his amazing career. Here the displays tell the Elvis story: his first records, his famous TV appearances, and press accounts that include an October 1956 *Variety* announcing how Elvis had become a millionaire in less than a year. You learn about his years in the army, his movie career, during which he made 33 films, his 1968 TV appearance known today as his "Comeback Special," and the Las Vegas performances. Items include a gold lamé suit from 1957, posters and props from his movies, and all kinds of the Elvis-theme merchandise: billfolds, shoes, I LIKE ELVIS buttons, I HATE ELVIS buttons.

Even the most world-weary visitor can't help being dazzled by the dozens of gold and platinum records as well as the plaques that recognize his 14 Grammy nominations (with three wins, all for gospel), adulation from fan clubs, and gratitude from the charities he supported. Elvis is one of the best-selling artists of all time, with gold, platinum, or multiplatinum records for almost 150 albums and singles. The collection is so big it spills over into another building.

The tour ends in the Meditation Garden, where Elvis and family members are buried. The graves are adorned with flower arrangements and other embellishments that fans send even though it has been more than 25 years since his death.

Once back across the street, you can check out Elvis's two private jets, the *Lisa*

Marie and *Hound Dog II*, which aren't that impressive beyond the gold seat-belt buckles and gaudy bathrooms aboard the *Lisa Marie*.

More interesting is the Elvis Presley Automobile Museum, which you won't want to miss if you're a car buff. You'll see the 1960 red MG convertible from the movie *Blue Hawaii*, several Stutz Black Hawks, and, of course, the 1957 Pink Cadillac, called Gladys's car because even though Elvis's mother, Gladys, didn't drive, it was her favorite. There are also a few motorcycles and a collection of golf carts and other vehicles that Elvis and his buddies used to drive around the grounds of Graceland.

The Sincerely Elvis Museum houses Elvis's personal effects, including his records and sneakers.

Graceland and related attractions are open every day. You can buy a ticket to the mansion, or pay more for Graceland's Platinum Tour Package, which gets you into the mansion, Automobile Museum, airplanes, and Sincerely Elvis Museum. Reservations can be made and tickets purchased in advance, a good bet during the summer months or other busy times, especially if your time is limited. Call or check www.elvis.com for details. Parking is $2.00.

Lichterman Nature Center $$
5992 Quince Road
(901) 767-7322
www.memphismuseums.org/nature
Lichterman Nature Center provides 65 acres of preserved forest and lake habitat in the middle of East Memphis. Roomy, paved paths wind through the forest and across the meadows. Along the paths, different species of trees and plants as well as birds, insects, and small creatures are identified so that you can fully appreciate what you see. Lichterman's lush preserve is a wonderful place to slow down, take a quiet walk, and enjoy wildlife. In short, it lives up to its description of itself as "a home for wildlife and a haven for humans." Various kids' camps and workshops are offered throughout the year.

Graceland: Shrine to the King

Each year, hundreds of thousands of people flock to Memphis to visit Graceland, and on the anniversary of Elvis's death in August, thousands—including fans from all over the world—participate in the Candlelight Vigil, many of them passing through the gates of Graceland to Elvis's grave to pay their respects. (See the Annual Events chapter for details on this and other events of Elvis Week.)

Clearly, Elvis has grown into something larger than the simple man from Memphis. He changed modern music forever, earned almost 150 gold and platinum records, and sold out some 837 shows in Las Vegas. More than that, he is one of the most enduring icons of the 20th century, and like Marilyn Monroe, John F. Kennedy, and James Dean, he appeals to devoted fans as well as ordinary people. At present more than 500 recognized Elvis Presley fan clubs flourish in 44 states and 45 different countries, despite the fact that their idol has been dead for more than 25 years. Thousands of Elvis impersonators throughout the world keep the image alive in their own personal way.

What's the appeal? Fans speak of the Elvis world, in which everybody belongs, drawn by their love of one man.

They admire his rags-to-riches rise, his charm and good looks, his generosity, his humble attitude, and how much he gave to his fans, even though his success may ultimately have destroyed him. They say they feel as though they've met him, that they know him.

Of course, others simply love Elvis's music, whereas still others like to poke fun of the kitschy, gaudy elements that were popular in the 1970s: the white jumpsuits, the sideburns, the flamboyant Jungle Room with its carpeted ceiling.

You'll learn plenty about Elvis at Graceland, the home where he sought refuge from fans and the rigors of performing. Fans should also check out Sun Studio, where he made his first record, and Beale Street, where he hung out to hear R&B. There's also his high school (Humes High School), his early homes, the church he attended (First Assembly of God Church), and the shop where he bought records (Poplar Tunes). You can also drive 100 miles to Tupelo, Mississippi, to see Elvis's birthplace and other related sights. (See the Day Trips chapter for more information on Tupelo.)

For a tour of these and other Elvis-related sights, see the sidebar on Offbeat Tours of Memphis in this chapter.

Note: This is a great spot for adults, but unless they're participating in a camp or workshop, kids tend to become bored after a short while.

Open 9:00 A.M. to 4:00 P.M. Monday through Thursday, 9:00 A.M. to 5:00 P.M. on Friday and Saturday, and noon to 5:00 P.M. on Sunday.

Main Street Trolley $
Main Street, various stops
(901) 274-6282
www.matatransit.com
Riding the Main Street Trolley is great for getting to places downtown so that you can take a break from the car. And for 50 cents a ride, it's the best entertainment

value in town. The train runs along Main Street and up Madison Avenue to Cleveland Street but also loops around for a great view of the Mississippi River. (See the Getting Here, Getting Around chapter for more information about the Main Street Trolley and other transportation.)

Tickets are 50 cents per ride for all ages, except seniors and disabled persons, who pay 25 cents. You can also get a $2.50 daylong pass or a $6.00 three-day pass. Exact change is required.

Memphis Botanic Garden   **$**
750 Cherry Road
(901) 685-1566
www.memphisbotanicgarden.com
Situated in the heart of East Memphis in Audubon Park, Memphis Botanic Garden consists of 96 acres planted with all kinds of flowering plants, trees, and other flora. Starting in late February, when tens of thousands of daffodils begin flowering on Daffodil Hill, you'll find something in bloom every time you visit until the first frost (usually October or November). Cherry trees become clouds of pink blooms in March, dogwoods flower in April, and, for much of the summer, roses, daylilies, and cactus are spectacular. Also notable are the Tennessee Bicentennial Iris Garden, which celebrates the state flower, and a Japanese tranquillity garden open year-round. A number of these gardens date from the 1950s and 1960s.

The botanic garden is a popular spot for picnics and strolls for everyone, and gardening enthusiasts can take advantage of its extensive education program. The main building, Hardin Hall, is a popular place for parties, weddings, meetings, and other events and also has a small gift shop. A series of popular evening concerts and other events take place on the grounds in the summer.

It's open every day, and admission is free after noon on Tuesdays.

Memphis Queen Riverboats   **$$$**
45 Riverside Drive (at the foot of Monroe Avenue)
(901) 527-5694 or (800) 221-6197
www.memphisqueen.com
Don't miss your chance for an up-close-and-personal experience of the Mississippi River. The Memphis Queen Line's riverboats, complete with paddle wheels, have daily cruises, dinner cruises, and all kinds of special trips. Plan to arrive 30 minutes before departure to get your picture taken as a souvenir. Once everyone is aboard, the captain gives a tour, complete with historical facts and important sites on the river. There's also a piano player and a snack bar on board, but the main attraction is the view of the river and the city. Cruises are available daily at 2:30 P.M. and 5:00 P.M. Be sure to ask about dinner cruises and special events. (See the Kidstuff chapter for more details.)

Memphis Zoo   **$$$**
2000 Galloway
(901) 725-3452
www.memphiszoo.org
This excellent zoo, with its Egyptian decorations, newly arrived giant pandas from China, and exhibits such as Cat Country and Animals of the Night, is the city attraction that locals like to brag about. More than 400 species of animals from all over the world reside in renovated natural habitats. A favorite event is seal feeding, which takes place at 2:30 P.M. every day.

Open daily. To see the pandas, you must buy a $3.00 timed ticket, either in advance by calling the zoo or visiting its Web site, or at the gate. It's best to reserve ahead, since tickets are first-come, first-served for this popular exhibit. Sometimes, though, you can walk right in, so it doesn't hurt to ask. *Note:* If you have a large family, it might be more economical to purchase a Memphis Zoological Society membership. Parking is $3.00. (For more information about the zoo, see the Kidstuff chapter.)

Mud Island River Park Free
125 North Front Street
(901) 576-7241, (800) 507-6507
www.mudisland.com
This attraction, although geared more toward kids, is full of interesting information about Old Man River. One of the main draws is a detailed replica of the Mississippi River, which flows through the park. For a detailed chronology of the history and culture along the great river, visit the Mississippi River Museum. You can see a reconstructed 19th-century steamboat, witness a battle aboard a Civil War gunboat, and listen to the river hollers and work songs of the river roustabouts. Guided tours are available.

To get to Mud Island, go to the ticket office on Front Street; then either walk across the pedestrian bridge or take the monorail across the Mississippi to the island.

Open daily. The park is free, but there's an admission charge ($8.00 for adults) for the museum. Parking is available near the Front Street side of the monorail for a charge. The monorail is $2.00 round-trip, free with your museum ticket.

The Peabody Ducks Free
149 Union Avenue
(901) 529-4000
www.peabodymemphis.com
In the lobby of The Peabody hotel, you'll find one of Memphis's most popular attractions, the famous Peabody ducks. Every day at 11:00 A.M., five mallard ducks march down a red carpet from the elevator to the lobby's fountain, to music by John Philip Sousa. Then, at 5:00 P.M. the carpet is unrolled again, and these lucky ducks—after a strenuous day of swimming in an Italian marble fountain—march back to the elevator, then up to their penthouse home on the hotel's roof. (For more about the Peabody ducks, see the Close-up in the Accommodations chapter.) Parking is on your own, although you can use the hotel's pricey valet parking.

Wonders: The Memphis International
Cultural Series $$$
The Pyramid Arena, Front Street at
Auction Avenue
(901) 312-9161, (800) 2MEMPHIS
www.wonders.org
Organizing blockbuster exhibitions for Memphis audiences and/or bringing them to Memphis from other cities is the mission of Wonders, which was established after a 1987 exhibit of artifacts surrounding the rule of Rameses the Great drew some 675,000 visitors to downtown Memphis. With proof that if you build it, they will come, Wonders has continued to produce exhibitions, ranging from a show of Egyptian artifacts from the British Museum to Titanic: The Exhibition, featuring relics brought up from wreckage of the mighty ship.

For an idea of the diversity of Wonders exhibitions, look no further than the most recently organized shows, Masters of Florence: Glory and Genius at the Court of Medici in 2004 and The Art of the Motorcycle, scheduled for 2005. The exhibits typically run from April through September at the Pyramid Arena in downtown Memphis.

If there's a Wonders exhibition open during your trip to Memphis, chances are you won't want to miss it. Call Wonders or check out its Web site when you plan your trip. It's usually advisable to make reservations, as the tickets are sold for entry at a particular day and hour. During the popular shows it's tough to get tickets for the same day, but it's worth checking if you didn't plan ahead. The gift shop is worth a look, as the operators usually do a good job of selecting merchandise.

Hours and admission prices vary.

MUSEUMS

Art Museum of the University of
Memphis Free
3750 Norriswood Avenue
(901) 678-2224
www.amum.org
Tucked away in a quiet corner of the University of Memphis Communication and

Fine Arts Building, the museum features two small but excellent permanent exhibitions as well as shows of contemporary work that change frequently. Its Egyptian art, from the university's Institute of Egyptian Art and Archaeology, includes sculpture, religious and funerary objects, jewelry, and other items, some of it excavated at a cemetery near Memphis, the city on the Nile for which the city on the Mississippi River is named. An authentic mummy is displayed under glass, with his feet and face exposed so that you can see how well preserved the body is (teeth and some toenails are still intact after several thousand years). There are also tiny snake mummies, which priests once sold to be used as votives to the gods. A painted wood model of a boat, which includes stiff-armed figures of servants standing onboard, is in remarkably good shape, considering that it dates from at least the 18th century B.C.

The other permanent exhibit is Spirit of Africa, which displays masks, figurines, and other items from West Africa. Particularly interesting are the forest-spirit masks, donned for special ceremonies in the belief that the wearers would become the spirits represented by the mask.

The museum is open Monday through Saturday except during university holidays and while exhibitions are being changed over. It's best to stop at the university's information office, a small, round building at Central Avenue and Patterson, to get directions to the museum. Ask about parking, which can be scarce on campus.

A number of Memphis museums have Free Days, including the National Civil Rights Museum (Mondays, 3:00 to 5:00 P.M.), the Pink Palace Museum (Tuesdays, 1:00 to 4:00 P.M. for exhibits only), Memphis Zoo (Tuesdays, 2:00 to 5:00 P.M.), Memphis Brooks Museum of Art (Wednesdays, all day), Lichterman Nature Center (Tuesdays, 1:00 to 4:00 P.M.), and Memphis Botanic Garden (Tuesdays, noon to 6:00 P.M.).

The Children's Museum of Memphis $$
2525 Central Avenue
(901) 458-2678, (901) 320-3170 for recorded information
www.cmom.com

Memphis has an excellent children's museum that allows kids to pretend to drive, to shop in a grocery store, to be firefighters racing to a fire, and to participate in other interactive entertainment. There's also a vertical maze and other activities. The museum has some 20,000 square feet of exhibition space, with truly something for everyone, including children ages 10 through 12.

Open Tuesday through Sunday. Parking is free. (For more information see the Kidstuff chapter.)

The Dixon Gallery and Gardens $$
4339 Park Avenue
(901) 761-2409
www.dixon.org

The Dixon, as Memphians call this small museum, is a pretty, quiet oasis compared with its busy Park Avenue surroundings. Once a private estate, the museum features a Georgian-style mansion, with traditionally furnished galleries, as well as pleasant gardens and a lawn used for performances and other events. Most notable, though, are the special exhibitions, in particular its 2004 exhibition of the work of Mississippi visionary painter Walter Anderson. Others have included the Painters of Normandy, an exhibition of French paintings, and the art of Dr. Seuss. This privately funded museum also has a number of permanent collections, including French and American Impressionist and Postimpressionist paintings donated by the Dixon family as well as one of the most extensive collections of decorative pewter pieces in the world.

The gardens are particularly nice in spring, when the azaleas are in bloom, adding bright splashes of color and white all around the museum and its grounds. The south lawn is a popular spot among Memphians, who flock there to enjoy concerts, plays, and the Dixons' annual family picnic.

Getting Married in Memphis

Thinking about getting married during your trip to Memphis? If you're a U.S. citizen age 22 or older, all you need is your social security number and $32 for the marriage license. There's no waiting period, and the license is good (only in the state of Tennessee) for 30 days. If you're not a U.S. citizen, the same criteria apply, except you need to present your passport rather than social security number. If you are 18 years old and a U.S. citizen, you need to present your birth certificate, and you do not need parental consent.

You can get your marriage license at the Memphis County Clerk's office at 150 Washington Street in downtown Memphis. Justices of the peace are not readily available to perform marriages, so you must make prior arrangements for a justice of the peace or other official/clergyman to perform the ceremony.

One popular option is to call Ministers in a Minute (901-754-4700,

www.ministersinaminute.com), a group of mobile ministers that has been performing weddings on short notice for more than 10 years. They prefer three days' notice, but are generally very accommodating if you're only in town for a day.

For something unique, contact the Center for Southern Folklore (901-525-3655). Someone can arrange for you to be married at the center in front of the First Church of the Elvis Impersonator, a one-of-a-kind mechanized Elvis shrine. Or you can arrange to say "I do" in the tiny Mississippi Delta church that's an exhibit at the Stax Museum of American Soul Music (901-942-7685).

For a more conventional preplanned wedding, there are many options, ranging from the Chapel in the Woods at Graceland to the Memphis Botanic Garden to the National Ornamental Metal Museum.

The museum is open Tuesday through Sunday.

Fire Museum of Memphis $$
118 Adams Avenue
(901) 320-5650
www.firemuseum.com
The museum, housed in a 1910 firehouse that at one time housed fire horses, tells the story of how fire fighting developed, complete with early fire engines on display. You can also learn important fire-safety information, and uniformed firefighters are on hand to answer questions.

Open Monday through Saturday. The museum has two-for-one admission on

Tuesdays. There is no parking available at the museum, so look for a space in a nearby lot or take the trolley, which stops a block west of the museum on Main. (For more information see the Kidstuff chapter.)

Memphis Brooks Museum of Art $$
1934 Poplar Avenue
(901) 544-6200
www.brooksmuseum.org
The state's largest and oldest fine-arts museum, the Brooks (as locals call it) was originally built in 1916 in the Beaux-Arts style. Since then it has been expanded three times, with the final addition (1989) including a rotunda and

first-rate amenities such as a restaurant and auditorium. In summer the distinctive white structure stands out from its lush green Overton Park setting, well back from the street and close to both the Memphis College of Art and Memphis Zoo.

The museum has three levels, where it displays items from its own extensive collection as well as traveling exhibitions. The ground-floor galleries feature 17th-, 18th-, and 19th-century items from the permanent collection, much of it British and American furniture plus paintings by Anthony Van Dyck, Winslow Homer, and Gilbert Stuart, among others. You get a sense of how Italian painting styles developed from the Brooks display of medieval religious art and works from the High Renaissance and Baroque periods. Look for special exhibits on the ground floor or lower level. The museum has had an incredible variety of exhibits, with works ranging from segregation-era and civil-rights period photographs by Memphian Ernest Withers to originals used in Absolut vodka advertisements to jewels of Russia's Romanov Dynasty. Don't miss the upper level, where the Global Galleries include beautiful African masks and sculptures, a Roman head of Nero from A.D. 50, Chinese figures from the Han and Tang dynasties, and a reconstructed suit of jade squares dating from the Han era. You'll also find a tiny collection of French Impressionist and Postimpressionist paintings by Camille Pissarro, Eugène Boudin, and others.

Off the rotunda where you enter the museum, you'll find a first-rate lunch restaurant, the Brushmark, and a great museum shop with all kinds of imaginative, funky objects in addition to the usual art books and note cards.

The museum is open Tuesday through Sunday. It's also open until 9:00 P.M. the first Wednesday of each month for a festive celebration of art that includes live music, drink specials, and gallery tours and talks.

The museum has an extensive program of film, art classes, and other stuff, so just ask.

Memphis Police Museum   Free
159 Beale Street
(901) 579-0887

At the Memphis Police Museum, which is also a working police station, you can see an actual jail cell, confiscated weapons, and old newspaper clippings relating how Machine Gun Kelly was captured in Memphis in 1933 and how crowds were controlled at Elvis Presley's funeral.

Open every day until 10:30 P.M. No parking on the premises. (For more information see the Kidstuff chapter.)

National Civil Rights Museum $$$
450 Mulberry Street
(901) 521-9699
www.civilrightsmuseum.org

The National Civil Rights Museum, which celebrated its 10th anniversary in 2001, provides a realistic and thoughtful look at the struggle to bring about racial equality and how that continues throughout the world. *USA Weekend,* a magazine supplement of *USA Today,* named the museum as one of the top-10 places to visit to gain a better understanding of our country. It's housed at the Lorraine Motel, where Dr. Martin Luther King Jr. was killed, and at the building across the street, from which the shot was fired.

Open daily. Parking is free. (For more information see the African-American Heritage section of this chapter.)

National Ornamental Metal Museum $
374 Metal Museum Drive
(901) 774-6380
www.metalmuseum.org

This small, unique museum is dedicated exclusively to the collection and exhibition of fine metalwork, such as iron gates, swords, and other items. You'll find it in a quiet pocket of land overlooking the Mississippi River, which seems a step back in time. Across the street are Native American ceremonial mounds, converted into bunkers during the Civil War. Local legend has it that this is the spot where explorer Hernando DeSoto first saw the great river. The museum is housed in the former 1930s nurses' dormitory of the U.S. Marine Hospital, and although it has its own collection, what you'll see are temporary exhibits, which in 2004 included a show of recycling evangelist Harriete Estel Berman's jewelry and sculpture, and a display of traditional kama Japanese teakettles. A popular annual event is the museum's repair days in October, when you can bring in silver or other metal items to the blacksmith shop for a free repair estimate (which also gets you into the museum for free). Consult the museum Web site or call ahead for details. When you visit, check out the museum gift shop for unusual jewelry and other metal items. Don't miss an opportunity to stroll the grounds, a great spot for a picture that features a spectacular view of the river. Check out the working blacksmith shop, which once restored Graceland's famous gates. Picnickers should bring their own everything (including bug spray!), as there are no restaurants or food stores in the area. The museum is open Tuesday through Sunday. Free parking.

Note: Finding the museum can be tricky. From downtown take Riverside going north (left if you're facing the river) and turn onto the I–55 North exit. Take the first right off the ramp (you'll see a sign); then follow the signs to the museum.

Peabody Place Museum $$
119 South Main Street
(901) 523-2787
www.belz.com
You have to hunt for this museum, located in the basement of the Pembroke Building on Main Street, but it's worth it for its collection of Chinese sculpture, mostly 19th-century (Ching Dynasty) works of jade, ivory, and agate. Intricately carved, often from one piece of stone, the works include dragon boats and a 10-story pagoda with 1,000 carved figures on the various levels. Don't miss the colorful two-by-two lineup of horses, camels, tigers, and other creatures—all the size of carousel animals—or the large gilt bronze temple lions. These artifacts, which include other items such as Mongolian silver and interesting rock for-

mations, come from the collection of Memphis developer Jack Belz, who spearheaded the redevelopment of downtown Memphis. The museum includes five large galleries and provides a cool, peaceful respite if you want to take a break from outdoor sightseeing.

Open Tuesday through Sunday. Parking is on your own.

The Pink Palace $–$$$
3050 Central Avenue
(901) 320-6362
www.memphismuseums.org
The Pink Palace is actually three attractions housed in one large pink mansion: the Pink Palace Museum, the Union Planters IMAX Theater, and the Sharpe Planetarium. The lavish mansion dates from the 1920s, when it was built of pink marble for Clarence Saunders, a Memphian who opened the world's first supermarket and founded the Piggly-Wiggly grocery chain. Sadly, Saunders went bankrupt, and no one ever lived in his pink marble palace.

You can buy a ticket separately for each attraction ($8.00 for the museum, $7.50 for IMAX, and $4.25 for Sharpe Planetarium for adults), but a combination ticket ($16.75 adults for everything, less for other combinations) is a far better value.

Pink Palace Museum: The permanent exhibition of the Pink Palace traces the natural history of the Mid-South region from prehistoric dinosaurs to the present. The artifacts are diverse, ranging from fossils and dinosaur bones found in the area to Indian artifacts to life-size dioramas illustrating the life of the early European settlers. Along the way you will learn about Memphis's connection with the Trail of Tears, the Civil War, Elvis and rock and roll, the modern chain supermarket as we know it, and much more. Don't miss the Clyde Park Miniature Circus. Mr. Park spent 50 years carving and motorizing this circus replica before donating it to the museum. The circus is turned on most days at 10:30 A.M. Ask about temporary exhibits, too.

Union Planters IMAX Theater: At an IMAX theater, instead of watching a movie, you experience it on a screen four stories high and five stories wide while actually feeling the vibrations from the sound system.

The IMAX allows you to swim with dolphins, scream with the others as the most outrageous roller coaster tests your thrill tolerance, or descend to the depths of the ocean in search of the *Titanic*. Films change constantly, so call (901–763–IMAX) for updated listings and show times.

Sharpe Planetarium: The Sharpe Planetarium allows you to glorify in the beauty and bounty of the constellations as you have never seen them before. Pointing with a laser light, guides explain the stories and history behind the stars and other astrological discoveries. Right before your eyes, the sky changes with the seasons so that you can see the movement of the stars. Call ahead for show times and ticket information.

The Pink Palace, IMAX theater, and planetarium are open daily. Check for show times for IMAX and the planetarium.

Fans of the band Pink Floyd and laser shows should not miss the LaserRock show at the Pink Palace Museum's Sharpe Planetarium. The shows feature "Money" and other Pink Floyd hits choreographed with lasers and other lighting special effects on the planetarium dome. For more information, call the LaserRock hotline at (901) 320–6333 or check out www.memphismuseums.org.

Wonders: The Memphis International Cultural Series $$$
The Pyramid Arena, Front Street at Auction Avenue
(901) 312-9161, (800) 2MEMPHIS
www.wonders.org
We include Wonders here because its exhibitions are always of museum quality. Wonders produces blockbuster exhibitions, including 2004's Masters of Florence: Glory and Genius at the Court of Medici and The Art of the Motorcycle, set for 2005.

If there's a Wonders exhibition open during your trip to Memphis, chances are you won't want to miss it. Call Wonders or check out its Web site when you plan your trip. It's usually advisable to make reservations. Hours and admission prices vary. (For more information see the General Attractions listing in this chapter.)

MEMPHIS HISTORY

Chucalissa Archaeological Museum $$
1987 Indian Village Drive
(901) 785-3160
www.chucalissa.org
In 1939, while excavating the site to develop a city park, workers discovered the ruins of a Choctaw Indian village. They named the village Chucalissa, which means "abandoned house." The park is dedicated to educating visitors about the Choctaw Indians who populated this area before European settlers arrived. A modest museum and reconstructed village have been developed over the years from the information and artifacts that archaeologists discovered on the site. On-site demonstrations of traditional dancing, food, and crafts help visitors imagine the village as it was when the Choctaw lived there. The museum is geared toward children, who love learning about Native Americans here. Chucalissa is off the beaten path, but worth the detour if you are interested in Native American history and archaeology.

To get there from downtown, take Riverside Drive (which turns into I-55 South). Take the Third Street exit and go south. Turn right onto Mitchell (you should see a sign) and follow the signs. It's about a 30-minute drive from downtown.

Chucalissa is open Tuesday through Saturday.

While in the area, you might want to check out Interstate Bar-B-Q & Restaurant, one of the city's best for a sit-down meal or drive-through order. It's at 2265 South

Third Street, just on the other side of the interstate (hence its name). (See the Restaurants chapter for more information.)

Davies Manor Plantation House $$
9336 Davies Plantation
(901) 386-0715
www.daviesmanorplantation.org
This is the oldest log house in Shelby County, built by an Indian chief in the early 1800s. In 1851 the Davies family bought the house, expanding it into a country farmhouse that sits on a 2,000-acre plantation. The construction is log-and-chink, and the interior is outfitted with early family furnishings.

Open Tuesday through Saturday or at other times by appointment for tour groups.

Historic Elmwood Cemetery Free
824 South Dudley Street
(901) 774-3212
www.elmwoodcemetery.org
Historic Elmwood Cemetery, which opened in 1852, covers 88 acres and includes a large collection of Victorian funeral sculpture and many beautiful old trees. The real attraction, though, is the past, since a tour of Elmwood is a tour of Memphis history. Buried in the cemetery are 12 Civil War generals (including two from the Union side), a madam who maintained a "resort of commercial affection," governors, senators, and E. H. Crump, the man who dominated Memphis politics for much of the 20th century. Some 5,000 people interred here died in the three yellow-fever epidemics that plagued Memphis, including many who came to Memphis to nurse the sick and others who stayed behind to care for loved ones. University of Tennessee maintains a plot for people who've donated their bodies to science. Confederate general Nathan Bedford Forrest was buried here, but later was moved to a park created in his honor near downtown Memphis.

Both blacks and whites are buried at Elmwood, so you'll find the graves of many African Americans, including many of the city's most important leaders. The most visible is the mausoleum in which Robert Church and his family are entombed. He was the South's first black millionaire, and he established Beale Street as a mecca for African Americans. There are also the graves of Beale Street blues singer Ma Rainey II; the Martin brothers, doctors who owned the Red Sox Negro Baseball League team; and Rev. Samuel Augustus Owen, founder of what is now LeMoyne Owen College in Memphis. About 300 slaves were buried here between 1857 and 1865, most of them marked with such designations as NEGRO MAN instead of names.

At the cemetery office, you can rent an hour-long recorded tour to play in your car as you drive through or buy a detailed map and informational brochure. Both cost $5.00 and will direct you to the graves of the more prominent and interesting people whose remains are buried at Elmwood. The office is open Monday through Saturday. Keep in mind that Elmwood is still an active cemetery, so show respect if there is a funeral taking place or mourners present when you visit.

The Magevney House Free
198 Adams Avenue
(901) 526-4464
www.memphismuseums.org
While millionaires lived in mansions such as the Mallory-Neely and Woodruff-Fontaine houses up the street, this pre–Civil War home shows how the middle class lived. It was built sometime before 1837, the year Eugene Magevney, a schoolteacher who emigrated from Ireland to the United States, bought it and later added on. The home looks tiny from the street but has a large backyard, at one time home to the kitchen, privy, stables, and slave quarters. Decorated with furniture and reproduction wallpaper typical of about 1850, it houses some of the family's possessions, including portraits of the owner and his family as well as a mahogany desk that served as an altar in the city's first Catholic Mass. Magevney eventually became wealthy from real-

estate holdings but continued to live in this house until his death from yellow fever in 1889.

Open Tuesday through Saturday. Donations (suggested: $2.00 for adults, $1.00 for children) are appreciated.

The Mallory-Neely House $$
652 Adams Avenue
(901) 523-1484
www.memphismuseums.org

This mansion, built in 1852 by insurance executive Isaac Kirtland and redecorated in high Victorian style in the 1890s, was home to two prominent Memphis families. The last resident was Daisy Mallory, who died in 1969 after living there for 86 years, leaving instructions that the house was to be a museum. Most of the furnishings are original to the house, including stained-glass windows, a Chinese prayer chest bought at the St. Louis World Fair, and two beautiful crystal chandeliers in the parlor, each with 12 lights and 250 prisms.

The exterior of this three-story house has elements of Italian Villa architectural style, including arched windows and a stucco facade designed to look as if it were made from stone blocks. A porch runs along the front of the house.

Inside, the house has colorful, ornate hand-stenciled walls and parquet flooring downstairs, with ceiling paintings, ornate plaster moldings, and other frills. These have been restored carefully to remove

If you love Victoriana or need to get into the holiday spirit, don't miss the Victorian Holiday Walk in downtown Memphis's Victorian Village the first Sunday in December. The Mallory-Neely House, the Woodruff-Fontaine House, and the more modest Magevney House, as well as private homes that are usually closed to the public, are all lavishly decorated for Christmas and open to tourists and locals alike.

years of dirt and soot, and a few untouched spots allow you to see how the house was decorated differently throughout the years.

Open Tuesday through Sunday. (Ticket office and gift shop are in the carriage house behind the mansion.) On days that both are open, you can tour both this home and the Woodruff-Fontaine House two doors down for $1.00 off if you buy a special ticket.

Memphis Belle $
8101 Hornet Avenue, Millington
(901) 412-8071
www.memphisbelle.com

The legendary *Memphis Belle* is probably the most famous airplane of World War II, as the first bomber to safely complete 25 missions. Pilot Robert Morgan named his B-17 bomber after his Memphis sweetheart, Margaret Polk. He had her likeness painted on the side of his plane as good luck, and good luck she was. The *Memphis Belle* had a distinguished combat record, completing its quota of 25 missions over Nazi-occupied territory.

A few years ago the celebrated bomber was moved from Mud Island River Park, where it had made its home for many years. This proud survivor is currently undergoing restoration, but it can still be seen by the public. Visiting the *Belle* involves a detour to suburban Millington, where you can see the disassembled plane undergoing restoration, and visit workshops where the engines, machine guns, and other components are being cleaned and repaired. This work will continue through 2005. After that, call or check the Web site for information on the *Memphis Belle*'s new home.

The schedule changes, so call ahead for hours and days of operation. To get there from downtown Memphis, take Danny Thomas Boulevard north (U.S. Highway 51) about 14 miles to Millington, turn right onto Navy Road, and then left onto Hornet Avenue just past the navy base.

Woodruff-Fontaine House　　　　$$
680 Adams Avenue
(901) 526-1469

This gem of a Victorian house, which dates from the days when Adams Avenue was the city's "Millionaires' Row," has a mansard-roofed tower, from which its merchant-owner could watch boats come in from the river. The house has its original hardwood floors and ceiling paintings as well as floor-to-ceiling windows that helped to cool homes in the days before air-conditioning. The house is outfitted mostly with Victorian furniture donated by Memphis's elite, including a Wooten desk and courtship chairs designed to keep a courting couple from getting too close. Original to the house is a stained-glass fanlight over the front door that depicts a bird's nest with four eggs, a reference to the fact that the owner had four children. Don't miss the pretty playhouses in the back and the garden area, complete with fountain, a popular place for summer weddings. Check out the small gift shop, which has jewelry, cut-glass vases, and other items culled from local estate sales by a volunteer, at good prices.

Call ahead for days of operation. On days that both are open, you can buy a special ticket to save $1.00 and tour both this home and the Mallory-Neely House just two doors down.

MEMPHIS MUSIC

Beale Street　　　　Free
Downtown Memphis, between Lt.
George W. Lee Avenue and Peabody
Place
www.bealestreet.com

Musical history was made on this famous street several times over, and you'll find historical markers along the street that tell part of the story as well as statues of W. C. Handy in Handy Park and of Elvis Presley (on the south side of the street, near Second). (Check out the Memphis Music chapter for the whole story.) At night you can check out all the neon signs, enjoy people watching, and hear the music Beale Street made famous at the clubs. (See the Nightlife chapter for details.) During the day you can visit shops, restaurants, and attractions that include the W. C. Handy Performing Arts Center at Handy Park and Memphis Police Museum, but otherwise, you'll learn a lot more about Memphis's musical history by visiting the Memphis Rock 'n' Soul Museum a block south of Beale. (For more information on the museum, see the write-up in this section.)

Center for Southern Folklore
& Cafe　　　　Free
119 and 123 South Main Street
(901) 525-3655
www.southernfolklore.com

The Center for Southern Folklore is devoted to keeping the South's music, crafts, and other traditions alive. One of the biggest draws is live music performances that feature such legends as the Fieldstones, barrelhouse-musician Mose Vinson, and Blind Mississippi Morris. (Sometimes there is a cover.) Contact the center for a schedule, or visit the Web site. (For more information, see the General Attractions listing in this chapter.)

The center's Folklore Store is on Main just in front of the Peabody Place trolley stop. To access everything else (including the performance hall), enter through the double doors facing Main Street and nearest to Gayoso, and go to the back of the lobby. Parking is on your own. (For more information about the music, see the Nightlife chapter.)

Full Gospel Tabernacle　　　　Free
787 Hale Road
(901) 396-9192

This small brick church, located south of Graceland Mansion in the Whitehaven area, is well known for its famous pastor, soul legend Al Green. He has led the church for more than 25 years, following an incredibly successful recording career during the late 1960s and early 1970s that

Offbeat Tours of Memphis

See the town in style by riding in a 1955 pink Cadillac, an old-fashioned biplane, or a horse-drawn carriage. Of course, you can always opt for a bus tour of Memphis attractions from operators that include Blues City Tours (901–522–9229) and Gray Line of Memphis (901–382–6366 or 800–222–0089).

American Dream Safari
(901) 274-1997
www.americandreamsafari.com
Tad Pierson can take you on a three-hour tour of the city, a gospel church tour, or a daylong excursion to the Mississippi Delta to explore the roots of the blues. Best of all, you ride in a 1955 pink Cadillac, just like the one Elvis drove. This is very popular, especially during summer months, so book ahead.

Belle Air Biplane Rides
(901) 481-1935
www.belleairtours.com
Get a bird's-eye view of Memphis and the Mississippi River from a biplane that looks like an antique but is actually state of the art. They supply the goggles and cap; you supply the adventurous spirit for this two-passenger tour.

Carriage Tours of Memphis
(901) 527-7542
www.carriagetoursofmemphis.com
You can find horse-drawn carriages lined up in front of The Peabody on Union Avenue, some of them with lavish decor and all of them with canine mascots. Each carriage can accommodate four adults or two adults and up to four children.

Memphis Explorations
(901) 761-1838
www.elvistyle.com
Mike Freeman and Cindy Hazen literally wrote the book about Elvis's Memphis (*Memphis Elvis-style*), so who better to show you where the King lived, worked, and played. They offer a driving tour as well as a walking tour that meets at the Elvis statue on Beale Street. They can also show you Elvis's Tupelo, or the homes, studios, and hangouts of other Memphis musicians. If you want to know every little thing about Elvis, this tour's for you. Reservations are required.

resulted in 16 top-10 hits. In 2003 he recorded his first album since those days, *I Can't Stop*, which drew critical acclaim, but he's still a preacher first. Services are held here at 11:00 A.M. every Sunday, and when he's in town, Reverend Green preaches and fronts for the Full Gospel Tabernacle choir. It's an electrifying and joyful experience to hear Green's charismatic preaching, if you are lucky enough to visit when he's in the pulpit. Visitors are welcome, but be aware that this is a

church, not a tourist attraction. Behave with respect (no cameras) and remember to put a few bucks in the collection plate.

Gibson Guitar Factory $$$
145 Lt. George W. Lee Avenue
(901) 544-7998
www.gibsonmemphis.com
Drawn by the mystique of Memphis music, Gibson Guitar opened a factory here just a block from Beale Street. Gibson makes electric guitars here, including custom-

made instruments for B. B. King, Prince, and others. It also makes the bright Beale Street Blue guitar, a special-edition instrument that commemorates this location. You can take a 25-minute tour of the Memphis Gibson Guitar Factory, and watch as the musical instruments are crafted by hand at various workstations throughout the factory. You see each step, as wood forms are transformed into about 100 finished musical instruments each day, ready to ship to guitar stores all over the world. Because the groups are limited, you might want to call ahead for reservations; otherwise, factory operations are closed to the public. You can buy a guitar at the Gibson Guitar shop as well as a T-shirt or other souvenir. Check out The Lounge, a bar that features uptown atmosphere and great live music in the evenings. Cost of the Gibson guitar tour is $10 per person, age 12 or older. Younger children are not allowed on the factory tour. Parking is on your own.

Graceland Mansion $$$
3734 Elvis Presley Boulevard
(901) 332–3322, (800) 238–2000
www.elvis.com

This was the home of Elvis Presley, the young Memphis man who bought the mansion in 1957 after his first hits had made him a millionaire and an international superstar. The mansion itself sheds some interesting light on the man behind the legend, but music fans shouldn't miss the impressive collection of gold and platinum records as well as memorabilia from every phase of Elvis's career. (For more information on Graceland, see the General Attractions section of this chapter.)

Ask at the guest services counter about the free shuttle service from Graceland to Sun Studio, the Memphis Rock 'n' Soul Museum, and the Stax Museum of American Soul Music.

Open daily. You can opt for the more expensive Platinum Tour Package, which gets you into the mansion, Automobile Museum, the two custom airplanes, and the Sincerely Elvis memorabilia museum.

Memphis Rock 'n' Soul Museum $$
200 South Third Street
(901) 543–0800
www.memphisrocknsoul.org

Housed inside the new FedExForum just south of Beale, the Rock 'n' Soul Museum is a great introduction to Memphis music and a good first stop before seeing Sun Studio and other music-related attractions. The exhibits tell the story of how the musical traditions drifted from the cotton fields and hills around Memphis into local recording studios and finally into America's musical mainstream as rock and roll, rhythm and blues, and soul. A short video sets the stage and features interviews with Carl Perkins, B. B. King, and Sam Phillips, who first recorded Perkins, Elvis, and others. The early part of the exhibition shows how the rural people, black and white, lived, before many of them left the farm for the city as part of the great migration that cut the rural population of Tennessee, Mississippi, and Arkansas from 3.7 million in 1930 to less than a million by 1969. The rest of the exhibition shows what happened when they got to Memphis, the importance of Beale Street as the heart of black Memphis, and the role of early radio. Much of the exhibit is devoted to the record labels that brought these musicians into the mainstream, first Sun Studio with the rock and roll of the 1950s. You learn plenty as well about the Memphis soul sound that emanated from here in the 1960s, as Hi Records first recorded Al Green and Ann Peebles and Stax Records recorded soul greats Otis Redding, Isaac Hayes, and Sam and Dave. The experience is enhanced by a portable CD player, free with admission, which in addition to providing a running narrative also allows you to listen to full-length recordings of the music you're learning about.

The museum is open daily until 7:00 P.M., later on event nights. Parking at market rates is available at FedExForum.

Stax Museum of American Soul Music $$
926 East McLemore Street
(901) 946-2535
www.soulsvilleusa.com

This is hallowed ground indeed, where Otis Redding, Sam and Dave, Booker T. & the MGs, Isaac Hayes, and numerous other soul artists recorded on the Stax label. The museum opened in 2002 at the same address where Stax made musical history. This upbeat party house of a museum tells the story of how this legendary recording studio came to be. You learn about the music makers and, most important, enjoy the music that topped the charts then and still remains popular. The tour begins upstairs, where you can see early recording equipment, Elvis's high-school yearbook, and more.

The museum is a replica of the Capitol Theater, the former movie house where Jim Stewart and Estelle Axton started Stax Records. The museum also includes a 500-seat auditorium, facilities for the LeMoyne-Owen College music department, and a music academy for school-age children.

The museum is part of a larger revital-ization program for this south Memphis neighborhood, known as Soulsville USA. (For more information go to the African-American Heritage chapter.)

The museum is open daily.

Sun Studio $$
706 Union Avenue
(901) 521-0664, (800) 441-6249
www.sunstudio.com

It's hard to believe so much musical his-tory was made in this small, simple studio, but that's what makes Sun Studio fasci-nating. This is where African-American music crossed over into the mainstream, changing music forever. Elvis was discov-ered here, the first rock-and-roll song ("Rocket 88") was recorded, and a leg-endary roster of rockabilly and blues musicians made records here. They include Jerry Lee Lewis, Carl Perkins, Johnny Cash, B. B. King, Howlin' Wolf, Lit-tle Milton, and many others.

Buy your tickets (and refreshments and gifts, too, if you like) in Sun Studio Café on the corner.

Open daily. Tours start every hour on the half hour. Free parking is available behind the studio.

W. C. Handy House $
352 Beale Street
(901) 527-3427 or (901) 522-1556

The tiny house you see set back from Beale Street was home to the blues giant W. C. Handy. He didn't invent the blues, but because he was the first to write down the music so the world could enjoy it, he has gone down in musical history as the "Father of the Blues." He lived here with his family from 1905 to about 1918, when he moved to New York to further his career. Moved from its original location to Beale Street in 1985, this was his home when he wrote "Memphis Blues," "St. Louis Blues," and "Beale Street Blues." While in Memphis, Handy started his own music-publishing company, Handy & Pace, at 392 Beale Street, which still exists in the form of New York–based Handy & Brothers. The house contains memorabilia and photo-graphs as well as furnishings and musical instruments of the period. Open Tuesday through Sunday. Parking is on your own.

AFRICAN-AMERICAN HERITAGE

Beale Street Free
Downtown Memphis between Lt. George W. Lee Avenue and Peabody Place
www.bealestreet.com

Beale Street was the center of African-American cultural and commercial activity during the segregated era that took up most of the 20th century. You'll find his-toric markers with information about important black Memphians, including Ida Wells, Nat D. Williams, and Robert Church. You can also see the oldest brick-constructed, multistory church for blacks (now First Baptist Beale Street), and

Church Park and the Old Daisy Theatre. (See the African-American Heritage chapter for more information about Beale, and the important people and places that made history.)

National Civil Rights Museum $$$
450 Mulberry Street
(901) 521-9699
www.civilrightsmuseum.org

Opened in 1991, the National Civil Rights Museum focuses on the major events of the civil rights movement, including events surrounding the integration of Central High School in Little Rock and the march on Selma. *USA Weekend,* a magazine supplement of *USA Today,* in 2001 named the museum as one of the top-10 places to visit to gain a better understanding of our country.

The museum is housed in the Lorraine Motel, where Dr. Martin Luther King Jr. was shot in 1968, as well as the building across the street, from which the shot was fired. The assassination of Dr. King and the Memphis sanitation-workers strike that brought him here are also a focal point. (For background on Dr. King and the strike, see the African-American Heritage chapter.)

The museum features photos, documents, and descriptions, as well as interactive experiences to illustrate civil rights history. An audiotape tour, narrated by actors Ozzie Davis and Ruby Dee, helps to keep up the tempo and to put a human face on what you're seeing. There's also a separate audiotape for children. (See the Kidstuff chapter for details.)

The main museum exhibit briefly describes developments from the 1600s, when slaves were first brought to this country, through the first half of the 1900s. The main focus, though, is on the major events of the civil rights movement, from the *Brown v. Board of Education* decision that outlawed segregation in public schools in 1954, to Dr. King's assassination in Memphis in 1968. There are pictures, photos, and descriptions, as well as inter-

Sun Studio operates a free shuttle service, a great way to get to key music attractions without a car. Eight times a day the Sun Studio bus makes a loop starting at Heartbreak Hotel near Graceland, then stopping at Graceland Plaza (where tours begin), Sun Studio, Memphis Rock 'n' Soul Museum, Beale Street, and Stax Museum of American Soul Music. It's first-come, first-served.

active experiences, to illustrate events surrounding the integration of Central High School in Little Rock, the Montgomery, Alabama, bus boycott, and the 1964 Freedom Summer's black-voter registration drive in Mississippi. You can sit on a bus with a seated statue of Rosa Parks, whose refusal to give up her seat sparked the Montgomery bus boycott. You feel firsthand what it's like to be ordered to the back of the bus.

In 2002 the museum opened its Exploring the Legacy annex in the building from which the fatal bullet was fired at Dr. King. Here, the museum details what happened after the assassination, including the investigation of the murder and the trial of James Earl Ray, who was convicted of killing Dr. King. Other exhibits focus on civil rights struggles outside the United States, including events in South Africa.

Open Wednesday through Monday.

Slave Haven Underground Railroad
Museum $$
826 North Second Street
(901) 527-3427

This five-room house, the home of Jacob Burkle, was a stop on the Underground Railroad, the path by which runaway slaves escaped to the North. Burkle, a German immigrant who owned a thriving stockyard, built the house in 1855 just a few blocks from the Mississippi River in what was then the countryside. The basement of the house, which has a secret door, is where the slaves are said to have hidden as they rested during their long journey, with easy access to the river. The house, decorated with furnishings from the period, also has displays about the realities of slavery: the hardship of traveling by boat from Africa, the lifestyle they were forced to lead, and even shackles once used to prevent slaves from escaping. Particularly intriguing are handmade quilts, with patterns that were actually coded directions for fellow slaves on how to make their way north. No documentation exists to confirm that the house was part of the Underground Railroad. Burkle would have been careful to keep it secret and avoided the risk of writing about it. Still, it's a compelling story, which Burkle's descendants have confirmed, especially when paired with displays that remind the viewer of the realities that drove slaves to escape.

To get there go north on Third to Chelsea; turn left and then right onto Second. It's best to drive, and there's street parking available.

Open Monday through Saturday.

Stax Museum of American Soul Music $$
926 East McLemore Street
(901) 946-2535
www.soulsvilleusa.com
This jewel of a museum occupies the site of the legendary Stax Records, which turned out hits by Otis Redding, Carla Thomas, Isaac Hayes, and others in the 1960s and 1970s. By 1974 Stax was the fifth-largest black-owned business in the country, according to *Black Enterprise* magazine. The lively exhibits tell the Stax story, and they also provide a look at (and a listen to) the music of Memphis's Hi Records and soul music produced in other cities.

The museum is open daily. (For more details about Stax Museum, see the Memphis Music section of this chapter.)

W. C. Handy House $
352 Beale Street
(901) 527-3427 or (901) 522-1556
This tiny two-room house is where W. C. Handy, considered the "Father of the Blues," lived with his family from 1905 to 1918. Open Tuesday through Sunday. (See the Memphis Music section of this chapter for details.)

KIDSTUFF 👫

Memphis is a kid-friendly place with plenty of attractions and activities for youngsters of all ages, from IMAX films and skating to the oldest operating wooden roller coaster in North America and the famous Peabody ducks. In addition to visiting a world-class zoo and children's museum, kids can ride a trolley along the Mississippi River or eat at a restaurant that lets you write on the walls and blow toothpicks into the ceiling through a drinking straw.

Traveling with kids has its challenges, and sometimes that's not so much finding interesting stuff as it is locating nearby clean restrooms, gauging how much more walking a kid can stand before imploding, and finding a restaurant that serves both chicken fingers and arugula. (You'll find tips throughout this chapter on these points.)

The biggest challenge, though, can be the familiar complaints from the back seat: "This is so boring!" or "Not another museum!" and the proverbial "We never get to do anything we want to do!" Doing things that offer something for everyone is the secret to pleasing both children and parents. Of course, it never hurts to have an arsenal of kid activities to use as bargaining chips to exchange for what Mom and Dad want to do. Ice cream and amusement parks can buy a lot of art-museum time.

If your family is relocating to Memphis, these activities and sights will help you get acquainted with the best of what the city has to offer for kids. We list fair-weather options as well as rainy-day options, just in case the weather's not cooperating when you venture out.

Don't forget to check other chapters in this book for ideas. In particular, take a look at Parks and Recreation, where we list the area's bowling lanes, swimming pools, places to skateboard and/or roller-skate, and even a stable where you can rent horses and ponies for riding. The chapter also tells you where you can join a youth league team, and it lists the largest parks, both in the city and nearby. For more detailed information on where to find a convenient park with a playground, call the Memphis Parks Commission at (901) 454-5200, or visit www.cityofmemphis .org. To find the list of parks with playgrounds, click on "Community," then "Park Services," and then "Park Locations." You have to scroll down a bit to reach the "parks with play equipment" listing, but it's down there. Of course, you can always ask at your hotel, or find out from neighbors if you've just moved to Memphis. Other chapters worth a look include the Spectator Sports chapter, where you can find out when and where to catch a Redbirds baseball game in spring and summer or a Grizzlies basketball game during the NBA season. The Attractions chapter has a more complete list of things to see, whereas we stick to the most popular kids' attractions for this chapter.

The days of operation listed are in effect during summer months. They may be different at other times, so call ahead if you are visiting at other times of the year.

PRICE CODE

The following price code is the admission charge for one adult. Almost all the attractions charge less for senior citizens and children ages 6 through 12, while children younger than 6 years of age usually are admitted free of charge. Some attractions are free to everyone, and we identify those in the individual write-ups.

$	**Less than $5.00**
$$	**$5.00 to $9.50**
$$$	**$10.00 and up**

ATTRACTIONS
Downtown

If you're centering your visit in downtown Memphis, you'll find it's a happening place for kids, too. In the last decade, this area has been transformed from a desolate, forgotten wasteland to a lively city center. If you have only a few days to explore Memphis culture and history, spend them here. You may want to park your car and take the Main Street Trolley to the different sights.

Carriage Tours of Memphis   **$$$**
393 North Main Street
(901) 527-7542
www.carriagetoursofmemphis.com
In the afternoon horse-drawn carriages line up on Union Avenue in front of The Peabody hotel and on Beale Street at Second Street. Each driver decorates his own carriage, some with gaudy plastic flowers or an all-Elvis theme. All the carriage drivers have their dogs with them atop the driver's seat, so kids are immediately drawn there, giving the drivers a chance to sell you the tour. The usual tour takes you along Main Street (much of which is closed to cars), up to Confederate Park to see the riverboats, and past many other downtown sights. Drivers provide entertaining trivia and stories about Memphis. Tours are especially fun in cold weather, when everyone has to snuggle under blankets.

Most carriages can accommodate two adults and up to four children. A number

ℹ️ *Before you come to Memphis, check your hometown zoo and museum memberships. Reciprocal agreements abound, and you may be eligible for free or reduced admission at the Memphis Zoo, the Children's Museum of Memphis, and other attractions. Don't forget to bring your membership card to show at the ticket booth.*

of other operators do carriage tours, too, and you'll find them all lined up at The Peabody or on Beale Street. Expect to pay $45 for a 30-minute tour, not including the driver's tip.

Fire Museum of Memphis   **$$**
118 Adams Avenue
(901) 320-5650
www.firemuseum.com
The museum, located in a 1910 firehouse that once housed fire horses, is a big hit with children, who often are fascinated with firefighters as real-life heroes. From its authentic stall a talking fire horse narrates film clips about the development of fire fighting during the last century. On display are a horse-drawn steam pumper and two early fire engines, sparkling and shining as if a child's toy fire-truck collection had magically become the real thing. Two modern fire engines and an ambulance are available for kids to climb on, to imagine themselves as firefighters rushing to the biggest fire ever. Uniformed firefighters serve as the museum educators and patiently answer questions.

The most memorable and moving exhibit is the Fire Room, where you experience a fire in real time. Smoke fills the scene and the room becomes uncomfortably hot as the fire rages behind a glass screen. The film lasts only six minutes, but it makes a lasting impression of the seriousness and danger of fires. It's so realistic that it could be frightening to some children. Ask museum educators if you're unsure about whether it's right for your kids.

Open Monday through Saturday. Tuesday is two-for-Tuesday. There is no parking available at the museum, so look for a space in a nearby lot.

Main Street Trolley   **$**
Main Street, various stops
(901) 274-6282
www.matatransit.com
Riding the Main Street Trolley is great for getting places downtown so that you can take a break from the car. And for 50 cents a ride, it's the best entertainment

value in town. Kids love everything about it—looking down the tracks for a trolley, dropping correct change into the metered coin box, and pulling the cord over their heads to signal your stop. The trolley windows are usually open, and kids always want to hang their heads out to catch the breeze, a definite no-no.

The trolley runs along Main Street but also loops around for a great view of the Mississippi River. Save the Riverfront Loop ride (ask the driver if he's making the loop) for an afternoon when the kids have had enough and could use 45 minutes of down time. Just sitting, looking out the window, taking in the cityscape can revive even the most frazzled child. Now that the trolley line has been extended, you can go east along Madison Avenue. Except for the cool mosaics at each stop, though, there's not much to keep kids entertained.

Tickets are 50 cents per ride for all ages, except seniors and disabled persons, who pay 25 cents. You can also get a $2.50 daylong pass or a $6.00 three-day pass. Exact change is required.

(See the Getting Here, Getting Around chapter for more information about the Main Street Trolley and other transportation.)

Memphis Queen Riverboats $$$
45 Riverside Drive (at the foot of Monroe Avenue)
(901) 527-5694, (800) 221-6197
www.memphisqueen.com

The best place to see the river and the only way to be on the river, other than bringing your own boat, is to take a Memphis Queen Riverboats cruise. Plan to arrive about 30 minutes before departure and just take in the atmosphere. Upon boarding, each group poses for a photo. A 5 x 7 print commemorating your voyage is available after the cruise for $5.00. The photos, actually, are pretty good.

The captain narrates the tour, pointing out historical facts and locations on the river, but kids much prefer rambling around from the top observation deck to the second-level snack bar and down to

the first level, where a crew member sings and plays the piano. You'll hear everything from traditional river ballads and blues to Elvis's greatest hits. It may seem unlikely that kids would go for something as laid-back as a 90-minute riverboat ride, but you may be surprised at the impression the piano player, paddle wheel, and view of the river can make.

Cruises leave at 2:30 and 5:00 P.M. daily.

Mud Island River Park Free
125 North Front Street
(901) 576-7241, (800) 507-6507
www.mudisland.com

Think you could walk the length of the Mississippi in a day? Of course not, yet that's the main attraction of Mud Island River Park. A detailed replica of the Mississippi River flows through the park. You can take your shoes off and walk in the water as the Mississippi twists and turns on its way to New Orleans, where it pours into the Gulf of Mexico. When you make it to New Orleans, reward yourselves with ice cream or lemonade from the snack bar.

For a detailed chronology of the history and culture along the Mississippi, visit the Mississippi River Museum. Kids can climb aboard a reconstructed 19th-century steamboat, witness a battle aboard a Civil War gunboat, and listen to the river hollers and work songs of the river roustabouts. Guided tours are available.

To get to Mud Island, go to the ticket office on Front Street. You can walk across the pedestrian bridge, but it's much cooler for a few bucks to take the monorail across the Mississippi to the island.

Open daily. The park is free, but the museum is $8.00 for adults and $6.00 for children ages 5 through 17. Parking is available for a fee.

National Civil Rights Museum $$$
450 Mulberry Street
(901) 521-9699
www.civilrightsmuseum.org

If you are thinking about not visiting the National Civil Rights Museum because your kids won't like it, reconsider. The museum offers an exceptionally engaging audio tour for children, narrated by Linda Rosa Brown, a fictional young girl with a fresh, upbeat voice. She's named for two civil rights figures, Linda Brown of *Brown v. Topeka Board of Education* and Rosa Parks, who helped to spark the movement when she refused to give up her bus seat. Linda Rosa explains the history of the civil rights movement from the perspective of the "commitment, courage, cooperation, and responsibility" of the participants, some of whom were teenagers and children.

The museum is interactive, with exhibits like a real bus to enter and sit in, with a seated sculpture of Rosa Parks, and a bridge to march over with the marchers in Selma. The facts and visuals can be disturbing as the kids struggle to understand segregation, but, overall, the museum is positive, powerful, and affirming.

The National Civil Rights Museum offers free parking. Open daily. (For more information see the Attractions and African-American Heritage chapters.)

The Peabody Ducks   **Free**
149 Union Avenue
(901) 529-4000
www.peabodymemphis.com
Kids love watching these famous mallards march from the elevator to the ornate lobby fountain at 11:00 A.M. every morning, then back to the elevator at 5:00 P.M. Get there early, since it's not unusual for hundreds of people to show up for this peculiarly Memphis tradition. (See the Close-up in the Accommodations chapter for more details.)

Beale Street

Any trip to Memphis will undoubtedly include Beale Street. It's the second-most-visited street in America after Bourbon Street in New Orleans and is like a calmer Bourbon Street with smoke-filled clubs but no strip joints. With kids the best time to visit Beale is during the day or the early

evening. Later in the evening it becomes rowdier, and after 11:00 P.M. no one younger than age 21 is allowed on the street because of city liquor laws.

A. Schwab   **Free**
163 Beale Street
(901) 523-9782
A. Schwab is the oldest establishment on Beale. It was founded in 1876 by Abraham Schwab, an immigrant from Alsace, France, whose descendants still mind the store.

For kids, Schwab's is a treasure trove. The first floor is full of such tourist trinkets as Memphis bumper stickers, key rings, souvenir license plates, and more. Don't miss the Elvis playing cards featuring a different Elvis photo on each card. The other two floors carry, well, everything. You can find straight razors, cast-iron griddles, ladies' bloomers, lye soap, and men's pants up to size 74. From all ends of the store, kids are saying, "Mom, look at this!" "Mom, what is this?" and "People really used to wear these?" Browsing at A. Schwab is an adventure worth the couple of bucks you'll spend on tourist trinkets or maybe even something useful.

Open Monday through Saturday. (For more information see the Attractions and Shopping chapters.)

Beale Street Visitors Center   **Free**
200 Beale Street
(901) 543-2200
This small store on the edge of Handy Park has all kinds of souvenirs and tourist information, and, most important, large, clean bathrooms. It also sells cold drinks, bottled water, and snacks.

Memphis Police Museum   **Free**
159 Beale Street
(901) 579-0887
The Memphis Police Museum is small and not sophisticated in its presentation, but kids love the simple displays and the stories about cops and robbers. The museum houses memorabilia that ranges from a collection of guns and other confiscated weapons to period uniforms and an actual

jail cell from an old women's prison. Old newspaper clippings highlight events in Memphis history in which police played an important role, such as the riots following the assassination of Dr. Martin Luther King Jr. and Elvis's funeral. Did you know that the legendary "Machine Gun" Kelly was captured in Memphis? George Kelly Barnes came home to Memphis when he escaped from prison in 1933 and hid out at the home of his wife and mother-in-law. You'll find newspaper articles, mug shots of Kelly, and the scales on which he was weighed after he was arrested—a coveted item among Machine Gun Kelly collectors.

You wouldn't think this place is an actual operating police station, but it is, even if the officer at the tall dispatch desk wears an old-fashioned police uniform. Tucking in here for a look-see is a nice reprieve from the street.

Open every day.

Elsewhere in Memphis

The Children's Museum of Memphis $$
2525 Central Avenue
(901) 458-2678, (901) 320-3170
(recorded information line)
www.cmom.com

Kids wouldn't call this place a museum because they don't just walk around and look at boring stuff. Instead they get to touch and explore everything in what feels like a kid-size city.

Kids can "drive" the family minivan and even "fill it up" with gas or check out a dismantled car to see how the steering wheel controls the axles. They can set up an account at the bank and immediately withdraw play money to use at the Kid Market, a stocked, kid-size grocery store where they can pick out grocery items or pretend to be cashiers, actually scanning bar codes.

Elsewhere in the museum there's a real fire engine and a police motorcycle with a working siren. A 40-foot vertical maze called the Skyscraper intrigues kids as they slip through various-size holes to reach the top of the tower. Like any maze, many routes are dead ends, and it requires patience and industrious backtracking to get through it.

An art area with bins full of recycled lids, tubes, and paper awaits budding artists and sculptors. Glue, crayons, scissors, and hole punchers are supplied at each table, and the museum takes care of cleaning up the mess.

A separate enclosed area is especially geared toward toddlers and kids younger than age five. Here they can enjoy toys and climbers appropriate for their age group, and there are no bigger kids stepping on them.

The museum's $6-million expansion a few years ago added 8,000 square feet of exhibition space. It includes galleries aimed at older children, especially the 'tweeners, ages 10 through 12, who may think they're too old to enjoy the museum. There's a 50-foot slice of the Mississippi River, where visitors can manipulate bridges, dams, and barges. Elsewhere kids can climb into a real aircraft cockpit or a flight simulator. As always, scattered throughout are computer terminals with a variety of games available.

As for parents there are numerous benches, and the open environment makes it easy to sit and keep an eye on your child from a distance. Children can explore freely and independently and enjoy playing

If you travel with in-line skates, Tom Lee Park (downtown, next to the Mississippi River) is the best place to go, with free parking and open, paved pathways. If you cross the footbridge that goes over Riverside Drive, you'll find the Riverbluff Walkway, known locally as Riverwalk. It has smooth sidewalk with some slight hills as well as a fabulous view of the river. There's also Shelby Farms, the large suburban park, which has lots of paved paths tailor-made for in-line skates. Be sure to check the Skating listing in the Parks and Recreation chapter for more options.

with lots of other kids. The gift shop is as much fun as the museum, and there's also a snack area with vending machines.

Open Tuesday through Sunday.

Chucalissa Archaeological Museum $$
1987 Indian Village Drive
(901) 785-3160
www.chucalissa.org

In 1939, while excavating the site to develop a city park, workers discovered the ruins of a Choctaw Indian village. They named the village Chucalissa, which means "abandoned house." The park is dedicated to educating visitors about the Choctaw Indians who populated this area before European settlers arrived. A museum and reconstructed village have been developed over the years from the information and artifacts that archaeologists discovered on the site. On-site demonstrations of traditional dancing, food, and crafts can be seen during the Choctaw Festival the first week in August, or at other special events. The museum and reconstructed village are modest, to be sure, but for some reason kids find this attraction fascinating.

To get there from downtown, take Riverside Drive (which turns into I-55 South). Take the Third Street exit and go south. Turn right onto Mitchell (you should see a sign) and follow the signs.

Chucalissa is open Tuesday through Saturday.

Memphis Belle $
8101 Hornet Avenue, Millington
(901) 412-8071
www.memphisbelle.com

The legendary *Memphis Belle* is probably the most famous airplane of World War II, as the first bomber to safely complete 25 missions. After years of being on display at Mud Island River Park, the *Belle* is undergoing restoration in suburban Millington through 2005. But you can still visit the *Belle* and, in fact, enjoy a rare opportunity to see a state-of-the-art restoration in progress. Be sure to call ahead before you make the 14-mile trip to

see the *Memphis Belle*. (See the write-up in the Attractions chapter for more details.)

Memphis Zoo $$$
2000 Galloway
(901) 725-3452
www.memphiszoo.org

Kids of all ages flock to this world-class zoo to see exotic animals, watch the giant pandas from China, and ride the train and carousel. Situated in Overton Park just off Poplar Avenue, this attraction incorporates Egyptian decorations borrowed from the original Memphis that once flourished on the Nile. You can see this especially well at the zoo's entrance, a sight that impresses children with its sheer grandeur. Its exotic look immediately transports you to far-away landscapes where unfamiliar animals roam. You then walk along a promenade flanked by huge sculptures of safari animals. Each statue has signs that clearly ask you not to climb on the animals, but many kids (and even parents) can't resist.

Inside, among Egyptian carvings and sculptures, more than 400 species of animals from all over the world reside in renovated natural habitats. Just left of the entrance is Cat Country, where visitors stroll through overgrown plantings to peer at lions and tigers that surround the pathway. Huge screens of barely visible piano wire are all that separate you from these wild beasts.

At the Animals of the Night exhibition, you'll enter a dark and eerie exhibit hall with nocturnal animals in full motion. Given the darkness, the symphony of animal sounds, the intimidating closeness of the animals to the glass, and the many bats that swoop overhead, you may be glad to see the light of day again. If you have young children, scout ahead first to see whether this exhibit is too intense for them.

Not for the fainthearted is the Dragon's Lair, home to the world's largest lizards, the deadly Komodo dragons. Also known as dragon lizards, they can grow to a length of 10 feet. They look slow and real creepy but, actually, are quick to attack, and their bite is deadly. They're scary despite the thick glass wall separating them from visitors.

The newest addition is the zoo's China exhibition, a three-acre area that includes a pagoda and different animals from China. The stars, though, are two giant pandas, Le Le and Ya Ya, acquired from China in 2003. You must buy a special ticket ($3.00 for those age 2 and older), which admits you at a specific time. It's a good idea to reserve ahead during the busy summer season, but sometimes if it's not busy, you can go right in.

Be sure to check the information board near the main entrance that tells you about the zoo events for the day, which can include snakes or other animals on display for kids to touch and hold. Always fun is the seal feeding at 2:30 P.M. every day, where the sea lions are guided through their tricks, and their trainers tell you all about them.

It's easy and enjoyable to spend a whole day at the zoo, given its beautifully landscaped grounds and plentiful run-around room for kids. Picnic areas are marked, and the pleasant playground outside the Cat House Cafe is always popular with kids. The cafe has hamburgers, old-fashioned soft-custard ice cream, and other kid-friendly treats. Strollers are available for rent, which may come in handy for young children who get tired of walking.

Open every day. *Note:* If you have a large family, it might be more economical to purchase a Memphis Zoological Society membership.

The Pink Palace $-$$$
3050 Central Avenue
(901) 320-6362
www.memphismuseums.org
The Pink Palace is actually three attractions housed in one large pink mansion: the Pink Palace Museum, the Union Planters IMAX Theater, and the Sharpe Planetarium. The lavish mansion dates from the 1920s, when it was built of pink marble for Clarence Saunders, a Memphian who opened the world's first supermarket

and founded the Piggly-Wiggly grocery chain. Sadly, Saunders went bankrupt and no one ever lived in his pink marble palace.

The Pink Palace, IMAX theater, and planetarium are open daily. Adult tickets are $8.00 for the museum, $7.50 for IMAX, and $4.25 for the planetarium, or you can get a combination ticket for all three for $16.75.

Pink Palace Museum: The permanent exhibition of the Pink Palace traces the natural history of the Mid-South region from prehistoric dinosaurs to the present, as well as temporary exhibits that have included The Lost Spacecraft: Liberty Bell 7 Recovered. You can see fossil and dinosaur bones found in the area, Native American artifacts, and, best of all, a real shrunken head. This is easily the coolest (and grossest) thing in the museum, and you want to be sure to ask how they shrink it. You can also visit a kid-size replica of the very first supermarket, the invention that made Mr. Saunders rich enough to build his pink palace. One of the kids' favorites is the Clyde Park Miniature Circus. Mr. Park spent 50 years carving and motorizing this circus replica before donating it to the museum. The circus is turned on most days at 10:30 A.M., and kids stand on platforms to watch the delightful performance.

Union Planters IMAX Theater: At an IMAX theater you experience a movie on a screen four stories high and five stories wide while actually feeling the vibrations from the sound system.

The IMAX allows you to swim with dolphins, climb Mount Everest, or ride on the most outrageous roller coaster. There are no bad seats in the theater, but kids especially love the extra sensation and excitement of sitting in the thrill seats at the bottom of the screen. Films change constantly, so call (901-763-IMAX) for updated listings and show times.

Sharpe Planetarium: Too many of us are able to see only a few stars in the night sky these days, given air pollution and light in our cities. The Sharpe Planetarium, though, allows you to see the constellations as you have never seen them before. Guides explain the stories and history behind the stars and other astronomical discoveries and manipulate the sky so that you can see the movement of the stars. Lying back in a reclining chair, you will be amazed by the vastness and mystery of our galaxy.

RAINY-DAY ACTIVITIES

Don't let a little rain spoil your vacation. Story hours and pottery studios offer great rainy-day fun for families who've had their fill of museums, or check out the local movie listings for some big-screen fun.

Story Hours

Many bookstores and libraries in the area host story hours for children. These places also tend to have extensive children's sections and kid-friendly staffs as well as cafes for lunch at the bookstores, so you'll probably want to hang around before or after the story. Be sure to call ahead to verify story-hour times because times change throughout the year.

Barnes & Noble Booksellers, 2774 North Germantown Parkway, Cordova, (901) 386-2468: Tuesdays and Saturdays at 11:00 A.M.

Borders Books Music and Cafe, 6685 Poplar Avenue, Germantown, (901) 754-0770: Saturdays at 11:00 A.M.

Davis-Kidd Booksellers, 387 Perkins Road Extended, (901) 683-9801: Tuesdays and Wednesdays at 10:00 A.M., Thursdays, Fridays, and Saturdays at 11:00 A.M. (during the week for children age four and younger, all ages on Saturdays)

Memphis/Shelby County Public Library, Central Branch, 3030 Poplar Avenue, (901) 725-8819: Mondays and Tuesdays at 10:00 A.M. (preschoolers), Wednesdays at 10:00 A.M. (toddlers), and Tuesdays at 7:00 P.M. (families)

Pinocchio's Book Store, 688 West Brookhaven Circle, (901) 767-6586: Fridays at 10:30 A.M.

Pottery Studios

Both of these studios are next to shopping areas, so family members who don't want to paint pottery can go shopping or find a snack without going too far. Paint-a-Piece is next to the Old Navy store in Wolfchase Commons shopping center (there's also Gelato Café next to Home Depot in the center) and just down Germantown Parkway from Wolfchase Galleria Mall (which has a movie theater). Seize the Clay is just across a busy parking lot from Oak Court Mall.

**Paint-a-Piece Pottery
8075 Giacosa Place, Cordova
(901) 387-3473**

**Seize the Clay
555 Perkins Road Extended
(901) 683-2529**

Amusements and Activities

**Jillian's
Free admission, pay for activities
Second Street at Peabody Place
(901) 543-8000
www.jillians.com**
Jillian's is sort of an electronic three-story playhouse with something for everyone, even teenagers. On the top floor is the arcade to beat all arcades, with a huge variety of game and virtual experiences. (The games are pricey, something that's not immediately apparent with Jillian's system of buying and spending points.) One of the most popular activities is virtual bowling, with amazingly realistic graphics. For the real thing check out the cosmic bowling on the first floor. The electronic atmosphere of lights, hip music,

food, and drink make this cooler than ordinary bowling. For younger kids you can program your lane to sprout bumpers so their experience isn't a continuum of gutter balls. The second floor has big-screen TVs with sports, pool tables, Ping-Pong, and a full-service restaurant.

The best time for younger kids and teens to have maximum access to the games and activities is during the day until about 6:00 P.M. Jillian's is not a good bet for kids later in the evening.

Libertyland Amusement Park $$$
940 Early Maxwell
(901) 274-1776

This old-fashioned theme park opened on July 4, 1976, in honor of the Bicentennial, thus the name. It's the largest amusement park with the best selection of rides in town and something for all ages. Its two roller coasters offer the best of the old and the new. The Revolution takes only 22 seconds but you spend half of that time upside down. It's one of those rides that is so scary and "thrilling" that you will want to ride it again and again. The Zippin Pippin, the oldest operating wooden roller coaster in North America, may look lame compared with the high-tech Revolution, but riding it may change your mind. The noise of the cars against the wooden tracks makes you think the whole structure will collapse any second, and as an unintended thrill, the cars' wheels actually leave the tracks a few times as if it were getting a running jump on its grand descents.

Other Libertyland attractions include a spectacular carousel, live stage shows, a playground, and shade provided by the mature landscaped grounds. The Grand Carousel, built in 1909 by the Dentzel Carousel Co., is listed on the National Register of Historic Places.

For hungry families Libertyland offers the best of "fair" food, such as pronto pups and cotton candy, as well as on-site restaurants with sit-down meals and plenty of air-conditioning.

Libertyland is open Wednesday through Sunday during most of the sum-

If the weather isn't cooperating, one indoor spot in downtown Memphis has something for everyone in the family. At Peabody Place Entertainment and Retail Center on Second Street at Peabody Place, you'll find Jillian's and the Putting Edge for games; Gap Kids, Claire's, DAPY, and Tower Records for shopping; Starbucks for the grown-ups; and best of all, ice cream and pizza for everyone.

mer. Ask about the unlimited ride ticket, perfect for kids who can't ride the roller coaster often enough.

Entertainment Centers and Laser Games

An outing to play miniature golf used to be just that, but now, the miniature-golf parks have turned into something-for-everyone "entertainment centers." The main one in Memphis is Golf and Games Family Park, situated just off I-240. Formerly called Putt-Putt Family Park, it truly has something for everyone: miniature golf, bumper boats, go-karts, kiddie rides, batting cages, arcade games, and party rooms. There's also a driving range and LaserTron. You can pay for activities a la carte, but the best deal is a wristband for about $20 that gets you into almost all the activities. The arcades at this park are happenin' and include basics such as air hockey as well as the newer simulator games. All the games give out tickets, which you can exchange for those junk-toy prizes that kids love.

Golf and Games is open every day. In addition to the LaserTron there, Laser Quest offers laser tag and an arcade at Poplar Plaza shopping center, situated at the eastern edge of midtown. These high-tech games are good bets if you are trying to amuse teenagers.

Golf and Games Family Park
5484 Summer Avenue
(901) 386-2992
www.putputtmemphis.com

Laser Quest
Poplar Avenue at Highland Street
(901) 324-4800
www.laserquest.com

KID-FRIENDLY DINING

In truth, most casual restaurants in Memphis are used to kids and reasonably accommodating to families. But the places we list here are truly unflappable. Of course, you'll also find the usual lineup of kid-friendly chains, from McDonald's and Chuck E. Cheese to Chili's and On the Border. They offer not only children's plates, but also coloring books, crayons, or other amusements to help keep everybody happy. Most of these can be found in the suburban areas, particularly along Germantown Parkway in Cordova. Our list is a bit skewed to downtown, since that's where so many people stay when they are visiting Memphis. As always, the challenge of eating out with kids is to find restaurants that welcome children but also have good food for adults. Many of these are winners on both fronts, and all of them have an easygoing, casual atmosphere.

See the Restaurants chapter for the explanation of the price codes.

The Arcade $
540 South Main Street
(901) 526-5757
One of the oldest restaurants in Memphis, the Arcade has great pizza available by the pie or by the slice. This downtown favorite also serves a good breakfast anytime and has great milkshakes.

Bol a Pasta $-$$
2200 North Germantown Parkway
Cordova
(901) 384-7988

3160 Village Shops Drive, Germantown
(901) 757-5609
Of all the Memphis restaurants operated by the Grisanti family, these are the ones designed and operated with an eye to keeping families with kids happy. These brightly appointed suburban restaurants serve pastas of all kinds, so the kids can have spaghetti and the parents can enjoy something a bit more gourmand such as scampi, steak, or the house specialty, sirloin steak carbonara with pasta alfredo.

Brontë $
387 Perkins Road Extended
(901) 374-0881
www.daviskidd.com
Situated inside Davis-Kidd Booksellers, this restaurant is a favorite for families and especially for moms and kids at lunch. Many families like to make an outing of visiting the store's kid-friendly children's area, then stopping at Brontë, where salads and other fare appeal to parents and kid plates are a hit with younger diners. There are a lot of yummy desserts, too, and espresso drinks for mom and dad. The restaurant can be really crowded after story hours.

Dyers Burgers $
205 Beale Street
(901) 527-DYER
Dyers is a kid-friendly place to eat on Beale Street, with shiny, 1950s diner decor and hamburgers fried in Memphis's most famous grease. (See the Restaurants chapter for the full story.) It's open all afternoon, so take a rest from sightseeing. Try an old-fashioned milkshake or a Coke float, or if you're hungry, have a burger, fries, or chili.

El Porton $
65 South Highland Street
(901) 452-7330

1805 North Germantown Parkway
Cordova
(901) 624-9358

2095 Merchants Row, Germantown
(901) 754-4268

1016 West Poplar Avenue, Collierville
(901) 854-5770
This kid-friendly Mexican restaurant is generous with the chips and has a nice outdoor eating area. It gets crowded especially around happy hour, so go early.

Garibaldi's $
3530 Walker Avenue
(901) 327-6111
Garibaldi's is a little on the grungy side, but kids love the combination of pizza and game arcade. It's located in the University of Memphis area between midtown and East Memphis.

Hard Rock Café $-$$
315 Beale Street
(901) 529-0007
If your kids are clamoring for Hard Rock Café, you'll find it at Beale and Fourth, with the usual menu, rock memorabilia, and merchandise shop. Incidentally, the chain was started by a Memphis native, Isaac Tigrett, but a Hard Rock didn't open up here until the 1990s.

Huey's $
77 South Second Street
(901) 527-2700
www.hueys.cc
Look up when you enter. Yes, those are toothpicks in the ceiling. Each has been spit there through a straw—a challenge that appeals to adults and kids alike. Also bring a Sharpie marker to write on the walls, another Huey's tradition. The menu includes great burgers, sandwiches, salads, and a kids' menu that features the ever-popular chicken on a stick. There's also a midtown location, as well as several in the suburbs. (See the write-up in the Restaurants chapter for details.)

Memphis Pizza Cafe $
2087 Madison Avenue
(901) 726-5343
Young sports teams and families with children all flock to this casual pizza joint, which serves up thin-crust pizza with the toppings of your choice. This is the midtown location closest to downtown Memphis, which has a pleasant back deck in addition to its dining rooms, but there are other Pizza Cafes in East Memphis, Cordova, and Bartlett, too. (See the write-up in the Restaurants chapter for details.)

The Peanut Shoppe $
24 Main Street
(901) 525-1115
Okay, you probably couldn't make a meal here, but hot roasted peanuts, snow cones, and candy are a great treat after riding the trolley or taking in the sights.

Sean's Deli and Smooth Moves $
75 South Main Street
(901) 529-1000

1651 Union Avenue
(901) 274-3917
This Greek deli serves great gyros, a huge cheeseburger with fries, and a variety of fruit smoothies (be sure to drink them slowly to avoid a brain freeze).

Sekisui Downtown $-$$
160 Union Avenue
(901) 523-0001
This sushi bar, located in the Holiday Inn Select, is a good compromise play because it has a sushi menu, a Japanese menu, and an American menu. Sushi lovers will be happy, and nonsushi eaters can choose from a menu of great burgers, fries, grilled cheese, and clam chowder. Other Sekisui locations, while they don't have an American menu, are reasonably child-friendly. (See the write-up in the Restaurants chapter for details.)

Spaghetti Warehouse $
40 West Huling Street
(901) 521-0907
The atmosphere of this family-oriented restaurant, where you can eat in a trolley car or a king-size bed/booth, is big excitement for kids, even if adults may find the food a little dull. You can take the trolley to get here, as it's located next to the tracks.

ANNUAL EVENTS

From a celebration of Elvis Presley's birthday and Dr. Martin Luther King Jr.'s birthday in January to the giant New Year's Eve party on Beale Street, Memphis has a respectable calendar of annual events. There's truly something for everyone, and some events also include elements of the bizarre. After all it's not everywhere you find female, Japanese, and dwarf Elvis impersonators (Elvis Week), or a stage full of people competing for who can best squeal like a pig (World Championship Barbecue Cooking Contest). Although many events are organized around sports and the arts, it's not surprising that the main events are organized around the things Memphis is best known for: Elvis, music, and barbecue.

Certainly the most international event is Elvis Tribute week, the August anniversary of Presley's death in Memphis in 1977. Each year, despite the sweltering temperatures, fans from all over the world roll into town for a three-ring circus of official and unofficial events, culminating with the candlelight vigil in front of Graceland Mansion on August 15, the eve of the anniversary of his death. A more modest celebration in January commemorates Elvis's birthday.

In terms of live music, the big event is the Beale Street Music Festival, which takes place in early May. It attracts national acts as well as local talent for a three-day, four-stage party next to the Mississippi River. Also notable are the annual W. C. Handy Awards, which around that time honors blues musicians and attracts a who's who of that universe to the presentation ceremony (and to Beale Street clubs later). Other favorites include the Beale Street Zydeco Festival in February and the Memphis Music and Heritage Festival during Labor Day weekend. Just about any other weekend, though, you'll find plenty of music on Beale Street and elsewhere. Check out local papers or just ask around.

A highlight on the events calendar is Memphis in May, a monthlong celebration that gives locals a chance to shake off the winter doldrums and attracts many out-of-towners. It includes about 100 events, big and small, as the city honors a different country each year and puts on three main events. The music festival takes place during the first weekend, then the World Championship Barbecue Cooking Contest two weeks later. To wrap things up, Sunset Symphony takes place during the final weekend. It's an outdoor performance by the Memphis Symphony Orchestra along Old Man River, coupled with fireworks.

As for professional sports events, the Kroger St. Jude and the Cellular South Cup tennis championship takes place in February, attracting a who's who of tennis stars, while in May the FedEx St. Jude Classic is a stop on the PGA Tour, which attracts top players to Memphis. College-football fans flock to the city each year for the Southern Heritage Classic in September, an annual matchup between Tennessee State University and Jackson State University, and for the AutoZone Liberty Bowl in December, when the Conference USA champion takes on the top team of the Mountain West Conference.

Another focal point for annual events is black history, as the National Civil Rights Museum commemorates both the birthday of Dr. Martin Luther King Jr. and the anniversary of his assassination in Memphis in 1968. In October there's the Pink Palace Crafts Fair, featuring local artists and artisans as well as their counterparts from all over the country.

In this chapter we list Memphis's top annual events, but you can find great stuff to do on just about any given weekend. Beale Street has a number of other music festivals each year, including events during Labor Day weekend and on St. Patrick's Day, and it offers great music even on ordinary weekends. Plus, there are neighborhood festivals, 10K races, fund-raising events, parades, independent film festivals, and outdoor concerts. For more information, check the *Memphis Flyer,* the city's free alternative weekly, or the Memphis Playbook section of the city's daily newspaper, the *Commercial Appeal,* which comes out on Fridays. Their Web sites are www.memphisflyer.com and www .commercialappeal.com.

JANUARY

Elvis Presley Birthday Celebration
Graceland Mansion
3734 Elvis Presley Boulevard
(901) 332-3322, (800) 238-2000
www.elvis.com
For Elvis fans who can't celebrate their idol enough, every year Graceland Mansion sponsors a weekend-long series of events to commemorate Elvis Presley's January 8 birthday. The events vary but always include a traditional proclamation of Elvis Presley Day ceremony on the front lawn of Graceland. In prior years the events have included a dance party, free birthday cake to Graceland visitors, and a special musical event. It's a miniversion of the big event, Elvis Week, which takes place in August to commemorate the King's death.

Dr. Martin Luther King Jr.'s Birthday
National Civil Rights Museum
450 Mulberry Street
(901) 521-9699
www.civilrightsmuseum.org
Every year on the Martin Luther King Jr. federal holiday weekend, the National Civil Rights Museum sponsors activities that include programs aimed at educating children about the life and work of Dr. King. A highlight is always a celebration of Dr. King's birthday, which takes place at the museum on that Monday. In April on the anniversary of his death, there's also a candlelight vigil or other event to commemorate his untimely death in Memphis in 1968.

FEBRUARY

Beale Street Zydeco Festival
Beale Street
(901) 529-0999
www.bealestreet.com
The street gets a dash of Louisiana spice at this popular festival, which features small family bands as well as zydeco stars such as Wayne Touts and Chubby Carrier. An annual event since 1989, the festival also brings you Cajun cooking, a fitting accompaniment to the music. Some years, Mardi Gras falls on the same weekend, which means a big parade and other festivities. It's a wristband event, so $15 gets you into most of the clubs on Beale, where the bands put on their shows.

The Memphis Convention & Visitors Bureau publishes a detailed calendar of events four times a year, which is available free. Call (901) 543-5333 to have one mailed to you.

Kroger St. Jude and the Cellular South Cup
The Racquet Club of Memphis
5111 Sanderlin Avenue
(901) 765-4400
www.krogerstjude.com
This annual men's and women's tennis event, which takes place in mid-February, brings in some of the biggest names in tennis as they compete on state-of-the-art indoor courts at the Racquet Club of Memphis. It's the only indoor tournament in the world to host a men's and women's combined event, attracting 32 men's singles players and 32 women's singles players, as well as 16 men's and 16 women's doubles teams to compete for more than $800,000 in prizes. The tournament organizers point out that of the 12 men who have finished the year ranked No. 1 in the world since 1976, 9 of them have played and won the Memphis tournament. Past winners have included Andy Roddick, Lisa Raymond, and Michael Chang, who

made this his first pro tournament in 1988. The event, which had been the men's Kroger St. Jude International Indoor Tennis Championship, became a men's and women's tournament in 2002 when its organizers acquired the Cellular South women's event that had been held in Oklahoma City.

Singles and doubles matches are played Monday through Sunday, with women's finals on Saturday night and men's finals on Sunday afternoon. Daily tickets range from $5.00 to $45.00, week-long tickets are $175.00 to $280.00, and weekend tickets are $170.00 and $200.00.

APRIL

Africa in April Cultural Awareness Festival
Robert Church Park
Beale and Fourth Streets
(901) 947-2133
www.africainapril.org
This three-day festival is a point of pride for the city's African Americans, who gather here to reconnect with their African roots. The festival, which honors a different country in Africa each year, includes children's activities, performances by color-fully costumed African dancers and musicians from the honored country and elsewhere, as well as storytelling, both onstage and in booths. Visitors of any heritage enjoy browsing the marketplace—with vendors selling jewelry, artifacts, and colorful African-made shawls and other clothing—and taking in performances that might include Jamaican reggae or African-American gospel. An annual event since 1986, Africa in April takes place in and

![i]
Many of these annual events have special days or hours during which seniors, children, or in some cases all ages get discounted or free admission. Call the numbers listed with each event, or check their Web sites for more information.

around Robert Church Park, having out-grown the smaller W. C. Handy Park far-ther down Beale Street. Admission is free.

MAY

Beale Street Music Festival
Tom Lee Park
Riverside Drive at Beale
(901) 525-4611
www.thebealestreetmusicfestival.com
For music-minded Memphians and a growing number of visitors, attending the annual Beale Street Music Festival is a rite of spring not to be missed. Held the first weekend in May along the Mississippi River at the foot of Beale Street, the festival celebrates Memphis music and the musical sounds it has produced or influenced, including blues, rock, gospel, R&B, alternative, and soul. The event, which outgrew Beale Street years ago, has become a three-day, four-stage extravaganza with performances by some 60 bands. The lineup generally includes a remarkable range of performers, from headliners such as Willie Nelson and Sheryl Crow, or the latest chart-topping alternative band to homegrown gospel and blues groups. The 2003 lineup, for example, included Joe Cocker, Steve Winwood, Booker T. & the MGs, Sheryl Crow, KoKo Taylor, Jerry Lee Lewis, Big Star, LL Cool J, Little Milton, and the North Mississippi Allstars. In addition to the music, there's a great view of the Mississippi River (particularly at sunset), plenty of people watching, cold beer, and vendors selling barbecue, pronto pups, grilled corn, and other festival food. Do bring cash, a blanket, and a photo ID (if you're drinking), but don't bring your own food and drink, cameras, or lawn chairs.

The festival, part of the monthlong Memphis in May International celebration, attracts more than 140,000 people over the three days. Recently, tickets began to sell out in advance, so it's a good idea to buy them early. Tickets are $22.50 per day at the gate or $19.50 if purchased in advance. The best deal, though, is to buy a three-day pass in advance, which costs $45 but must be purchased before April 23.

Memphis Kemet Jubilee
Various locations
(901) 774-1118

Formerly known as the Cotton Makers Jubilee, this annual event has a rich history dating from 1936, when the city's African American community, excluded from Memphis Cotton Carnival across town, created a celebration of its own. The highlight is the Jubilee parade, the city's largest. The parade, which goes along Second Street from Exchange Street to Beale Street before turning east, features more than 100 marching bands from Tennessee and surrounding states as well as floats carrying Jubilee participants, including its king and queen. It's mainly a family event and features a youth leadership program as well.

World Championship Barbecue Cooking Contest
Tom Lee Park
Riverside at Beale
(901) 525-4611
www.memphisinmay.org

This is Memphis's biggest, craziest, most eccentric party of the year. Some 250 barbecue teams, with names like Pork Me Tender and Squealer Dealer, gather in mid-May to compete for cash prizes at this, the largest pork-barbecue cooking contest in the world. While team members tend to the serious business of cooking prize-winning ribs and other pork delicacies in preparation for the judges' visits on Saturday morning, there's plenty of time for fun. Its organizers describe it as "the Super Bowl, Mardi Gras, and one bodacious party rolled into one," but one might just as easily describe it as bizarre. There's a hog-calling contest, the Ms. Piggy contest (contestants tend to be hairy and male despite the makeup and dresses), and other eccentricities such as the Viva Las Porkas chapel for renewing wedding vows.

The atmosphere is reminiscent of an oversized fraternity cookout, producing clouds of barbecue aroma that permeate downtown Memphis as well as your clothes. One of the oddities of the festival is that unless you are invited by a team, you won't get to taste the barbecue you smell cooking. Organizers have remedied that situation by setting up vendors, including contest winners, to sell barbecue. Other festival food and cold beer are available as well.

It goes without saying that if anyone invites you to visit his or her barbecue team, say "Yes!" immediately and get passes if possible. Although it's fun to people watch, see the entertainment, and check out the sometimes outrageously decorated team sites, it's a better party if you hang out with a team.

Admission is $7.00 per day for adults and children ages 7 through 12, and free for children age 6 and younger. On Thursday and Friday admission is free during lunchtime (10:00 A.M. to 2:00 P.M.). The party atmosphere gets rowdy later at night, so plan an early visit if you're bringing the kids.

W. C. Handy Blues Awards
Downtown Memphis
(901) 527-2583
www.handyawards.com

The blues' highest honor is bestowed at this annual awards presentation, also known as the Blues Grammys. The awards, presented in the city where the blues first became famous, attract the best-known names in blues: B. B. King, Taj Mahal, Bonnie Raitt, Ruth Brown, and Little Milton. Named after the Father of the Blues (W. C. Handy wrote the first blues music when he lived in Memphis), the awards show takes place in downtown Memphis in late April or May, usually around the time of the Beale Street Music Festival. This is a great time for blues fans to go club-hopping on Beale Street, as many of these stars find their way to the birthplace of the blues after the ceremony. The Handy Awards, put on by the Memphis-based Blues Foundation, celebrated its 25th anniversary in 2004.

Volunteering can be a great way to enjoy some of these annual events, while meeting some new people and helping organizers put on a successful show. Even if there's no money involved, there's usually a free T-shirt and free admission. Call organizers of the individual events for more information.

FedEx St. Jude Classic
Tournament Players Club at Southwind
3325 Club at Southwind
(901) 748-0534
www.hushyall.com
This annual stop on the PGA tour brings top players to Memphis every year, along with television cameras. An estimated 150,000 spectators watch as the players compete for a $4.7 million purse. The FedEx St. Jude Classic is played at Tournament Players Club at Southwind in the southeastern suburbs in late May. The current date represents a switch from the early days, when the tournament was in August amid the 90-plus temperatures and high humidity that plague Memphis at that time of year. The tournament was started in 1958 as the Memphis Open and changed names as TV-actor Danny Thomas, then St. Jude Children's Hospital, and finally FedEx sponsored the event. The event has raised more than $14 million for St. Jude Children's Research Hospital since 1970. Among the tournament's highlights was in 1977, when golfer Al Geiberger shot a 59, a PGA-tour one-round record. Memphis fans have a soft spot for hometown players, including John Daly, Loren Roberts, and Shaun Micheel, who won the PGA championship in 2003.

One-day tickets are $20 in advance (before April 15) and $25 at the gate for adults. Season tickets, which are good all week, are $65 in advance and $80 at the gate for adults, and $15 in advance and $18 at the gate for youth (ages 5 through 16).

JUNE

Carnival Memphis
Various locations
(901) 278-0243
www.carnivalmemphis.org
Established in 1931 as Memphis Cotton Carnival to draw attention to the cotton industry and to promote business, this yearly event mimics New Orleans Mardi Gras festivities by featuring a royal court with king and queen as well as krewes, the participating clubs. Each year Carnival honors an industry that has had a major impact on the local economy, and participants come from all over the Mid-South. It continues largely as a society event, although at one time it was much more visible, with public festivities such as a parade and fireworks. At present most of its parties and events are invitation only, taking place in early June.

Germantown Charity Horse Show
Germantown Charity Horse Show Arena
7745 Poplar Pike, Germantown
(901) 754-0009
www.gchs.org
This five-day event, held in early June, is one of the largest all-breed horse shows in the country, with more than 300 classes. As a Mid-America States Cup (MASCUP) event, it draws the top national riders and features Tennessee walking horses, saddle horses, and hunter jumpers as well as amateur events such as horse-drawn carriages. A major highlight is the awarding of the $25,000 Lincoln Grand Prix of Germantown. For spectators there's plenty of picnicking room in the grassy natural bowl in which the arena is built, as well as cotton candy, barbecue, snow cones, and other goodies for sale. The events take place in an arena built in 1954 especially for the horse show, where 35,000 to 40,000 people gather over the five days to watch the horses, and to see and be seen. Admission is $5.00 for adults and $3.00 for children. Box seats are also available.

Ducks Unlimited Great Outdoors Festival
Agricenter International
7777 Walnut Grove Road
(901) 758-3825
www.ducks.org
This three-day festival, which takes place in early June, is geared toward hunters and other outdoors enthusiasts, with interactive exhibitions and demonstrations of the latest in sporting equipment. You can check out canoes, camping equipment, bows and arrows, fishing gear, and other equipment. There are even special tracks for testing ATVs, bikes, and climbing equipment. The sponsor is Ducks Unlimited, a wetlands conservation group whose members are mostly waterfowl hunters. Its headquarters is in Memphis, just a stone's throw from the festival location.

Tickets are $10.00 for adults and $5.00 for children (ages 6 through 12) in advance; at the gate, tickets are $15.00 for adults and $8.00 for children. Kids younger than age 6 and dogs on leashes are free (rabies tag and cleaning up after dogs are required), as is parking.

JULY

July 4th Fireworks
Various locations
In Memphis, instead of one main event, you'll find a number of fireworks exhibitions, usually coupled with a concert or other festivities, all over the Memphis metropolitan area. Some take place on July 4th proper, whereas others take place the night before. Check local newspapers for the exact locations, dates, and times. The two major fireworks displays are held downtown and in Shelby Farms. Among the most popular is the annual WMC Star-Spangled Celebration, which after years downtown has moved to Shelby Farms near Germantown. Taking its place downtown is the Red, White & Blues celebration at Tom Lee Park. Both events also feature musical entertainment and are free to the public. In East Memphis the Memphis Botanic Garden hosts a pops concert that features fireworks; lawn seats are $15. Other free fireworks exhibits take place in Millington, Bartlett, Germantown, and Collierville. Don't forget about Tunica, Mississippi, where you'll see a splashy fireworks show done in fine Las Vegas style.

AUGUST

Elvis Week
Graceland Mansion
3734 Elvis Presley Boulevard
(901) 332-3322, (800) 238-2000
www.elvis.com
At a time when Memphians are hitting back-to-school sales or looking to escape the heat, thousands of Elvis Presley fans are pouring into Memphis from all over the world to commemorate the anniversary of the King's death. It has been more than 25 years since Elvis left the building, but the flame still burns bright in the hearts of his fans. Usually about 30,000 to 35,000 come through Graceland that week. The highlight is the candlelight vigil in front of Graceland Mansion the evening of August 15. The street is closed off that night, as mourners line up in front for their turn to walk up the driveway of Graceland, candles in hand, to pay their respects at his grave in the Meditation Garden. Everyone should see this ritual once, but remember, it's as serious as church for many, so if you go to observe, be respectful to the true faithful who've saved all year to be here for this moment.

Dozens of other events take place during the week, many of them sponsored by Graceland, such as Elvis—The Concert. This virtual-reality show at the Mid-South Coliseum features vintage footage of Elvis singing, along with former band members who perform the music live. "Tribute artists" from all over the world compete in what most of us would call an Elvis-impersonator contest, which runs for several days.

All over Memphis locals get into the act as well. The Orpheum summer film series features the 1970 classic concert film, *Elvis, That's the Way It Is,* this week, while the Pink Palace's Sharpe Planetarium puts on its annual Elvis: Legacy in Lights laser show. Various forums are held around town to allow fans to hear about their hero from professional and personal associates of the late King. There's no charge to visit the grounds of Graceland Mansion on vigil night, and charges vary for other events. You'll find a calendar of Elvis Week events and ticket information in local newspapers.

SEPTEMBER

Memphis Music & Heritage Festival
Downtown Memphis
(901) 525-3655
www.southernfolklore.com
If you are interested in hearing the music that originated in Memphis and the surrounding Delta area, don't miss this Labor Day weekend festival held each year by the Center for Southern Folklore. The organizers bring together a remarkable collection of musicians, ranging from local gospel quartets and homegrown bluesmen to the original Sun Records rockabilly hit-makers and Memphis soul royalty such as Carla Thomas. But it's not just music from the past, since contemporary young musicians also perform blues, new soul, gospel, and other current music at the festival. With modest stages set up in and around the Center for Southern Folklore, the event is on a much smaller, more human scale than the Beale Street Music Festival in May. You may not hear the latest, slickest chart-toppers, but you won't miss them, not with performers such as blues performer Blind Mississippi Morris, Memphis music guru Jim Dickinson, Mississippi-bred folksinger Kate Campbell, rockabilly legends Eddie Bond and Billy Lee Riley, and the Last Chance Jug Band. Best of all, the performances are all free.

Southern Heritage Classic
Liberty Bowl Memorial Stadium
(901) 398-6655
www.southernheritageclassic.com

This mid-September football contest between archrivals Tennessee State University and Jackson State University fills the Liberty Bowl and spills over into one of the biggest party weekends of the year. Alumni of these historically black colleges and other football fans pour into the city for the Saturday-night game and other activities, ranging from concerts and tailgate parties to the Ed "Too Tall" Jones Golf Classic and the Classic Fashions & Brunch event. The weekend is also an opportunity for informal reunions of the schools' alumni, many of whom live in the region. Many of the events are fund-raisers that funnel tens of thousands of dollars to the two schools and to charities, so very few of them are free. A highlight is the Dr. Pepper High School Battle of the Bands, which features top high-school show bands and their dance routines. During the game's halftime show, the contest moves from football to music as the JSU Aristocrat of Bands and TSU Sonic Boom of the South strut their stuff. Tickets for the game range from $10 to $30 for box seats.

Cooper-Young Festival
Cooper Street at Young Avenue
(901) 276-7222
www.cooperyoung.com
This is the biggest street party in midtown, as the hip, artsy Cooper-Young neighborhood rolls out the red carpet every fall. The festival, started in 1988, today draws more than 40,000 people, who flock here to enjoy the arts and crafts, food vendors, people watching, and, of course, beer. Booths line the streets, and local musicians take to the stages at this all-day event. Admission is free, and parking is every man for himself.

The Mid-South Fair
Mid-South Fairgrounds
(901) 274-8800
www.midsouthfair.com
The Mid-South Fair, a Memphis tradition since 1856, attracts about half a million people each fall, as Memphians and

country-come-to-town visitors alike pour in to check out carnival rides, pronto pups, and other junk-food classics, exhibitions, concerts, and rodeo events. The fair starts in late September and runs for 10 days, usually coinciding with the welcome arrival of cooler weather.

There's truly something for everyone at the fair, which has more than 60 rides, 150 food vendors, 200 exhibitors, youth programs that include 4H competitions, the largest amateur youth talent contest in the world, and the Championship Rodeo. Many go for the rides and the dazzling array of carnival favorites such as candied apples and funnel cakes, whereas others are there to compete in livestock shows, homemade-ice-cream contests, and other events. Agriculture continues to be the backbone of the fair, so you'll find livestock exhibits, sheep-dog trials, farm-and-garden-produce exhibits, and horticulture educational programs. The fair takes place at the 176-acre fairgrounds, bound by Central Avenue, East Parkway, Southern Avenue, and Hollywood. Parking is $5.00 and can be accessed from all sides except from Eastern Parkway.

Admission is $7.00 for adults (48 inches and taller), $3.00 for children (under 48 inches), and free for children age 3 and younger. Ask about Wristband Days, when in addition to the admission you can also buy a wristband that admits you to unlimited rides.

OCTOBER

Pink Palace Museum Crafts Fair
Audubon Park
(901) 320-6320
www.artsandcraftsfestival.org
This big, yearly fund-raiser for the Pink Palace Museum System, a favorite since 1973, draws at least 30,000 people each year. Held early in October and organized by the Friends of the Pink Palace, this four-day event features craftspersons

from all over the country selling one-of-a-kind jewelry, fused and blown glass, pottery, and other handmade goods. You can watch artisans making baskets, spinning and weaving, turning wood, and demonstrating other crafts. There are also children's activities, including a petting zoo, as well as a culinary tent where fairgoers can buy handmade preserves and other goodies. If you have a sweet tooth, don't miss the Friends' Donut Tent, featuring fresh, homemade donuts.

Advance tickets are $5.00 for adults, $3.00 for seniors, and $2.00 for children. Admission at the door is $7.00 for adults, $4.00 for seniors, and $3.00 for children. Two-day adult passes are available for $8.00 in advance, $12.00 at the door. Parking is $2.00.

DECEMBER

AutoZone Liberty Bowl Football Classic
Liberty Bowl Stadium
(901) 795-7700
This annual matchup between the winners of the Conference USA and the Mountain West Conference draws thousands of college-football fans to Memphis in late December to cheer on their team. Okay, it's not the Sugar Bowl or one of the more prestigious football contests that take place around the New Year, and it rarely fills Liberty Bowl Stadium, but it's a great party for fans of the two teams. AutoZone took over sponsorship in 2003 for what had been the AXA Liberty Bowl. The Liberty Bowl originated in Philadelphia, which explains the name, and was moved to Memphis in 1965, when its founder decided the Northeast was too cold. This bowl game made history in 1982, when legendary University of Alabama head coach Paul "Bear" Bryant ended his career with a game against University of Illinois. *Note:* If the University of Memphis Tigers, a Conference USA team, ever make it to the Liberty Bowl, expect the party of the century.

Beale Street New Year's Eve Celebration
Beale Street
(901) 526–0110
www.bealestreet.com
On New Year's Eve Beale Street is to Memphis what Times Square is to New York City, namely, the place where crowds gather to bring in the New Year. It's a huge, rowdy outdoor party, whether there's an organized event or not. The clubs on Beale Street are sure to be hopping as well, offering live music as well as libations and respite from the cold, while there are often bands such as the North Mississippi Allstars playing in W. C. Handy Park, too. Most years sponsors set up a stage, on which an official Countdown on Beale program takes place.

THE ARTS

Memphis has a very active arts scene for a city its size, with a range that takes you from the classics to a funky, homegrown alternative scene energized by the presence of a major art school, Memphis College of Art. The symphony, ballet, and opera are all represented by major professional companies, and, in fact, there are two symphonies currently performing in the city. Local theater, which is very strong, dates from at least 1920, when Front Street Theater (now Theatre Memphis) began featuring local stage talent. The historic Orpheum Theater and other venues bring in a steady stream of Broadway shows and other national acts, something that has been a tradition in this river-port town throughout its history. Visual arts can be enjoyed at local museums, most notably, the Memphis Brooks Museum and Dixon Gallery and Gardens, and galleries range from snob to funk.

Filmgoers will want to catch the city's two independent film festivals each year and may recognize Memphis as the backdrop in several movies, as it has become a popular place to shoot films. Among those filmed here are the movies made from the John Grisham novels, including *The Firm, 21 Grams* with Sean Penn, and Jim Jarmusch's cult film *Mystery Train*. A few of the city's independent filmmakers have received national recognition, including Craig Brewer for *The Poor and Hungry,* and self-styled exploitation author John Michael McCarty, director of *Teenage Tupelo* and *Elvis Meets the Beatles*. During summer moviegoers can see classic movies such as *Gone with the Wind* on the big screen at the Orpheum.

A number of actors and actresses have come from Memphis. Some, including Kathy Bates and Cybill Shepherd, grew up here and developed their careers elsewhere, whereas actress Dixie Carter got her start in local theater. A major claim to fame is that Tennessee Williams wrote his first play, *Cairo! Shanghai! Bombay!,* in the 1930s while visiting his grandparents at their home near what is now Rhodes College.

Theater continues to be strong, with Playhouse on the Square (the city's professional company) and Theatre Memphis putting on more mainstream productions that have included *A Chorus Line* and *Deathtrap*. Circuit Playhouse focuses on off-Broadway fare, and Theater Works provides a stage for several smaller theater companies.

Memphis is rich in other performing arts and currently supports two symphonies. Memphis Symphony Orchestra, an excellent regional symphony, gives 80 performances a year, mostly at its new home at the Cannon Performing Arts Center downtown. IRIS, a chamber orchestra formed in 2000, performs eight times a year, under the baton of Michael Stern, an internationally known musician who's also the son of the late violinist Isaac Stern. Opera Memphis, under the direction of savvy American composer Michael Ching, produces classics such as *Aida* and new compositions as well. Internationally known soprano Kallen Esperian makes her home in Memphis and occasionally makes guest appearances in Opera Memphis productions.

Ballet Memphis is a professional dance company that performs full-length classical works, a yearly production of *The Nutcracker,* and some avant-garde work. There are also some smaller companies.

For visual arts South Main Street, a historic district once home to the hustle and bustle of the city's major train station, has become the center for art galleries. The most festive way to check out these galleries is the Art Trolley Tour, which takes place on the last Friday of every month. From 6:00 to 9:00 P.M. you can ride the Main Street Trolley for free between the Orpheum Theater at Beale and Central Station at G. E. Patterson. The galleries, shops, and stained-glass manufacturers are open, so you can browse the artwork and sip a glass of wine. This is a favorite party spot among the Memphis artsy set, so people turn up as much to see and be seen as they do to enjoy the artwork.

In East Memphis you'll find many of the city's serious galleries, those that represent artists from the region with national recognition. Many feature changing exhibits and opening receptions for the artists that are open to the public (usually Friday nights). Others are open by appointment only. Among the artists with national and international reputations are painters Burton Callicott and Brenda Joysmith, well known for her pastels and prints of daily life among African Americans. Two legendary photographers hail from Memphis: William Eggleston, whose color photographs have been shown at the Museum of Modern Art, and Ernest Withers, whose black-and-white photographs chronicle the civil rights movement in Memphis as well as life on Beale Street during segregation.

The more avant-garde arts scene is centered on Marshall Avenue near Sun Studio, sometimes called "the edge" because it's on the eastern edge of downtown, and at the Memphis College of Art, which shows the work of its students and faculty mainly. The city is home to dozens of working artists—painters, potters, sculptors, and others—many of them graduates of the art college. We list the days of operation for galleries, but hours vary.

Remember that in Memphis visual art isn't limited to galleries and museums. Artwork can be found in restaurants, shops, theater lobbies, and office buildings all over town, and often it's for sale.

Arts groups in Memphis, no matter what the discipline, usually incorporate a strong educational element into their programs, offering lessons (and sometimes scholarships) and performing in schools for students. And speaking of education, don't forget that University of Memphis, Rhodes College, and other colleges have strong programs in the arts, which include theater productions, concerts, and art

shows by their students and faculty as well as programs that bring in important nationally known artists. These are usually listed in local newspapers.

As is the case in any city, the Memphis arts scene changes, as established arts groups shift gears and newer ones emerge. Be sure and check out the listings in the *Commercial Appeal* Memphis Playbook section or the *Memphis Flyer* for general information as well as the ticket information, hours, and other specifics on current performances and art shows.

GALLERIES
South Main/Downtown

Art Village Gallery
410 South Main Street
(901) 521-0782
www.artvillagegallery.com
This gallery is the permanent home for the work of Ephraim Urevbu, a Nigerian-born artist who has been in Memphis for many years. Urevbu's contemporary abstract paintings are afire with bright colors. The gallery also features exhibitions of work by other artists. Art Village Gallery is open by appointment.

Center for Southern Folklore
119 and 123 South Main Street
(901) 525-3655
www.southernfolklore.com
The center's SOFO gallery features folk art and other pieces by Mississippi Delta folk artists. The gallery is in the back, but there's also the Folklore Store in front, where you can buy some of the work. This is also a cafe, music venue, and all-around friendly place.

D'Edge Gallery
550 South Main Street
(901) 521-0054
Featuring the work of internationally known artist George Hunt, as well as other artists including N. J. Wood, Deborah Edge, and Emery Franklin, D'Edge Gallery

displays a colorful collection of original art, prints, posters, and folk art. Open every day except Tuesday, or by appointment.

Delta Axis at Marshall Arts
639 Marshall Avenue
(901) 458-4207
www.deltaaxis.org
Established in 1992 as a nonprofit contemporary visual-arts organization, Delta Axis stages its local art shows at Marshall Arts, an artists' workspace the organization started to support the city's working artists. The focus is on new and emerging artists from this region, as well as artists from other parts of the country and abroad. Examples include a show of artist sketchbooks, a group show of artists from Arkansas State University at Jonesboro, and Ghosts, an exhibit that involved taking works by out-of-town artists out of the gallery and placing them in various places around the South Main Street district. The gallery is usually open Monday through Saturday, but call (901) 522-9483 since hours can be sporadic.

Durden Gallery
408 South Front Street (entrance on Huling Avenue)
(901) 543-0340
www.durdengallery.com
The Durden Gallery, part of the Galleries of Huling Row, features the work of local, regional, and national emerging and established artists. With a traditional and contemporary mixture of paintings, glass, and sculpture, the gallery highlights the mastery of Delores Justus, L. Gordon, Chuck Zimmer, and David George Hinske. Open every day.

Hollis Art Studio/Gallery
408 South Front Street (entrance on Huling Avenue)
(901) 522-8300
Featuring the work of Mickey Hollis, the Hollis Art Studio/Gallery, which is part of the Galleries of Hurling Row, operates as a working studio with an array of contempo-

rary, abstract, and figurative artwork that is diverse in style and medium. Open Tuesday through Friday or by appointment.

Jay Etkin Gallery
409 South Main Street
(901) 543-0035
www.jayetkin.com
When New York–born Jay Etkin moved his gallery from the Cooper-Young historic district to South Main in 2000, it was a big boost to the downtown arts scene. You could say that this is the flagship gallery in the area, given the many artists and the variety of styles represented. Etkin is considered a major player, and at any given time this three-story, Soho-style space is filled with the work of some 35 different artists, which sometimes includes local sculptor Roy Tamboli and painters Annabelle Meacham and Pam Cobb. The gallery also handles the work of New York artist Tim Rollins & K.O.S. and others to Memphis market, not to mention Etkin's own abstract paintings and conceptual art. A large collection of ethnographic art also is available. Open every day except Tuesday.

Joysmith Gallery
46 Huling Avenue
(901) 543-0505
www.joysmith.com
This gallery, situated between South Main and Front Streets, features the work of African-American artist Brenda Joysmith, who moved from her studio in northern California with her husband, Robert Bain, to her hometown of Memphis in 2000. Joysmith, one of the artists credited with creating the market for African-American art during the 1980s, sells her work all over the world. One of her paintings even hung on the walls of the Huxtable home on TV's *Cosby Show.* The gallery features Joysmith's works, both limited and open editions, as well as works by other black artists, who have included painter Claude Clark, Sr. Joysmith Gallery is open Tuesday through Sunday or by appointment.

Patio Gallery
408 South Front Street (entrance on Huling Avenue)
(901) 281-2257
This is the exhibition space and workshop of artist Ed Vining, who makes furniture and other works with fine woods, leather, and clay. Open by appointment.

Power House
45 G. E. Patterson Boulevard
(901) 578-5545
www.deltaaxis.org/powerhouse
This is easily the most dramatic exhibition space in the South Main arts district. Housed in the cavernous interior of the brick-and-glass plant that once produced steam power for Central Station, it's an initiative of the arts group Delta Axis. Power House has four solo shows each year, featuring artists such as sculptor Marc Quinn and sculptor/video artist Bruce Nauman, as well as other perform-ances and exhibitions. Even if you're not that interested in the artwork, don't miss a chance to explore the Power House, in itself a work of art. Open on weekend afternoons or by appointment.

Rivertown Gallery
119 South Main Street
(901) 527-7573
www.packcraig.com
Offering a wide range of eclectic artistry, Rivertown Gallery displays everything from abstract and realistic work to photography to water colors. The gallery also features monthly displays and exhibi-tions, as well as the artistic work of 10 to 12 local artists. Open Monday through Friday or by appointment. Call for sum-mer schedule.

Robinson Gallery/Archives
44 Huling Avenue
(901) 683-1132
www.robinsongallery.com
The work of *Vogue* and *New York Times* photographer Jack Robinson is exhibited here in Memphis, where he spent the last years of his life. The collection includes the late photographer's images of 1960s and 1970s icons such as Bob Dylan and Jack Nicholson as well as a collection of fashion and other photographs.

Second Floor Contemporary
431 South Main Street
(901) 521-1514
www.2ndfloorcontemporary.com
This second-floor alternative space holds four to six shows a year, featuring mostly local artists. Past exhibitions have included the work of Hamlett Dobbins, who paints large, abstract oils, Greeley Myatt, who creates a variety of sculpture and installa-tions, and Terri Jones, a conceptual artist who does installations. The gallery is open Monday through Friday and by appoint-ment on the weekends.

Universal Art Gallery
111 G. E. Patterson Boulevard
(901) 522-9398
www.universalart.com
This galley features the work of contem-porary artists from all over, including the painterly photographic images of Indi-anapolis artist William Rasdell and the illu-sional paintings of gallery-owner Arnold Thompson. Open Tuesday through Satur-day or by appointment.

Willis Gallery
156 Beale Street
(901) 526-3162
This gallery has operated on Beale Street since 1989, featuring artwork that's the visual counterpart of the blues and other music you hear at the clubs. Willis fea-tures original works, prints, and posters by local Southern artists, including George Hunt, Don Allen, Danny Broadway, and the Twins. Closed on Tuesday.

Midtown/East Memphis

Albers Fine Art Gallery
1102 Brookfield Road
(901) 683-2256
www.albersgallery.com

This East Memphis gallery was established in 1984 by Kathy Albers, a respected art dealer, and features both two- and three-dimensional works by artists from the Southeast as well as a few with national reputations. Among the artists represented are Ann Kobdish, a Texan who paints tranquil landscapes, and Michael Barringer, a painter who often uses mixed media on paper. William Morris is a maker of glass vessels and sculpture, with works at the Metropolitan Museum of Art, widely considered one of the foremost glass artists of the 20th century. The gallery has six shows a year and is open Tuesday through Friday or by appointment.

Clough-Hanson Gallery
2000 North Parkway
(901) 843-3442
www.rhodes.edu

Located on the campus of Rhodes College, the Clough-Hanson Gallery is dedicated to providing opportunities to explore the visual arts in a setting that promotes learning, discovery, and appreciation. Each year between September and March, the gallery presents four professional exhibitions of the work of regional, national, and international artists. In March and April the gallery also presents a show of student work. Recent artists include Nikki S Lee and Thomas Nozkowski. The gallery is open Tuesday through Saturday. To find the gallery, ask the guard at the campus entrance on University Street for directions.

David Lusk Gallery
4540 Poplar Avenue
(901) 767-3800
www.davidluskgallery.com

Situated in Laurelwood Shopping Center near Grove Grill restaurant, this gallery was established in 1995 by Memphis art dealer David Lusk. The gallery specializes in the work of established regional and Southeastern artists with national recognition. Among them is Carroll Cloar, the late painter whose realism is compared with Edward Hopper's, and Memphis-born pho-

tographer Huger Foote, whose work is featured in magazines such as *Interview* and in his book, *My Friend from Memphis.* (Incidentally, he's the son of Shelby Foote, the Civil War historian who lives in Memphis.) Other painters include Robert Rector and Mary Sims. David Lusk Gallery is open Monday through Saturday or by appointment.

David Mah Studio
888 South Cooper Street
(901) 272-8880
www.davidmahstudio.com

This Cooper-Young neighborhood gallery, principally the studio and show space for Memphis painter David Mah, is also the site of about six shows each year by other contemporary Memphis artists. They include Bryan Blankenship, who does paintings and ceramics, and landscapist Matthew Hasty. Mah's work is mixed media on board in a minimalist style with Asian influences. Open by appointment only.

Lisa Kurts Gallery
766 South White Station
(901) 683-6200
www.lisakurts.com

Lisa Kurts Gallery prides itself on being the city's oldest, established in 1979, and represents some 30 artists from the United States, Canada, and Europe. The gallery has 10 to 12 shows each year, featuring artists such as landscape-painter Wade Hoefer, sculptor Anita Huffington, and Marcia Myers, a New Mexico painter influenced by works found in Pompeii and other excavation sites in Italy. Although the focus has traditionally been on Memphis artists, presently the focus is moving

---

Want to find out what's happening in the arts or what movies are playing during your visit? The Memphis Flyer *(www.memphisflyer.com) and the Memphis Playbook section of Friday's* Commercial Appeal *(www.commercialappeal.com) are good places to begin.*

away from the city and to Impressionist works. Apropos of that, the gallery has one Impressionist painting show each year and operates Lisa Kurts Ltd., a business that advises collectors of late 19th-century and early 20th-century paintings by Monet, Picasso, and others. The gallery is open Monday through Saturday.

Memphis College of Art
1930 Poplar Avenue
(901) 272-5100
www.mca.edu
The gallery at Memphis College of Art mainly exhibits the work of its students and faculty but also exhibits other work, which has included a show of black-velvet art by local artists. Here you can get a fix on what the next generation of artists is up to. The gallery is open Monday through Friday. For more information about the college, check out the Education chapter.

Perry Nicole Fine Art
3092 Poplar Avenue
(901) 405-6000
www.perrynicole.com
Tucked away in the Village at Chickasaw Oaks shopping center in midtown, this gallery was opened in 1999 by Nicole Haney and David Smith, alumni of Lisa Kurts Gallery. The focus of this gallery is to find artists who have already had shows in markets similar to the Memphis market such as those in New Orleans and St. Louis, and to market their works here. Among the artists represented are Seattle abstract-painter Adele Sypesteyn, New Orleans glass-artist Mitchell Gaudet, and Andy Reed, a local landscape artist. Perry Nicole has a new show each month. The gallery is open Monday through Saturday or by appointment.

ART MUSEUMS

You can learn more about all of these museums by checking out the Museums listings in the Attractions chapter.

Art Museum of the University of Memphis
3750 Norriswood Avenue
(901) 678-2224
www.amum.org
This quiet museum in the University of Memphis Communication and Fine Arts Building houses a gallery displaying works by students, faculty, and other artists as well as an excellent small exhibition of Egyptian artifacts.

The Dixon Gallery and Gardens
4339 Park Avenue
(901) 761-2409
www.dixon.org
The Dixon is a former private estate with a small permanent collection of Impressionist art and decorative arts as well as temporary exhibitions that include a recent show of Walter Anderson paintings.

Memphis Brooks Museum of Art
1934 Poplar Avenue
(901) 544-6200
www.brooksmuseum.org
The state's largest and oldest fine-arts museum, the Brooks displays works from its own extensive collection as well as temporary exhibitions that range from Russian Romanov jewels to the art of Warner Brothers cartoons. Situated in Overton Park, this Beaux Arts–style palace also hosts lectures, musical performances, and other events.

National Ornamental Metal Museum
374 Metal Museum Drive
(901) 774-6380
www.metalmuseum.org
This small, offbeat museum is the only institution in the United States dedicated exclusively to the collection and exhibition of fine metalwork, such as iron gates, swords, and other items. On display you'll find exhibitions on some type of ornamental metals, such as Japanese Kana teakettles.

Peabody Place Museum
119 South Main Street
(901) 523-2787
www.belz.com

Tucked away on the lower level of the Pembroke Building on Main Street, this museum has an extensive collection of Chinese sculpture, mostly 19th-century (Ching Dynasty) works of jade, ivory, and agate.

Wonders: The Memphis International Cultural Series
The Pyramid Arena, Front Street and Auction Avenue
(901) 312-9161, (800) 2MEMPHIS
www.wonders.org
It's always worth checking to see if there's a Wonder exhibition coinciding with your visit. This group organizes blockbuster exhibits with themes ranging from the Renaissance to the Russians to motorcycles.

DANCE

Ballet Memphis
7950 Trinity Road
(901) 737-7322
www.balletmemphis.org
This 24-member professional company performs full-length classical works such as *Giselle* and *Swan Lake* as well as modern ballet by top choreographers. Ballet Memphis was started in 1985 by Dorothy Gunther Pugh, who remains its artistic director. There is a season of four major productions in Memphis, most of them at the Orpheum Theater, in addition to participating in local arts festivals and touring. In 2001 the company received national exposure when it traveled to New York to perform at the Kaye Playhouse as one of nine dance companies. The company also performs original works, such as *The Rescue,* a piece about local hero Tom Lee, in 2004. Its yearly performance of the holiday classic *The Nutcracker* is always a favorite among Memphians. Ballet Memphis also reaches out into schools and teaches 500 adults and children each year at all levels.

Memphis Dance Group
60 Perkins Road Extended
(901) 537-1483, (901) 537-1486 (box office)

This small dance company presents ballet as well as modern, jazz, and latino dance at the Buckman Performing and Fine Arts Center at St. Mary's Episcopal School. The dance group features two main stage performances a year, which have included El Beso, a blend of salsa and flamenco, as well as community outreach performances.

FILM

Indie Memphis
Muvico Theaters, 150 Peabody Place
(901) 246-7086
www.indiememphis.com
Indie Memphis was started by a University of Memphis film student in 1998 to provide a voice and forum for the local film community. The group sponsors a juried competition each year entitled the Indie Memphis Film Festival: The Soul of Southern Film, focusing on films with a Southern connection. The weeklong event, which takes place in October, includes screenings, symposiums, and other events, with the action centered around Muvico Theaters downtown. Through its partnership with the arts group Delta Axis, Indie Memphis works to promote film as artistic expression.

Memphis Film Forum
517 South Main Street
(901) 626-9685
www.memphisfilmforum.org
This nonprofit organization is dedicated to promoting cinema arts, most visibly with the Memphis International Film Festival it launched in 2000. The festival, held every spring, features independent films by local filmmakers as well as films with international scope, including shorts, animation, documentaries, and foreign films. In 2003 actors Morgan Freeman and Holly Hunter made appearances to discuss their film *Levity*. The film forum also sponsors the Spike and Mike Animation Festival in the fall, featuring animated short films, and other events, such as special premieres, throughout the year.

The Orpheum Classic Movie Series
203 South Main Street
(901) 525-7800
www.orpheum-memphis.com
Every summer this historic theater presents a series of classic films on Friday
nights, including such favorites as *Gone
with the Wind, North by Northwest,* and
One Flew over the Cuckoo's Nest. The
films are shown on the big screen and
usually include a concert of organ music
from the silent-movie era.

Paradiso
584 South Mendenhall Road
(901) 682-1754
www.malco.com
Malco's Paradiso, named after the Italian film
Cinema Paradiso, is one of the city's largest
and most comfortable movie theaters, with
stadium seating and 14 screens, including an
extra-wide 50-foot screen. But what sets
this East Memphis theater apart is its Italian
look, created with fresco-type finishes and
other Italian architectural details. That
makes the lobby, with its pizza cafe/coffee
bar and concessions that include chicken
tenders and fried mozzarella as well as beer
and wine, a comfortable place to hang out
before or after the movies.

Studio on the Square
2105 Court Street
(901) 725-7151
www.overtonsquare.com
Opened in 2000 at Overton Square entertainment district in midtown, Malco's Studio on the Square generated great
excitement by bringing the movies back
to midtown. The theater caters to film
buffs who prefer independent and foreign
films to the latest commercial blockbuster.
Unlike the city's other movie houses, Studio on the Square, in addition to its five
screens, also has lounge areas and tables
and serves specialty coffees, beer, wine,
desserts, and light appetizers. The theater
gets involved with the local film scene,
sponsoring special events promoting *Poor*
& Hungry, a film by Memphis filmmaker
Craig Brewer, and festival screenings.

Summer Quartet Drive-In
5310 Summer Avenue
(901) 767-4320
Okay, maybe this isn't high art, but Summer Quartet is one of the few drive-in
theaters left in the country. Here, you can
pretend it's the fifties as you park, get
refreshments, and take in a double feature. For parents of young children, it's a
great way to get to the movies, because
the kids usually crash in the back seat
pretty early in the evening. Open on the
weekends.

CLASSICAL MUSIC

Calvary and the Arts
102 North Second Street
(901) 525-6602
www.calvaryjc.org
Every fall Calvary Episcopal Church downtown presents a concert and lunch series,
featuring free musical performances and a
$6.00 lunch prepared by area restaurants
or the church's own chefs. Performers are
various. They always include Navy-band
Mid-South and Kirk Whalen, and in the
past have also included soprano Kallen
Esperian, local chanteuse DiAnne Price,
and former Stax musicians.

Concerts at Lindenwood
4600 Union Avenue
(901) 458-1652
www.lindenwood.net
For more than 25 years Lindenwood
Christian Church in midtown has hosted
an acclaimed concert series. Throughout
the years the series has included an
incredible range of music, from the U.S.
Marine Band and Metropolitan Opera stars
to singer Debbie Boone and local
favorites, including the Gary Beard
Chorale. All performances take place in
the church sanctuary.

Concerts International
Harris Concert Hall
3775 Central Avenue
(901) 527-3067
home.midsouth.rr.com/webs/Concerts
International

For more than 30 years, Concerts International has been bringing in internationally acclaimed chamber music to Memphis through its annual concert series. The performances usually take place at Harris Concert Hall on the University of Memphis campus. The series has included performances by the Orpheus Chamber Orchestra and the Academy of St. Martin's in the Fields Chamber Ensemble.

IRIS: The Orchestra
Germantown Performing Arts Center
1801 Exeter Road, Germantown
(901) 757-7256
www.gpacweb.com

During the time that Memphis Symphony Orchestra was performing at a local church while waiting for its sleek, new concert hall to open downtown, this young upstart chamber orchestra burst onto the scene in 2000. With internationally known conductor Michael Stern at the podium and guests such as cellist Yo Yo Ma, IRIS immediately attracted sellout crowds. It's smaller than MSO and is composed mostly of out-of-town musicians. Eight performances are given each year at the Germantown Performing Arts Center. Local music lovers are hoping that there's room in this town for both orchestras.

Memphis Chamber Music Society
Various locations
(901) 758-0150

Some of the city's most beautiful and historic private homes open their doors to aficionados of chamber music for a series of nine yearly concerts. The concerts range from duos to 12 musicians, and although most of the performers are local musicians, there are sometimes national and international artists. Subscriptions and single tickets both sell out quickly, as audiences are limited to about 100 people.

The performances are at 3:00 P.M. Sundays, followed by a reception.

Memphis Symphony Orchestra
3100 Walnut Grove Road
(901) 324-3627
www.memphissymphony.org

Founded in 1952, the Memphis Symphony Orchestra is one of the country's premier regional orchestras, with 85 musicians who present 80 performances each year. Under the leadership of David Loebel, who became musical director and conductor in 1999 after a decade with the Saint Louis Symphony Orchestra, the musicians perform everything from classical masterworks to pops to premiers of original works. Highlights each year include Handel's *Messiah,* a Mad about Mozart program, and outdoor performances at the Dixon Gallery and Gardens. The orchestra frequently welcomes guest performers, who have included violinist Pamela Frank and the Eroica Trio. In 2003 MSO began performing in its new home, the Cannon Center for the Performing Arts, an intimate, 2,100-seat concert hall that's part of the newly rebuilt and expanded Memphis Cook Convention Center in downtown Memphis. MSO also sponsors the volunteer Memphis Symphony Chorus as well as Memphis Youth Symphony.

The Beethoven Club, which dates from 1888, brings together music lovers of all ages to listen to classical-music performances, usually by local musicians. You can learn more about the club, which welcomes new members, by calling (901) 274-2504.

Memphis Vocal Arts Ensemble
Buckman Performing and Fine Arts Center
60 Perkins Road Extended
(901) 458-9766
www.stmarysschool.org

This vocal group has been performing in Memphis for more than 10 years, under the directorship of founder Thomas Machen. The ensemble gives four concerts each season, usually at Buckman Performing and Fine Arts Center at St. Mary's Episcopal School in East Memphis. The programs range from Broadway show tunes and popular music to opera and holiday favorites. The concerts are usually on Friday nights and Saturday afternoons.

Opera Memphis
6745 Wolf River Parkway
(901) 257-3100
www.operamemphis.org
Memphis has a long tradition of opera, dating from when Jenny Lind sang here in 1851. Formed in 1956, Opera Memphis is the largest opera company in Tennessee, led by general and artistic director Michael Ching, also a well-known composer of operas such as *Buoso's Ghost.* Opera Memphis serves the greater Mid-South community with three major main-stage productions every season at the Orpheum Theater or Cannon Center for the Performing Arts. Small productions, concerts, and other events are held at the company's new home, the Clark Opera Memphis Center, which also houses its administrative offices and rehearsal hall. Productions have included classic favorites such as *The Magic Flute* and *Aida* as well as new American works. The operas are usually sung in their original language, with English subtitles, and are accompanied by the Memphis Symphony Orchestra. Renowned soprano Kallen Esperian makes her home in Memphis and sometimes makes guest appearances with Opera Memphis, always a sellout event.

Wolf River Singers
2310 Hickory Path, Cordova
(901) 758-8634
www.wolfriversingers.org
This auditioned group of singers performs choral music ranging from Renaissance to the contemporary composer Dan Gawthrop, much of it a capella. The group does three concerts a year in various churches and other venues around town.

THEATER

Circuit Playhouse
1705 Poplar Avenue
(901) 726-4656
www.playhouseonthesquare.org
Circuit Playhouse is a year-round theater that stages eight different plays each year. The focus is on off-Broadway and experimental theater, but not exclusively. Productions have included *From the Mississippi Delta, The Spitfire Grill,* and *Sophisticated Ladies.* Its home in midtown since 1979 is a 140-seat theater, although the theater company has been active since 1969. Circuit is a sister theater to Playhouse on the Square.

Ewing Children's Theater
2635 Avery Avenue
(901) 452-3968
Established in 1949, the Ewing Children's Theater presents eight shows each year, which have included *Charlotte's Web* and *Jungle Book.* The theater's management encourages young people to participate in all aspects of putting on a play, not just acting but also writing, stagecraft, lighting, costume design, and other elements of theater production. The theater also offers drama classes for children ages 5 through 18, which include a talent showcase.

Germantown Community Theatre
3037 Forest Hill Irene Road
Germantown
(901) 754-2680
www.germantowncommunitytheatre.org
Considered one of the best small community theaters in the state, this local theater makes its home in a converted turn-of-the-century schoolhouse, where it puts on seven productions a year in its 116-seat theater. Founded in 1972, Germantown Community Theatre has staged performances of *The Glass Menagerie, Deathtrap, Catfish Moon,* and the musical *Pearlie.* Every year the theater puts on *The Best Christmas Pageant Ever,* a favorite among local theatergoers during the holiday season.

Playhouse on the Square
51 South Cooper Street
(901) 726-4656
www.playhouseonthesquare.org
This professional resident year-round theater presents mainstream fare, with performances of such plays as *Ragtime* and
Wizard of Oz. The company makes its
home in the former Memphian Movie Theater in the Overton Square area, which
has seating for an audience of 258 people.
During the holidays Playhouse on the
Square puts on performances of *A Tuna
Christmas,* always a favorite among Memphis audiences. A number of Playhouse
alumni have gone on to successful acting
careers in Hollywood and New York,
including Michael Jeter (who won an
Emmy for his work on the TV show
Evening Shade), Chris Ellis, and Shannon
Cochran (active with Steppenwolf Theater
in Chicago).

Sleeping Cat Studio
655 Marshall Avenue
(901) 728-4262
www.sleepingcatstudio.org
This tiny independent theater company,
under the direction of Virginia playwright
Jim Esposito, presents works by established dramatists such as David Mamet as
well as Esposito's own plays, which are
edgy dramas with an element of dark
humor. There's also a cafe and weekend
cabaret shows.

Theatre Works
2085 Monroe Avenue
(901) 274-7139
www.theatreworksmemphis.com
Here you'll find some of the city's more
avant-garde productions. Situated at
Overton Square just around the corner
from Playhouse on the Square, this 110-
seat theater provides a home to emerging
artists and groups who don't have their
own performing spaces. Currently, it's
home to Emerald Theatre Company, Our
Own Voice Theatre Troupe, Playwrights'
Forum, Voices of the South, New Moon
Theatre Company, and the dance company

*In Memphis you can enjoy theater even
if you're on a budget. For each of their
productions, Circuit Playhouse, Theatre
Memphis, and Playhouse on the Square
have a "pay what you can" performance,
where you can pay any sum for a ticket.
For more information call the theater
box office.*

Project: Motion. Built in 1995 by Playhouse
on the Square, Theater Works is intended
as an artistic incubator for the local performing-arts community.

Theatre Memphis
630 Perkins Road Extended
(901) 682-8323
www.theatrememphis.org
Theatre Memphis is one of the oldest community theaters in the country, dating from
1920. Since 1974 it has made its home at an
East Memphis facility that has two stages,
The Main Stage, with seating for 424, and
its Little Theater, with seating for 75 to 120.
The Main Stage features Broadway shows
and plays that have included *Mame, A
Funny Thing Happened on the Way to the
Forum,* and *Deathtrap.* The Little Theater
features off-Broadway fare, including
Betrayal and *Little Shop of Horrors.* In addition, Theatre Memphis's ShoWagon program features a troupe of young
professional actors who perform seven or
eight shows a year at schools. There's also
a kids' program, where kids can audition for
plays such as *Charlotte's Web.*

VENUES

The theaters and performing-arts centers
listed here are where you'll find performances of the orchestra, ballet, opera, traveling Broadway shows, and some popular
artists. For more venues that feature popular music, including rock, country, and
R&B, refer to the listings in the Nightlife
chapter.

Bartlett Performing Arts and Conference Center
3663 Appling Road, Bartlett
(901) 385-6440
www.bpacc.org

Built in 1998, this suburban venue sponsors a regular season lineup that has featured such artists as singer/songwriter Iris DeMent, the Cashore Marionettes, and the Nashville Mandolin Ensemble. This is also home to the Lucy Opry, a regular forum that features bluegrass music.

Buckman Performing and Fine Arts Center
60 Perkins Road Extended
(901) 537-1483, (901) 537-1486 (box office)
www.stmarysschool.org

This 288-seat theater at St. Mary's Episcopal School is where you'll find some of the more diverse performing arts in the city. Through the Buckman Concert Series, the center has presented performances by flamenco dancers from Spain and Russian gypsies as well as Celtic music and Tibetan music and dance. Buckman is also home to the Memphis Dance Group.

Cannon Center for the Performing Arts
255 North Main Street
(901) 576-1200
www.thecannoncenter.com

This beautiful 2,100-seat, acoustically superior concert hall is part of a major expansion and renovation of the Memphis Cook Convention Center in downtown

Memphis. The performing-arts center, completed in 2003, is the permanent home for the Memphis Symphony Orchestra, and it also plays host to other concerts as well as some Opera Memphis productions. A modern hall finished with handsome wood veneers, it is designed so that the stage extends into the audience, creating an intimate ambience.

Germantown Performing Arts Center
1801 Exeter Road, Germantown
(901) 757-7256
www.gpacweb.com

This acoustically perfect theater, which opened in 1994, provides an intimate venue for performances of all kinds. The center, which locals refer to as "G-Pac," hosts a series of popular performances that have included artists such as Nitty Gritty Dirt Band, Alison Kraus, and actor Hal Holbrook as Mark Twain. It's also the artistic home to the chamber orchestra IRIS and brings in ballet companies and other performers as well. The theater seats 824 people, and no seat is more than 55 feet from the stage.

The Orpheum Theater
203 South Main Street
(901) 525-7800
www.orpheum-memphis.com

The lavish Orpheum Theater, built in 1928 as a venue primarily for vaudeville, holds court at the foot of Beale Street in downtown Memphis. At present the theater hosts performances of Broadway shows, Opera Memphis, and Ballet Memphis as well as other acts that have included David Copperfield and Garrison Keillor's "Prairie Home Companion." Bedecked with crystal chandeliers, gilded moldings, and brocade draperies, the Orpheum also sponsors a popular film series in summer (for more details see the write-up under the Film section in this chapter). The theater was renovated in 1983 and 1997, to the tune of $15 million, so now it can accommodate traveling Broadway shows that have included *The Producers* and *Rent*. The Orpheum sells tickets at the

---

Tickets for concerts and other events can be purchased from one or two companies: Ticketmaster (901-525-1515, www.ticketmaster.com) and New Era Tickets (887-639-3728, www.NewEra Tickets.com). Both have specific locations in or near Memphis where you can buy your tickets in person. Of course, you can buy tickets directly from the venue's box office if you don't want to pay the extra fees.

theater's box office or at a satellite box office at Davis-Kidd Booksellers.

SUPPORT GROUPS

Germantown Arts Alliance
1930 Germantown Road South
Germantown
(901) 757-9768
This nonprofit group, whose mission is to develop, support, and strengthen the area's cultural environment, was spun off from the governmental Germantown Commission in 1992. The group's main function is to raise money and give out matching grants to local arts groups as well as to local schools for arts programs. In 2003 the Alliance gave out $41,000 in grants. Among the arts groups it supports are Germantown Community Theatre, the Germantown Symphony Orchestra, and the Germantown Community Chorus.

Greater Memphis Arts Council
8 South Third Street
(901) 578-2787
www.memphisartscouncil.org

Started in 1963 to foster improvements in the artistic and cultural quality of the area, the Greater Memphis Arts Council typically raises $3 million each year, which it reallocates to some 20 local arts groups and about 30 special-arts programs. An important focal point is the council's Arts for Children and Teachers education initiative, which brings the arts to tens of thousands of schoolchildren each year through subsidized tickets for performances, after-school arts programs, and other activities. This initiative is available to all city and county public schools. Among the council's past achievements is the launch of the UrbanArts Commission, a program that brings works of art by local artists to public buildings and outdoor spaces. The council depends on gifts from individuals and companies. It recently gave $3.6 million to help fund the construction of the Cannon Center for the Performing Arts. Although many organizations have their own support groups, such as the Memphis Symphony Orchestra with its Memphis Symphony League, much of the city's arts-support activity is under the Arts Council umbrella.

PARKS AND RECREATION

Those who like to get out and enjoy the outdoors will find many options in Memphis. The city has some 187 parks and 34 walking trails that encompass nearly 6,000 acres, and beyond the city limits there's Shelby Farms, the largest urban park in the United States with more than 4,500 acres. Best of all, because of the area's relatively mild winters, parks, golf courses, and other amenities can be enjoyed year-round.

Parks have been part of city planning since the city fathers first laid out the town of Memphis in 1819, and Memphians have not been afraid to fight to preserve their favorite parks. For example, in the 1960s and 1970s government leaders planned to build I-40 right through midtown's Overton Park, but popular opposition, which led to a Supreme Court ruling to block the plans, saved the park. At present conservationists are working to block construction of a major highway through the heart of Shelby Farms Park. They're also keeping a sharp eye on plans to develop the downtown Mississippi riverfront, to make sure the waterfront remains accessible to the public.

Local parks offer a variety of amenities and activities, from walking trails and fishing lakes to swimming pools, tennis courts, and golf courses. The parks also have large stately oaks, cottonwoods, and other trees that make the city green and beautiful.

The largest city parks are Overton Park in midtown, M. L. King/Riverside in south Memphis near downtown, and Audubon Park in East Memphis. There are numerous others, ranging in size from a block to more than 300 acres. We can't list them all, but you can get a complete listing or find out which parks are nearest you by calling the Memphis Parks Commission

(also known as the City of Memphis Division of Park Services) public information line at (901) 454-5200 or go online to www.cityofmemphis.org and click on "Park Services." The suburbs Germantown, Bartlett, and Collierville each maintain parks, services, and recreational activities of their own. Contact the Germantown Parks and Recreation Department at (901) 757-7375 or visit www.ci.germantown.tn.us. For more information on Bartlett parks, call (901) 385-5590 or visit www.cityof bartlett.org. Collierville parks details are available by calling (901) 853-0889 or by visiting www.collierville.com.

Just outside the city you'll find two large parks, Meeman-Shelby Forest State Park and Shelby Farms, each with fishing lakes, hiking and bike trails, and a host of other amenities. If you're willing to venture out farther from the city, you'll find a number of state parks where recreation facilities abound. Because Memphis is at the extreme southwest corner of Tennessee, bordering Mississippi and Arkansas, Memphis residents and visitors have access to three state park systems. There are no major national parks in west Tennessee, with the exception of Shiloh National Military Park, which is described in the Day Trips and Weekend Getaways chapter.

As for recreation you'll find many options, both in the city and within an easy drive. Tennis buffs will find a number of tennis complexes operated by the parks commission. The city also operates seven golf courses around the city, and a wide array of daily-fee courses are scattered throughout the metropolitan area and farther.

City community centers are also a part of the park system, and many of them have pools. Admission to the pools is free, and lessons are available for anyone age three or older. Other activities for young people at community centers include basketball and volleyball, while for senior citizens there are cultural and educational activities.

Organized sports activities are available under the auspices of the Memphis Parks Commission. It sponsors amateur adult sports leagues for baseball, softball, basketball, and touch football as well as youth sports programs for baseball, basketball, and volleyball. Other leagues are organized through area churches, and, of course, schools have sports teams.

As for indoor activities you'll find a whole host of options to keep you busy, including skating and bowling. There are also driving ranges, which tend to be family-entertainment centers that also have go-karts, batting cages, and video games on-site.

Water sports are also popular, no surprise given the mild climate and the proximity of the Mississippi River. Old Man River can be a dangerous guy, though, given its currents, whirlpools, and the huge waves that towboats leave behind. It's for experienced boaters only, so you may want to opt for one of the lakes in the area, several of which are less than an hour's drive from the city. Check the listings for state parks. For canoeing we suggest some rivers in the area that are picture perfect for paddling.

We also list options for fishing and hunting, two popular activities in this part of the country. Finally, we include some information on great places to enjoy hiking and mountain biking.

So get out there and have some fun.

PARKS
City Parks

These are the largest of the city parks, each with more than 100 acres and a variety of amenities. Call the Memphis Parks Commission at (901) 454-5200 or check out www.cityofmemphis.org for other

options. You can click on "park locations" to find what smaller parks are nearby or on "community centers" to learn more about activities such as ceramics or martial arts if that's your interest.

Audubon Park
4145 Southern Avenue

When the city bought this land in the late 1940s to establish what is now the second-largest park in Memphis, it was just east of the city limits. At that time it took some vision to believe city leaders' claims that it would rival Overton Park in 25 years. At present, Audubon Park is in the heart of East Memphis, where residents flock to enjoy the walking trails, picnic areas, 18-hole golf course, and large indoor tennis facility. You'll also find a lighted baseball field, a soccer field, and a seven-acre fishing lake, where kids delight in feeding the ducks. In 2004 the city began making improvements to the park, adding a new playground, extending its walking trail to 1 mile, and adding two exercise stations to the trail. A specially designed park area dedicated to cancer survivors is being added, and at some point the golf course will be redesigned. The park is also home to Memphis Botanic Garden, which includes the Japanese garden, the municipal rose garden, and others that had been established in the park. An annual arts-and-crafts fair is held here every October, and on Sunday mid-afternoons one of the more intriguing sights is the medieval-style jousting by members of the local chapter of the Society for Creative Anachronism, often in costumes of the period.

Kennedy Park
4577 Raleigh–LaGrange Road

The city bought the 310 acres on which to establish Kennedy Park in 1962, but the first order of business was to fill in the gravel pits on the property before developing the amenities. Situated on Raleigh–LaGrange Road just beyond the I–240 loop, the park is set so far back from the street that it's hard to see. Just take the Covington Pike exit from I–240 and turn left onto Raleigh–LaGrange Road, and the park is about a mile on the left. Kennedy Park is geared toward softball, with several lighted baseball and softball diamonds. Each of them has stands, and there are concessions during the summer games, which make it a popular place during the season. You'll also find four lighted soccer fields, a junior football field, and plenty of parking near all the fields.

Martin Luther King Jr. Riverside Park
South Parkway West and Riverside Drive

This is one of the city's oldest large parks, established at the turn of the last century when the city acquired property on a bluff overlooking the river. It's a historic site, and there are indications of burial sites from multiple periods. Originally named Riverside, it was renamed for Dr. King in 1968. Amenities include playground equipment and a baseball field as well as a 9-hole golf course, tennis, nature trails, and boat ramp access to McKellar Lake. The 388-acre park is adding a clubhouse facility as part of its golf course.

Overton Park
2080 Poplar Avenue

When the Memphis Parks Commission was formed in 1899, one of its first major steps was to purchase 300-plus acres in what was then the city's extreme northeast corner for a major park. At present it's the green heart of midtown. Until then, city parks were in downtown Memphis, because that's where most people lived, and they tended to be much smaller. At Overton Park the city established its first municipal golf course and, throughout the years, also added a clubhouse, the Memphis Zoo, the Memphis Brooks Museum of Art, and Overton Park Shell (where a young Elvis Presley gave one of his first performances). All of them are still operating. In the 1960s the state wanted to route I-40 through the park, and city officials were so sure their efforts would succeed that they demolished almost 200 homes to pave the way. But they underestimated

local opponents, who fought to preserve the park. The result was a historic U.S. Supreme Court decision against the highway plan. (This decision put Overton Park in the law books, as this decision set a new standard for review of administrative decisions by the court. It also threw a monkey wrench into plans for I-40, which to this day is still routed onto the northern portion of the I-240 loop.) Finally city officials gave up their efforts. Now visitors can enjoy one of the city's treasures, an old-growth forest that's preserved within the park, with nature trails and a paved path available for hiking, running, skating, or cycling. Amenities include a wide expanse of soccer fields, a baseball field, and a pond, as well as pavilions and other areas for picnics. It's also home to the Memphis College of Art, an outstanding school for aspiring artists.

River Parks

Memphis has a number of parks and trails along the Mississippi River, where you can take in the beauty and majesty of Old Man River. It's not that easy to get a glimpse of the river from the central downtown area, that is, unless you seek out one of these parks. One of the best places to access these parks is at the foot of Union Avenue at Riverside Drive. Cross Riverside Drive and you'll be at the historic cobblestones, where riverboats first landed to unload passengers and goods and to take on bales of cotton bound for European markets. Originally these stones served as ballast in the many boats that plied the river. When a load of goods or people was taken on board, the ballast was lightened and the stones were placed at the landing. As the largest remaining cobblestone landing in the country, it's listed on the National Register of Historic Places. From here go south to reach Tom Lee Park and the Riverbluff Walk or go north to find the Tennessee Welcome Center and Jefferson Davis Park. For views from the bluff, check out Confederate Park on Front Street, or you can cross the Auction Avenue bridge to Mud Island and walk or jog along the river at Greenbelt.

City leaders are planning to redevelop the Memphis riverfront, so one day soon the riverfront might have a whole new look.

Confederate Park
Front Street between Court and Jefferson Streets
This is one of the city's oldest parks, where during the Civil War Memphians came in carriages to watch the Battle of Memphis between Confederate cannon on the bank and Union gunships. It was used as a dump during the latter part of the century, until in 1900 the parks commission brought it back to life. This small park offers a great view of the river from atop the bluffs, as well as a statue of Confederacy president Jefferson Davis and cannon from World War I. It's easily accessible on foot to visitors who are exploring downtown Memphis and may not want to take the downhill walk to the cobblestones and other parks adjacent to the river.

Greenbelt Park
Harbortown Road (Mud Island)
This paved, 1.5-mile walkway along the Mississippi River starts at a convenient parking area just north of where the Auction Avenue bridge crosses from downtown and continues north to another parking area at the other end of the peninsula called Mud Island. It's a popular spot for residents, who flock there to walk, jog, skate, ride scooters and bikes, or walk animals. The walkway forms a loop surrounding a long, flat grassy lawn, and you can get a great view of the river from here.

Martin Luther King Jr. Riverside Park
South Parkway West and Riverside Drive
This 388-acre park, near South Parkway and about 3 miles south of Beale Street, is home to a 9-hole golf course. (See the listing in City Parks for more details.)

Tom Lee Park
Riverside Drive and Beale Street
Situated below the bluffs and just across Riverside from downtown Memphis, Tom Lee Park offers great views of the Mississippi River. There's plenty of room for picnics, walking, or tossing a Frisbee. During the 1990s the park was expanded to 24 acres, landscaped, and equipped with a parking lot, restrooms, and sidewalks. The park, originally named Astor Park, was renamed in honor of Tom Lee, a black laborer who saved 32 passengers in 1925 when the USS *Norman* sank in the river near Memphis. In May the park is closed to visitors and given over to the events of Memphis in May, which include a music festival and a massive barbecue cooking contest (see the Annual Events chapter for more details). After dark the park morphs into a youth hangout, as parades of cars continually cruise the lot.

County Parks

Shelby Farms
Germantown Road and
Raleigh-LaGrange/Mullins Station Road
(901) 382-0235
www.shelbyfarm.com
Situated in the middle of Shelby County and overseen by the county government, Shelby Farms is popular with Memphians and county residents seeking an escape from the hustle and bustle of city life. With more than 4,500 acres of land, Shelby Farms is the largest urban park in the United States, far bigger than Central Park in New York City and the Golden Gate Recreational Area in San Francisco put together. The land had been originally used for the county penal farm, and the county penal facility is still located near the western edge of the park. The county decided to turn over the acreage for public use, and for years politicians, developers, and conservationists debated what to do with the land, finally agreeing on an urban park in the 1970s.

Shelby Farms has at least five small lakes, a special wheelchair-accessible trail, and a 1,000-acre conservation area called Lucius East Burch Jr. State Natural Area, where hiking, wildlife watching, and cycling are allowed. Elsewhere in the park you can find the largest range of amenities and activities around, including horseback riding (you can rent horses; see the Recreation section in this chapter), pistol and rifle ranges, soccer, walking and bike trails, BMX bicycle area, roller-blading, a 10K cross-country running course, exercise trails with 21 exercise stations, and playgrounds. In addition, you can fish, raft, canoe, sail, or windsurf on 60-acre Patriot Lake or the smaller lakes. The paved pathway around Patriot Lake is a very popular exercise loop. Despite all of this activity, there's still plenty more land for hiking, picnicking, or just enjoying nature. The upland part of this park is referred to as Plough Park.

State Parks

Here we list the parks that are within a couple hours' drive of Memphis, but Tennessee, Mississippi, and Arkansas offer many more options if you are amenable to a longer trip. For more information on Tennessee parks, check out www.tnstateparks.com or call (888) TENN–PKS, the centralized reservation system; that is the number you must call in order to reserve accommodations at any Tennessee state park. For more on Mississippi's state parks, call (800) GO–PARKS or check out www.mdwfp.com. The state of Arkansas also has a number of state parks, but few of them are very close to Memphis. For information about Arkansas

In summer have plenty of water with you whatever outdoor recreation you're enjoying. Temperatures frequently push 100 degrees, and the oppressive humidity can be a serious health issue if you don't stay hydrated.

state parks, call (888) AT–PARKS or check out www.arkansasstateparks.com. We list a few of these in the Fishing and Canoeing/Paddling sections of this chapter. Many parks charge an entry fee and other nominal charges.

TENNESSEE STATE PARKS

Tennessee has 54 state parks and a handful of national parks, the best known of which is Great Smoky Mountains National Park way over in east Tennessee. We list the parks closest to Memphis, which have fishing lakes, hiking, and other amenities, but here you won't find the mountains that are commonplace in east Tennessee. Those interested in the Civil War may also want to visit Shiloh National Military Park or Fort Pillow State Park. (Turn to the Day Trips and Weekend Getaways chapter for details on these historic parks.) Be sure to call ahead about the days and hours of operation for all of these state parks, as they can change.

Big Hill Pond State Park
984 John Howell Road, Pocahontas
(731) 645–7967
This hidden jewel, located about two hours east of Memphis, is small and lightly used. Thirty miles of hiking trails with overnight shelters line the hills that surround a lake and the Dismal Swamp. A wooden boardwalk 0.8 mile long will take you through the swamp. Only electric motors or paddling are allowed on the 165-acre lake, and fishing is okay. The 14 miles of horse trails attract riders with their own horses, and mountain bikes are allowed to use some of these trails, too. In addition to RV and primitive campsites, you'll find a nice bathhouse. To get there go east on Highway 57 for about 80 miles, and about 7 miles past its intersection with U.S. 45, look for the entrance on the right.

Chickasaw State Park
20 Cabin Lane, Henderson
(731) 989–5141
Also known as Chickasaw State Rustic Park, this facility is situated about 90 miles

from Memphis on some of the highest terrain in west Tennessee. The recreation areas take up only a portion of the park's 14,384 acres of timberland and include tennis courts, basketball courts, an archery range, a horseshoe pit, volleyball courts, and a lighted baseball field. The park is also a golfer's delight, given the 18-hole championship course designed by Jack Nicklaus (see the Golf section in this chapter). There's also a 50-acre lake, hiking trails, and horseback-riding trails with a rental stable. Ask about mountain biking, too.

As for other amenities the park has a restaurant, with Southern cooking on weekends, and 13 cabins overlooking the lake. Three campgrounds offer modern bathhouses, RV hookups, or primitive camping. The park is within easy reach of Shiloh National Military Park.

From Memphis take I–64 east, then turn east onto Highway 100 at Whiteville and follow signs to the park.

Meeman-Shelby Forest State Park
910 Riddick Road, Millington
(901) 876–5215

This 13,500-acre park is just half an hour's drive from Memphis, making it very accessible for a country getaway. Located north of the city on the Mississippi River, two-thirds of the park consists of bottomland hardwood forests of large oak, cypress, and tupelo. The park and its museum/nature center are named for Edward J. Meeman, the conservation editor of Scripps-Howard newspapers who helped establish this park and the Great Smoky Mountains National Park.

The park contains two lakes for boating and fishing and many miles of hiking trails, as well as a boat ramp on the Mississippi River. There's plenty of wildlife here, including deer, turkey, beaver, and about 200 species of birds. You'll find paved bike trails, a swimming pool, pavilions and tables for picnics, a 27-hole disk golf course, and playgrounds. The park also has six two-bedroom cabins and a swimming pool that's open during the summer months. You can rent a boat, too. Other

attractions include a nature center, with exhibits of live snakes, a fish aquarium, a stuffed animal exhibit, a "touch table," and a Native American exhibit. Special programs at the center include making bird feeders and homemade ice cream, watching nature videos, and taking pontoon boat rides. Directions: From I–40, take exit 2-A, go right, and proceed through six stoplights to Watkins Road and turn left. Drive until the road ends, turn left, and then go right at the General Store. The park entrance is 1 mile on the left.

Pickwick Landing State Park
Park Road, Pickwick Dam
(731) 689–3129, (731) 689–3135 (inn)

Many years ago the Tennessee Valley Authority built numerous dams along the Tennessee River in order to bring electricity to an impoverished region. Another benefit was created at the same time: huge lakes made to order for recreation. Pickwick Dam made a 46-mile-long section of the river into a boating paradise. Pickwick Landing Park sits on the site of a former riverboat stop, that is, before the dam was built. TVA operates the dam and lake, which borders Tennessee, Mississippi, and Alabama. This 43,000-acre lake is probably the number-one watersports destination for Memphians. During Friday afternoons in summer, a steady stream of vehicles towing boats heads east on Highway 57 (Poplar Avenue) toward the big lake, and many folks buy second homes or condos here for weekend getaways. This park includes a great and inexpensive 18-hole golf course, a resort inn and conference center, cabins with central heat and air and fireplaces, camping, a marina and free boat ramps, and rental fishing boats and pontoon boats. Swimming is encouraged, plus you'll see all types of boats, including sailboats, on this busy lake. Numerous other parks, campgrounds, and conservation areas dot the lake's boundaries in all three states. For complete listings contact the relevant state-park system for the desired area either in Tennessee, Mississippi, or Alabama.

Reelfoot Lake State Park
Route 1, Box 2345, Tiptonville
(731) 253-7756, (800) 250-8617
This shallow, 15,000-acre lake was created in the winter of 1811–1812 as a result of the New Madrid earthquake. This is the famous massive quake, centered in Missouri, that rang church bells in Philadelphia and caused the Mississippi River to flow backwards for 15 minutes as the lake filled. Today Reelfoot can be very rewarding if you are a bird-watching enthusiast or angler. Its claim to fame is the population of golden and American bald eagles, which spend the winter here and in a nearby wildlife preserve. For that reason, this is one park you'd definitely want to visit in January, February, or early March, when park personnel conduct bus tours to see the eagles. (You can go on your own, but the rangers know best where to find the eagles.) Reservations are a must. There are daily pontoon-boat tours May through October, and special arrangements can be made for a group tour in spring and fall. Road biking, a boardwalk, and three hiking trails are popular activities, and the fishing here is excellent, especially for crappie. The lake is shallow, so boating is done slowly so that stumps can be avoided. Accommodations are available at the Airpark Inn, which has minifridges and microwaves in every room, a good thing since the hotel restaurant may or may not be open when you visit. In addition, there's a boat ramp, a visitor center, and camping. Campsites have RV hookups, showers and toilets, and fish-cleaning areas. Primitive camping is also available. This is a large area, so amenities can be miles apart. Take U.S. 51 north from Memphis, and the park is about 25 miles north of Dyersburg on U.S. 78.

T. O. Fuller State Park
1500 Mitchell Road
(901) 543-7581
This state park is also within easy reach, just 11 miles from downtown Memphis. The park is named for Dr. Thomas O. Fuller, a minister, writer, and teacher who spent his life empowering and educating African Americans during the late 1800s and early 1900s. In 1898 he was the only black senator in North Carolina. When Fuller opened in 1942 as Shelby Bluffs State Park, it was the first park for African Americans east of the Mississippi River.

The park has a softball field, basketball and tennis courts, playground equipment, and a swimming pool. There's also plenty of open fields for Frisbee and other games, as well as places to hike and camp. One of the best-kept secrets is the T. O. Fuller State Park Golf Course, an 18-hole course that's challenging and a bargain (see the Golf section in this chapter for details). Near the park is Chucalissa Indian Village, a reconstructed and partially excavated Native American village with an archaeology museum. (See the Attractions and Kidstuff chapters for more details.)

To get to Fuller Park, go south from the U.S. 61/Third Street exit from I-55 (north of the I-240/I-55 interchange) and turn right (west) onto Mitchell Road in south Memphis. Continue a couple of miles, and the road will go straight into the park.

MISSISSIPPI STATE PARKS
If you're looking for a lake or reservoir to enjoy boating, waterskiing, sailing, or fishing, you'll find some excellent options in Mississippi. Many of these parks also have cabins, plenty of birds and wildlife, and other attractions. For more information about Mississippi state parks, call (800) GO-PARKS or visit www.mdwfp.com.

Arkabutla Reservoir
3905 Arkabutla Dam Road, Coldwater
(662) 562-6261
Forty-five minutes south of the city is a recreation lake that can satisfy many outdoor appetites. More than 300 campsites and 420 picnic places grace 13 different recreation areas, swimming is available at three beaches, and eight boat ramps give access to watercraft. Some of the acreage is open to public hunting, and the remainder is lake or flooded timber. Call (662) 362-9212 for fishing and hunting license information. There is also a 5-mile hiking trail. To get

there take I-55 south to Hernando, then 304 west to Eudora, then South 301 to Pratt Road, and follow the signs.

John West Kyle State Park
Sardis
(662) 487-1345

This park is centered around 58,500-acre Sardis Reservoir, well suited to boating, Jet Skiing, or almost any other water activities you can think of. The Sardis Lower Lake has several beaches for swimming. The park also includes a facility for your large group's activities. If you want to stay overnight and you didn't bring your tent, ask about the park's cabins. There's also a swimming pool, tennis courts, and a recreation building in the park. The group campsite can hold 150 to 200 people on Sardis Lower Lake, and there are adjacent swimming beaches and nature trails. There's also a new marina with docking amenities (662-578-7922). John West Kyle State Park is located 9 miles east of Sardis off Highway 315. From Memphis take I-55 south and get off at exit 252.

J. P. Coleman State Park
Iuka
(662) 423-6515

Another nice park on the Tennessee River at huge Pickwick Lake, this is a wonderful place to practice your backstroke, put your boat in the water for some skiing or fishing, or just stroll peacefully along the bank. Cabins and motel rooms are available for overnight stays if you aren't prepared to pitch a tent or bring an RV; and if you'd prefer a pool to the lake, there's one of those here, too. A complete marina is on-site to serve you as well, plus miniature golf and a playground for the children. There's also a convention center that can accommodate up to 150 people. The park is located in the northeast corner of the state, 13 miles north of Iuka. Take U.S. 72 past Corinth, Mississippi, and go north on Route 25.

Wall Doxey State Park
Holly Springs
(662) 252-4231

The 45-acre, spring-fed lake at Wall Doxey State Park is an excellent location for numerous water sports. The park has excellent facilities to accommodate large groups. Within the park, visitors will find a large activity field, a playground, a nature trail, a visitor center, and productive fishing spots. Also, there are two 20-hole disk golf courses.

Lodging facilities include a group campsite (which can accommodate 104 people), 9 cabins, 64 improved campsites, and 18 tent camping pads. From Memphis take U.S. 78 south, turn right off the Holly Springs exit onto Highway 7, and follow the signs to the park 6 miles south.

RECREATION

Adult Recreation Leagues

Whether your game is softball, basketball, soccer, or Ultimate Frisbee, you'll find plenty of team action in the Memphis area. Here are details on specific sports and how to find a team.

BOWLING

You'll find plenty of spots around Memphis to go bowling, most of them open until midnight during the week and into the wee hours on the weekends. All of them rent shoes, and most offer cosmic bowling, so you can play under wild, psychedelic lights during set hours. All of the lanes have their own leagues, but if you want more information about Memphis bowling, check the Memphis Bowling Association Web site, www.memphisbowling.org.

Bartlett Lanes
6276 Stage Road, Bartlett
(901) 386-7701
www.bartlettlanes.net

This 32-lane, 25-year-old facility was remodelled in 2004 and in recent years has gotten all new lanes and a new scoring system. It offers league play at all levels all week and cosmic bowling Friday and Saturday. There's also a cocktail lounge. Bartlett Lanes is big on birthday parties, company parties, and other gatherings and will gladly cater them.

Billy Hardwick's All Star Lanes
1576 White Station Road
(901) 683-2695

For more than 20 years, this East Memphis alley has been the most convenient for people living or staying in midtown and East Memphis. There's league play and open bowling, and All Star Lanes also has hourly specials and group discounts. Amenities include a snack bar, a lounge, and a game room.

Cordova Bowling Center
7945 Club Center Cove, Cordova
(901) 754-4275

One of the newer alleys in the area, Cordova Bowling Center has 36 lanes of league play Sunday through Thursday. The center features automatic scoring scoreboards, a pizza parlor, a snack bar, and a game room with a virtual golf machine. Bowling specials are run weekly.

Cotton Bowl Lanes
9091 Highway 51 North, Southaven
(662) 342-2695 (no area code needed to call from Memphis)

This 34-lane bowling alley has a snack bar, a lounge, and a game room and features cosmic bowling. In the wee hours on weekends, for a set price you can bowl as much as you want until closing time.

Fun Quest Lanes
440 Highway 72, Collierville
(901) 850-9600

This all-purpose 32-lane facility features leagues most days and neon bowling on weekends. Fun Quest has a pro shop, a snack bar, a lounge, a restaurant, a rollerskating rink, and a game room, as well as meeting and party rooms. It closes earlier than most other bowling alleys around town.

Imperial Bowling Center
4700 Summer Avenue
(901) 683-5224

This is one of the oldest alleys in the city, established in 1958. It's open around the clock, with 48 lanes. There's league play all week from 6:00 to 9:00 P.M., with open bowling the rest of the time at various rates. Imperial also has a snack bar, a game room, and a pro shop.

Jillian's
150 Peabody Place
(901) 543-8000
www.jillians.com

This downtown sports complex features Hi Life Lanes, cosmic bowling that has a definite party atmosphere and features multimedia shows on giant video screens and a retro-style lounge. While not for the serious bowler (the lanes are not regulation, and you're not allowed to use your own equipment), Jillian's location makes it convenient to those who live downtown or are staying there during their visit to Memphis.

Winchester Bowl
3703 South Mendenhall
(901) 362-1620

Winchester Bowl features 40 lanes with league play every day, but open bowling is in the afternoons and after 9:00 p.m. There's a pro shop, a snack bar, auto scoring, and, on the weekends, cosmic bowling.

SOCCER

The Mike Rose Soccer Complex is a testament to the growing popularity of the sport here and to the dedication of Mr. Rose and others who share a dream for the youth of this community. Located in Collierville and visible from the Nonconnah Parkway, this state-of-the-art facility features 16 lighted, regulation-size fields of the latest hybrid Sports Bermuda grass. These fields are supported by the best drainage and irrigation technology there is, and the plan is that the 2,500-seat stadium will be home to tournaments, special events, exhibitions, and clinics for years to come. Facilities for participants include showers and a food court, and, in addition to the fields at this 136-acre site, you'll find a picnic and recreation area and a three-acre lake. The Complex (www.mikerose soccercomplex.com) is owned by the Shelby County government and run by OS Memphis in a public/private partnership. To get here take I-240 to Nonconnah Parkway (385). Follow the parkway 7 miles east to the Forest Hill-Irene Road exit; then turn right onto Forest Hill-Irene Road. Take your first right into the Complex on Cindy Parlow Drive.

Soccer clubs in the area include, for adults, the Greater Memphis Soccer Association (901-321-3333); for youth, Collierville Soccer Association (901-854-8724), Germantown Soccer Club (901-755-6688), and Memphis Futbol Club (901-327-9444).

OTHER TEAM SPORTS

The parks and recreation divisions of Memphis (901-454-5220 for adult athletics, 901-767-4580 for youth athletics), Germantown (901-757-7375), and Bartlett (901-385-5599) offer adult and youth team sports such as softball, basketball, and touch football. But how do you locate a team to play on? Start by contacting the Park Service in your area; they might be able to hook you up with a team. If you're affiliated with a church or other large organization, chances are there is already an existing team looking for fresh players. Another good possibility is playing on the team for the company you work for. Some of the larger businesses in Memphis field numerous teams, both single-sex and coed, or, if you can round up enough players on your own, start your own team. Again, call the city to find out about fees and other regulations.

The following sports aren't big enough to warrant a local league, but they are part of larger national leagues:

**Memphis Blues Rugby Football Club
(901) 568-8338
www.memphisbluesrugbyclub.com**

This club was founded in 1998 with the combining of the University of Memphis RFC and Memphis Old #7, at one time sponsored by the Jack Daniels Distillery, hence the name "Old #7" (talk about great parties!). Scrums are held at the University of Memphis or Tobey Field at Central Avenue and Hollywood (hours vary, so check), and tournaments are held twice yearly.

**Memphis Ultimate Frisbee Team
(901) 278-7456
www.memphisultimate.com**

These zany but dedicated athletes have been going at it since 1988, when the "Prairie Squids" first formed. Regional tournaments begin early in the year, so practice continues year-round on the big field at Overton Park. During the short days of winter, they meet on Sundays and some Saturdays at 2:00 P.M. The rest of the time practices are Tuesdays and Thursdays after work and Sunday afternoons. The team hosts its yearly Dead Elvis-A-Go-Go tournament the third weekend in August, which coincides with Elvis Week.

Canoeing/Paddling

You can canoe on all the fishing and park lakes, but paddling nearby rivers is often more satisfying for canoe and kayak enthusiasts. Unfortunately, you have to drive two to three hours to reach many of the best rivers in this area. Close at hand, though, is the Ghost River. Situated roughly 20 miles east of Collierville, it is unspoiled and easy-going, with quiet, shallow waters.

You'll notice that we haven't mentioned what you might think is an obvious choice for paddling: the Mississippi River. Think again. Old Man River can be quite dangerous, with its treacherous undercurrents, entire trees and other debris floating downstream, and huge wakes from the constant stream of barges that are often the size of football fields. Paddling or operating a recreational boat of any kind on the Mississippi should be attempted only by experienced boaters, and swimming is highly dangerous for anyone. Now that you've been sufficiently warned, you should know that the most complete local outfitter, Outdoors Inc. (800–370-1224, www.outdoorsinc.com), sponsors a yearly canoe and kayak race on the Mississippi that is part of the Memphis in May festivities. (See the Shopping chapter for more details about Outdoors Inc.) Every May hundreds of paddlers line up at the starting line, located where the Wolf River empties into the Mississippi. They race downstream to the southern tip of Mud Island, then into the harbor and to the finish line. You might also want to seek out the Bluff City Canoe Club (www.bluffcity canoeclub.org), which organizes canoe trips year-round for paddlers at all experience levels.

These area rivers, excellent for canoeing, are really much more beautiful than the Big Muddy and far less threatening.

Buffalo National River
Jasper, Arkansas
Buffalo River Outfitters
(800) 582-2244
www.buffalonationalriver.com
This breathtaking river, also the first National River, comes tumbling out of the Ozark Mountains of north-central Arkansas. It's home to black bear and elk, and you can hear howling coyotes that send chills up your spine. The main attraction, though, is the tall limestone cliffs for which the river is famous and the incredible beauty that's all around. Paddlers will find that sharp bends and fast shoals interrupt the slower stretches, but it's an enjoyable Class I trip. Buffalo River Outfitters in Jasper (800–582-2244) is your best bet for renting a canoe, and the staff can give you directions from Memphis. The drive takes a little more than three hours, but it's worth it because of the beautiful wilderness.

Buffalo River
Flatwoods Canoe Base
Highway 13, Flatwoods, Tennessee
(931) 589-5661
www.flatwoodscanoe.com
This lovely and clean Class I and II river is well suited to beginners and anyone who enjoys a lazy float. Smallmouth bass, catfish, and bluegill are some of the fish to be caught on the 43 miles of river running through Perry County. Holiday weekends during the peak season tend to be busier, so to avoid crowds, consider other times. You can rent a canoe, kayak, or inner tube for the day.

To get there travel east on I-40 to Jackson, take the Law Road/Highway 152 South exit and go 1 mile to Highway 412. Turn left and go east through Lexington and Parsons, and into Linden. At the four-way stop in Linden, go right onto Highway 13 South. Go 12 miles south and into Flatwoods, and it's on the left. The entire trip is about two and a half hours.

Eleven Point River
9931 Highway 93
Pocahontas, Arkansas
(870) 892-9732
Not far from the Spring River in northeast Arkansas is the beautiful Eleven Point River, originating just across the state line in Missouri. Small, spring-fed, and quiet, this is a generally peaceful alternative to the Spring River, because far fewer people come here. The wildlife is abundant, especially if you venture into a backwater slough, and fish of all kinds are in the water. The water temperature is cold, which can be welcome during the hot summer. Just about all the property along the river is private and marked, but seldom inhabited, and plenty of sandbars provide places to stop and picnic or just relax. No waterfalls have to be negotiated, and rapids are few, mild, and short, so beginners should be comfortable. Woody's Camp and Canoe Rental near Pocahontas is your best bet if you need a campground and canoe outfitter.

The Ghost River (Upper Wolf River)
Moscow and La Grange, Tennessee
Wolf River Canoe Trips
(901) 877-3958

A meandering channel through breathtaking cypress wetlands and a lush lily-pad swamp are just a couple of the habitats to be experienced in the gentle Ghost River section of the upper Wolf River in Fayette County, just a short drive east from Memphis. Wise and vigilant guardians at The Wolf River Conservancy (901-452-6500, www.wolfriver.org) established the canoe trail in 1990, marked by blue and silver signs at regular intervals, and they do group trips for beginners. Rated a Class I run, few if any rapids will be encountered. Depths are shallow, and sometimes low water can require that you get out and pull across sandbars or over fallen trees. Occasional motorized fishing boats will navigate the river, and a popular fishing destination is the swamp, rumored to be the favorite local hole for Collierville resident and fishing-superstar Bill Dance. Largemouth bass, crappie, and catfish are some indigenous species.

To get there go east from Memphis on Poplar Avenue (Highway 57); as you approach the city of Moscow, you'll cross a bridge, and to the right is a gravel parking lot and boat ramp. This is the lowermost access point, and depending on which float you decide on, you might want to leave a car here. Continue into Moscow, go 2.5 miles farther to Bateman Road and turn south, or right. Another 2.5 miles on the left is a small gravel lot and ramp just before the bridge. Putting in here and floating downstream is a two- to three-hour trip through grassy chutes. For a longer float keep going east on Highway 57 about 10 minutes to the small town of La Grange. Turn right and proceed down the steep road less than a mile to the bridge. Before you cross it look for the dirt parking and launch area on the right. The float from here to Bateman Bridge takes roughly six hours and traverses several different kinds of wetlands. For a longer paddle, La Grange to below Moscow takes around nine hours.

Sarah and John Wilburn operate the only nearby outfitter, called Wolf River Canoe Trips. The six-hour float runs $35, and the three-hour one is $30, including the shuttle ride. If you have your own canoe, they'll be glad to drive your car to the get-out spot for a small fee. Wolf River Canoe Trips operates from late March until the end of November. Efforts continue to protect the river through land purchases, and if you're going downstream between the La Grange and Bateman points, everything on the left is now public and open. On the right there are parcels still privately held, so no trespassing or camping is advised.

Spring River
Mammoth Spring, Arkansas
(870) 856-3451

Located in north-central Arkansas about three hours from Memphis is this very popular river. Summertime sees flocks of youthful partyers, many from Memphis, especially on weekends. A huge spring that wells up out of the ground in Mammoth Spring, Arkansas, feeds the river with millions of gallons of chilly water every hour, and if you have the chance, definitely go there and look at the spectacle. Bass and trout are fished out of these waters. Modest rapids and short falls make paddling pretty easy, and several outfitters service visitors. Many Islands Camp Canoe Rental (870-856-3451) is the biggest company and probably has the best amenities and selection of trips. You can rent a canoe or kayak, and camping is available.

To get there from Memphis, cross into Arkansas on either I-40 or I-55, then continue north on I-55 until you reach the Highway 63/Jonesboro exit, and then continue north. About 7 miles north of the town of Hardy, you'll see signs for Many Islands Rentals.

Cycling/Mountain Biking

Because the terrain is as flat as a pancake, road biking can be done anywhere in Memphis. Unfortunately, the city hasn't yet recognized the merits of cycling over automobiles; therefore, bike lanes are all but nonexistent. The city did recently set up five neighborhood bike-route tours, each one with signs to keep you on track and maps available on the Internet (www.cityofmemphis.org). You are, however, sharing the road with cars on these routes. The famous Mississippi River Trail passes through here on its way south to New Orleans and also includes sights such as Alex Haley's boyhood home in Henning. Many area roadies prefer the asphalt of Shelby Forest, where traffic is light. An excellent club and an outstanding resource for rides and social events for individuals and families is the Memphis Hightailers Bicycle Club (www.memphis hightailers.com). The club arranges regular weekly rides all year, and you don't have to join the club to ride with them.

Off-road trails in the area range from easy to expert. Not to be missed is October's Tour de Wolf, which attracts the sport's biggest stars, like Tinker Juarez, to Shelby Farms. This is Tennessee's biggest mountain-bike event, sponsored by Outdoors Inc. Numerous racing classes fit every skill level and age, and vendors from all the big bike companies set up display booths and tents to showcase their latest innovations. Contact Outdoors Inc. (901–755–2271 or www.outdoorsinc.com) for registration information. You can also ask for more details about the following trails.

MOUNTAIN-BIKING TRAILS

Arkabutla Reservoir, Mississippi

Five miles through woods and plenty of charm characterize this trail 45 minutes south of Memphis. Autumn is a good time to enjoy the fall colors around this lake. To get there take I-55 south to Hernando, then take 304 west to Eudora, turn onto South 301 to Pratt Road, and follow the signs. (See the State Parks section of this chapter for more details about Arkabutla Reservoir.)

Herb Parsons State Park

Tucked inside Herb Parsons State Park is this 6.5-mile trail that features abundant tree crossings as the route takes you around the lake. Be sure to wear long pants, as the poison ivy can be brutal. To get there take Macon Road in East Memphis east past the town of Fisherville, go right onto Fisherville Lake Road, and then follow the signs. It's less than an hour's drive.

Shelby Farms

The 5.5-mile trail at Shelby Farms on which the Tour de Wolf is held is undoubtedly the most popular in the area. Single-track, fire roads, and open prairie with slight elevations make for a fast ride, which favors a "hard-tail" bike. Another section of the park is home to the White Trail, a technical and narrow singletrack through the woods. The starting point of this 8-mile trek is under the Walnut Grove bridge on Germantown Road, about 0.5 mile south of the intersection of Walnut Grove and Germantown Roads.

Stanky Creek

Only a few years old, this collection of three loops and a cool jump area is awesome. The name comes from the bottomlands that the trails occupy, but the smell isn't nearly as bad as the name suggests. This collection of narrow and technical singletracks in the middle of Bartlett will test all your skills, and all three trails offer jumps and tight twists. Riding these trails when they're wet is nearly impossible because they get really slick. Also, it's easy to get lost without an experienced rider along, so a detailed map of the trails can be found at www.midtownbikeco.com. Directions: From I-40 take the Sycamore View exit north toward Bartlett. A couple miles up and just past Freeman Park (on the left), turn left before the barbecue place and continue past the old town center to the four-way stop sign. Turn left, and the parking lot is about 200 yards on the right.

Disk Golf

Meeman-Shelby Forest State Park
910 Riddick Road, Millington
(901) 876–5215

This is probably the city's most convenient disk golf course, recently expanded to 27 holes. Shelby Forest, in addition to being open to players seven days a week, also hosts an annual tournament. Be sure to check out the general store right at the park's entrance, where you'll find a good selection of disks for sale.

Wall Doxey State Park
Holly Springs, Mississippi
(662) 252–4231

If you don't mind a bit of a drive, venture down to Wall Doxey and check out its two 20-hole disk golf courses. It's open every day, and once you pay the $2.00 entry fee to the park, you can play the course as much as you want for free. The second course, which was added recently, is the more challenging of the two.

Fishing

TENNESSEE WILDLIFE RESOURCES AGENCY LAKES

The Mississippi River can be sport fished for monster catfish, but eat 'em at your own risk and don't take a boat out unless you are very familiar with the treacheries of Old Man River. A better bet is one of 17 TWRA-managed lakes in middle and west Tennessee, open year-round. Some of these lakes are operated by private concessionaires under contract and offer complete services for the fishing public. Lakes open one-half hour before sunrise to one-half hour after sunset, except Garrett Lake, which is open 24 hours a day. Camping may be permitted after obtaining permission from the lake manager and only in designated areas. A daily lake permit of $3.00, in addition to the regular fishing license, is required to fish most of these lakes. All residents 16 through 64 years of age, except holders of a Sportsman License or Lifetime Sportsman License, and all nonresidents (regardless of age) must have this permit, obtainable at the lake office. The lakes are open to fishing all week. Some concessionaire-operated lakes may be closed on Thanksgiving Day and Christmas Day. Speed boating, waterskiing, and swimming are not permitted, nor are houseboats, sailboats, and inboard cruisers. On Bedford, Marrowbone, VFW, and Williamsport Lakes, only trolling motors can be used. Boats may be rented at many lakes. Statewide creel and size limits apply with the following exceptions: Only rods and reels, poles and hand-held lines, and jugs may be used. Cast nets are illegal on agency lakes. For more information, call TRWA (731–423–5725) or visit www.state.tn.us/twra and click on "Fishing in Tennessee."

STATE AND COUNTY PARK LAKES

In addition to the TWRA lakes, nearly every single park and reservoir has at least one fishing lake, if not more. Crappie (pronounced "croppy"), large- and smallmouth bass, catfish, sauger, and other species are plentiful around the Memphis area. You'll need appropriate licenses for whichever state you're fishing in, as well as day-use permits for most state park lakes. (See the State Parks write-ups in this chapter for directions and details.) You can also fish on the Wolf and Buffalo Rivers.

Under County Parks, see Shelby Farms. Under Tennessee State Parks, see Big Hill Pond State Park, Chickasaw State Park, Meeman-Shelby Forest State Park, Pickwick Landing State Park, and Reelfoot Lake State Park. Under Mississippi State Parks, see Arkabutla Reservoir, Sardis Reservoir (see John West Kyle State Park), and Wall Doxey State Park.

OTHER FISHING LAKES

Chewalla Lake Recreation Area
Holly Springs National Forest
Mississippi
(662) 236-6550
**www.southernregion.fs.fed.us/
mississippi/hollysprings**

Just 7 miles south of Holly Springs is this nifty and quiet 260-acre lake, recently renovated to maximize its fishing opportunities and featured on TV by the well-known fisherman Bill Dance. A boat ramp, fishing pier, picnic sites, and tent camping as well as RV hookups await at this wooded location. If you decide to go, be sure to watch the southern sky after dark for a peek at the mysterious and unexplained colored dots of light that are rumored to sometimes flash and jump across the horizon.

Horseshoe Lake
Hughes, Arkansas

The west-central portion of the state is composed mainly of flat farmland, and most recreational lakes are found well to the west in mid-central Arkansas, like Greer's Ferry Lake north of Little Rock or Lake Hamilton near Hot Springs. If you absolutely must splash around in nearby Arkansas, consider Horseshoe Lake. Situated about 30 minutes south of West Memphis, this big oxbow lake is home to a small community made up largely of weekend places owned by Memphis families. Two thousand five hundred acres of water produce all the standard local varieties of fish, and waterskiing can be popular, along with Jet Skiing. Amenities are spare, but at the main entrance to the lake, there's a boat ramp and a fishing dock (small fees) and a homey little country restaurant. The food is good, and the owners and servers are friendly. You can't go wrong when you stop in after a long day on the water, sit at the counter facing the lake, and order a piece of the fresh pie du jour with coffee. To get here cross the Mississippi River on I-40 to West Memphis and take exit 271. Pick up Highway 147 South here and follow it all the way to the lake, about 25 miles.

Tunica Lake
Tunica, Mississippi
www.tunicalake.com

Created by the Corps of Engineers for flood control, this large oxbow lake is large enough to support lots of anglers easily. Although the lake is well known for crappie, lots of other fish lurk these waters, including the toothy alligator gar, and white, yellow, and largemouth bass. With a small chute to the Mississippi River, the lake is able to replenish constantly, so nourishment for fish is abundant. You'll find several places here that operate bait shops and ramps that require a small fee. To get here follow Highway 61 South past the casinos and look for the signs to the lake off to the right. The trip takes about 45 minutes from Memphis.

WORLD-CLASS TROUT FISHING IN ARKANSAS

Avid flyfishermen in Memphis consider themselves to be extremely fortunate to live so close to the generous streams and rivers of north-central Arkansas, in particular the White River, the North Fork River, and the Little Red River. The current world-record brown trout, weighing in at 40 pounds, 3 ounces, was hauled out of the waters of the Little Red River, located two hours (100 miles) west of Memphis. Thanks to an aggressive trout-stocking program and well-managed rivers, Arkansas is home to some of the best trout fishing in the country. Fish hatcheries grace the Little Red, White, and North Fork Rivers, among others. Brook trout ("brookies"), German brown, cutthroat, and rainbow trout can all be landed from the same bit of water on a really good day. Most anglers stick to the traditional fly-fishing techniques, but trout caught from the bank with a plain old rod and reel are fun, too! Several dollars at most docks will cover the cost of fishing, but not your license. For a fee guides can be hired to float you down the river in a shallow boat and tell you how to catch 'em. Keep an eye out for grocery stores.

They're a good place to get a license and fishing regulations, and you can pick up food and supplies at the same time.

Sometimes a good day on the river is defined as a day when the water is slow and shallow, as upstream dams manipulate water flow for electricity generation, and heavy power demand can mean that heavy water flows are needed to turn turbines. Nonetheless, veteran and novice fly fishermen from far and wide descend upon these waters in hopes of tricking wily Mr. Trout into biting a hook. During peak season folks line the middle of the rivers for long stretches, so plan ahead and make reservations if you want to fish holidays or summer weekends.

Caution: Listen for loud blasts from the air horns blown by the dams to warn fishers of impending water releases. Count the number of blasts, and that will tell you how many turbines will be operated and, consequently, how high and fast the water will become. Always know how far you are from the dam because only a few minutes' warning is given, and even for single or double blasts, you'll have to get out of the water fast.

For lists of trout docks and guide services on all the rivers, contact the Arkansas Department of Tourism at (888) AT-PARKS or go to www.arkansas.com. One favorite place to rent a cabin or hire a guide for a float-fishing trip is Gene's Resort (870–499-5381) in Salesville, on the North Fork River. Just a little south of Mountain Home, Gene's is a neat, clean establishment that is staffed by knowledgeable people. Cabins and RV spots can be rented, but even if you pitch a tent at the park down the road (at the base of the dam), go by Gene's to find out how the fishing's been. By the way, on the other side of the dam is the long and deep Norfork Reservoir, also full of fish, as well as people who are sailing, waterskiing, fishing, sunning, and the like. To get to Gene's from Memphis, cross the Mississippi River on I-40 and turn north on I-55 on the far side of West Memphis. After roughly 25 minutes look for the Highway 63/Jonesboro exit and continue north on Highway 63 toward Jonesboro. Stay on this road through Jonesboro to Hardy, then take Highway 62/412 West all the way to the city of Mountain Home. From there follow Highway 5 South to Highway 177 and turn left. The Norfork Dam and Gene's are right down the road; just look for the signs.

Golf

Golfers in Memphis are a lucky lot, thanks to an abundance of courses and weather that permits essentially year-round play. Whether you prefer economical municipal courses, the latest name-brand designer links, or something in between, there are choices aplenty.

Memphians are proud of their contributions to the game as well. The late Dr. Cary Middlecoff, winner of 40 PGA tournaments, an early Masters winner and two-time U.S. Open Champion, was a native Memphian. Some active PGA players who call Memphis home are "The Boss of the Moss" Loren Roberts, 2003 PGA Championship winner, Shaun Micheel, and occasional resident John Daly.

Every year the PGA Tour stops here for the FedEx St. Jude Classic. (See the Annual Events chapter for more information.) During the week of the tournament, tour pros can be spotted all over town, and because so many local hackers are at the Classic watching great golf, area courses are wide open and deserted.

Always call ahead before setting out to play, and ask about tee times, specials, and course conditions (especially in summer, when bent-grass greens can suffer from the heat). Virtually all area courses offer an array of discounts for juniors and seniors, and for weekday, winter, and afternoon play.

MEMPHIS PARK SERVICES MUNICIPAL GOLF COURSES

"Muni" golf is thriving in the city, thanks to the seven courses operated by Memphis Division of Park Services. Modest in cost and conveniently located, almost all these mature courses are located inside or near the I-240 loop, with the exception of the hilly and tight Davy Crockett course situated about 10 minutes north of the loop in Frayser. All have a good selection of equipment and lessons as well as sandwiches, snacks, sodas, beer, and electric and pull carts. Most of these courses have been open for many years and were built at a time when Bermuda grass was the norm for tees and fairways. Accordingly, some allow metal spikes, but since that policy is subject to change at any time, it's better to call ahead and ask. Several have driving ranges, practice greens, and lessons. It's best to call ahead about the condition of the course, lest you arrive at the course only to find out the greens have just been aerated. Tall, healthy trees line generally wide fairways at many of the facilities, making for moderately challenging holes that are ideal for mid- to high-handicappers and even beginners. Walking will set you back about a buck a hole in summer, and cart riders will pay $30; expect slightly better prices in the off-season. Overton is a nine-holer, as is M. L. King, which recently added a new clubhouse. It would be hard to find two better beginner's layouts, and they cost about half as much as the full-size layouts. The epicenter for Memphis muni golf is Galloway, which hosts more rounds than any other, so definitely call and make sure you can get a tee time! A major overhaul and update were completed in spring 2002, as the holes were redesigned, bunkers and

water hazards added, some sick trees eliminated, and a smart-looking new clubhouse sits where the old snack bar rested. A great "new" place to begin your Memphis golfing experience!

**Audubon, 4160 Park Avenue
(901) 683-6941**

**Davy Crockett, 4380 Rangeline Road
(901) 358-3375**

**Fox Meadows, 3064 Clarke Road
(901) 362-0232**

**Galloway, 3815 Walnut Grove Road
(901) 685-7805**

**M. L. King Jr., 465 South Parkway West
(901) 774-4340**

**Overton Park
(2100 block of Poplar Avenue)
(901) 725-9905**

**Pine Hill, 1005 Alice Avenue
(901) 775-9434**

OTHER GOLF COURSES

**Edmund Orgill Golf Course
9080 Bethuel Road, Millington
(901) 872-3610, (901) 872-7493 for tee times
www.orgillpark.com**

This Millington bargain is another very playable muni-type layout, located in a 442-acre park of the same name. The only course operated by Shelby County, it's the site of regular high-school district and regional competitions. Most fairways are wide and accommodating, and the course is generally in good shape. A few holes are next to a magic lake that eats golf balls and spits out catfish! Bermuda greens and fairways mean that this is one of the few courses that allows metal spikes. Par is 70, and length is 6,400 yards from the back tees. Rates: $31 with cart included, but ask about junior, senior, and twilight discounts. Lessons are available. There is a driving range and modest clubhouse, and walking

Greg Pickett (7948 Winchester, 901-757-1112) is the preeminent golf-club technician to the local pros. He has a shop (laboratory?) that any wizard would be proud of, and he can perform first-class jobs on any club. His specialty is custom fitting clubs to your swing, and he's proud to feature True-Temper shafts, made right down the road in Olive Branch.

18 holes is common at this course, situated near a naval base. Directions: From downtown take I-40/I-240 east to the Millington exit and continue north on U.S. 51 for 11 miles. At the second light turn right onto Navy Road and proceed 3.3 miles to Bethuel Road and turn left. From there the course is 2.5 miles on the right.

T. O. Fuller State Park Golf Course
1400 Pavilion Drive
(901) 543-7771
www.state.tn.us/environment/parks/ tofuller/golf.htm

The only local course run by the state park system can be found at T. O. Fuller State Park in the southwest corner of Shelby County. Another older-style Bermuda course, it's nestled among some hills originally hunted by the Chickasaw Indians centuries ago. Recently, funds were spent here to improve the overall condition, and as a result the course was honored by the state in 1998 as the Best State Park Golf Course. Several holes capitalize on the terrain by running along the tops of ridges, along the dales, or both. One of the hardest par-3s ever conceived is hole number 4, affectionately called "The Volcano." It's 196 yards to a small green, if you hit it! Par is 72 on this 5,986-yard course, and there is a practice green near the first tee, but no driving range. Costs run $16 weekdays and $18 on weekends in summer, and add $11 for a cart. This is a great course to walk for exercise, and pull carts are available for a nominal fee. The clubhouse is home to a modest selection of apparel, balls, gloves, and a few clubs. Nice folks run the snack bar, and they serve a mean cheeseburger and soda, but because it's a state park, no alcoholic beverages of any kind are allowed on the grounds. If you like hilly, frequently deserted golf courses, this is a good spot, and the rates fit many budgets. Directions: Head south on Third Street, either from downtown or I-55, and turn right onto Mitchell Road. After a few minutes the road runs straight into the park. Once in the park, take your first right and then bear right at the top of the hill.

SEMIPRIVATE COURSES

Most Tennessee and Mississippi suburbs boast one, if not several, "daily-fee" golf courses, generally of excellent quality and surrounded by residential developments. These courses frequently offer memberships at a moderate cost (usually worth it if you play two or three rounds a week) in addition to tee times for the nonmember public. Fees are higher than those at municipal courses, and dress codes are stricter; collared shirts are usually required, and cut-off shorts are frowned upon. All these higher-quality facilities offer lessons from PGA professionals and have ranges and putting greens, nice clubhouses, and well-stocked pro shops. Yardages stated are from the back tees, so subtract a bit for regular and ladies' tees. The highest weekend and holiday rates with carts are listed, but expect to pay less if you're walking or playing weekdays or during the off-season (winter). About walking: Most of these places don't allow it on weekends in order to keep the speed of play faster, and all prohibit metal spikes on your shoes.

Cherokee Valley Golf Club
6635 Crumpler Boulevard
Olive Branch, Mississippi
(901) 525-4653
www.olivebranchgolf.com

Cherokee is another of the younger courses on the local golf scene, and one of the best. Plenty of time was allowed for the grass to mature before play started, and it shows: The Zoysia fairways are sweet, and the bent-grass greens (like those at Plantation) are area favorites, with lots of tricky, hidden breaks! This is a relatively short course, 6,054 yards, with ample water hazards and bunkers. In fact, there are 78 bunkers scattered around the course, a tribute to U.S. 78, which runs right past a couple of holes. Number 12 is a par-4 dogleg right around a pond to a green with a backdrop of sorts. Confident longer hitters might try to fly the pond to set up an eagle putt. Good luck! A fee of

$46.50 will get you on this beautiful course, which can yield some low scores.

The Club at Big Creek
**6195 Woodstock Cuba Road, Millington
(901) 353-1654
www.golfnorthcreek.com**

This semiprivate facility is several miles north of downtown in a community called Woodstock. The greens have recently been upgraded to Champion Bermuda, and the fairways are still Standard Bermuda. Almost 7,100 yards from the tips, the front 9 of this long course is made up of basically flat, pine-lined, wide, back-and-forth holes. The back 9 snakes through wooded hills and requires more precision off the tee. In warm weather bring your bug repellent to thwart monster mosquitoes bred in the nearby creek bottoms. Numerous ponds, traps, and wooded OB's can paste extra strokes to your score, and if the greens happen to be lightning fast, you'd better watch out! Lots of membership packages are offered, and nonmember summertime greens fees reach $42 plus tax. To get here ride the I-240 loop to its northwest corner and follow the signs to U.S. 51 and Millington. Go north on Thomas Street 5.5 miles and turn left onto Fite Road (across the highway from the DuPont plant). Go straight until the road comes to a T, and turn left. Turn left again soon onto Woodstock Hills Road and then immediately right; the course is about 0.25 mile on the right. Affiliated with Big Creek is the Club at North Creek in Southaven, Mississippi.

The Club at North Creek
**8770 North Creek Boulevard
Southaven, Mississippi
(662) 280-4653
www.golfnorthcreek.com**

This sister course to Big Creek is still a relative newcomer but has matured over the last few summers. Some holes are open; more are framed by woods and water hazards. Think before you tee off: Lots of the holes require shorter and more precise tee shots than a driver can deliver, and

some long hitters could even leave their biggest drivers at home. Play your approach shots with care, too, lest your ball slide off one of the slick greens. Carts come equipped with GPS systems that really help describe the holes and nail down yardages! The completed clubhouse is handsome, with all the standard amenities. Fees are $45.

Fair Oaks Golf Club
**220 Fair Oaks Drive, Oakland
(901) 466-1445**

Located in the newest, farthest reaches of the ever-expanding metropolitan area, this daily-fee course has generally wide-open Bermuda fairways and modern TifEagle Bermuda greens of generous size. Accuracy keeps the ball out of the rough, but misses aren't penalized too much. Par is 72 on these 6,970 yards, designed by Kevin Tucker of Nashville. John Lisman is the PGA golf professional. He owns the course, and he might just be the one who loads your clubs on the cart, sells you your greens fees, tells you where not to hit, and what kinds of sandwiches are on hand. You gotta like that! Plenty of homesites are still vacant, and given how quickly the memberships have sold, buying a homesite is the only way remaining to wiggle into a membership. The clubhouse has not yet been built, so operations run from a temporary structure. Daily-fee players trade $40 for a greens fee and cart in summer, $35 in winter.

Plantation Golf Club
**9425 Plantation Road
Olive Branch, Mississippi
(901) 525-2411
www.olivebranchgolf.com**

Slightly west of Southaven is the city of Olive Branch, Mississippi, home to Plantation, its sister course Cherokee Valley, and others. Plantation is a long test from the back tees (6,773 yards from the tips) but still a joy to play. Par is 72, and only slight elevation changes interrupt this largely flat layout. Zoysia fairways provide fluffy, upright lies, and water hazards abound.

Be sure to enjoy hole number 18. A par 4, it makes a sharp dogleg left over a wide pond to an elevated and sloping green. One reason this club hosts so many tournaments is that it has one of the best finishing holes in the city. A spacious and airy clubhouse contains one of the better-stocked pro shops. Greens fees are $42.50 including cart during summer weekends. The nice people at this club also operate Cherokee Valley, just a little way down the road.

Quail Ridge Golf Course
4055 Altruria Road, Bartlett
(901) 386–6951
Here is a nifty 18 located northeast of the city in the suburb of Bartlett. Tree-lined fairways (some wide, some narrow) demand careful tee shots because you'll be looking to set up your ever-important approach shots on most of these holes. All the par 3s demand good shot-making, taking advantage of moderate elevation changes that set up large and well-maintained greens. Length from the back tees is only 6,314 yards and par is 71, but this deceiving layout will drive many golfers to overconfidence. It's difficult to put a finger on what exactly makes this spread such a favorite—perhaps the friendly staff, the design? Rates are in line with comparable area courses, at $42 plus tax during busy summer times (includes cart) and $35 plus tax in winter. Memberships are available. The clubhouse at this busy place is attractive and pretty new and includes a snack bar and pro shop.

Stonebridge Golf Club
3049 South Davies Plantation Road
Lakeland
(901) 382–1886
www.stonebridgegolf.com
This 6,743-yard gem is adjacent to I-40, but only a couple of holes abut the interstate, and there is ample vegetation to block most noise. This layout can be quite a challenging test. In winter overseeded rye makes for green fairways, and the bent-grass greens can be deadly fast any-

time! Many holes feature water hazards, and a healthy breeze is a frequent adversary. George Cobb is well-known for designing "Amen Corner" at Augusta, but not many locals know he did this layout as well. Lots of corporate tournaments are held here, so always call ahead. Being close to the freeway means quick and easy access from most of the city, so that adds to the course's popularity. Weekend rates including cart (with GPS) run $46.

Wedgewood Golf Club
5206 Tournament Drive
Olive Branch, Mississippi
(901) 521–8275
www.wedgewoodgolfersclub.com
Another Olive Branch spread, and not too far from Plantation, is Wedgewood. The holes here are flat and wide for the most part, but many are adjacent to wide, deep ditches that will devour any ball that enters, so beware! Steep sides and thick kudzu prevent any retrieval whatsoever. Fast bent-grass greens are generally in good condition. The slick green on number 17 is maybe the toughest in the Memphis area, with a steep grade and three tiers. Number 18 features a very narrow fairway lined with trees to keep you honest, and a pond guards the front of a steep two-tiered green. Fees are in line with other similar courses at $45 with cart in summer.

Leaderboard Golf is a great place to buy grips, shafts, clubheads, or many other golf components. Located on National Avenue, they no longer have a brick-and-mortar retail shop, but you can go to www.leaderboardgolf.com for a look at their truly gigantic selection of replacement and upgrade items for your golf clubs at wholesale prices. Or you can call (901) 948–8190; they may answer the phone with their former name, Memphis Golf.

WORTHY GOLF OUTINGS

Several outstanding layouts are within an hour's drive (give or take) of the city limits. Because they are in the countryside, they offer a more relaxed setting for swinging away without the fear of plunking a golf ball into someone's living room. These include two casino "resort" courses near Tunica, Mississippi.

The Bear Trace at Chickasaw State Park
9555 State Route 100
Henderson, Tennessee
(888) 944-2327
www.beartrace.com

Opened in spring 2000, this Jack Nicklaus design is already building a sterling national reputation. This and four other Nicklaus courses comprise Tennessee's Bear Trace "golf trail" of outstanding yet affordable layouts. About 1 hour and 15 minutes away, this is the nearest one to Memphis so far, but there are rumors of one to be built even closer. Carved out of the woods in massive Chickasaw State Park, characteristics include the marshy wetlands of Piney Creek and its tributaries and gentle rolling hills. The gorgeous holes total over 7,100 yards from the tips, with a slope of 134, so this is no cakewalk. The clubhouse, handmade from logs, looks like a mansion where Davy Crockett would be right at home. Bermuda fairways and bent-grass greens stay in good shape, which they should, considering top rates of $57 including cart in summer; however, winter and twilight fees are substantially lower. As with all Bear Trace courses, packages are available.

The Cottonwoods Golf Course
13615 Old Highway 61 North
Robinsonville, Mississippi
(662) 357-6079
www.grandcasinos.com

River Bend Golf Links
205 Nine Lakes Drive
Robinsonville, Mississippi
(888) 539-9990
www.riverbendlinks.com

These two courses are owned and operated by the casinos in Tunica County, Mississippi. River Bend's manicured course was created by the collaboration of Harrah's, Hollywood, and Sam's Town. Wide open and without trees, the grass-covered dunes are indeed reminiscent of true Scottish links. Opened in 1998, the architect is Clyde Johnston. Fees run $60 with cart. Cottonwoods is owned by the Grand Casino. A touch longer than River Bend (6,999 yards vs. 6,923 yards), it is a links-style course as well. Hale Irwin designed this resort course, and peak-season fees are $115 for nonguests and $100 for guests. Packages are available through the casinos. (For more information see the Casinos chapter.)

Kirkwood National Golf Club
Highway 4
Holly Springs, Mississippi
(662) 252-4888
www.kirkwoodgolf.com

Possibly the most outstanding daily-fee course in this area is Kirkwood National Golf Club, just south of Holly Springs. From the Memphis city limits, it should take about 50 minutes to reach this devilish spread. Use the highway time to polish your mental game because you'll need it. Every hole is a tribute to the game. Take number 4 for example, a long and narrow par 5 with a 90-degree dogleg at the end, where you'll then have to fly a creek and bunkers to reach the elevated two-tier green. Not for the faint of heart! A bit farther on, number 6 is another par 5, this one curving nearly 180 degrees to the left, leaving a short shot to a green surrounded by water on three sides and sand on the fourth side. Champion Bermuda greens welcome well-placed shots from Bermuda fairways at this grand layout. Despite the hearty fairway grass, leave your metal spikes at home, and don't plan on walking this 7,100-yard beast on weekends. The fairly new clubhouse, though not huge, is nicely appointed and can be a great postgame place to soothe your ego with a sandwich, a bubbly beverage, and the understanding words of other golfers. Rates: $35 during the week and $45 weekends, including cart and range balls; lessons are extra. There's also a driving range. From I-240 South, take the Lamar Avenue exit south. This road will become U.S. 78, so continue south about 30 miles to the Holly Springs/Oxford exit and then turn right, or south, onto Highways 7 and 4. Go 1 mile and make a right onto Highway 4 West. From there the course is 1 mile on the left. Check out the Web site for information on rental cottages and cottage rental/greens fee specials.

Mallard Pointe Golf Course
John West Kyle State Park
Sardis, Mississippi
(888) 833-6477
www.mallardpointegc.com

Perfectly situated on hilly land overlooking Sardis Lake, this is the type of course that can lead to severe golf addiction! No pushover, this 7,000-yard Bob Cupp–designed treat wears gloves most of the time. But when the wind blows off the lake, be ready for a test of your game. Number 3 is a moderately long dogleg par 4, easily reachable in two, but the green is nestled up against a pond. There is nothing but shaved grass along the edge, so if your ball hits anywhere near the slope, goodbye! Number 17 is a potentially drivable par 4 for long hitters, but the sheer front face of the elevated green is covered with sand traps that offer only difficult and nearly vertical recovery shots. The clubhouse is small, with a walkup snack and sandwich window where soda and beer is available, too. Cheerful youngsters bring carts to your car and load your bags for you, the driving range is really nice, and so is the practice chipping green behind it—all of this for only $36 including cart, even on weekends and holidays. Ask about other discounts, and if you want to play a second round it's only $12 more! To get here go south on I-55 to exit 252, which only takes about 50 minutes, and from there head east about 3.5 miles to the park entrance.

Tunica National Golf & Tennis
1 Champions Lane, Tunica, Mississippi
(662) 357-0777, (866) 833-6331
www.tunicanational.com

This is the area's newest course, a 7,210-yard, par-72 championship course designed by renowned course architect Mark McCumber. The course features five sets of tees to provide a challenging game for all levels, and its incredible 365-degree driving range is only one of the tools at the course's golf academy to help improve your game. Amenities include a huge new clubhouse featuring a bar and grill as well as a fully stocked pro shop.

DRIVING RANGES

Golf and Games Family Park
5484 Summer Avenue
(901) 386-2992
www.puttputtmemphis.com

This entertainment complex has both artificial and grass tees, and the artificial tees are heated in cold weather. There is a pro shop full of goodies and a PGA-certified teacher on hand to correct your duck-hook. The range balls are kept fresh, and the cart that retrieves the balls is protected by wire mesh should you *accidentally* hit in that direction. Batting cages, go-karts, miniature golf, and a video arcade round out this facility, located just east of the I-40/I-240 interchange on Summer Avenue.

Hiking

Most state parks have hiking trails that can be enjoyed at all times of the year. See the State Parks listings for more information. The Memphis Chapter of the Tennessee Trails Association (www.tennesseetrails.org) sponsors hikes. See the Sporting Life listings in Friday's *Commercial Appeal* Memphis Playbook section. Alternatively, ask at Outdoors Inc. (901-755-2271, www.outdoorsinc.com), an outfitter that sells hiking boots and equipment; the staff is knowledgeable and up to date about good places to hike.

Wolf River Bottomlands
Highway 194, Rossville
(901) 452-6500
www.wolfriver.org
Eight miles west of Moscow is the town of Rossville, where a new half-mile board-walk gives walkers access to one of the few remaining cypress-forest swamps that used to characterize the entire Mississippi Basin. It's the work of the Wolf River Conservancy. To get there from Memphis, follow Poplar Avenue (Highway 57) East to tiny Rossville and turn left at the local bank onto Highway 194. Just a little bit north of the city limits is the parking lot for the boardwalk.

Horseback Riding

Shelby Farms Park
5000 Pine Lake Drive
(901) 382-4250
www.shelbyfarm.com
The place to ride horses is at Shelby Farms, the large park east of Memphis. You can rent horses for all types of riders and ride over 450 acres of land for $15 an hour for riders age nine and older. Younger kids can ride the ponies. The stables are open seven days a week, and because no reservations are taken, it's first-come, first-served.

Hunting and Shooting

HUNTING

The Tennessee Wildlife Resources Agency (731-423-5725 or www.state.tn.us/twra) assures equal access to publicly held land for all uses, including hunting, and they can tell you what to do to gain access to the best public-hunting areas. Because there aren't enough public-land permits to go around, drawings are held in order to select recipients. The applications are available from TWRA or can be downloaded from their Web site. Tennessee

licenses can be ordered online or at Wal-Mart, K-Mart, and other retailers of sporting goods. Remember, Memphis is in the middle of the Mississippi River Flyway, so the surrounding area has some of the best waterfowl hunting in the country, and lots of public land is located in Mississippi and Arkansas, too. Numerous private landowners outside the city operate hunting resorts for all kinds of game, not just waterfowl. In fact, hunting leases have become a significant source of income for cash-strapped farmers. The classified ads in the local newspaper include a hunting/fishing section, and there are almost always ads offering land for lease, clubs looking for members, and offers for guided or "pay" hunts and full-service hunting resorts. One good bet is to contact the knowledgeable staff at the local hunting store Tommy Bronson Sporting Goods (901-458-5458) for a recommendation or look over the pamphlets pinned to the big bulletin board at Buck & Bass Sports Centre (901-660-3515).

SHOOTING RANGES

Venues for honing your shooting skills are plentiful around town, and the local government even operates one for the general public at Shelby Farms. The Memphis Sport Shooting Association, which used to be called Memphis Rifle and Revolver Association, was incorporated in 1936. Their 185-acre facility, which is just outside town in Arlington at 9428 Old Brownsville Road, includes several pistol-range and rifle-firing points, five skeet and trap fields, two sporting clay courses, and more. Call (901) 867-8277 for current membership fees and requirements. Here are some other shooting options.

Range Master
2611 South Mendenhall Road
(901) 370-5600
www.rangemaster.com
This indoor, full-service pistol range offers classes, information for getting permits, memberships, and more. The range is

open to nonmembers for $15 an hour; memberships, which start at $149 a year, will reduce the usage fee.

Shelby Farms Public Shooting Range
6791 Walnut Grove Road
(901) 379-4492
This is an outdoor facility run by the local government on park property, but it's across the street from the main park area. It features rifle and pistol ranges, as well as muzzle-loading and trap shooting areas. The cost to fire a gun is $12, but senior discounts may apply. Eye and ear protection is mandatory, and shooters must bring their own. The range is closed Monday and Tuesday.

Top Brass Sports
4788 Navy Road, Millington
(901) 873-2264
www.top-brass.com
In addition to their indoor handgun range, this place also sells and even rents firearms for use at their facility. No membership is needed, training is available, and range rates are only $8.00. Open seven days a week.

The Willows Sporting Clays
Grand Casino
Tunica, Mississippi
(662) 357-3118
www.caesars.com/GrandCasino
This fast-growing sport, sometimes described as golf with a shotgun, is available at Grand Casino in Tunica. The game, conducted in a controlled atmosphere, simulates a hunting environment, providing a variety of targets. Reservations are required. The Grand also offers trap and skeet shooting, and quail hunting in season.

Racquetball

Public courts can be found at the Fogelman Downtown YMCA (901-527-9622) and Collierville's Schilling Farms YMCA (901-850-9622). One for-profit athletic

club that has six courts for members is Wimbleton Sportsplex. It offers a whole range of membership options (901-388-6580).

Skating and Skateboarding

Whether you go for skateboarding, rink skating, or outdoor roller blading, you'll find places in Memphis where you can skate to your heart's content. For roller-skating rinks, there's Skateland Summer (901-683-6991) and East End Skating (901-363-7785), both in East Memphis. There's also Cordova Skating Center (901-755-0221), situated in the suburbs off Germantown Parkway, and Funquest Skating Center (901-850-1124) in Collierville. For outdoor skating, Tom Lee Park in downtown Memphis and Shelby Farms in the suburbs are good options. See the Insiders' Tip in the Kidstuff chapter for details.

The best place to get the goods on local skateboarding is Cheapskates (1576 Getwell Road, 901-744-1312). A visit or call to Memphis's oldest skateboard store is a good way to stay on top of the latest local news or just hang out with the "crusties."

Be sure to ask for the Cheapskates map of area skate parks. Favorite skateboarding venues include Skate Park of Memphis (901-737-8448) in Cordova and Kullison (pronounced "collision," believe it or not) Park (901-323-3888) in midtown. The skating is free behind Houston High School in Germantown and Horn Lake High School in the Mississippi suburb of Horn Lake.

Swimming

CITY POOLS

The city of Memphis operates 15 outdoor swimming pools for nine weeks during the summer. Hickory Hill and Bickford, the

city's only indoor swimming pools, are
open year-round. Admission to the pools
is free, and swimming lessons are available. Hours and days of operation vary.

Bickford
321 Henry Street
(901) 578-3732

Charlie Morris
1235 Brown Avenue
(901) 272-0327

Douglass
1616 Ash Street
(901) 323-3542

Fox Meadows
3064 Clarke Road
(901) 365-0527

Frayser
2907 North Watkins Street
(901) 353-0627

Gaisman
4223 Macon Road
(901) 763-2920

Gooch
1974 Hunter Street
(901) 276-9685

Hickory Hill
3910 Ridgeway Road
(901) 566-9685

L.E. Brown
617 South Orleans Street
(901) 527-3620

Lester
Tillman at Mimosa Streets
(901) 323-2261

Orange Mound
2430 Carnes
(901) 458-9035

Pine Hill
973 Alice Avenue
(901) 947-2978

Raleigh
3678 Powers Road
(901) 372-1930

Riverview
1981 Kansas Street
(901) 948-7609

Tom Lee (Carnes Pool)
328 Peach Street
(901) 527-3748

Westwood
810 Western Park
(901) 789-6275

Willow
4777 Willow Road
(901) 763-2917

Tennis

The city of Memphis operates public tennis centers throughout the city, with
courts that are open seven days a week
and cost a nominal fee. The centers are
open year-round and offer indoor and
outdoor courts, with the exception of
Frayser, Raleigh, and Wooddale, each of
which have eight outdoor courts, open
March through October only. Most accommodate children as well as groups. While
Memphis has a number of private,
members-only clubs with tennis courts
and related amenities, we do not include
them in this listing.

Bellevue Tennis Center
1310 South Bellevue Boulevard
(901) 774-7199

Frayser Tennis Center
2907 North Watkins Street
(901) 357-5417

Leftwich Tennis Center (East Memphis)
4145 Southern Avenue
(901) 685–7905

Raleigh Tennis Center
3680 Powers Road
(901) 372–2032

Whitehaven Tennis Center
1500 Finley Road
(901) 332–0546

Wolbrecht Tennis Center (East Memphis)
1645 Ridgeway Road
(901) 767–2889

Wooddale Tennis Center (Parkway Village)
3390 Castleman Street
(901) 794–5045

YMCAs

The Memphis area YMCAs offer an array of services, equipment, and programs. While all of them have before-school and after-school programs for kids, other amenities vary from location to location. For example, the East Memphis Y has access to a wooded walking/jogging trail at adjacent Lichterman Nature Center, while the Medical Center Y has cardiac and other rehabilitation programs. For more information on available amenities, or to find the Y nearest you, contact the YMCA of Memphis and the Mid-South at (901) 850–0987 or log onto www.ymca memphis.org.

The Abe Scharff YMCA
254 South Lauderdale Street
(901) 521–9622

DeSoto County Family YMCA
1471 Highway 51
Hernando, Mississippi
(662) 449–0500

East Memphis YMCA
5885 Quince Road
(901) 682–8025

Fogelman Downtown YMCA
245 Madison Avenue
(901) 527–9622

Mason YMCA
3548 Walker Avenue
(901) 458–9622

Medical Center YMCA
777 Washington Avenue, Suite 405
(901) 572–5622

Millington Family YMCA
7725 East Navy Circle, Millington
(901) 873–1434

Sweeney YMCA
5959 Park Avenue
(901) 765–3105

Thomas B. Davis Family YMCA
4727 Elvis Presley Boulevard
(901) 398–2366

YMCA at Schilling Farms
1185 Schilling Boulevard, Collierville
(901) 850–9622

SPECTATOR SPORTS

You might say it's a brand-new ball game for spectator sports in Memphis. After decades of having to watch underfunded minor-league teams play in barely adequate facilities, Memphians are finally seeing how the other half lives. And they are showing their approval by purchasing tickets in record numbers.

The new dawn came at perhaps the city's darkest sports hour. Memphis, which has enjoyed professional baseball—usually at the Double A level—for more than 100 years, lost its team in 1997, when the ownership moved it about 95 miles east to Jackson, Tennessee. However, less than a year later, a new ownership team won a Triple A franchise and announced plans for a new downtown ballpark. And to make it even better, the new owners landed a major-league affiliation with the St. Louis Cardinals, the lopsided favorite of Memphis baseball fans. When AutoZone Park opened in 2000, it was the best of all worlds for the Memphis fan: a Triple A (not Double A!) franchise with a Cardinals affiliation in a facility widely regarded as the best in the minor leagues. One member of the St. Louis Cardinals, playing in the exhibition game that inaugurated the ballpark, said, "This is not a great minor-league park—it's a great major-league park for minor-league baseball." During the next three seasons, Memphis finished second in attendance for all of minor-league baseball, missing first place by just a few thousand tickets each year.

AutoZone helped launch the revitalization of downtown Memphis, and the trend has continued since then. University of Memphis basketball, fueled by the arrival that year of coach John Calipari, saw a dramatic rise in ticket sales for its games at the nearby Pyramid Arena. Then came the arrival of the NBA Grizzlies: Finally, after a seemingly endless parade of fly-by-night pro basketball leagues, Memphis had

its very own honest-to-goodness major-league team. Even better, the Griz made the playoffs during the 2003–2004 season, and starting with the 2004 NBA season, the team plays in the new FedExForum, another downtown facility that has won raves nationally. Almost lost in all the good news from downtown Memphis is the area's professional hockey team, the RiverKings. This Central Hockey League team is playing in a beautiful new facility in the nearby suburb of Southaven, Mississippi, where they, too, are setting attendance figures and winning league championships.

As if to validate Memphis's rise to national sports prominence, the Mike Tyson–Lennox Lewis title fight—one of the richest prizefights in boxing history—was held in the Pyramid in 2002. Of course, to many the real spectacle was the three-ring circus surrounding the bout, as celebrities and television crews poured into town, and Memphis found itself squarely in the media spotlight.

The city also boasts a calendar of annual sports events, starting in February with the Kroger St. Jude and the Cellular South Cup indoor tennis championship. The event features top tennis stars in a weeklong tournament that's steeped in tradition. In summer professional golfers of national prominence play here in a PGA stop, the FedEx St. Jude Classic, which has taken its place as one of the most competitive on the tour. There's also the Germantown Charity Horse Show in June, which draws top riders.

The annual matchup between two top area historically black universities, Tennessee State University and Jackson State University, fills the Liberty Bowl for the Southern Heritage Classic in September. In December the Liberty Bowl is the site of the AutoZone Liberty Bowl Football Classic, an annual college football game pitting the champions of Conference USA and Big West. One of the oldest bowls in college football, the Liberty brings national exposure to the city.

(See the Annual Events chapter for details on all of these sporting events.)

As for other spectator sports, boxing matches take place monthly on Beale Street at the New Daisy Theater, and there's also wrestling from time to time at the Mid-South Coliseum. This retro arena near the Liberty Bowl has a rich tradition of professional wrestling, and it's here that Sputnik Monroe and Jerry "The King" Lawler built their careers. (For more information see the Close-up in this chapter.) Across the river in West Memphis, Arkansas, "The Sport of Kings," greyhound racing, is a nightly attraction at Southland Greyhound Park. North of the city in Millington, auto racing makes itself heard at the Memphis Motorsports Park.

It's worth mentioning that even though they don't play here often, a number of Southeastern Conference teams have a huge Memphis following. You'll see scores of alumni and other fans in the bars when the teams play. Easiest to spot are University of Tennessee fans, often clad in bright Volunteers orange, but there are also lots of Ole Miss Rebels (University of Mississippi) fans, and to a lesser extent devotees of University of Arkansas and Mississippi State University. Then there are the Titans, the NFL team that played briefly in Memphis in the late 1990s before making their home in Nashville. Although they're called the Tennessee Titans, Memphians tend to view the team as a Nashville thing.

Amateur sports thrive in the city under the auspices of the Memphis Parks Commission, which operates baseball, softball, soccer, and basketball leagues for all ages, and of the city and county schools. (Check out the Parks and Recreation chapter for more information about these leagues.)

BASEBALL

Memphis Redbirds
AutoZone Park
8 South Third Street
(901) 721–6050 (for tickets)
www.memphisredbirds.com
The hottest summer sports ticket in town gets you into AutoZone Park, the crown jewel of downtown Memphis, where you can watch the Memphis Redbirds take on their Pacific Coast League (Triple A) rivals. The Redbirds play 72 home games between April and Labor Day. The Redbirds are the St. Louis Cardinals farm team, and a number of players are now with their major-league parent club. The park itself is a prince among minor-league baseball parks, with a design that looks and feels like Baltimore's Camden Yards.

The Redbirds have built on a strong baseball tradition in Memphis, which dates from the old Memphis Chicks of the Southern Association. That Double A team won a league championship, then captured the Dixie Series in the 1950s. Major-league rosters were dotted with former Chicks such as Luis Aparicio, Jim Landis, and Sammy Esposito. After the decades-old Russwood Park burned down in a spectacular Easter Sunday fire in 1960, the Chicks played at Tim McCarver Stadium, named for the famous Memphis-born player and current TV commentator, as did another Triple A team, the Memphis Blues.

AutoZone Park opened on April 1, 2000, to a sellout crowd of 15,000 as the team hosted its major-league parent, the

---

One of the most pleasant ways to take in a Redbirds baseball game—especially if you have young children—is to buy lawn seats for just $5.00 each. You can spread out a blanket and relax on the sloping, grassy bank behind left field to watch the game. Your ticket will also admit you into the ballpark to buy concessions, T-shirts, or just wander around.

St. Louis Cardinals. Sellout crowds that first year were the rule rather than the exception as fans flocked to the new park. Sellouts were no fewer in 2001 as 900,000 flocked to the park to watch the beloved Birds and fan-favorites Stubby Clapp and Lou Lucca.

Ticket prices range from $5.00 to $15.00, and various ballpark facilities are available to accommodate groups of up to 2,500.

For a sampling of the basketball talent for which Memphis has long been known, check out the annual Jerry Dover Memorial Classic, a three-on-three basketball tournament held each summer at Southwest Community College gym. Here, the big college players who hail from Memphis come home to play each other in this annual charity event. You can watch old high-school rivalries being rekindled, as well as some great basketball action.

BASKETBALL

Memphis Grizzlies
FedExForum
200 South Third Street
(901) 205–1234, (901) 888–HOOP (for tickets)
www.grizzlies.com

The Grizzlies first season (2001–2002) created great excitement in Memphis, with highlights that included the team's at-home win over the L.A. Lakers. Much of the excitement came from the perform-ances of top players like Pau Gasol, named conference rookie of the month several times during the season; Shane Battier, the Duke University star forward, and Jason Williams. True, the team didn't excel in its NBA division, the Midwest divi-sion of the Western Conference, but coaches attribute that performance to the fact that the first season was more about developing a team.

The team's prospects, morale, and visi-bility got a big boost in 2002 when former L.A. Lakers executive Jerry West signed on as the team's president of basketball oper-ations. One of the 50 greatest players in NBA history, West as an executive led the Lakers to eight NBA Championships.

The team, which had been the Vancou-ver Grizzlies, landed in Memphis during the 2001 off-season, bringing to the city its first major-league sports team. Before the first game was played, the team scored points with Memphians by drafting Battier and by choosing hometown favorite St. Jude Children's Research Hospital as one of its featured charities.

The Grizzlies had built a tradition of losing while in Vancouver but began to improve upon their arrival in Memphis. The improvement accelerated with the arrival of West, who brought in Hubie Brown as coach for the 2002–2003 season. The Griz finished that season with the best record in franchise history, although still a losing one. However, building on that momentum and capitalizing on West's keen eye for tal-ent, the 2003–2004 season was a dra-matic turnaround. Memphis was one of the hottest stories of the year. The Grizzlies finished with one of the best records in the NBA and made it into the playoffs. With-out an established superstar, the Griz play with passion and fire. Brown, who has molded the Griz into an unselfish unit, takes advantage of the team's fine chem-istry and hustle by giving most of the players equal playing time and sending fresh units at the opposition in waves that gradually wear on the opponents. Brown was named NBA Coach of the Year for his role in transforming the Griz into a winning team. Memphis fans enjoy the Griz style of play, and tickets for many games are hard to come by.

Grizzlies fans can take advantage of some of the lowest ticket prices in the NBA. Tickets are available through Ticket-master (901–525–1515), $9.00 to $125.00 for individual tickets and $405.00 to $5,625.00 for season tickets.

CLOSE-UP

Wrestling: A Memphis Thing

For years and years grunts and groans emitted from the Mid-South Coliseum on Monday nights, as a pair of broad, burly, hairy-chested men (or women) clashed in yet another wrestling match.

Although some people may argue that it's more show than sport, professional wrestling is one sport in which Memphis has played a huge role for more than 40 years, developing such talents as Sputnik Monroe, Hulk Hogan, and Randy Savage.

Over the years Memphians—and wrestling fans everywhere—have come to know Sputnik Monroe, Jack Dundee, Jerry "The King" Lawler, and Sid Vicious. This is where in the 1980s the late comedian Andy Kaufman, after years of wrestling women, came to take

on the local wrestling establishment, only to leave it with his head pile-driven into the floor by Lawler. More recently, World Wrestling Federation stars The Rock and Kurt Angle wrestled in Memphis on their way to WWF fame.

Now that Monday Night Wrestling is no longer a fixture at Memphis's Mid-South Coliseum, you can still see live wrestling when the WWF comes here a few times each year. WMC-TV 5, the station that broadcasts wrestling on Saturday mornings, also sponsors some live matches. Both capture the theatrics that wrestling audiences of all ages love.

Make no mistake: Wrestling is definitely a Memphis thing, along with barbecue, Elvis Presley, soul music, and walks along the Mississippi.

University of Memphis Tigers Basketball
FedExForum
200 South Third Street
(901) 678-2346, (888) 867-8636
www.gotigersgo.com
The University of Memphis basketball team boasts a strong, local following. Coach John Calipari has brightened the team's fortunes after several lackluster seasons under a myriad of coaches. Already Calipari helped the Tigers to their first national title, with an NLT win in 2002, and a first-round win in the 2004 NCAA tournament.

Fans have to go all the way back to the 1980s to remember when the Tigers, under Coach Dana Kirk, were consistent winners. Before that, in 1973, another leg-

endary Tiger coach, Gene Bartow, led the school to its first Final Four appearance in history. In St. Louis the Tigers lost to the eventual national champions, UCLA. A dozen years later, Kirk would once again lead the team back to the Final Four, where it lost to Villanova in a semifinal game.

Today's Tigers tip off at FedExForum against Conference USA opponents such as Louisville, Cincinnati, and St. Louis University. Memphis also has hosted several conference tournaments and served as hosts of early-round NCAA games.

In 2000–2001, the team's first season under Calipari, the Tigers advanced to the NIT semifinals before being knocked out. A big reason was high-school All-American

Dajuan Wagner, son of Tiger assistant Milt Wagner, who joined the team in 2001. Among other distinctions, Wagner was named Conference USA's Freshman of the Year. The team has regrouped since Wagner left to pursue his NBA career. In the past U of M squads have included other All-American players such as Penny Hardaway, Keith Lee, Eliot Perry, and Lorenzen Wright, now a member of the Memphis Grizzlies.

Individual game tickets are $18 and $13, while season tickets are $205 and $280.

BOXING

Boxing on Beale
New Daisy Theater
(901) 525-8979, (901) 525-8981
Boxing on Beale, a longtime tradition, takes place the first Tuesday of every month at the New Daisy. Memphis boxing fans, who sometimes include some of the city's top executives, gather to watch the action. There are usually four to six fights—some good, some bad—but the best entertainment may be watching the family and friends of the local boxers vociferously weighing in for their fighter.

On boxing night you'll see a main event and several undercards, in weight classes that can include heavyweight, middleweight, junior-middleweight, and welterweight divisions. It's quite a scene, complete with "ring babes" in bikinis, beer, cigars, popcorn, and, of course, great boxing.

Most Memphians don't realize that the national racquetball championships are played at the Racquet Club of Memphis each November. More than 800 professional and amateur players meet to do battle at this event, officially named the Choice Hotels U.S. OPEN Racquetball Championships and sponsored by USA Racquetball. For more information call (800) 234-5396 or check out www.usra.org.

Ringside seats are $15, and general admission seats are $12.

FOOTBALL

University of Memphis Tigers
Liberty Bowl Memorial Stadium
335 South Hollywood Street
(901) 678-2341, (901) 729-4344 (tickets)
www.gotigersgo.com
After floundering for more seasons than Tiger fans care to remember, the University of Memphis appears to be headed in the right direction. In his third season as head coach, Tommy West led the 2003 Tigers to an 8-4 regular season record, including a win over Ole Miss. The U of M celebrated its best finish in decades with a win over North Texas in the New Orleans Bowl—its first bowl appearance in more than 30 years.

West, former head coach at Clemson and player at the University of Tennessee, not only is producing more wins for the Tigers, he also has established growing fan support. Games that once drew less than 20,000 now are drawing more than 30,000. His teams also are drawing more national attention, even receiving mention in top-25 polls. Obviously, this is a dramatic departure for the Tigers, who, under a number of different coaches, suffered through losing season after losing season. Playing in Conference USA, the team is eligible for an automatic spot in the Auto-Zone Liberty Bowl matchup in December if they are champions of their league. The conference also has tie-ins with other bowls for second- and third-place finishers.

Despite yearly disappointments Memphis schedules two or three SEC teams each season. It has been playing both Ole Miss (University of Mississippi) and Mississippi State University since the 1950s and can show wins over those schools plus Auburn University, Vanderbilt University, University of Alabama, and University of Tennessee. Memphis fans still talk about the 1996 home game with Tennessee, in which U of M scored a dramatic last-second win over the Volunteers, its first in 16 meetings.

Individual tickets are $10 to $30; season tickets run from $60 to $135. The school also offers various ticket packages.

HOCKEY

Memphis RiverKings
4560 Venture Drive
Southaven, Mississippi
(662) 342-1755
www.riverkings.com

The RiverKings, the longest-running professional indoor team in Memphis sports history, plays 35 home games each season beginning in October. The Central Hockey League team, which moved to the new DeSoto County (Mississippi) Civic Center in 2000, had played for many years in the Mid-South Coliseum in Memphis.

The current RiverKings team is not the original professional hockey team in Memphis. In the 1960s the Memphis Wings and their successor team, the Memphis South Stars, were members of the Central Hockey League, which at the time was a developmental league for the NHL. Presently the Central Hockey League is unaffiliated, and its teams are stocked mostly with free agents and players just out of college who are looking for a way into the NHL. Also, the league owns the teams, sells the franchise to local ownership, and has local personnel to take care of the day-to-day tasks.

Tickets are $9.00 to $20.00. Game times are 7:15 P.M. and, on Sundays, 2:35 P.M.

RACING

Memphis Motorsports Park
5500 Taylor Forge Drive, Millington
(901) 358-7223, (866) 407-7333
www.memphismotorsportspark.com

The area's racing fans can listen to the roar of the engines, smell the gas fumes, and see the races at the Memphis Motorsports Park, located 7 miles north of Mem-

If you are a big race fan, ask about the Memphis Motorsports Park NASCAR season pass (866–40–SPEED, www. memphismotorsportspark.com). Available early in the year, the $99 pass entitles you to great seats at both of the park's NASCAR weekends as well as other perks. If you order early, they'll throw in a free junior season ticket, too.

phis in Millington. Some of the featured races are the NASCAR Craftsman Truck Series Memphis 200 in June, the NHRA AutoZone Nationals in September, and the Sam's Town 250 Busch Series, a NASCAR event, in October. In addition, Memphis Motorsports Park hosts the Winston Drag Racing Series, weekly racing, and special events throughout the season.

From April to September the Mid-South's top racers gather for Friday Night Thunder at the quarter-mile, high-banked dirt track. This weekly series features four classes of cars including mini stocks, hobby stocks, open-wheel modifieds, and winged-sprint cars. These racers try to follow in the footsteps of other legendary racers such as Hooker Hood, Sammy Swindell, Jeff Swindell, and Greg Hodnett.

Each Thursday the park's quarter-mile drag strip becomes a drag-racing haven for its popular Test-N-Tune event. This gives the serious drag racer a final chance to tune his car before the weekend's competition and gives the novice a chance to come out and put his personal car to the test.

Saturday night at the park features the finest drag racing in the area as the E.T. Bracket Racing Series takes center stage. Drivers from all over the Mid-South converge on Memphis to compete in four different classes—Super Pro, Pro, Junior Dragster, and a Trophy Class—as the racers vie for weekly titles.

The Thursday, Friday, and Saturday events continue into fall.

Gates open about two hours before race time. Ticket prices vary, depending on the event.

Southland Greyhound Park
1550 North Ingram Boulevard
West Memphis, Arkansas
(800) 467–6182, (870) 735–3670
www.southlandgreyhound.com
Long before the casinos began opening up in Tunica, Memphians have been crossing the bridge into Arkansas to watch the greyhounds race and to indulge in pari-mutuel wagering. Southland has live races every day except Sunday and simulcasting of greyhound races from other tracks daily.

You can watch the action trackside or on TV monitors in a clubhouse environment. Southland also has a family-seating area and arcade to accommodate families with kids. The park has an adoption program for its past-prime racers, so don't be surprised if you occasionally see the sleek greyhounds on leashes around the city.

There's free admission to the park and $1.00 admission to the clubhouse level.

WRESTLING

Mid-South Coliseum
996 Early Maxwell Boulevard
(901) 274–3982 (tickets)
The days are gone when Monday Night Wrestling was a fixture at the Mid-South Coliseum, but you can still catch some live wrestling there when the World Wrestling Federation comes to town a few times a year. Memphis has a rich tradition of wrestling, producing stars from Sputnik Monroe to Jerry "The King" Lawler. (See the Close-up in this chapter for details about pro wrestling in Memphis.)

DAY TRIPS AND ⊖
WEEKEND GETAWAYS

We include this chapter not because there isn't enough to do in Memphis. We believe the city has enough attractions, nightlife, and good food to keep any visitor entertained and happy, but if you're in the mood for a road trip, there are plenty of excursions you can take to experience rural and small-town life in the Deep South.

You can venture down to the Mississippi Delta, to see firsthand where the blues were born, and across the river to Helena, Arkansas, home of the "King Biscuit Time" radio show and annual blues festival. Elvis fans may want to visit Tupelo for a look at the King's birthplace, with a stop in Holly Springs to visit the shrine assembled by the world's most committed Elvis fan. Oxford, Mississippi, where writer William Faulkner lived and worked, is the quintessential small Mississippi town, a favorite day trip among Memphians (and especially Ole Miss fans, as Oxford is home to the University of Mississippi). West Tennessee has plenty to offer, including Civil War battlefields and the birthplace of *Roots* author Alex Haley.

If you like gambling, you can check out the nine world-class casinos in Tunica County, Mississippi, all within about a 45-minute drive from Memphis. (See the Casinos chapter for details.) There's an abundance of hotel rooms at Tunica, which could come in handy given the dearth of accommodations options in nearby towns such as Clarksdale.

These destinations are within two hours' drive of the city. If you wish to venture farther for the weekend, Hot Springs, Arkansas, is a favorite getaway for Memphians. At this historic resort, you can bathe in the natural hot-springs water at bathhouse spas, enjoy live horse racing in season, and tour lavish restored bathhouses dating from the 1920s.

Hikers, anglers, and others who like the great outdoors can learn more about state parks and other getaway options in the Parks and Recreation chapter.

Before you set out, it's a good idea to call ahead to make sure the attractions you want to visit will be open, and to see if there's anything special going on. It would be great if your visit to Clarksdale, for example, just happened to coincide with the annual Sunflower River Blues and Gospel Festival, but not so great if you were counting on a room for the night. If you visit some of these towns and attractions on Sunday or Monday, virtually everything will be closed. Also, word of mouth is important in these rural areas, so once you arrive, start asking questions. Otherwise, you might not learn about a great local bluesman who's performing at a nearby juke joint, or that a dumpy-looking restaurant has fabulous fried catfish.

BIRTHPLACE OF THE BLUES

Head south from Memphis on the legendary Highway 61 (now four lanes all the way through Clarksdale), and you'll be in the heart of the Mississippi Delta, the land where the blues were born. From downtown Memphis take Third Street to the south, which eventually turns into U.S. 61; otherwise, take I–40 to I–55 North and take the exit to U.S. 61 South. Once you leave the city, you'll drive past cotton fields (you'll actually see the white stuff on the plants in late summer and fall), plantation houses, sharecropper shacks, and simple country churches. (The casinos at Tunica are a relatively recent development.) These were the fields where workers' hollers gradually evolved into the blues as we know them, and many of the greatest bluesmen in the world once lived and worked in the fields you're seeing. (See the Memphis Music chapter for a full account.) If you're looking for the legendary crossroads, where blues-great Robert Johnson made his mythical deal with the devil to get a guitar, you'll find many intersections claiming to be The One. A likely candidate is where Highway 61 crosses U.S. 49, the road that takes you across the Mississippi River into Helena, Arkansas. It's about 75 miles from Memphis to Clarksdale and about 65 miles to Helena, home to the "King Biscuit Time" blues show.

Blues fans may want to time their visit to coincide with one of the Delta's annual blues festivals. King Biscuit Blues Festival (870–338–8798, www.kingbiscuitfest.org), one of the world's largest blues festivals, takes place in October in Helena. There's also the August Sunflower River Blues and Gospel Festival in Clarksdale (662–627–6820, www.sunflowerfest.org), or the Mississippi Delta Blues and Heritage Festival in Greenville (888–812–5837, www.delta blues.org). Book accommodations in the local area well in advance, or expect to drive back to Memphis after the festival.

Clarksdale, Mississippi

If you're looking to experience the raw feel of the Mississippi Delta, this town of 20,000 is the place. As you approach Clarksdale, take a right turn onto U.S. 61 (which becomes State Street) to north Clarksdale and follow the road as it meanders through town. Look for signs to the **Delta Blues Museum** (1 Delta Blues Alley, 662–627–6820, www.deltabluesmuseum .com), a good first stop in your tour. The museum, established by the Carnegie Library after members of ZZ Top and other musicians raised the necessary money, is housed in the Clarksdale railroad depot (a separate building houses the archives, which also are open to the public). You enter the museum proper through double screen doors, which every Delta country store once had, and into a rustic exhibit space. The museum recreates the plantation lifestyle that produced the blues, with old photos, guitars, and harmonicas that belonged to blues greats including John Lee Hooker and Sonny Boy Williamson II. You'll also find the original headstone from the grave of Mississippi Fred McDowell, the sign from the Three Forks juke joint where Robert Johnson played and was poisoned, and the shack where Muddy Waters lived (with a life-size statue of the man inside). From the displays you learn exactly where W. C. Handy heard the blues for the first time and the name of the Delta plantation where locals say the blues originated. The museum is open Monday through Saturday. Admission is $6.00 for adults and $3.00 for children ages 6 through 12 (this may seem steep for a small museum, but think of it as your contribution to keeping the blues alive). The museum occasionally gets traveling exhibitions, which may cost extra and may displace some of the permanent collection. The museum director or other staff can tell you about live music, both at the museum and in area clubs, taking place during your visit. Just west of the blues museum (to the left as you leave the building) is a former grocery store/cotton seed company that has been converted into **Ground Zero Blues Club** (0 Delta Blues Alley, 662–621–9009, www.groundzerobluesclub.com). Co-owned by actor Morgan Freeman and named for Clarksdale's position as "ground zero for the blues," the lofty, old-fashioned club serves home cooking and burgers for lunch and most nights for dinner. Live music (mostly local blues acts but it varies) usually cranks up about 9:00 P.M. on Wednesdays and weekends.

Just beyond Ground Zero is **Cat Head Blues and Folk Art** (252 Delta Avenue, 662–624–5992, www.cathead.biz), where you can buy blues CDs and folk art by locals. Store-owner Roger Stolle is a great source for information on what's happening in Clarksdale, and he also maintains an up-to-the-minute Web site.

Another claim to fame is that playwright Tennessee Williams lived in Clarksdale as a child with his grandfather. You can see the brick church, St. George's Episcopal Church (106 Sharkey Avenue), where Rev. Walter Dakin was rector for many years. True fans may want to attend the yearly Mississippi Delta Tennessee Williams Festival, when there is usually a walking tour of places associated with the playwright and his work.

Clarksdale food options include Abe's Bar B Q (U.S. 61 at U.S. 49, 662-624-0047), one of the Delta's oldest barbecue joints where you also can get hot tamales. Farther south on U.S. 61 is Chamoun's Rest Haven restaurant (121 Issaquena Avenue, 662-627-5554), a diner that features Southern home cooking, Lebanese specialties, and great homemade meringue pie. For fine dining that seems far too elegant for a place like Clarksdale, have dinner at Madidi (164 Delta at Second Street, 662-627-7770, www.madidires.com), a swank restaurant that serves dishes such as oven-roasted local striped bass with cheddar grits. Like Ground Zero, it's partly owned by actor Morgan Freeman, who frequently stops in when he's not filming or making appearances out of town.

As for accommodations Clarksdale boasts the swank Belle-Clark bed-and-breakfast inn, a beautifully restored 19th-century home (662-627-1280, www.belleclark.com), and has a few chain hotels on U.S. 61 such as Comfort Inn. The most unusual accommodations are found at Hopson Plantation's **Shack Up Inn** (662-624-8329, www.shackupinn.com), where you can stay in a sharecropper shack, complete with the corrugated tin roof as well as modern amenities such as indoor plumbing, which the sharecroppers never had. The shacks are near the former plantation commissary, now a blues club with a bar, occasional live blues music, and errant hours. It's worth checking out for the cool old signs, cash register, and other antique stuff, but it's sometimes reserved for private parties.

For more information about Clarksdale, call (800) 626-3764 or check out www.clarksdale.com.

Note to steak lovers: You can't be this close and not check out the legendary grocery-store-turned-steak-joint in Greenville, Mississippi, **Doe's Eat Place** (662-334-3315). Greenville is about 85 miles as you continue south on U.S. 61; then go west on U.S. 82. You may be eating in the kitchen, but it will be the steak of your dreams. Be sure to try the hot tamales, too. Reservations are recommended. If you spend the night, the Greenville Suites and Inn (662-332-6900) next to the levee is a good bet or try the Hampton Inn. Literary buffs will want to visit McCormick Book Inn (825 South Main, 662-332-5068) to learn about the many local writers, including historian Shelby Foote and novelist Walker Percy. For more information about Greenville, check out www.thedelta.org.

Helena, Arkansas

Incorporated in 1833, this small, historic river town caught the eye of Mark Twain for its picturesque perch above the river. To get here take U.S. 61 from Memphis, then go west on U.S. 49, going about 10 miles past the Isle of Capri Casino and across the Mississippi River bridge into Arkansas. Although you may want to first take a detour to the Visitors Information Center, to get to historic Helena, turn right at the end of the bridge. Once in town, check out the **Delta Cultural Center** (141 Cherry Street, 870-338-4350, www.deltaculturalcenter.com), where staff can answer your questions about the area. The center is actually two buildings, one of which is housed in a former railroad depot. In that regard it's like Clarksdale, but it differs in that the exhibits are new and modern looking, not rustic in a Delta sort of way. The depot's exhibits give the history of the area, including photos and descriptions of life on the river. The second building, a storefront on Cherry Street, is a visitor center with temporary art exhibitions as well as a permanent exhibit highlighting blues musicians who came from or passed through the Arkansas Delta. One of its eccentricities is that the center mentions only Arkansas blues artists. So you'll find plenty about Sonny Boy Williamson, but nary a word about Muddy Waters. The main attraction, though, is the "King Biscuit Time" radio show, broadcast from the visitor center every day at 12:15 P.M. by Sonny Payne. The blues show, broadcast from local station KFFA since the 1940s, launched the careers of Williamson and Robert Jr. Lockwood. Importantly, it brought blues music to many Deltans, including B. B. King and others who went on to become blues greats. Although there's occasionally live music, as in the program's early days, today Payne usually spins CDs and spins yarns during the half-hour show. You can hear the program at www.kingbiscuit.com. Payne likes mingling with visitors, and he might even invite you to be on the radio show. King Biscuit also lends its name to the annual blues festival, which has grown into a huge event with a who's-who of performers. The lineup has included Robert Jr. Lockwood, Sam Carr, Alvin "Youngblood" Hart, Pinetop Perkins, and Marcia Ball. Best of all, it's free. You can see footage of the most recent festival at the center.

Elsewhere downtown are antiques and gifts shops to browse, as well as Bubba's Blues Corner (105 Cherry Street, 870–338–3501), a shop inside a shop that buys and sells blues records and CDs. There are few questions that owner Bubba Sullivan can't answer, and he can direct you to places such as the restaurant around the corner where the soul food is the real thing, but there's no telephone.

For barbecue try Armstrong's Pit Barbecue (303 Valley Drive, 870–338–7746).

When it comes to accommodations, Helena has some exquisite antiques-filled, historic bed-and-breakfast inns, all with large verandas, private baths in the rooms, and full breakfasts. The Edwardian Inn (317

Biscoe Street, 870–338–9155 or 800–598–4749, www.bbonline.com/ar/edwardian) is a 1904 colonial revival mansion that features quarter-sawn oak woodwork on the interior. Magnolia Hill (608 Perry Street, 870–338–6874, www.bbonline.com/ar/magnoliahill), is a Queen Anne Victorian home with original fireplaces that at one time served as a club for World War II soldiers. Foxglove, 229 Beech (870–338–9391, www.bbonline.com/ar/foxglove), is a 1900 home with beautiful interior woodwork that overlooks the city of Helena from Crowley's Ridge. These are just a few of more than 30 Helena homes found on the National Register of Historic Places. You can also get a free tour of some homes, including the Pillow-Thompson House (718 Perry Street, 870–338–8535, www.pccua.cc.ar.us/pillowthompson).

If bed-and-breakfast inns aren't your thing, try the Isle of Capri Casino (888–782–9582), across the river in Lula, Mississippi, or the Best Western Inn in neighboring West Helena.

For more information about Helena, get in touch with the Helena Tourism Commission at (877) 899–3263.

ELVIS'S BIRTHPLACE AND MISSISSIPPI TOWNS

If you drive southeast from Memphis out U.S. 78, the four-lane highway to Holly Springs and Tupelo, you'll discover the hilly terrain of Mississippi's piney-woods area. It's a marked contrast to the flat farmland of the Mississippi Delta, and Mississippians will tell you that people from the hills are a different breed from the party-loving Delta folk. Holly Springs is the closest of the towns we list here, about a 45-minute drive from Memphis, whereas Tupelo is about 100 miles from Memphis. Oxford is about a 30-minute drive east of Holly Springs. It would make for a long day to try to see all three towns in one day, but it can be done if you plan carefully. The towns form a triangle, so once you get to Holly Springs, you can continue east on U.S. 78 to Tupelo, from Tupelo west on Mississippi Highway 6 to Oxford, then from Oxford back to Holly Springs via Highway 7 and U.S. 78 back to Memphis. Alternatively, from Oxford you can go east on Mississippi Highway 6 to I-55, then north to Memphis. Of course, you can choose to concentrate on one or two of these towns or make it an overnight trip. If you are spending the night, keep in mind that Tupelo, by far the biggest of the three towns, has the largest concentration of accommodations.

Tupelo

Probably every person in the world knows that Tupelo is the birthplace of Elvis Presley, who lived there until moving with his parents to Memphis at age 13. Tupelo, a vibrant town of 35,000, also has other things going for it, including a furniture-making industry that's one of the largest in the world and a convention arena (BancorpSouth Center) that seats 10,000 people. To go straight to the Presley house from U.S. 78, you pass a number of Tupelo exits and take the Veterans Boulevard exit and follow the signs to the **Elvis Presley birthplace and museum,** 306 Elvis Presley Drive (662-841-1245). The house is a tiny two-room shotgun shack that Elvis's father, Vernon Presley, built himself for $180, which he borrowed for materials. Elvis was born there on January 8, 1935. You'll see a wood-burning stove, an icebox, and furnishings of the era, although none is original to the house. Behind the house is a museum with a collection of memorabilia from the collection of Janelle McComb, a family friend of the Presleys. You find notes written by Elvis and childhood photos as well as photos, outfits, and mementos from his rise to fame through his Las Vegas days. There's also a large gift shop, and a statue of Elvis at age 13. Just over from the museum is a modern chapel, built with funds from Elvis fans and dedicated two years after his death. Admission to the home is $2.00 for adults and $1.00 for children ages 7 through 12; admission to the museum is $5.00 for adults and $2.50 for children. If you're hungry and don't want to venture far, check out Johnnie's Drive-In Bar-B-Q, a 1950s-style place that serves barbecue sandwiches and other fare. When you leave the birthplace, turn left onto Veterans Boulevard, and look for the drive-in at the corner of Main Street. For a map with other Elvis points of interest, including his schools, go to the Tupelo Convention and Visitors Bureau at 399 East Main Street at Franklin Street (662-841-6521, 800-533-0611, tupelo.net). Main Street is also Mississippi Highway 6, the highway that links Tupelo to Oxford.

As for other attractions, you can continue west on Main Street/Mississippi Highway 6 to check out the **Oren F. Dunn Museum** (662-841-6438), a modest but interesting town museum with a mishmash of displays and artifacts. You'll find a 1949 bookmobile, a space suit worn on the *Apollo 15* mission and other items related to the U.S. space program, Civil War artifacts, and a dogtrot house built in 1870. Admission is $1.00 for visitors age five and older.

One of the city's newest attractions is the Tupelo Automobile Museum (399 East Main Street, 662-842-4242, www.tupeloautomobilemuseum.com), which boasts more than 100 restored classic and antique cars. It's near the convention and visitor bureau and the city's state-of-the-art convention center. Near the airport you'll find Tupelo Buffalo Park (662-884-8709, www.tupelobuffalopark), home to several hundred of these formidable creatures as well as exotic animals including monkeys and a tiger. There's a petting zoo as well.

Tupelo is home to one of Mississippi's top bed-and-breakfast inns, the **Mockingbird Inn,** 305 North Gloster Street (662-841-0286, www.bbonline.com/ms/mockingbird). Situated in the heart of the city within walking distance of several restaurants and across the street from Milam School, where Elvis attended the sixth and seventh grades, the Mockingbird Inn features seven rooms, each with a geographic theme. The Africa room has rattan furniture, mosquito netting, and faux zebra skins; the Venice room has a tapestry of Venetian gondolas and European styling—you get the idea. A hot breakfast is served, and nonalcoholic beverages are available throughout the day. No children younger than age 12.

Other accommodation options include chains such as Ramada Inn and Hampton Inn.

The best restaurants are on or near Gloster Street. There are two fine-dining establishments within walking distance of the Mockingbird Inn, the best of which is Park Heights at 825 West Jefferson (662–842–5665). Around the corner is Gloster 205, at 205 North Gloster Street (662–842–7205). Both are open for dinner.

Other dining options in Tupelo include Vanelli's (1302 North Gloster Street, (662–844–4410), a large family-owned restaurant/pizzeria that serves lunch and dinner. It's kid-friendly, with a huge menu that has something for everyone. For lunch try Harvey's, a bustling downtown eatery at 424 South Gloster Street (662–842–6763).

While in Tupelo you can also check out the historic **Natchez Trace Parkway,** which goes from Nashville to Natchez, Mississippi. This famed highway was originally an Indian trail, which two centuries ago became a key route for early pioneers, travelers, and post riders carrying mail between the two cities. Unfortunately for those early travelers, it was popular among robbers, too. The parkway fell into disuse with the advent of steamboat travel, but now it is part of the National Park system. For more information contact the Natchez Trace Parkway Headquarters and Visitors Center at Tupelo (662–680–4025, 800–305–7417).

Oxford

This college town, with its charming square and stately homes, has become one of the South's most celebrated small towns, and not just among University of Mississippi fans. It was also home to William Faulkner, the novelist who won the Nobel Prize in literature in 1950. Many of his novels were set in Yoknapatawpha County, a fictional stand-in for Lafayette County, where Oxford is the county seat. You'll probably want to see Faulkner's home, Rowan Oak, but also spend plenty of time at Courthouse Square, where you'll find great restaurants, shops, and Square Books, an outstanding independent bookstore. The popular Double-Decker Festival, usually the last Saturday in April, attracts lots of craft vendors, food booths, and great live music—not to mention plenty of festivalgoers. Check the football calendar if you are visiting in the fall. You will probably want to avoid an Ole Miss home football weekend, unless, of course, you don't mind sharing your experience with hundreds of football fans.

To get to the square, take the downtown/South Lamar exit off Mississippi Highway 6 and stay on Lamar, which runs right into the handsome, white Lafayette County Courthouse, with its statue of a Confederate soldier facing south. On the east side of the square is the Oxford Tourism Council (107 Courthouse Square, 662–234–4680, 800–758–9177, www.tour oxfordms.com), where you can pick up a map and brochures and ask about tours. If you're interested in Faulkner, ask for the *Faulkner Country* brochure.

On the south side of the square, you'll find **Square Books,** with its extensive selection of Southern literature and other fiction and nonfiction. Go up the stairs, lined with photos of writers who have done book signings here, and you'll find a quiet cafe, where you can linger over coffee, espresso, dessert, or a light meal. Its upstairs porch is nice during good weather. There are plenty of other shops to browse on the square as well.

Take South Lamar and then go right onto Old Taylor Road to visit **Rowan Oak** (662–234–3284), the antebellum home Faulkner purchased in 1930 and occupied until his death in 1962. He wrote some of his most acclaimed novels here, and you can still see the outline for his novel *A Fable* scrawled on his study wall.

To see the **Ole Miss campus,** take South Lamar from the square, turn onto University Avenue, and you'll drive through the main part of campus. Ole Miss, incidentally, has one of the world's most extensive collections of blues recordings and related materials at J. D. Williams Library (662-915-7091).

As for dining in Oxford, **Courthouse Square** offers many of the best options, particularly City Grocery (152 Courthouse Square, 662-232-8080), an urbane restaurant with a good wine list and a changing menu that includes imaginatively prepared fresh fish, quail, and its famous shrimp and grits. This is a hands-down favorite among local gourmands. (Upstairs at City Grocery is a casual bar, a good hangout for happy hour or later.) Another uptown option is Downtown Grill (upstairs at 110 Courthouse Square, 662-234-2559), which features a piano bar overlooking the square. On the more casual side is Old Venice Pizza Company (1112 Van Buren Avenue, 662-236-6872), which serves gourmet handmade pizzas, and Proud Larry's (211 South Lamar Boulevard, 662-236-0050), a bar just south of the square that serves good sandwiches. Bottletree Bakery (923 Van Buren Avenue, 662-236-5000), an excellent bakery, also serves breakfast, lunch, and specialty coffees. However, you will have to order ahead if you want to sample Bottletree's apple tart, made famous when celebrity Oprah Winfrey declared it best of the best. Steak lovers might want to seek out Doe's Eat Place (1536 University Avenue, 662-236-9003), a satellite of the original. A short drive to the country brings you to the Yocona River Inn (842 Highway 334, 662-234-2464), a former general store that's now a fine-dining restaurant.

There are a number of quaint bed-and-breakfast inns. The most popular are two restored antebellum mansions: The Oliver-Britt House (512 Van Buren Avenue, 662-234-8043), which is 2 blocks from Ole Miss campus, has five rooms with private

baths; and Puddin' Place (1008 University Avenue, 662-234-1250) has suites with private baths. Both are within walking distance of the square. The Tree House (53 County Road 321, 662-513-6354, 887-849-8738) is a modern log cabin with fireplace and nice rooms, situated about 4 miles from the square.

Other lodging options include Best Western Downtown Oxford Inn and Suites (400 North Lamar Boulevard, 662-234-3031), a renovated motel within walking distance of the square, and several chain hotels on the outskirts of town, including Holiday Inn Express and Hampton Inn.

Holly Springs

Situated about 45 minutes' drive from Memphis, this quaint town boasts 64 antebellum homes, mainly because Gen. Ulysses S. Grant decided to spare Holly Springs from the usual torching. The town may be familiar to moviegoers as the backdrop for the Robert Altman film, *Cookie's Fortune,* and it's home to Rust College, Mississippi's oldest historically black college. The best time to see the homes—and the only time for many—is during the Holly Springs Pilgrimage, which takes place the last weekend in April each year. These gracious homes open their doors to show off their period furnishings, with guides in period costumes giving history and other information. Some other properties, including several historic churches, open for the Holiday Tour of Homes the first weekend in December.

Otherwise, stop by the Holly Springs Tourism and Recreational Bureau (104 East Gholson Avenue, 662-252-2515, www.visit hollysprings.org), which makes its home in an 1832 house known as the Yellow Fever House. The staff can supply you with a map for a driving tour of the homes. They'll know what homes you might be able to tour, although it's best to make those arrangements ahead of time.

You'll see the exteriors only of most of these antebellum structures, although a

If you are planning a day trip on Sunday, call ahead to make sure the attractions you want to visit will be open. Many businesses in the outlying areas are closed on Sundays, and unsuspecting day-trippers might find they've made the trip for nothing.

few are open to visitors by appointment. They include Montrose, an 1858 home maintained by a local garden club, and the Yellow Fever Martyrs Church on East College Avenue. Ask, too, about Strawberry Plains (662-252-4143), an antebellum home that serves as headquarters for the Mississippi Audubon Society and is not only magnificent but also offers wildlife educational programs for children.

The **Holly Springs town square** also is very well preserved, with a pre-Civil War courthouse and streets built double wide in order to accommodate large cotton bales. You might want to check out Booker Hardware (119 South Market Street, 662-252-2331), an old-fashioned general hardware store, or Tyson Drug Company (145 East Van Dorn Street, 662-252-2321), a vintage drugstore with a soda fountain.

By far the most bizarre attraction in Holly Springs is **Graceland Too** (200 Gholson Avenue, 662-252-1918), which might be described as the world's most intense personal shrine to Elvis Presley. Paul MacLeod, the generously sideburned, self-proclaimed number-one fan of Elvis, has converted his 1853 home into a museum of Elvis minutiae, including the King's report card, all his albums, and stacks of TV Guide magazines with every mention of Elvis marked with colored paper clips. He and his son, Elvis Aaron Presley MacLeod, monitor TVs to make note of all references to the King. The senior MacLeod will not only show you around, with rapid-fire commentary (just try to interrupt this man), he'll also take your picture (to join the 200,000-plus others he has collected) and entertain you by singing along with Elvis records. Your enjoyment of Graceland Too

depends on the strength of your interest in Elvis and tolerance of personal eccentricity. Graceland Too is open 24 hours a day every day, as the MacLeods sleep near the door to be ready for guests. As you come into Holly Springs after turning off U.S. 78, go through the first stoplight and then take a right onto Gholson.

The most famous place to eat in Holly Springs is **Phillips Grocery** (541 East Van Dorn Street, 662-252-4621), known for its hamburgers. It's housed in a rustic grocery store decorated with early 1900s memorabilia. Ask for directions, as it can be hard to find. However, locals swear by Copper Kettle (170 North Memphis Street, 662-252-1022). Also on or near the square are City Café (135 East Van Dorn Street, 662-252-9895), a plate-lunch restaurant, and Annie's (198 North Memphis Street, 662-252-4222), which serves a good lunch buffet.

For accommodations try the Hampton Inn on the outskirts of town.

WEST TENNESSEE TRAVELS

As you venture into west Tennessee from Memphis, you pass some great little towns and plenty of cotton fields and other agrarian sights. We recommend two loops, one of which will take you to Shiloh National Military Park, the site of one of the bloodiest battles in the Civil War. It's a little more than 100 miles from Memphis, going east on Highway 57, and on the way you'll pass some interesting old towns, a state park, and an off-beat museum devoted to hunting dogs. Shiloh is only a short drive from Pickwick Lake, one of the largest lakes in the area. (See the Parks and Recreation chapter for details about the lake.)

Although you can retrace your steps back on Highway 57 to Memphis, a faster, but not particularly picturesque, option is to swing south to Corinth, where another important battle took place, then back to Memphis via U.S. 72. Either way your best route in and out of Memphis is to take Nonconnah Parkway, getting on or off at the

Collierville exit. If you plan to stay overnight in the Shiloh area, bear in mind that there are very few accommodations.

A second west Tennessee loop takes you north from Memphis on U.S. 51, where you'll pass the picturesque town of Covington on the way to Henning, the boyhood home of Alex Haley. From Henning go west on Highway 87 to Fort Pillow State Park. On the way back, via Covington, take Highway 59 south to Mason to Gus's for some of the best fried chicken on the planet. Even though they are probably not worth a detour, other points of interest include Nutbush, the birthplace of Tina Turner, and Benton County, where singer Patsy Cline died in a plane crash.

The Road to Shiloh National Military Park

Once you pass the Memphis suburbs, the first point of interest is the historic town of LaGrange, worth a short jog off the highway, given its old storefronts and antebellum homes. Just a few miles down Highway 57 you'll come to Grand Junction, home of the **National Bird Dog Museum** (731-764-2058, www.fielddog .com). Believe it or not, West Tennessee is recognized as the birthplace of America's pointing-dog field trials and is home to the National Field Trial Championship. The museum pays homage to the canine worker that finds birds, rousts them from their hiding places, and retrieves them for the hunter. It features art, photography, and memorabilia highlighting the accomplishments of more than 40 breeds of bird dogs, including pointing, flushing, and retrieving breeds. A highlight is its version of Mona Lisa, featuring a bird dog in the familiar pose. Field trials take place at nearby Ames Plantation in February.

Continue traveling east on Highway 57, and you'll see signs directing you to **Shiloh National Military Park** (Shiloh, 731-689-5275, www.nps.gov/shil). The Battle of Shiloh was fought here on April 6-7, 1862,

between 45,000 Confederate soldiers and 66,000 Union soldiers. It was the bloodiest battle in American history, resulting in more than 23,000 casualties, more than all casualties in previous American wars put together.

History buffs will recall that Confederate general A. S. Johnston began concentrating men at Corinth, with the intention of moving against Gen. U. S. Grant's Union Army of the Tennessee. The plan was to attack the Union army before it could be reinforced by Gen. D. C. Buell's Army of the Ohio. When Johnston's army attacked the Union camps around Shiloh Church on the morning of April 6, it was a complete surprise, and the South advanced throughout the morning. Then the Union finally held a line, which was dubbed the "hornets nest" because the fighting there was so ferocious. It resisted many Confederate attacks but later fell under fire from 62 cannons, at that time the largest artillery concentration ever seen on a North American battlefield. The fighting ended for the day, but during the night, unbeknownst to the Confederates, Buell's army arrived. As a result, by the following day, the Union force far outnumbered the Confederates. The next day things went well for the Confederates initially, but the army withdrew once its leaders realized the strength of the Union numbers. The Rebels fell back to Corinth.

Start your visit by stopping at the visitor center for a self-tour map of the park as well as a look at Civil War soldiers gear and a 25-minute film about the battle. Nearby is a bookstore with souvenirs as well as books and videos about the war for Civil War buffs. The map will guide you to key locations, including Pittsburg Landing (where Buell's troops arrived), the Hornets Nest, and the peach orchard, where witnesses say bullets cut down peach blossoms that fell like snow over the battlers. The entrance fee is $5.00 for a single-family car or $3.00 for an individual, both good for seven days. Every year near the anniversary of the Battle of Shiloh, the park has a special program that includes reenactors portraying parts of the battle and others demonstrating such skills as rifle-musket firings. Pickings are slim in terms of dining, but one local favorite is Hagy's Catfish Hotel (731–689–3327).

If you plan to spend the night, try the Hampton Inn or accommodations at Pickwick Landing State Park (see the Parks and Recreation chapter for details), but reserve ahead, as this is a popular spot in the summer. You can also try Savannah, where you'll find a gorgeous Queen Anne–style bed-and-breakfast inn, the White Elephant (731–925–6410, www.bbonline.com/tn/elephant), as well as Days Inn and Comfort Inn. Continue about 20 miles to Corinth, where you'll find Hampton Inn, Holiday Inn Express, and other chains along U.S. 72.

Fort Pillow, Alex Haley's Boyhood Home, Gus's Fried Chicken World Famous

Take U.S. 51 north through Millington, home of the USA Olympic Baseball Team stadium, journeying north through the suburbs until you reach Covington, a picturesque town about 40 miles from the city. This charming town features a well-preserved town square complete with two vintage movie theaters, antiques shops, a few restaurants, and other businesses. Another 7 miles brings you to Henning, where you can follow the signs to the **Alex Haley House Museum** (200 South Church Street, 901–738–2240). This 10-room bungalow was built by Will East Palmer, Haley's grandfather and manager of a local lumber mill. Haley lived with his grandparents as a child, hearing accounts of family history from his grandmother and aunts that later inspired him to write *Roots*. Tours are given by Fred Montgomery, the town's mayor and a boyhood friend of Haley. Admission is $2.50 for adults, $1.00 for students.

From Henning take Highway 87 west toward the Mississippi River about 20 miles to **Fort Pillow State Historic Park** (3122 Park Road, 901–738–5581, www.state.tn.us/environment/parks). Fort Pillow was set on a bluff high above the Mississippi River, although the river has since shifted away from the bluff. The South held the fort during the Civil War until 1862, when the Confederates evacuated and the Union took it over for the next two years. Fort Pillow is best known, however, for the raid by Confederate general Nathan Bedford Forrest, who in 1864 with 1,500 soldiers attacked the fort, where some 550 federal troops—almost half of them African American—were stationed. Because of the high casualties, particularly among the black soldiers, controversy continues to surround the raid. At the time some considered it acceptable wartime action, whereas others considered it a massacre, enough so that Congressional hearings were held to investigate Forrest's actions.

If all this sightseeing has worked up an appetite, you're in luck. Take U.S. 51 back to Covington, then Highway 59 to Mason, home of **Gus's Fried Chicken World Famous** (520 U.S. 70, 901–294–2028). This small shotgun shack has three big skillets working overtime to turn out perfect mahogany chicken that makes Mason a favorite road trip for hungry Memphians. In 2001 *GQ* magazine named Gus's as one of the 10 restaurants in the world worth flying to for a memorable meal. Open every day for lunch and all afternoon. No credit cards. If Gus's is full, try Bozo's Hot Pit Bar-B-Q (901–294–3400) down the road, which serves up great barbecue sandwiches and other menu items in a diner atmosphere that's like a trip back in time.

ARKANSAS TRAVELS

Hot Springs, Arkansas, is a favorite weekend getaway for Memphians, who flock here for live horse racing at Oaklawn Park as well as spas that feature local hotsprings water and massages, and the charms of the vintage Arlington Hotel. To get to Hot Springs, take I–40 west to Little Rock, then take I–30 south, following the signs to Hot Springs via U.S. 270.

If you want to check out Little Rock as long as you're passing through, get off I–30 at exit 10 and follow the signs to the Little Rock Convention and Visitors Bureau at Markham Street and Broadway (501–376–4781, 800–844–4781, www.little rock.com). Given its wealth of local information as well as its location in the heart of the city, it's a good first stop. Ask about the sights, including such Hillary and Bill hangouts as the elegant governor's mansion and the former Excelsior Hotel, made infamous by the Paula Jones incident (it's now the Peabody Little Rock). If you're hungry, there are restaurants along Markham Street, or check out River Market for more choices as well as shopping.

As for Hot Springs, it was a popular resort, particularly in the early part of the 20th century, and one of the first areas to be preserved by the U.S. government as a national park. Although we focus on the historic downtown area of Hot Springs National Park, there are many other reasons to visit this part of Arkansas, including five beautiful lakes, each dotted with resorts, cabins, and rental homes, and attractions for families that range from the Arkansas Alligator Farm & Petting Zoo to the Magic Springs and Crystal Falls Theme Park. You can get more information from the informative Hot Springs National Park Web site at www.hotsprings.org.

If the horses are running at **Oaklawn Park** (2705 Central Avenue, 501–623–441, 800–OAKLAWN, www.oaklawn.com), you should definitely spend a day watching the thoroughbred races and betting on your favorites. You can do it uptown style by going up to the boxes, or you can mix with the regular folks on the grandstand level. Wherever you are at Oaklawn, don't miss the legendary corned-beef sandwiches and jumbo shrimp. Admission to the track is a few dollars, and minimum bets are usually $2.00. Boxes and club member-

ships are generally available for the season only, but sometimes boxes become available the day of the race, if you're in the mood for a splurge. The season lasts generally from early January through March, and at other times of the year you can enjoy simulcast racing at Oaklawn.

You should also spend some time exploring the historic area of **Central Avenue,** where you'll find shops, restaurants, and eight huge, exquisite bathhouses, built at the turn of the last century and carefully restored. The entire area is part of Hot Springs National Park.

You can tour **Fordyce Bathhouse Museum** (501–623–1433) to get an idea of what the bathhouses were like during their heyday and to learn about the lifestyles of those who frequented them back when hot springs were considered the best available treatment for arthritis and other ailments. This is also the park's visitor information center, where you can inquire about other attractions and amenities including hiking trails.

Buckstaff Bath House (509 Central Avenue, 501–623–2308, wwwbuckstaff baths.com) is the only remaining continuously operating bathing facility on Bathhouse Row, and you can still get baths, massages, or other treatments here. They don't take reservations, however.

Also check out the park areas, where you can see the steaming springs water bubbling forth, as well as other attractions, which include the Josephine Tussaud Wax Museum (250 Central Avenue, 501–623–5836), where, of course, you can see a wax likeness of Hot Springs native-son Bill Clinton, and the Mountain Valley Spring Water Co. (150 Central Avenue, 501–623–6671), where you can get a free sample.

The park also includes an extensive network of hiking trails, where you can experience anything from an easy walk to a challenging mountain hike.

By far the most popular place to stay is the **Arlington Resort Hotel & Spa** (239 Central Avenue, 501–623–7771, www .arlingtonhotel.com), which feels like a step back in time with its opulent lobby bar, vintage elevators, and uniformed valets. The Arlington has its own bathhouse and spa, supplied with local thermal mineral water, and you take a private elevator from the hall of your room to this old-fashioned spa for your appointment. A hot-bath-and-massage combination is the most popular, although other services are available, and it's best to reserve ahead, especially during weekends. Definitely spend some time in the lobby, where there's a great bar, great people watching, and, later in the evening, Big-Band music and dancing. Restaurants, shops, and the bathhouses are a short walk away.

If you are a fan of bed-and-breakfast inns, you will find a number of elegant choices. A number of them are in historic homes, including the Stitt House (824 Park Avenue, 501-623-2704, www.bbonline.com/ar/stitt), built in 1875, the 1890 Williams House (420 Quapaw Avenue, 501-624-4275, www.1890williamshouse.com), and Gables Inn (318 Quapaw Avenue, 501-623-7576, www.gablesn.com). Contact the local tourism office at (888) 772-2489 or check out www.hotsprings.org for more ideas.

Other accommodations include the Majestic (101 Park Avenue, 501-623-5511, www.themajestichotel.com), another historic resort hotel with its own springs-fed spa. Hot Springs also has its share of chain hotels, including Comfort Inn (501-623-1700) and a Best Western that's close to Oaklawn Park (501-624-2531).

For fine dining Belle Arti Ristorante (719 Central Avenue, 501-624-7474) is a warm, elegant family-run restaurant that features a large menu of Italian specialties and live piano music. Hamilton House (130 Van Lyell Terrace, 501-525-2727) is a memorably romantic restaurant on nearby Lake Hamilton with continental cuisine. In the historic downtown area is the Pancake Shop (719 Central Avenue, 501-624-9465). Don't miss this bustling breakfast diner that serves great pancakes, omelets, and other favorites.

CASINOS

Tunica County, Mississippi, which calls itself the South's casino capital, has grown into one of the largest gaming destinations in the United States. Nine casinos operate in this rural county 30 miles south of Memphis, including Grand Casino, Harrah's, and Sam's Town. They offer 24-hour-a day Las Vegas–style gaming with no limits, 40 different restaurants, their own luxury hotels, and amenities that include nightly live entertainment, PGA golf courses, and health spas.

It has been more than a decade since the arrival of casinos transformed this quiet rural county. Yet longtime residents still occasionally rub their eyes when they behold the mini–Las Vegas in their midst, with its high-rise hotels and neon lights. After all, until the casinos started flocking to Robinsonville in the early and mid-1990s, Tunica County was an expanse of cotton and soybean fields, with a handful of restaurants and a rich blues history but little else to recommend it to visitors.

The situation changed, however, when authorities voted to allow riverboat gambling, and Splash Casino opened in October 1992, a few miles south of the present-day cluster of casinos. When locals and Memphians flocked here—standing in line and paying a cover to come in and lay their money down—it got the attention of the major casino operators, who quickly moved in. To date the casinos have invested more than $3 billion in their Tunica County operations.

The present clientele is a combination of locals, Memphians, and a growing number of out-of-towners, both people who drive from their hometowns and those on group tours. The crowd is pretty consistent from casino to casino, and during the week it consists mostly of retirees. On the weekends there's usually a good crowd, with a steady stream of traffic pouring in from Memphis. Some come in for the evening or

the day; others spend the night in one of the 6,300 hotel rooms in Tunica County.

The differences among the casinos lie in their decor, comp policies, size, and number of slot machines and tables; otherwise, they're pretty similar, with the same games—blackjack, craps, and roulette—and the same types of slot machines. The electronic din as hundreds of slot machines all jangle at the same time is standard as well.

Players are always attracted to casinos by the chance they'll win big, but the chances of that are, in fact, slim. The odds are in the casinos' favor, both at the table games and the slot machines, and the longer you play, the greater your chance of losing. The best approach is to decide before you go how much you can realistically afford to lose, then to walk away once you spend that amount. Some advise stricter rules: Leave your credit cards behind to avoid the temptation to continue beyond your budgeted amount or to stop playing when you're ahead.

Each casino issues comp cards, which it uses to calculate how much time and money you've spent there. Free meals, hotel rooms, and other comps are based on those amounts, although drinks are free to anyone who's playing. Points can also be used in gift shops, or some casinos will cash out the points. You can ask the casino's hostess about its policies (for example, how much do you have to play to get a free meal).

Another draw is live entertainment. The casinos bring in a variety of musicians, comedians, and other entertainers, from Mr. Las Vegas himself, Wayne Newton, to country legend George Jones and the Temptations. Although much of the entertainment consists of acts on the casino circuit, others are touring performers who in years past would have gone to Memphis instead of Tunica. The casinos advertise lavishly in Memphis newspapers, so it's not hard to find out who's playing down in the

Visitors to Tunica can learn all about the Mississippi River, thanks to a new $26-million river museum complex. Tunica River Park includes a museum, aquariums, a river overlook, and a levee with its own eco-trail (866–517–4837, www .tunicariverpark.com). Another way to experience the Mississippi is to take a river sightseeing tour on the Tunica Queen *(866–805–3535, www.tunica queen.com).*

Delta and how to get tickets.

Each casino also has at least three restaurants, including a buffet and a steak house or upscale eatery, and gives away meals to players under certain circumstances. Reservations are generally recommended for fine-dining restaurants only.

The hotels at the casinos are a favorite among Memphians for a quick weekend or overnight getaway. They generally fill up on the weekends, including Thursday, so booking ahead is a must. If you're venturing out from Memphis to see the Mississippi Delta, you might want to make Tunica an overnight stop. Tunica County is in the heart of the Mississippi Delta, which produced the blues and many of its legends, including Muddy Waters and Robert Johnson. It's just half an hour away from Clarksdale, where you'll find the Delta Blues Museum. Other Mississippi day-trip destinations are nearby, notably, Oxford, Holly Springs, and Tupelo. (See the Day Trips and Weekend Getaways chapter for more information.)

Remember, if you spend a lot of time in the casinos, you won't see much of the Delta, as the gaming halls have no windows, no clocks, or anything else to distract you from the gaming tables and slot machines. Often gaming patrons never even see the Mississippi River, which is less than a mile from the casinos. The recent addition of Tunica River Park, though, makes it easier for visitors to appreciate the river. See the Insiders' Tip on this page

for more information on this $26-million complex.

To get here take U.S. 61 from Memphis. You can take I–240 to I–55 north, then turn onto the U.S. 61 South exit, or take Third Street from downtown Memphis going south (it will eventually turn into U.S. 61). Or you can take I–55 South into Mississippi and turn west onto Mississippi Highway 304 at Hernando. The casino exits are well marked. Once here, you can take a shuttle between casinos for $1.00 per ride.

For more information about Tunica and its casinos, call the Tunica Convention and Visitors Bureau at (888) 4TUNICA or check out www.tunicamiss.com.

Here's a description of what the Tunica casinos have to offer in terms of gaming, dining, lodging, and amenities.

Bally's Casino Tunica
1450 Bally's Boulevard (off Casino Center Drive)
Robinsonville, Mississippi
(800) 382–2559
www.ballysms.com
One of the first casinos built in Tunica, Bally's has more than 1,200 slots and 40 tables as well as free live performances in an entertainment center that's built into an authentic grain silo. It also houses Bonkerz, the only comedy club in Tunica. Bally's has a country feel: The decor is down-home barn on the outside, with a rustic Delta theme inside, complete with exposed wooden beams and 1800s-style wallpaper. Gaming options include $2.00 and $3.00 blackjack tables. In terms of amenities Bally's has three restaurants, which include a buffet restaurant and a snack bar, and 230 hotel rooms, each with a whirlpool tub and minifridge, and a swimming pool for guests.

Fitzgeralds Casino/Hotel
711 Lucky Lane
Robinsonville, Mississippi
(800) 766–5825
www.fitzgeraldstunica.com
This is one casino where you can get a good look at the Mississippi River. Fitzger-

alds, the only one overlooking the river, touts the luck of the Irish to draw visitors. It's a favorite for its penny and nickel slots and $3.00 blackjack. The casino is built to resemble an Irish castle, with a whimsical ceiling painting of clouds, castles, and leprechauns in the gaming hall. The 500-room hotel is a modern style, with an indoor swimming pool and exercise room. It has three restaurants, including a steak house, and indoor parking, a welcome amenity during the summer hot-car season.

Gold Strike Casino Resort
1010 Casino Center Drive
Robinsonville, Mississippi
(888) 245-7829
www.goldstrikemississippi.com
With its marble floors, brass, and elaborate decor, Gold Strike draws the usual crowd as well as the high rollers. Its 31-story luxury hotel tower, with 1,200 rooms and suites, wins raves from visitors, who consider it to be one of the best. Players enjoy more than 50,000 square feet of gaming, with 1,400 slot machines and 40 game tables. Its 800-seat, state-of-the-art Millenium Theater attracts national acts such as Ann-Margret and Engelbert Humperdinck. Restaurant choices range from a food court featuring burgers, pizza, and Krispy Kreme donuts to the elegant Chicago Steakhouse. One of the Gold Strike's most popular amenities is its luxury spa.

Grand Casino
13615 Old Highway 61 North
Robinsonville, Mississippi
(800) 946-4946
www.grandtunica.com
Grand has the distinction of being both the largest casino in Tunica County and the closest one to Memphis. Four gaming areas—each with a different theme—feature 3,100 slot machines and 110 game tables for players. The amenities are more extensive here than at any other place in the area: Seven restaurants (plus two poolside cabanas in summer) include two steak houses and an Italian cafe, three hotels offer more than 1,500 luxurious

rooms, and an RV park provides 200 spaces for guests who bring their homes with them. The Grand also has a spa and salon for guests seeking to be pampered. Its 18-hole Cottonwoods Golf Course, designed by Hale Irwin, offers tee times as well as a golf school. Its Willows Hunting & Sporting Clays allows sportsmen to shoot a variety of targets in a controlled environment, one of the few places like it in the region. Deer and quail hunting are also available in season. Live entertainment at its event center includes such acts as Sinbad and the Doobie Brothers. The Grand also has its own convention center and an activity center for kids.

Harrah's Casino & Hotel
1100 Casino Strip Boulevard
Robinsonville, Mississippi
(662) 363-7777
www.harrahs.com
Harrah's, a big name in casinos, offers 50,000 square feet of slot machines and game tables at its Tunica property, as well as 200 hotel rooms and four restaurants, including Bourbon Street Bistro. Its 1,400 or so slot machines offer nickel, quarter, or $1.00 slots. There are 20 game tables as well. Harrah's, in partnership with Hollywood and Sam's Town, also offers River Bend Golf Links golf course, a links-style course designed by Clyde Johnston.

Hollywood Casino Tunica
1150 Casino Strip Boulevard
Robinsonville, Mississippi
(800) 871-0711
www.hollywoodcasinotunica.com
This casino has plenty of star quality, with 54,000 square feet of gaming (1,600 slots, 35-plus game tables). You'll find great movie memorabilia, including the DeLorean car from *Back to the Future,* and three restaurants, among them the ornate Fairbanks Steakhouse. For accommodations Hollywood has a hotel with almost 500 rooms and suites, upgraded in 2003 to the tune of $8 million, and an RV park with 123 spaces. There's also an indoor pool for guests to enjoy. Golf aficionados

will enjoy the River Bend Golf Links golf course, a challenging links-style course designed by Clyde Johnston, which Hollywood operates in partnership with Harrah's and Sam's Town.

Horseshoe Casino & Hotel
1020 Casino Center Drive
Robinsonville, Mississippi
(800) 303-7463
www.horseshoe.com
Horseshoe is a big favorite among Memphians, who rave about the friendly ambience, the generous comp policies, and its steak house. Fans of this Tunica casino are hoping things won't change much now that Harrah's acquired Horseshoe. Horseshoe has more than 2,500 slots and 90 tables as well as five diverse restaurants. The casino caters to high rollers as well as the more general player. Of all the casinos this is the one that pays tribute to the blues heritage of its Mississippi Delta location, with a tiny blues museum featuring memorabilia. Its Bluesville entertainment complex is a big draw, featuring rock and blues acts that have included Ringo Starr and Michael Bolton. Horseshoe's 15-story hotel tower has about 500 rooms and suites for guests.

Sam's Town Tunica
1477 Casino Strip Boulevard
Robinsonville, Mississippi
(800) 456-0711
www.samstowntunica.com

Expect to see some cowboy boots here. Although Sam's Town retains the exterior look of an Old West town, its interior was updated to the tune of $21 million in 2000, replacing the rustic look with a more polished ambience. The gaming area consists of two floors with 1,500 slots and 60 tables. Sam's Town is known for its country flair, both in the music and general ambience. A favorite among its restaurants is Corky's BBQ, where you can get your Memphis barbecue fix. The hotel has 850 rooms and suites, and a new RV park has 60 spaces and plenty of amenities. Sam's Town gets some of the hottest acts around, including James Brown and Merle Haggard, at its 1,600-seat arena. It also operates River Bend Golf Links golf course in partnership with two other casinos, an amenity that's popular with golf-playing visitors.

Sheraton Casino & Hotel
1107 Casino Center Drive
Robinsonville, Mississippi
(800) 391-3777
This casino resembles a Tudor mansion on the outside, with 31,000 square feet of gaming on the inside that includes 1,300 slots and 50 game tables. This one definitely has the most annoying ads of any Tunica casino, featuring a clown character touting its claim of loose slots. The Sheraton prides itself on its full-service spa and luxurious accommodations, with a whirlpool bath in every room.

RELOCATION

Memphis is a city of neighborhoods with all kinds of houses. You can find historic mansions, roomy new homes, charming bungalows, ranch houses, and cottages, not to mention apartments, town houses, and, in the outlying areas, farms. Plus, there's a pleasant surprise in store for people who move here from high-cost areas such as the East Coast or West Coast: You can get a lot of house for your money in Memphis. In fact, you can live well in Memphis for much less than in many other cities. The cost of living here is low, about 90 percent of the national average in 2003, according to the American Chamber of Commerce Researchers Association. Plus, there's no state income tax.

But that's not all Memphis has to offer. In a sense, the whole city is one big neighborhood, where people tend to be friendly and welcoming. It's easy to fall in with the spirit of things, whether that means rooting for the Grizzlies, griping about the weather, participating in a volunteer effort, or swapping celebrity-sighting stories while a Hollywood movie is being filmed around town. Many who have relocated here from high-stress lifestyles in larger cities find the living is easy in Memphis, and the commutes are shorter.

Memphis also has excellent health-care facilities, plenty of housing options and resources for retirees, colleges and universities with classes to accommodate any schedule, and hundreds of churches and other places of worship. In addition to the many fine schools in both the city of Memphis and Shelby County school districts, there's a variety of private and parochial schools. It's easy to stay informed, since the market is well served by newspapers, magazines, and electronic media. See the chapters that follow for details on health care and wellness, education, retirement, media, and worship.

One reason Memphis is so affordable is that home prices hold pretty steady here, so you can still find a good home in the $100,000 range, or of course you can pay more than $1 million. More recent figures show that the average sales price for a home inside the city was $118,800 in 2003, according to the Memphis Area Association of Realtors Multiple Listing Service. For the Shelby County suburbs outside the city, that figure is higher, ranging from $132,300 in Millington to $304,400 in Germantown.

The city of Memphis includes downtown Memphis, midtown, and East Memphis, as well as neighborhoods in north Memphis, including Raleigh, and south Memphis neighborhoods that include Hickory Hill and Whitehaven. The city is ringed by bedroom communities, including Millington, Bartlett, Cordova, Germantown, and the DeSoto County, Mississippi, suburbs of Southaven and Olive Branch. Among them is Collierville, the town named by *Money* magazine in 2003 as one of the top-10 best places to live in among cities with populations of less than 100,000 in the eastern United States. Outside this ring of suburbs, you'll find additional housing options in Tipton County, Arlington and elsewhere in northeast Shelby County, and Fayette County.

The most energetic new construction activity is taking place in downtown Memphis, which is enjoying an unprecedented revitalization, east Shelby County, north across the county line into Tipton County, and in DeSoto County, Mississippi. Much of this development is taking place along new major roads such as Highway 385, or other roads as they are widened into major arteries.

The city's population continues to grow, following 13 percent growth in the metropolitan statistical area (MSA) population during the 1990s to 1,135,614 in 2000, according to the U.S. Census Bureau.

As for property taxes, they vary greatly by county and by municipality. Property tax in Shelby County is $4.09 per $100 of assessed value ($4.04 within the Memphis city limits). If you live in Memphis proper or another municipality, there's city tax on top of that. Property tax in the city of Memphis is $3.23 per $100 of assessed value, whereas it's less than $2.00 per $100 of assessed value in the other municipalities.

Each municipality has room to grow under a comprehensive plan that gives each certain annexation reserves. These are areas of the county not currently within a city or town that may be annexed in the future by a designated municipality. That means if you own a home that's in an annexation reserve, you could be obligated at some point in the future to pay city taxes on top of county taxes should the area be annexed.

Property taxes in Fayette County, Tipton County, and DeSoto County are generally lower than in Shelby County. In Tennessee there's no state income tax, and although Mississippi does have a state income tax, that's somewhat offset for homeowners by the state's homestead exemption program. (See the section on DeSoto County, Mississippi, in this chapter.)

NEIGHBORHOODS
City of Memphis

DOWNTOWN

Residential development has been an important part of the revival of downtown Memphis in the last 15 years or so, and as a result, you can find beautiful homes ranging from lofty condominiums in renovated historic warehouses to spacious new houses with views of the river. A standout is Harbor Town, widely considered one of the most successful traditional neighborhood developments in the country. Situated on Mud Island just across the Auction Street Bridge, this neighborhood is easily accessible to downtown and its attractions but is self-contained, with its own grocery store and parks. The homes, some of which have river views, are beautifully designed and are frequently featured in the pages of *Southern Living* and other magazines. They feature updates of traditional Southern elements such as porches and columns, and the smaller ones are designed like a shotgun house—so called because a shot from the front door can go through the back door without piercing any walls. You can also find plenty of apartments and condominiums on Mud Island at a variety of prices. Whereas Harbor Town flourishes on the north end of downtown, neighborhoods on the south end, such as South Bluffs and Founder's Pointe, provide homes on the bluffs of the Mississippi River. Actress Cybill Shepherd has a home in this area, and more homes are under construction.

An alternative to these neighborhood houses with yards is downtown proper, where apartments have been developed in some of the historic buildings. They range from huge luxury penthouses to the moderate-income apartments in the Exchange Building. Also popular are loft-style apartments and condominiums that have become available as industrial buildings on South Main Street and elsewhere downtown are renovated. The average sales price for the downtown area in 2003 was $174,500, with some homes selling for as much as $1,750,000, according to the Memphis Area Association of Realtors Multiple Listing Service. Downtowners love the easy access to restaurants, bars, and other attractions, as well as proximity of the river and parks alongside it. It's one of the few areas where you can get along without a car except for long commutes or trips to the grocery.

MIDTOWN

If you like unique older homes with high ceilings and lots of charm, midtown is where you'll find them. Here the options range from historic mansions in Central

Gardens to modest bungalows built in the 1920s, and everything in between. It's a matter of opinion exactly where the boundaries of midtown fall. Interstate 240 West near the medical-center area is generally seen as the western border, and while the traditional eastern border is East Parkway, most Memphians think of midtown stretching farther than that. If you count Highland as the eastern border, the average price for a home in midtown in 2003 was $148,900, according to the Memphis Area Association of Realtors Multiple Listing Service. Midtown has the feeling of being a small town within a city and is more culturally and economically diverse. It's not unusual to see a $500,000 house on the same block as a $100,000 house. Memphians think of midtowners as being more avant-garde than their counterparts in the suburbs. That's probably overstating the case a bit. Although you'll find some punked-out artists and musicians living here, it's mostly families with kids who prefer the charms and quirks of midtown to the anonymity of the suburbs. Among the swanker neighborhoods in this area are Central Gardens and Hein Park, and you'll find more modestly priced homes throughout. The most typical architectural styles in this part of town are bungalows, with exaggerated porches and eaves, and foursquares, with four square rooms on the ground floor. In addition to the older homes, which are constantly being renovated by owners and investors, you'll also find new "infill" homes, so called because they are built to "fill in" areas of older neighborhoods. A notable collection of these homes were built near Overton Park in a portion of the city that years ago had been cleared for an interstate that never materialized. You'll find both Memphis City Schools as well as some parochial schools in midtown. Although homes can cost $1 million or more in midtown, it's also possible to find homes in comfortable neighborhoods for around $75,000, depending on the condition and if they have been recently renovated.

EAST MEMPHIS

East Memphis is the area that stretches between midtown Memphis and the I-240 loop. While there's a difference of opinion as to where East Memphis begins, the real estate community considers that midtown ends and East Memphis begins at East Parkway, just on the eastern edge of Overton Park, and continues east to Germantown. Given the fact, however, that the center of the city has shifted to the east over the years, Highland Street and the area around University of Memphis are generally thought to be more midtown than East Memphis.

East Memphis is the nearest suburb to central-business-district downtown and is convenient to shopping at Oak Court Mall, Laurelwood shopping center, and elsewhere as well as to excellent public and private schools. Public schools include White Station High School and Grahamwood Elementary, and private schools include St. Mary's Episcopal School and Memphis University School. Of the $1-million-plus homes that have changed hands in this area since 1999, most are situated in East Memphis. For the most part, the homes here are older, dating from the 1940s, 1950s, and 1960s, although some are brand-new "infill" homes. Families or developers buy lots and replace the existing home with brand-new structures, or they make a separate lot out of a large yard.

You'll find homes in all sizes and price ranges, with "starter" homes in the sought-after High Point Terrace neighborhood as well as near University of Memphis, where there's a concentration of 1940s homes built under the GI bill. In the middle range are ranch homes in neighborhoods along Mendenhall, White Station, and Yates.

The larger East Memphis homes are found in enclaves near Galloway Golf Course and elsewhere, along Walnut Grove, and in new areas such as Valley Brook, an area where huge new homes are being built.

Between I-240 and Germantown is where you'll find many of the new, million-dollar homes. If you count East Memphis as extending all the way west to Highland and east to the Germantown city limits, the average home price in 2003 was $186,228, with the most expensive costing $2.1 million, according to the Memphis Area Association of Realtors Multiple Listing Service.

Whatever the location or price range, the homes in East Memphis tend to appreciate in value, because the neighborhoods are so established. Plus, you'll find plenty of large trees and good-size yards.

NORTH MEMPHIS

This area of Memphis, north of downtown Memphis and tucked between the river and Bartlett, includes the working-class neighborhoods of Frayser and Raleigh. Frayser features many different styles of homes, such as bungalows and ranch homes, and enjoys easy access to the city. It's one of the hillier areas of the Memphis area, with plenty of stately trees, and homes are very affordable, with prices in the $50,000 range.

Raleigh dates from the early 20th century, when it was home to a popular mineral spring that attracted visitors from the city. It, too, with its rolling hills, is a refreshing break from the relatively flat terrain of Memphis. Raleigh, as home to Raleigh Springs Mall and numerous shopping centers, has plenty of shopping options.

Overall, homes in north Memphis had an average sales price of $75,400, according to the Memphis Area Association of Realtors Multiple Listing Service.

SOUTH MEMPHIS/HICKORY HILL

This part of Memphis consists of many neighborhoods, including Whitehaven, the South Parkway area, Oakhaven, and Hickory Hill, many of which have very affordable home prices. Whitehaven, best known as home to Graceland, is close to Memphis International Airport and I-55. Here you'll find subdivisions with homes built in the 1950s and 1960s. Homes in Whitehaven neighborhoods don't turn

over very often, as families tend to stay in the same house for a long time. Along South Parkway are beautiful old homes with grand trees and roomy yards. Oakhaven, adjacent to the airport, features moderately priced homes and subdivisions, although homes near Holmes Road are wooded and spacious. Average sales price for homes in south Memphis was $60,600 in 2003, according to the Memphis Area Association of Realtors Multiple Listing Service. Hickory Hill in southeast Memphis started becoming a suburb in the 1970s, as the first of many subdivisions was built. Since it encompasses a large, diverse area extending from the Mississippi state line all the way to Germantown and Collierville, it's not surprising to find homes in all price ranges. The average price in 2003 was $133,500, with some as high as $1,450,000, according to the Multiple Listing Service figures. Today you'll find Highway 385 in this area, open from I-240 to Collierville so that Hickory Hill residents have easier access to other parts of the city than ever before. One recent development is the closing of Mall of Memphis at I-240 and Perkins, at one time among the city's most prestigious malls. This has brought uncertainty to the immediate area, since it's to be razed and no one knows what will happen to the sprawling property.

Suburbs

SHELBY COUNTY, TENNESSEE

Arlington/Lakeland
Arlington is a quiet municipality in the northeast corner of Shelby County seen as an up-and-coming area that will soon be the next Cordova or Collierville in terms of development. Census figures show that Arlington's population grew nearly 70 percent between 1990 and 2000, as subdivisions began to spring up. The area is in the midst of a second wave of building homes, this time with prices in

the $160,000 to $280,000 range. Arlington sits a few miles beyond Lakeland off I-40, and as Lakeland has become more expensive, it's attracting families who want to pay less for their homes, send their children to brand-new Arlington High School, and enjoy a less-crowded environment. Arlington has few shopping centers or other commercial development, but that's expected to change as the number of rooftops grows. Most of the homes are in the $200,000 range, although the average sales price for a home in Arlington in 2003 was $173,300, according to the Memphis Area Association of Realtors Multiple Listing Service. Property taxes here are $1.00 per $100 of assessed value, in addition to Shelby County property tax. Arlington is served by Shelby County Schools, with two elementary schools, two middle schools, and a new high school.

Lakeland is closer to Memphis, and actually just 2 miles from Wolfchase Galleria Mall. It has been around for many years, but during the 1990s its population grew by 400 percent. As a result, you'll find more established neighborhoods as well as lots of new subdivisions to accommodate all the new residents. Homes are more expensive in Lakeland than in Arlington, with the average price at $231,400, according to 2003 Multiple Listing Service figures. Demand has pushed the prices up in recent years, so many more homes are above the $300,000 mark. Lakeland also offers the advantage of having no city property tax, only Shelby County property taxes.

Bartlett

This family-oriented suburb, with a population of 40,543, according to the 2000 census, is situated in the center of Shelby County and about 11 miles from downtown Memphis. It started off as a stagecoach stop in the 1820s and has grown dramatically, especially in the last 30 years, from a sleepy town into a thriving suburb that manages to keep its small-town feel. You'll find most homes in the $100,000 to $250,000 range, which makes it an

affordable option for first-time buyers. The average sales price of a Bartlett home in 2003 was $173,300, according to the Memphis Area Association of Realtors Multiple Listing Service. The older section of Bartlett is to the west, where you'll find the town proper, and to the east are newer subdivisions as well as a plethora of shopping centers and stores. There's continuing construction of new homes, which start at about $150,000. City property taxes are $1.38 per $100 of assessed value, in addition to Shelby County property tax. Bartlett is part of the Shelby County school system, and has six elementary schools, three middle schools, and two high schools. The town also boasts the new Bartlett Performing Arts Center, as well as lots of new retailers, including national chains.

Collierville

Collierville, situated about 10 miles east of the Memphis city limits and 25 miles from downtown, has become a popular bedroom community, particularly for families with children. During the 1990s it nearly doubled in population to 31,872, according to the U.S. Census Bureau, and an annexation is in the works that will add about 20 more square miles to this historic town. In 2004 Money magazine named Collierville one of the 10 best places to live in the eastern United States among cities of less than 100,000 people, based on population growth, cost of homes relative to local household income, and other criteria. Residents love its picturesque town square with shops and restaurants, as well as its family-friendly attitude, and there are plenty of shopping centers and other commercial businesses along West Poplar Avenue (U.S. 72), the main thoroughfare. The area economy benefits from the presence of FedEx's World Technology Center, but many residents commute to Memphis for work, too. The completion of Highway 385 (Nonconnah Parkway) a few years ago has made the commute between Memphis and Collierville much shorter, thus making this historic town more convenient to the city. As for homes, there is a lot of building going on in the area, as well as more established homes that change hands. Homes start around $90,000 and go all the way up to $2 million, but the average sales price for a home in Collierville in 2003 was $276,000, according to the Memphis Area Association of Realtors Multiple Listing Service. Property taxes here are $1.45 per $100 of assessed value, in addition to Shelby County property tax.

Cordova

This fast-growing suburb, tucked between Germantown and Bartlett, is where many young families with children choose to make their homes. The atmosphere is comfortingly familiar if you're at home in a modern American suburb; if not, it may seem overly homogeneous. The subdivisions of Cordova are convenient to a significant concentration of shopping and restaurants along Germantown Parkway, and you'll find many familiar chains represented both in the shopping centers and the mall, Wolfchase Galleria. Part of the suburb is in the Shelby County school district, parts are in various municipalities. It's subject to change, so be sure to ask around before you buy if schools are a key consideration. Cordova favors the first-time buyer, with homes that are more affordable than in neighboring Germantown, generally considered the swank suburban address. The average sales price for a home in Cordova in 2003 was $163,700, according to the Memphis Area Association of Realtors Multiple Listing Service. Most of the homes here were built fairly recently, and more are under construction, so they have oversize bathrooms and kitchens and other up-to-date amenities. Cordova is also adjacent to Shelby Farms, a large urban park with recreational activities available. Since Cordova is an area and not a true municipality, its residents pay only county property taxes, although those in annexed areas pay Memphis city taxes as well.

Germantown

Considered to be the area's premier suburb, Germantown is an established community with excellent schools and other amenities as well as careful city planning that makes sure even fast-food joints maintain a dignified look. Traditionally, it has had a reputation as home to the elite, horsey set, and each year it hosts one of the country's largest equestrian events, the Germantown Charity Horse Show. Today the population is more diverse.

Germantown began as a separate town in the 1820s but, throughout the years, has grown into a suburb of Memphis with a population of about 40,000, according to census figures. Homes can be spectacular and fairly expensive for the Memphis market. The average sales price for a home in this area in 2003 was $304,400, according to the Memphis Area Association of Realtors Multiple Listing Service, although more modestly priced homes can be found as well. Germantown is proud of its parks, its state-of-the-art performing-arts center, its annual charity horse show, and its shopping, including the Shops of Saddle Creek. The city of Germantown has exacting planning standards, so here expect businesses to have discreet signs rather than flashing neon. The area is well known for its horses, and both polo and fox hunting are still popular sports. Germantown schools are part of the Shelby County school system, which includes four elementary schools, two middle schools, and two high schools. There are also several private schools. The city's property tax is $1.70 for every $100 of assessed value, in addition to the county property tax of $4.09 per $100 of assessed value.

Millington

This community of 10,400 people, just 10 miles north of downtown Memphis, has traditionally been a navy town. Now it is home to the Bureau of Naval Personnel, although until the 1990s Millington's naval operation was a much larger air station engaged in training. People choose to live in Millington for its small-town ambience and easy highway access, both to the city and to I–40. Millington prides itself on being surrounded by greenbelt, and that includes the Loosahatchie River to the south. By buffering the Millington area from Memphis, the greenbelt allows it to retain its small-town feel. It's popular among retirees, many of them former navy officers who like having access to the base and its facilities and in some cases were once stationed in Millington. A number of subdivisions are new, ranging from neighborhoods with modest homes for first-time buyers to those with 3,500-square-foot homes that command prices near $200,000. In 2003 the average home sales price was $132,300, making it perhaps the county's most economical housing market, according to the Memphis Area Association of Realtors Multiple Listing Service.

Millington is in the Shelby County school system and has four elementary schools, a middle school, and a high school; there are also several private schools. Meeman-Shelby Forest State Park is nearby.

Taxes in Millington are lower than those in some municipalities, with a city property tax rate of $1.23 for $100 of assessed value plus county property tax.

FAYETTE COUNTY, TENNESSEE

Fayette County, which is just east of Shelby County, has grown into a bedroom community in recent years for persons who like rural or small-town living but want to be close to the city. Another attraction is that property taxes are lower here than in Shelby County. Fayette County property owners paid $1.74 per $100 as of 2004, less than half of what Shelby County property owners paid.

Most of the county's residential development has followed U.S. 64, and in the more densely populated west part of Fayette County, you'll find Hickory, Withe, and Oakland, towns where a lot of new homes and subdivisions have been built. Prices range from $100,000 for a starter home to $350,000 and more. There's very little commercial development here, mainly supermarkets and other retail stores, which are being built in the Oakland area. It's about a 20-minute drive away from Wolfchase Galleria Mall and the surrounding shopping area and an additional 15 minutes or more from Memphis proper.

But growth is expected to pick up dramatically when Highway 385 is completed between I–40 and Collierville around the beginning of 2006, sweeping through Fayette County as it creates an outer loop around the city. In some parts of the county, public amenities, including schools and a sewer system adequate for new residential and commercial building, are not as well developed as in other counties in the Memphis MSA.

As you go farther east, Fayette County becomes even more rural, appealing to homeowners who want more seclusion and more elbow room, whereas tiny Somerville is attractive to those who like small towns. This area is not growing as quickly as the western part of the county, but this trend could change in the near future.

TIPTON COUNTY, TENNESSEE

Situated 18 miles north of Memphis, this fast-growing county saw its population increase 36 percent during the 1990s to 51,271 people, according to the U.S. Census Bureau. For those who want country living, Tipton County fills the bill, so you'll find that many residents work in Memphis but live here, attracted in part by lower property taxes. There's plenty of new development, particularly along U.S. 51 in southern Tipton County, with new homes and subdivisions being built in the tiny towns of Munford, Atoka, and Brighton. Shopping centers and other commercial development has been slow but is beginning to pick up in the area. Farther north is Covington, a small town with a charming, vibrant downtown.

Property taxes in Tipton County, at $2.92 per $100 of assessed value, are lower than those in Shelby County. Modest municipal taxes are levied in some areas. The Tipton County school system has four elementary schools, three middle schools, and three high schools, located in Brighton, Covington, and Munford.

DESOTO COUNTY, MISSISSIPPI

Drawn by low housing prices and other factors, many people are opting to make their homes just south of Shelby County and across the Tennessee state line into Mississippi. As a result, DeSoto County was one of the fastest-growing counties in the country during the 1990s, with a 58 percent increase in population to 107,000 people in 2000, according to the U.S. Census Bureau. Most of the residential development is in the towns of Southaven, Olive Branch, Horn Lake, and Hernando, where you'll find numerous subdivisions with homes of all sizes and in all price ranges. There are also homes in the rural pockets in between these municipalities. A big draw is the state's homestead tax exemption, which can save a homeowner several hundred dollars in taxes each year. The exemption is much more generous for homeowners who are age 65 or older or disabled. Property taxes, which have been $3.64 per $100 of assessed value, will probably be higher by the time you read this, since in 2004 voters approved a tax increase to expand what has become an overcrowded county school system. Residents say they like the small-town feeling of the Mississippi neighborhoods while still being close enough to the city of Memphis to enjoy its offerings. Another draw is the DeSoto County school district,

---

ℹ️ *If you are looking at houses with an agent and think you would like to check out some of the cool older homes in midtown, speak up. Some agents are notorious for steering home buyers who don't know the city to the suburbs without even mentioning that there is a midtown.*

---

although the system has attracted so many families that it has been struggling to accommodate all the students. It's the second-largest system in the state of Mississippi and one of the state's best, and boasts above-average test scores. A huge expansion is in the works to accommodate all the new county residents. DeSoto County has well-developed amenities, including plenty of shopping centers with familiar chain retailers as well as locally owned stores and other commercial businesses—and more under construction.

REAL ESTATE

Existing homes are constantly changing hands, and new homes are always being built in the Memphis area, both in the heart of the city and in the surrounding suburbs. Of course, as in any other market, Memphis real estate is buoyed when times are good and quiets down a bit when the economy slows down. By and large, though, the local real estate market has been very strong, thanks in part to low interest rates. They've been below 8 percent for nearly a decade, and around 6 percent since about 2002 (as of early 2004). As a result, many Memphians have been able to buy their first home or trade up to a larger home. Memphis-area home sales had a total sales volume of $2.32 billion in 2003, according to the Memphis Area Association of Realtors Multiple Listing Service. That breaks the record, set in 2002, of $2.1 billion in sales. In January 2004, there was a 17.2 percent increase in home sales volume versus January 2003. At the same time, home prices have been holding steady. The median sales price actually decreased by 2.6 percent in 2003 to $125,600, while the average sales price decreased 0.001 percent to $153,300 in 2003, according to Multiple Listing Service information. By another measure, the city had one of the lowest house price appreciation rates among large cities. The Memphis metropolitan statistical area (MSA) ranked 202 out of the top 220 MSAs in terms of annual percentage change in house prices, with a 2.21 percent increase, according to the U.S. Department of Housing and Urban Development's House Price Index for the third quarter of 2003.

Real Estate Agencies

To help you find your way through the local real estate market, there are hundreds of real estate agents in all areas of the city and its surrounding suburbs who can help, whether you are buying or selling a home. Here we list the largest and best-known residential real estate brokerage firms. Bear in mind, though, that Memphis has dozens of other reputable and knowledgeable agents and firms, so this is by no means a complete listing. For more information about other companies, contact the Memphis Area Association of Realtors at (901) 685–2100 or visit its Web site at www.maar.org.

The Sunday edition of the city's daily newspaper, the *Commercial Appeal,* is an excellent source of information. It has listings of homes for sale or rent as well as news about the local housing market, real estate agents, and lenders. The weekly *Memphis Flyer* also features homes and apartments in its classified advertising section.

Century 21 River Oaks, Inc.
1926 Exeter Road, Germantown
(901) 756–1622
riveroaks.com

Opened in 1985, and part of the Century 21 organization since 1997, this real estate firm works mainly in Germantown, Collierville, and Cordova as well as East Memphis. Century 21 River Oaks specializes in relocation, as an affiliate of the large transferee network, Cendant Mobility. In addition, because it represents a large homebuilder, the company shows a lot of new homes. Its main office is in Germantown, but it also maintains an office in Bartlett. River Oaks is known locally for buying and selling properties in German-

town. With some 66 agents the firm has about $145 million in annual gross sales.

Coldwell Banker/Hoffman-Burke, Inc., Realtors
1709 Kirby Parkway
(901) 759–1651
www.coldwellbanker.com

This real estate company, with about 30 agents, prides itself on its work with upper-tier homes in Memphis, Germantown, and Collierville. However, the agency also serves other areas of Shelby County. The firm provides relocation services, as well as new construction and commercial real estate, and does about $100 million in gross annual sales.

Coleman-Etter, Fontaine Realtors
651 Oakleaf Office Lane
(901) 767–4100
www.cef-realtors.com

This full-service residential real estate company, which has been in operation since 1951, prides itself on its personal service to customers. One of the city's premier realty companies, it's best known for high-end properties in the downtown, midtown, and East Memphis areas but also works with first-time buyers and sellers of middle-income properties. The company is also knowledgeable about all aspects of Memphis and will help newcomers with recommendations for lenders, movers, day-care providers, or whatever else customers need. Coleman-Etter, Fontaine Realtors has about 35 realtors and does about $108 million in gross sales each year. The president and owner is Fontaine Taylor.

Crye-Leike, Inc.
6525 Quail Hollow Road
(901) 756–8900
www.crye-leike.com

Started in 1977 by two Memphians, Crye-Leike has become the largest real estate company in Memphis as well as the largest in Tennessee, with 2,600 agents in six states. You can count on finding a Crye-Leike office with knowledgeable agents in every neighborhood. That's because with 1,100 agents and 22 offices in the greater Memphis area, Crye-Leike covers every part of Memphis as well as much of the Mid-South region outside the metropolitan area. In addition to handling home sales and purchases, Crye-Leike also offers an array of services, including relocation (it's part of the RELO network) and home improvement. It also publishes its own home-buyer's guide with listings of properties for sale in Memphis and the surrounding suburbs. The company does about $1.8 billion in annual gross sales in the greater Memphis market.

John Green & Co., Realtors
108 Mulberry Street, Collierville
(901) 853-0763
www.johngreen.com
Based in Collierville, this realty company handles new and existing homes in Collierville, Germantown, Cordova, East Memphis, and other suburban areas. John Green is the owner and has 50 agents on his staff as well as a relocation department to take care of those types of client needs. The company works with properties in all price ranges, but most are $150,000 or more, given the home prices in the Collierville area.

Although primarily a residential real estate firm, the company also does some commercial and land transactions. John Green & Co. does about $102 million in annual gross sales.

The Hobson Co., Realtors
5100 Poplar Avenue
(901) 761-1622
www.hobsonrealtors.com
This family-owned residential real estate company is best known for buying and selling midtown and East Memphis properties at the upper price range but also handles homes in other areas of the metropolitan area as well as more moderately priced homes.

The company does about $150 million in yearly gross sales and prides itself on its 27 agents, each of whom averages $5 mil-

lion in sales and has an average of 15 years of experience in residential real estate. The company is owned and managed by Joel Hobson III, the son of the couple who founded it in 1972.

Lawrence Johnson Realtors
4222 Millbranch Road
(901) 345-1600
www.lawrencejohnson.com
Started and still operated by super-agent Lawrence Johnson, this company has about 110 agents, making it one of the largest agencies in Memphis. The focus is on properties in all neighborhoods in Memphis and northwest Mississippi, with plenty of homes below $100,000 as well as more expensive properties. The firm, which also offers relocation services and some commercial listings, does about $65 million in annual gross sales. Lawrence Johnson maintains offices in the Millbranch, Hickory Hill, and Raleigh neighborhoods.

Marx & Bensdorf Real Estate & Investment Co.
959 Ridgeway Loop
(901) 682-1868
www.marx-bensdorf.com
This is the city's oldest real estate agency, founded in 1868, and it continues to operate under the same name. With 33 agents Marx & Bensdorf covers all of Memphis and Shelby County, as well as Tipton and Fayette Counties, and sells homes in all different price ranges. Although the company retains the original name, the present principals are David Okeon and Jimmy Reed. As part of the RELO referral network, the firm reaches customers who are moving to Memphis, and it provides relocation services. The company does an estimated $122 million in annual gross sales.

Prudential Collins Maury, Inc., Realtors
1352 Cordova Cove, Cordova
(901) 753-0700
www.collins-mauryrealtors.com
This locally owned and operated franchise of Prudential, with offices in Cordova, Col-

lierville, and East Memphis, handles residential properties at all prices. Collins Maury is most active in Germantown, Cordova, Collierville, and Bartlett but works with properties in all parts of the metropolitan area. This agency, which has more than 100 agents with an average of 12 years of experience, does a good bit of relocation work, too. The owners are Doug Collins and Bill Maury. Annual gross sales are about $200 million.

RE/MAX at Mallard Creek
7556 Highway 70, Bartlett
(901) 372-9933
www.midsouthhometour.com
RE/MAX at Mallard Creek got its start in 1994 selling newly constructed homes. These days the firm continues to sell lots of new homes, particularly in the Collierville, Bartlett, Cordova, and Millington areas. Existing homes are equally important to them, however, and account for almost half of the agency's business. Those listings tend to be in the same area, although agents handle listings all over town. Mallard Creek has 50-plus agents, with an average of at least a decade of experience, and maintains offices in both Bartlett and Cordova. It does some $75 million in annual gross sales. The owner and founder is Stan Holmes.

RE/MAX Elite of Memphis
1335 Germantown Parkway, Cordova
(901) 759-9488
www.memphismidsouthhomes.com
RE/MAX Elite of Memphis has three offices, including locations in Collierville and Germantown, and has about 148 agents who specialize in all parts of the Memphis metropolitan area. The agency is independently owned and operated by Richard Sharpe and does quite a bit of relocation work as part of the RE/MAX referral network. The agency works mainly in residential real estate, buying and selling properties at every price. Annual gross sales are about $383 million.

RE/MAX On-Track
2075 Exeter Road, Germantown
(901) 758-1200
www.memphismidsouthhomes.com
Started in 1990, this residential realty company has about 60 agents who cover all areas of the metro area, including Germantown, Cordova, Collierville, Memphis, and Mississippi. The office is independently owned, but as part of the RE/MAX system, it does lots of relocation work, both for companies and individuals. The principal broker and owner is Peter Ritten. The company has annual gross sales of about $185 million.

Sowell and Co. Realtors
54 South Cooper Street
(901) 278-4380
www.sowellandco.com
This company, which has been helping customers buy and sell homes since the mid-1970s, has this motto: "We own Midtown but we buy and sell all over Memphis." Sowell and Co. has a specific interest in historic homes such as those found in the Central Gardens neighborhood of midtown. The homes range from starter homes in the hip Cooper-Young area to historic mansions in Central Gardens and other upscale midtown enclaves. The company also handles properties in suburban areas such as Germantown or Collierville. Founded by Linda Sowell, the firm has 33 agents and annual gross sales estimates at around $80 million.

Apartments and Rental Housing

Many residents opt to rent apartments or homes rather than buying, and there's something to satisfy every taste. You'll find large modern apartment complexes with every possible amenity, both in the suburbs and downtown Memphis, as well as charming older apartment buildings in midtown and downtown. You can also choose from duplexes, garage apartments, and carriage houses, most of which are peculiar to midtown, and loft apartments in downtown historic warehouses and other buildings. Whatever part of town you're interested in, you'll likely find plenty of freestanding houses available for rent, too, in all price ranges.

Apartments in Memphis are very affordable. In fact, of the 59 apartment markets in the country tracked by the National Real Estate Index, Memphis in 2003 had the fourth-lowest rents, with average monthly rent ranging from $471 to $535 for a typical 800-square-foot unit. The national average of the markets covered by the index ranges from $729 to $933, based on data as of September 2003. Memphis is among the cities with a glut of apartments, caused in part by the fact that many former renters, taking advantage of low interest rates and moderate home prices, have bought homes. So it's definitely a renter's market these days, with many apartment complexes lowering rents and offering deals to attract tenants.

Keep in mind, too, that there are a number of corporate housing companies that specialize in furnished temporary digs for those who aren't ready to choose an apartment or home. They include Bridgestreet Corporate Housing (901–737–3000, www.bridgestreet.com) and Executive Lodging (901–363–8894, www.ExecutiveLodging.com).

Memphis's local newspapers, the daily *Commercial Appeal* and the weekly *Memphis Flyer,* have listings of rental properties currently available, which is where many Memphians turn when they're looking for new digs.

Also look for the *Greater Memphis Area Apartment Guide* or *Apartments For Rent,* both free publications with plenty of information about the larger apartment complexes around town. They can be found in racks at supermarkets, library branches, and other locations. There's also a growing number of apartment Web sites,

where you can check out different properties online. They include Memphis Apartments (www.apartmentsmemphis.com), RENTNET (www.rentnet.com), and For Rent.com (memphisforrent.com).

CHAMBERS OF COMMERCE

The Memphis metropolitan area is well served by no less than 10 chambers of commerce. You will find a warm welcome and helpful staff at the suburban chambers of commerce, but don't be surprised if the largest of the group, Memphis Regional Chamber, is less attentive. Since it's more oriented toward business, you won't get much of a welcome—unless, of course, you are bringing a big company and many jobs with you to the Memphis area. That being said, the Memphis Regional Chamber does publish *Meet Memphis,* an annual guide that includes information for newcomers ($5.00 at area bookstores, or it can be ordered directly from the chamber), and it will send you a relocation package for a $15.00 charge. The chamber also maintains a Web site, www.memphischamber.com, with information useful to those relocating to the area.

Bartlett Area Chamber of Commerce
(901) 372–9457
www.bartlettchamber.org

Collierville Chamber of Commerce
(901) 853–1949
www.colliervillechamber.com

Fayette County Chamber of Commerce
(901) 465–8690
www.fayettecountychamber.com

Germantown Chamber of Commerce
(901) 755–1200
www.germantownchamber.com

Memphis Regional Chamber
(901) 543–3500
www.memphischamber.com

Millington Chamber of Commerce
(901) 872-1486
www.millingtonchamber.com

Olive Branch (Mississippi) Chamber of Commerce
(662) 895-2600
www.olivebranchms.com

Southaven (Mississippi) Chamber of Commerce
(662) 342-6114
www.southavenchamber.com

South Tipton County Chamber of Commerce
(901) 837-4600
www.southtipton.com

West Memphis (Arkansas) Chamber of Commerce
(870) 735-1134
www.wmcoc.com

MOTOR VEHICLE INFORMATION

Tennessee license plates must be obtained soon after establishing residency in the state. If you are a resident of Memphis or Shelby County, this is done through the Shelby County Clerk's office (901-545-4244, www.co.shelby.tn.us). You must bring your car's title or registration to one of its offices, and pay $113 in fees and taxes. If you live within the Memphis city limits, you have to get your vehicle inspected first at one of three inspection stations, then take your certificate of inspection with you to the county clerk's office. For information on inspection, con-

tact the Motor Vehicle Inspection Bureau (901-528-2904, www.mvib.org).

New residents of the state are required to get a Tennessee driver's license within 30 days of establishing residency. Those with a valid out-of-state license must take an eye exam and bring their current license and proof of residency to a driver testing center. However, all tests are required for those with a license that has been expired for longer than six months, and for new residents from other countries. The initial fee is $26.50. For more information call (901) 543-7920 or log on to www.tennessee.gov/safety.

LIBRARIES

The Memphis-Shelby County Public Library system operates 23 locations, the main one being the Central Library on Poplar Avenue between midtown and East Memphis. Memphians are proud of this splendid $70-million library, opened in 2001, which features original artwork as well as excellent resources that include some 120 computer terminals. It's also home to Memphis Shelby County Room, the best source around for local history. The system also maintains an excellent Web site at www.memphislibrary.org, which provides details about each location as well as other key information. Libraries in suburban DeSoto County, Mississippi, are operated by First Regional Library system, which serves eight counties in northwest Mississippi (www.first.lib.ms.us), and West Memphis Public Library (www.ci.westmemphis.ar.us/departments/library), which serves the population across the river.

HEALTH CARE AND WELLNESS

M emphis is one of the largest medical centers in the South, providing health care to a five-state region. It has changed dramatically with the times and is fast becoming one of the nation's premier centers for medical research.

Here, the practice of medicine is dominated by two large health-care systems, and it benefits from the presence of the state medical school, University of Tennessee Health Science Center. The city also is home to world-renowned St. Jude Children's Research Hospital, which boasts a Nobel Prize for medical research and treats children from all over the world. (See the Close-up in this chapter.)

The primary competitors in Memphis health care are Baptist Memorial Health Care Corp. and Methodist Healthcare, Inc. The two large systems operate hospitals, surgery centers, and health plans throughout the Mid-South. Whatever the name is on your insurance card, if you could peel the label back and peek, it would probably say Baptist or Methodist.

Baptist and Methodist each claim to be unique, but they both offer most of the same services and also compete on quality and price. This competition has proven to be very beneficial to the community because it has meant a wide range of services and access throughout the city. By virtue of the dominance of the Baptist and Methodist systems, the other hospitals in Memphis work on the fringes, filling their own niches.

Saint Francis Hospital, an additional provider on most health plans, controls about 18 percent of the market. Saint Francis recently built a new hospital in the suburb of Bartlett. Delta Medical Center specializes in behavioral health and is attractive to physicians who prefer a smaller, cozier atmosphere.

Baptist and Methodist have set aside their competitiveness when the community's needs have been great. Both systems have agreed not to pursue vital services provided at the Regional Medical Center at Memphis (The Med), such as its trauma center equipped to treat the sickest and most seriously injured patients or its world-class burn center. Competing in these areas would undermine The Med, which would be bad for everyone. The two systems also cooperate in a helicopter air ambulance, and they co-own a surgery center. Both work with the Church Health Center, which provides health care to the city's working poor (see the Close-up in this chapter).

Le Bonheur Children's Medical Center (no need to dust off your high-school French, because it's pronounced luh-BON-ner) is the region's primary provider of pediatric care. Courted by both health systems for several years, Le Bonheur merged with Methodist in 1995. Since then, Baptist has developed its own pediatric services so that now only about 3 percent of Baptist's pediatric patients are treated through Le Bonheur.

University of Tennessee Health Science Center keeps health care in the city both friendly and first rate. The med school operates in Memphis, even though the main university campus is in Knoxville.

Many of the region's physicians, nurses, and other medical professionals are graduates of UT, and more than 800 Memphis physicians donate their time to teaching students about the real world of medicine beyond the school's walls. Most of the faculty of UT also practice medicine in the community. Some 375 faculty members are part of UT Medical Group, Inc. and, as such, staff area hospitals, clinics, and surgery centers. The result is a dynamic, professionally charged environment where there is no barrier between academics and private practice.

University of Tennessee is also linked to St. Jude, which was started by 1960s TV star Danny Thomas. Here, no child is turned away, regardless of the seriousness of the illness or ability to pay. St. Jude is also unique in that almost all the scientists there have medical degrees as well as Ph.Ds. Most of St. Jude's scientists have dual appointments at UT, creating even more cross-pollination of medical creativity.

Like their counterparts elsewhere, the city's health-care providers have been pressed by rising health-care costs, resulting in the establishment of outpatient surgery centers. By far the biggest pressure has been from TennCare, enacted by the state in 1994 to put Medicaid under the discipline of managed care. What followed was financial chaos for several years and the effective disappearance of mental health care for the poor. At present, hospitals and doctors complain that TennCare covers only half of the actual cost of providing care to those patients. Efforts are ongoing to improve the program.

HISTORY

Memphis health care dates from 1855, the year that the first of a series of yellow-fever epidemics began. The disease killed off much of the population and earned Memphis a reputation as one of the three deadliest cities in the world, alongside Prague and the Chilean port of Valparaiso.

To the rescue came Catholic priests and nuns from three different orders, many of whom died while caring for the stricken during the epidemics of 1873 and 1878. In 1889 a priest and two nuns from Lafayette, Indiana, started the city's first civilian hospital. Fund-raising for the hospital was directed by Rabbi Max Samfield of Temple Israel. Thus, the religious tradition of health

care in Memphis was established at the very beginning, and it's still evident in the names of the primary health-care institutions: Baptist, Methodist, Saint Francis, St. Jude.

Baptist and Methodist started early in the 20th century, as much of the city's health care shifted to institutions. Previously, it was customary for all but the very poor to be treated at home by family physicians.

Since that time health care has grown dramatically, and as the city has grown, health care has followed the population growth. That movement led to the addition of suburban and regional hospitals, and the 2000 closing of what was once the world's largest private general hospital: Baptist Medical Center, near downtown Memphis.

As a sign of the times, the property is shifting over from patient care to research. In partnership with Baptist and the Memphis Biotech Foundation, UT Health Science Center is building the UT–Baptist Research Park, a new campus integrating research, teaching, and biomedical development. It includes a biotech business incubator, where scientists from UT can develop and commercialize their medical research.

Recognizing the city's strength in biotechnology, in 2003 the Department of Homeland Defense chose UT as a site for a $25 million biocontainment laboratory. It's one of just 10 such facilities to be built across the nation to work on problems related to bioterrorism.

HEALTH DEPARTMENT

Memphis and Shelby County Health Department
814 Jefferson Avenue
(901) 544-7600
www.shelbycountytn.gov
The health department provides a wide range of services, including primary care in poor neighborhoods and oversight of a wide range of public health matters. It also owns a nursing home, Oakville Health Care Center.

Although physicians can administer childhood immunizations, the Memphis and Shelby County Health Department operates five childhood immunization clinics throughout the metro area where the costs are less than $10 per visit.

HOSPITALS

Baptist Memorial Health Care Corp.
350 North Humphreys Boulevard
(901) 227–2727

Baptist Heart Institute
6019 Walnut Grove Road
(901) 226–2328

Baptist Memorial Hospital/Collierville
1500 West Poplar
(901) 861–9000

Baptist Memorial Hospital/DeSoto
87601 Southcrest Parkway
Southaven, Mississippi
(662) 349–4000

Baptist Memorial Hospital for Women
6225 Humphreys Boulevard
(901) 227–9000

Baptist Memorial Hospital/Memphis
6019 Walnut Grove Road
(901) 227–2727
www.bmhcc.org

Baptist, as locals call the local health-care system, has evolved into one of the world's largest and most comprehensive health systems since leaders from Tennessee, Arkansas, and Mississippi first opened their hospital here in 1912. At present, with about 8,000 employees in metro Memphis alone, Baptist operates 17 hospitals in three states. In Tennessee those hospitals are in Memphis, Collierville, Germantown, Covington, Ripley, Huntingdon, and Union City. In Mississippi they are in the Memphis suburb of Southaven plus Booneville, Columbus, New Albany, and Oxford. Arkansas hospitals are in Blytheville, Forrest City, and Osceola. In just the metro Memphis hospitals, Baptist treats more than 45,000 patients each year, a figure that doesn't include more than 60,000 emergency-room visits and 140,000 outpatient visits annually.

This expansion at the regional level reflects the desire among consumers to be treated closer to home. At one time, however, regional hospitals provided basic care to local patients but referred their most complex cases to Memphis, either to the facility traditionally known as Baptist Memorial Hospital/East or, until it closed in 2000, Baptist Medical Center near downtown Memphis.

At its peak the medical center was the nation's largest private general hospital, with a capacity of 1,800 patients, and until the mid-1980s it usually ran a full house. This was where Elvis Presley was pronounced dead after his untimely collapse and, during happier times, where his daughter Lisa Marie was born. The center opened more than 90 years ago as a nine-story, 150-bed hospital on land donated by Physicians and Surgeons College. Baptist Hospital ran into financial problems, and just two years after opening, a group of Methodists declined to buy the place for $1.00. They were already planning to build the new Methodist Hospital up the street. Today, Baptist and Methodist are the Coke and Pepsi of Memphis-area health care.

One reason for the medical center's demise is that during the 1990s, much of the system's health-care activity shifted to Baptist East, now the system's main hospital and renamed Baptist Memorial Hospital/Memphis.

In East Memphis, besides the main hospital, Baptist also operates a busy emergency department and recently expanded to bring its total capacity to 766 beds, including the 20-bed Hardin Pediatric Center.

In 2001 Baptist opened the 140-bed Baptist Women's Hospital, which has an adjacent physician's office building and its own secure parking. As one of only 17 women's hospitals in the United States, the facility has 36 birthing rooms and is capable of delivering 8,000 babies a year. There are also 6 operating rooms, a 40-bed neonatal intensive care unit, and a laboratory.

Nearby, Baptist recently opened a $86-million heart institute, which combines medical and surgical heart care, with one floor dedicated to cardiac research. The system also owns and operates Baptist-Trinity Home Care and Hospice.

The hospital also is strengthening its presence in north Mississippi. In 2003 it won permission from the state of Mississippi for a $175 million makeover of Baptist Memorial Hospital/DeSoto, with plans that include a 10-story tower that would bring the total number of beds to around 340. In 2004 the company acquired an 80-bed facility in Batesville, Mississippi, aligning it with Baptist Memorial Hospital/North Mississippi, in Oxford, Mississippi.

Crittenden Memorial Hospital
220 Tyler, West Memphis, Arkansas
(870) 735-1500
www.crittendenmemorial.org

Crittenden Memorial Hospital is a 152-bed facility about 7 miles from downtown Memphis. It's a full-service hospital with referral relationships across the river with Tennessee hospitals, and many of Crittenden's physicians also practice in Memphis.

Crittenden has a cardiac-imaging center, providing a service that formerly was routinely referred to Memphis. The hospital is the new home for the University of Tennessee School of Dentistry pediatric-residency program, as well as a medical education center that includes a 75-seat auditorium. The hospital also has a new children's health center and a new women's center that includes 6 birthing rooms and a high-security 14-bed nursery.

Delta Medical Center
3000 Getwell Road
(901) 369-8100
www.deltamedcenter.com

Delta Medical Center is a 134-bed hospital that has changed hands frequently over the years. It started more than 30 years ago as Doctor's Hospital, when a group of physicians sought to separate their professional fate from the two big systems, and it later operated as Eastwood Medical Center, a name that has stuck despite its most recent name change. Entrepreneurs Craig Watson and Neil McLean, who bought the hospital in 1999, have committed themselves to making the place a success. Under their control the hospital has expanded its behavioral-health areas, and they've recruited more physicians to take up shop in the neighboring office building and to practice at the hospital. As a result, activity has picked up at Delta Medical Center in recent years, so that today the hospital handles more than double the number of emergency-room visits it did in 1999.

Le Bonheur Children's Medical Center
50 North Dunlap Street
(901) 572-3000
www.lebonheur.org

Children are not just little adults, and that's the point behind Le Bonheur Children's Medical Center. At the 1952 dedication a key attached to a balloon was sent skyward, symbolizing that the hospital would always be open to sick and injured infants, children, and adolescents.

Presently Le Bonheur, with 225 beds and more than 1,600 employees, enjoys an international reputation for clinical care, research, and benevolence. It became part of the Methodist system in 1995 and treats more than 100,000 children each year. It also distributes about 38,000 popsicles and 13,000 crayons to patients each year.

A long list of accomplishments includes the city's first pediatric open-heart surgery in 1959 and the region's first intensive-care unit. At its main hospital Le Bonheur operates the only emergency and trauma unit in the Mid-South that's fully staffed and designed specifically for children.

Because it's home to the University of Tennessee Health Science Center's department of pediatrics, UT doctors staff the hospital and provide much of the high-intensity care. Between the university and the community, some 650 doctors practice at Le Bonheur in 42 different medical specialties. The hospital is also home to pediatric organ transplants, providing liver, kidney, heart, and lung transplants.

Other additions to Le Bonheur's services include the Sam Walton children's pediatric imaging center (opened in 1990) and a neurosciences center for children and adolescents (opened in 1995). The latter specializes in brain tumors, epilepsy, spinal-cord injuries, sleep disorders, and attention and behavioral problems.

Although all the heavy-duty surgery takes place at the main hospital, Le Bonheur also operates the Le Bonheur East Surgery Center at 786 Estate Place in East Memphis (901-681-4100). That's where many of the city's children have surrendered their tonsils or had other minor surgery.

Methodist Healthcare, Inc.
1265 Union Avenue
(901) 726-7000

Methodist–Le Bonheur/
Germantown Hospital
7691 Poplar Avenue, Germantown
(901) 754-6418

Methodist Healthcare/North Hospital
3960 New Covington Pike
(901) 384-5200

Methodist Healthcare/South Hospital
1264 Wesley Drive, (901) 516-3700
www.methodisthealth.org
This major health-care system includes a network of five Tennessee hospitals and surgery centers, the hub of which is Methodist University Hospital, a 917-bed medical center near downtown Memphis, newly affiliated with the University of Tennessee. It's the same location where 125-bed Methodist Hospital was first built in 1924, after John H. Sherard convinced fellow Methodists in the region to start a hospital.

Methodist operates, in addition to its central medical center, three other Memphis-area medical centers as well as a hospital in Somerville.

Methodist has aggressively expanded its other hospitals in Shelby County into freestanding medical centers. They provide most of the care people need, from advanced cardiac care to birthing centers, but close to home. That frees much of Methodist University Hospital to concentrate on the most complex cases, from heart transplants to brain surgery.

Methodist University Hospital has four Centers of Excellence, providing research, training, and treatment in cardiology, oncology, women's services, and neuroscience.

Reflecting its growing ties to UT, Methodist at the end of 2002 sold seven west Tennessee hospitals to a Nashville company, a logical step considering that 85 percent of its business already came from that metro area. The move was intended to allow Methodist to focus on building its relationship with UT.

Methodist took over management of UT Bowld Hospital, closing it and moving its transplant programs to University Hospital. In a parallel step, obstetric services at University Hospital are being merged with those of the Regional Medical Center, to eliminate duplication of birthing, neonatal intensive care, and related services. Methodist will also oversee the new Hamilton Eye Institute, a one-of-a-kind $70 million ophthalmology center that combines research, teaching, and advanced care.

Methodist University Hospital is also home to the Memphis Gamma Knife Center, which provides a specialized type of radiation for tumors too deep in the brain to be reached through surgery.

Its emergency department treats more than 48,000 patients each year.

Since merging with Le Bonheur Children's Medical Center, Methodist has expanded the reach of the pediatric hospital into many Methodist facilities.

Emergency and Information Numbers

Emergencies: fire, police, ambulance, 911
Al-Anon, (901) 278-5953
Alcoholics Anonymous, DeSoto County, (662) 280-3435
Alcoholics Anonymous, Memphis, (901) 458-7845
American Cancer Society, (901) 278-2000
American Diabetes Association, (901) 682-8232
American Heart Association, (901) 526-4616
American Lung Association, (901) 276-1731
Civil Defense, (901) 528-2780
Crisis Center, (901) 274-7477
Gamblers Anonymous, (901) 371-4083
LifeBlood: Regional Blood Center, (901) 522-8585
Memphis Light Gas & Water emergencies, (901) 528-4465
Memphis & Shelby County Health Department, (901) 544-7600
Narcotics Anonymous, (800) 677-1462
Overeaters Anonymous, (901) 458-5261
Red Cross, (901) 726-1690
Social Security Administration, (800) 772-1213
Southern Poison Center, (901) 274-7477

Physician Referral Services
Baptist Physician Referral, (901) 362-8677
Delta Medical Physician Referral, (901) 369-8293
Methodist Med Search Physician Referral, (901) 726-8686
Saint Francis Physician Referral, (901) 765-1811
UT Medical Group Physician Referral, (901) 448-6610

Regional Medical Center at Memphis
877 Jefferson Avenue
(901) 545-7100
www.the-med.org

The Med, as everybody calls this medical center, started in the 1980s as a partnership between the Shelby County government and the University of Tennessee. They wanted to organize a new kind of medical center, an academic and research hospital that would provide the most acute care possible.

The Med, with 321 beds, is part of the training ground for UT and serves as the county's safety-net hospital to the poor. It's also home to five Centers of Excellence, including its Level III trauma center, where the most seriously injured accident victims from a 150-mile radius are airlifted for emergency care.

The best known of the five is the Elvis Presley Memorial Trauma Center, where saving lives is a daily miracle. It was established in 1983 by surgeon Timothy Fabian, who remains medical director to this day. The center is staffed around the clock with on-site trauma surgeons, nurses, anesthesiologists, and other service personnel, all of them specially trained in severe trauma care.

The newborn center at The Med is one of the oldest and largest newborn intensive-care units in the United States. More than

1,300 premature or critically ill newborns are treated here each year. It is one of only 14 member institutions of the National Research Network, which is supported by the national Institute of Health's Child Development Program. Since its founding in 1968, this facility has successfully treated more than 40,000 premature babies, some weighing as little as one pound.

In general, The Med delivers more than 3,600 babies each year. More than a quarter of those mothers are considered high risk before birth and are therefore treated at the hospital's high-risk obstetrics center. This includes the 1,500-plus referrals of women with complicated pregnancies that The Med gets each year.

The 14-bed burn center treats adults and children with severe burns and cares for more than 300 patients a year. It also operates a skin bank used for transplants. The Med's wound-care center is an outpatient facility that treats slow-healing injuries, such as diabetic foot ulcers, and provides hyperbaric oxygen therapy. The center also has treatment vans that provide wound care to patients in area nursing homes.

Saint Francis Hospital
5959 Park Avenue
(901) 765-1000
www.saintfrancishosp.com

This 500-plus-bed hospital, on Park Avenue near the Germantown line, anchors a campus near the geographic center of the metropolis, which also has an on-site nursing home and two physician's office buildings. Saint Francis operates a trauma center, a chest-pain center, and an emergency stroke center. It is also

You'll get the most comprehensive eye exam of your life for $60 at the Southern College of Optometry (901-722-3250). But if they see something interesting, be prepared for several extra students to also take a look.

home to the Saint Francis/UT Family Practice Residency Center, staffed by University of Tennessee Health Science Center faculty and residents.

In 1994 the chain that is now Tenet Healthcare Corp. bought out the hospital for $100 million, a sum used to fund the Assisi Foundation of Memphis. Since then the foundation has awarded tens of millions of dollars in health-care and education grants.

Saint Francis recently built a new outpatient surgery center on the front lawn of its main campus. It's designed to be easy to get into and out of, so surgery patients don't have to navigate the hospital.

To serve the city's growing suburban population, in 2004 Tenet opened Saint Francis–Bartlett, a 90-bed acute-care, full-service facility. It offers an emergency room, intensive care, labor and delivery, and surgery. Some services were transferred from the main hospital.

St. Jude Children's Research Hospital
332 North Lauderdale Street
(901) 495-3300
www.stjude.org

This unique hospital focuses on childhood catastrophic diseases, such as leukemia, that were formerly considered hopeless, and it is at the forefront of medical research in many areas. More than 20,000 children from more than 60 countries have been treated at St. Jude, and no child has ever been denied care for lack of money. (See the Close-up in this chapter for more information.)

Veterans Affairs Medical Center
1030 Jefferson Avenue
(901) 523-8990

The city's VA hospital, with 322 beds and 1,500 employees, includes one of the best facilities for treating spinal-cord injuries in the entire VA system. Before moving to the medical district in the 1960s, local VA medical facilities were concentrated at Kennedy VA Hospital on Shotwell Road. Some people thought the street's name

St. Jude Children's Research Hospital

In the winter of 1940, an out-of-work comedian, with just $7.00 in his pocket and a pregnant wife at home, fell to his knees in desperation before a statue of St. Jude Thaddeus, the patron saint of hopeless cases. The entertainer, Danny Thomas, prayed, "Help me find my place in life and I will build you a shrine, where the helpless may come for aid."

Thomas remembered his vow, and as his career advanced, he used his position and fame to launch St. Jude Children's Research Hospital in 1962. True to its namesake, St. Jude has always concentrated on research that leads to survival of childhood catastrophic diseases that were at one time considered hopeless.

The survival rate today for most of these diseases is dramatically better, thanks to St. Jude research. For example, in 1962 the survival rate for leukemia was just 4 percent. Today it's 80 percent, due in part to the hospital's work.

St. Jude today operates 56 inpatient beds but provides nearly 50,000 outpatient treatments each year. It has more than 2,200 employees, including clinicians, scientists, social workers, and administrative staff. St. Jude is one of the most international places in town, with scientists from throughout the world. Thousands of children from more than 60 countries have been treated at St. Jude, and no child has ever been denied care for lack of money. Food, lodging, and transportation are provided free to families while there for treatment, with the help of Ronald McDonald House and Target House. Thanks to a $5 million gift from the Memphis Grizzlies, St. Jude recently opened a new residential facility for families, aptly named Memphis Grizzlies House.

The focus at St. Jude is still pediatric leukemia, solid tumor cancer, and biomedical research, but it has grown into basic and clinical research in bone-marrow transplantation, chemotherapy, the biochemistry of normal and cancerous cells, and other areas. Research at St. Jude has helped in understanding diseases such as AIDS and sickle-cell disease, which hopefully will also provide clues to treating childhood diseases. Scientists there are also at the forefront of the newest forms of gene therapy. St. Jude is also committed to sharing its knowledge to help children throughout the world, and it does so in many innovative ways.

Despite its accomplishments, which include a 1996 Nobel Prize for Medicine awarded to St. Jude researcher Peter Doherty for his work on the immune system, the research hospital is always looking ahead. A $1 billion expansion (with a 2005 completion date) is adding laboratory space and other facilities to attract the best minds in the world.

In 2003 St. Jude entered a new era of research with the opening of a $42 million Current Good Manufacturing Processes lab (GMP). The facility allows scientists to quickly whip up batches of novel drugs or experiment on viruses and germs in ways that were never possible before.

For example, when a scary new form of flu appeared in Hong Kong in 2003, the World Health Organization turned to St. Jude for help. A GMP virologist was able to isolate the virus in just four weeks, a task that typically takes several years. But the GMP lab also helps in less exotic ways, such as making flu shots work better.

unfortunate and thus moved to have it renamed Getwell Road, which it is still called today.

VA Memphis treats more than 35,000 patients each year, almost entirely on an outpatient basis. The hospital offers a full range of services to military veterans, many of whom have no place else to turn. The hospital is staffed primarily by University of Tennessee physicians, and many of the clinics there are operated by advanced-practice nurses who are also on faculty at the UT College of Nursing.

For a variety of reasons, veterans account for a disproportionate number of homeless persons and those with alcohol and drug addictions. VA Memphis has several programs specifically designed to find and treat these veterans.

WALK-IN CLINICS

Many Memphians turn to walk-in clinics when a sudden illness or injury comes up, but they can't get into their doctor's office and don't want to risk a long wait at a hospital ER, where ambulances have priority. Fast, convenient, and reasonably priced, these centers also are choices for getting treatment for colds, flu, bug bites, sprains, and cuts. As with most everything else in Memphis health care, the minor meds are dominated by Baptist and Methodist health-care systems. You may want to check your health insurance before your visit to make sure you are covered, as there may be some restrictions.

Baptist Memorial Health Care

All of the centers are open Monday through Saturday, 8:00 A.M. to 7:30 P.M.; two are also open the same hours on Sundays (see below). All are closed Thanksgiving Day and Christmas Day.

LOCATIONS

2087 Union Avenue, (901) 274-3336

6570 Stage Road, Bartlett, (901) 385-7817

5030 Poplar Avenue, (901) 683-7937 (open on Sundays)

584 North Germantown Parkway, Cordova, (901) 753-7686 (open on Sundays)

8990 Germantown Extended, Olive Branch, Mississippi, (901) 525-1160 or (662) 893-1160

Methodist Healthcare

The system operates three minor medical centers for adults and two Le Bonheur Urgent Care facilities devoted to treating children.

Cordova Minor Medical Center, 8045 Club Parkway, Cordova, (901) 758-6035: open seven days a week 9:00 A.M. to 10:00 P.M., including holidays

Winchester Minor Medical Center/Le Bonheur Urgent Care, 8071 Winchester Road
Methodist phone: (901) 756-6056, Methodist hours: 8:00 A.M. to 9:00 P.M. seven days a week, including holidays
Le Bonheur phone: (901) 756-9634, Le Bonheur hours: Monday through Friday, 6:00 P.M. to 10:00 P.M.

Methodist Medical Complex–Robinsonville, 11273 Highway 61 North Robinsonville, Mississippi, (662) 363-3224: open 24 hours a day, seven days a week, including holidays

Le Bonheur Urgent Care, 1335 Germantown Parkway, (901) 758-6000: open Monday through Friday 4:00 P.M. to 11:00 P.M. and Saturday and Sunday 8:00 A.M. to 11:00 P.M., including holidays

Church Health Center

Scott Morris is a doctor who preaches, and a preacher who heals, and the Church Health Center is both the result of his vision and the template of similar clinics across the United States.

While an associate pastor at St. John's Methodist Church, Dr. Morris set out to organize a clinic for the 150,000-plus Memphians who work yet lack adequate insurance. They often fall through the cracks in terms of health care, since they earn too much to qualify for Medicaid but can't afford their employer's health plan.

The Church Health Center opened in 1987 in a boardinghouse purchased by St. John's, and on its first day Morris and his nurse treated 12 patients. Today Church Health Center has more than 32,000 patients and employs 5 on-site physicians, a dentist, 6 nurses, and 2 pastoral counselors. There's also a network of more than 600 volunteer physicians, nurses, dentists, and other health professionals, who either volunteer their time in the clinic or treat the center's patients in their own offices. Hospitals set aside their competitiveness when it comes to the Church Health Center, making MRI units, CT scanners, even operating rooms available for center patients.

In keeping with its name, Church Health Center is funded almost entirely by 200-plus Memphis churches and synagogues, plus individuals, businesses, and other groups.

Morris has added two other successful programs, the Memphis Plan and the Hope and Healing Center. The Memphis Plan lets people who make $7.50 an hour or less pay $20 a month for a plan that gives them access to medical care, including specialty care and hospitalization. The Hope and Healing Center provides an attractive, affordable facility where people can go for exercise, yoga classes, cooking lessons, prayer time, and whatever else is needed for a healthy, balanced life.

Church Health Center is at 1210 Peabody Avenue, (901) 272-7170. Hope and Healing Center is at 1111 Union Avenue, (901) 259-4673, or online at www.churchhealthcenter.org.

Independent Walk-in Clinic

There is one independent clinic in the area, but it mainly handles work-related injuries.

Med-Emergency Clinic, 5270 Knight Arnold, (901) 362-2811: open Monday through Friday 7:00 A.M. to 5:00 P.M. and Saturday 9:00 A.M. to noon

ALTERNATIVE MEDICINE

Not all health care in Memphis is of the cut, sew, and medicate variety. As a large city with a particular focus on health care, Memphis offers alternative therapies, ranging from Christian Science healing and acupuncture to midwives who will deliver babies at home.

In addition, UT has developed techniques for most surgeries that can be performed without donated blood. The

Church of Scientology operates the Mission of Memphis, which includes classes on physical and mental health. Its focus is on health maintenance and preventive care, rather than treatment.

Memphis has more than 40 trained acupuncture specialists, many of them registered nurses who use acupuncture within a physician's practice. Most acupuncturists are also well versed in the uses of herbs, vitamins, and other nutritional interventions. The Healing Arts Center (see listing) combines acupuncture, internal medicine, massage therapy, and Eastern medicine.

For more information, or if you're seeking a specific type of treatment, you can do as many Memphians do and head for Wild Oats Market, the local health-food store. Get some gourmet coffee, scan the bulletin board, and ask around. Chances are somebody will be able to help you. Wild Oats is at 5022 Poplar Avenue, (901) 685-2293.

Acupuncture and Acupressure Center, 5733 Nanjack Circle, (901) 795-3900

Healing Arts Center, 6005 Park Avenue, (901) 763-0909

Chinese Acupuncture Center, 515 North Highland Street, (901) 323-1202

William L. Faulkner, MD (acupuncture), 969 Peabody Avenue, (901) 527-1153

Mid-South Center for Natural Medicine, 4515 Poplar Avenue, (901) 766-9355

Church of Scientology Mission of Memphis, 1440 Central Avenue, (901) 276-5686

Stone Center for Wellness, 8200 Old Dexter Road, Cordova, (901) 757-4646

EDUCATION

Memphis has more than a dozen institutions of higher education, including a major university (University of Memphis) and Tennessee's leading medical school (University of Tennessee Health Science Center). Colleges in Memphis are also at the forefront of the emerging world of online education, and it's possible to earn an entire degree in Memphis in front of a computer terminal.

For elementary and secondary education, there are two public-school systems: Shelby County Schools and Memphis City Schools. Although Shelby County schools are generally seen as better than those in the city, the Memphis system boasts a number of schools so outstanding that parents from outside the city pay tuition for their children to attend them. Parents can also choose from a roster of private schools for children of all ages, many with long-standing traditions of academic excellence.

In both the city and the county, many families base their home-buying decisions on the neighborhood's public schools, an important consideration given how dramatically different each school can be. Word of mouth among parents is often the best source of information about the schools, particularly city public schools, which vary significantly due to parental involvement and other factors.

Some families are drawn to Southaven, Olive Branch, and other parts of DeSoto County, the fast-growing Mississippi county just south of Memphis. The DeSoto County School District, which had 26 schools and 2 more under construction as of 2004, is the second-largest school district in Mississippi. The district, with 2003–2004 enrollment of 23,500, prides itself on the fact that some 30 percent of its teachers have advanced degrees, and that more than 90 percent of its students graduate.

PUBLIC SCHOOLS

Shelby County, which operates 48 schools with almost 50,000 students, includes the lion's share of middle- and upper-income areas, with virtually no poverty. Memphis City Schools is the largest school system in Tennessee and the 21st-largest school district in the nation, operating nearly 180 schools with an enrollment of nearly 120,000.

Memphis City schools are a mixed bag, so each school must be considered on its own merits. For example, White Station High School in East Memphis is considered one of the best college-prep schools in the United States and routinely has more National Merit semifinalists of any public school in Tennessee. Yet in 2001, after the Tennessee Department of Education toughened some of its criteria, some 64 city schools were identified by the department as low performing and in danger of being placed on probation. That spurred a statewide charter-school movement and in 2003, a master plan for improvement.

Many of these troubled schools face significant challenges, including locations in impoverished, crime-ridden sections of the metropolitan area and parents who in many cases don't get involved with their children's education or schools. The same schools usually have a high percentage of students qualifying for free or subsidized school lunches.

Memphis City schools encourage parents to take an ownership role in their neighborhood school and allow parents to develop programs based on local need. One example is a 501(c)3 nonprofit corporation formed by parents at Richland Elementary, which raised enough money to hire two extra reading assistants to help the slower readers catch up.

The system is working to improve the low-performing schools. In addition, more than 650 business and community partners give time and money to students at all the schools through the Adopt-a-School program. The school system also encourages parents to get involved with their child's school, and as a result many parents volunteer their time and help to raise money for improvements ranging from new playground equipment to extra teaching assistants.

The city school system also offers an optional program at 31 schools, with enrichment areas ranging from fine arts to engineering, and from international business to aviation technology. Optional programs are available at no extra charge to residents of the district, but others clamor and compete for a limited number of slots. Noncity residents pay $600 per year, Tennessee residents outside Shelby County pay $2,600, and out-of-state residents pay $5,300 to attend Memphis City schools.

For example, Overton High School offers the area's only creative- and performing-arts optional high-school program. Students must have good grades, conduct, and attendance records, plus they must pass rigorous audition standards to be admitted to the program. About 600 of Overton High's 1,400 students are enrolled in the creative- and performing-arts program at the school, which also offers honors, advanced placement, and standard courses in English, mathematics, and other subjects as well as business education and vocational courses.

One of the city district's most exciting programs is its charter schools, intended to improve the quality of education. Three of them began classes in 2003, including Memphis Academy of Science & Engineering, operated by the Memphis Biotechnology Foundation and University of Tennessee Health Science Center. There, the emphasis is on science, math, and engineering, with students spending part of each day with scientists and UT faculty. Other charter schools are being planned. Entry to these schools is competitive, and

parents are expected to take an active role.

The 2003–2004 operating budget for Memphis City Schools was $731 million. The system has also made extensive capital expenditures, including a six-year, $1-billion project to install air-conditioning in every school. That makes sense for a city where temperatures in August and September are often in the 90s. Schools that could be retrofitted were, but many older schools were replaced with modern facilities. Recognizing that each school is a long-term investment in neighborhood stability, Memphis City Schools officials designed each school to fit its particular neighborhood.

Capital improvements continue, with a number of new schools being added and existing schools being renovated or expanded.

In contrast new Shelby County schools have been less expensive to build, but they tend to look very much alike. The system includes all areas of the county outside the Memphis city limits, including the incorporated towns of Arlington, Bartlett, Collierville, Germantown, Lakeland, and Millington. It's the fourth-largest school system in the state, and in 2003–2004 it had a budget of $225 million.

The Shelby County government has spent at least $1.5 billion on public education since 1990: $1.1 billion in operations and $400 million in capital improvements. Because every property owner in the city of Memphis pays taxes to the city and the county, a major portion of tax collections from the county find their way back to city schools.

In order to comply with laws requiring county government to equally fund students in both systems, 70 percent of county tax collections for education go to the city. That means that half of every dollar collected in property taxes and 100 percent of the local sales taxes support public education.

For more information about Memphis City Schools, contact the student enrollment office at (901) 325-5830. You can also check out the city schools' Web site at www.memphis-schools.k12.tn.us, or call (901) 325-5628 for a free brochure. For more information on Shelby County Schools, contact the pupil services offices at (901) 321-2560 or check out the system's Web site at www.scs.k12.tn.us.

PRIVATE AND PAROCHIAL SCHOOLS

The Memphis area has more than 100 private elementary, middle, and secondary schools. Most are affiliated with a church or denomination, but some are purely academic. Tuition and fees can range from $3,000 a year to more than $10,000 a year.

A number of private schools also offer special education for children with various learning disabilities. By law, city and county schools are obliged to provide these services to residents at no additional charge. The reality is that the public-school systems do their best but are overwhelmed by the demand. Those who have grown weary of the struggles and the waiting have found refuge in private schools.

The Catholic Diocese of Memphis operates the single largest private-school system in Memphis, with 7,700 students at 25 schools. In 1999 the diocese launched an ambitious plan, the Jubilee Project, to reopen six inner-city schools beginning with kindergarten and first grade in each and adding one grade each year. The response from the neighborhoods has been overwhelming. Most Jubilee schools are 80 to 100 percent black and about 90 percent non-Catholic. The percentage of children qualifying for free or subsidized lunches is in the same range. The last of the six schools opened in 2002, but the Jubilee effort has been such a success that the diocese is considering an expansion.

Another major private-school system in Memphis is Harding Academy. Affiliated with the Church of Christ, Harding operates eight schools with a total enrollment of about 2,000.

Private Elementary/ Middle Schools

Holy Rosary Elementary School
4841 Park Avenue
(901) 685-1231
www.cdom.org
Holy Rosary is a Catholic school under the auspices of the Catholic Diocese of Memphis. It's a coed school founded in 1954, along with the founding of Holy Rosary Parish, and offers classes in kindergarten through the eighth grade.

The school has a reputation as being academically rigorous—and very Catholic. That's reflected in daily Bible studies, weekly Mass, and a faculty that is 85 percent Roman Catholic. It is one of the largest parochial grade schools in the diocese.

The East Memphis campus includes 29 classrooms, a library, a media center, a computer lab, a science lab, a music room, a gym, and athletic fields. The teacher-pupil ratio is 1 to 14 and virtually all graduating eighth graders are accepted into the high school of their choice.

The leading private schools in town take pride in having a student body that is diverse, both ethnically and socially, so if there's a school you really like, don't write it off because the tuition might be $7,000 or more. Most schools offer scholarships and grants based on need, and most will trade for services. That top school might be within reach with a combination of partial tuition, financial aid, and maybe painting the gym.

St. Ann-Bartlett Elementary School
6529 Stage Road, Bartlett
(901) 386-3328
www.cdom.org
St. Ann has been part of the Bartlett community since 1960, when the parish school opened with 150 students. Presently St.

Ann has an enrollment of nearly 700, and 95 percent are Catholic. It has classes for kindergarten through the eighth grade.

The school has a staff of 40 certified teachers, plus a full-time counselor and administrators. There are 30 classrooms, plus a library, a computer lab, a science lab, a music room, a band room, a full-service cafeteria, and a gym.

In addition to Catholic religious instruction, St. Ann puts a high value on enrichment activities. Those include academic competitions, community-service projects, sports, and music. The school also offers child care before and after school, as well as summer programs.

Private Elementary/ Secondary Schools

Briarcrest Christian Schools
6000 Briarcrest Avenue
(901) 765-4600
www.briarcrest.com
Briarcrest was founded in 1972 as a ministry of Briarcrest Baptist Church, and since then has evolved into a large, coed, nondenominational Christian school with an enrollment of nearly 1,700 students and a strong sports program.

The main campus is on 20 acres near Poplar and I-240 in East Memphis, with an elementary school (K–5), a middle school (6–8), and a high school (9–12). Briarcrest also operates an elementary school at 1620 Houston Levee Road in Cordova.

Briarcrest offers a wide range of sports, including soccer, football, and tennis. The school's sports complex is on 90 acres near Walnut Grove and Raleigh–LaGrange Roads in east Shelby County. The high school has moved to the Raleigh-LaGrange campus, and the rest of the school is expected to follow eventually.

Christian Brothers High School
5900 Walnut Grove Road
(901) 682-7801
www.cbhs.org

CBHS is an all-boys Catholic high school in East Memphis operated by the same LaSalle order that operates Christian Brothers University in midtown Memphis. The school, on a 32-acre campus on Walnut Grove near I-240, has a reputation for solid academics and college prep. It's one of the few schools in Memphis that still teaches Latin, and it prides itself on its commitment to technology, with a computer-learning center and computers also woven into other classroom areas. The curriculum is heavy on math, science, computers, fine arts, and even business, another rarity for a high school.

Christian Brothers has an enrollment of about 875, and a very intimate teacher-pupil ratio of 1 to 13. The students are required to perform 44 hours of community service in addition to satisfying academic requirements. The student body consists of grades 9 through 12.

Evangelical Christian School of Memphis
7600 Macon Road, Cordova
(901) 754-7217
www.ecseagles.com
Tucked away in a wooded area of Cordova, ECS is an independent, nondenominational, coed school with an enrollment of about 1,400. As its name implies, the school comes from the evangelical tradition, which means a strong emphasis on moral character, clean living, and service to others.

ECS teaches children from kindergarten through 12th grade. It's known for its rigorous science programs, especially in high school, where chemistry and biology get special attention. ECS operates elementary schools at 11893 Macon Road and 735 Ridge Lake Boulevard.

The school prides itself on the fact that 70 percent of the 2003 graduating class were offered academic, athletic, or achievement scholarships.

Harding Academy
1100 Cherry Road
(901) 767-4494
www.hardingacademymemphis.org

Harding Academy, affiliated with the Church of Christ, operates six schools across Shelby County with a total enrollment of about 1,900, including a high school at 1100 Cherry Street in East Memphis. Its system covers all ages, from prekindergarten through 12th grade.

The school, which was founded in 1952, has expanded by going into growing neighborhoods and adding schools to church campuses there. The newest addition is a 54,000-square-foot school in fast-growing Cordova, located on 6.1 acres next to the current building on Macon Road. The additional space provides 18 classrooms to serve 432 elementary students in grades 1 through 6.

Harding is unabashed about its Christian foundation and also seeks to instill a sense of pride in being an American and the responsibility that citizenship entails.

Hutchison School
1740 Ridgeway Road
(901) 761-2220
www.hutchisonschool.org

Hutchison is one of the premier, all-girls schools in the Mid-South, with a college-prep program. The school was founded in 1902 and is known for its high-quality, academically rich instruction. Enrollment is about 820, covering kindergarten through 12th grade.

The school has been expanding and adding new services recently, including a new athletic center and a learning and technology complex complete with a NASA satellite feed, interactive media, wireless technology, and an e-classroom. Hutchison completed a new early childhood center in 2001.

Foreign-language classes begin as early as age three, and hands-on science classes begin in the 1st grade. One popular area of study has been robotics.

Hutchison also provides instruction in fine arts and offers a summer program that's also academically rich. About 25 percent of the school's students each year are recognized as National Merit Scholars.

Lausanne Collegiate School
1381 West Massey Street
(901) 683-5233
www.lausannekth.com

Part of the 28-acre campus of Lausanne is the Blue Herron Lake, where students often gather to read poetry, paint, or discuss studies. And that reflects the Lausanne philosophy of incorporating learning into all of life's activities.

Lausanne is a coed, college-prep school with about 700 students and 110 faculty and staff. It offers classes in kindergarten through 12th grade.

The school has embraced technology in almost every way, from teachers who post assignments on the Internet so that parents can stay involved to word processing in English. Kindergartners use calculators in math instruction, and science labs are equipped with the latest devices. The school also provides a variety of athletic options, so all children can find something they enjoy. In addition to the usual soccer, basketball, and track, sports programs also include dance, karate, weight training, fencing, and lacrosse. Outdoor leadership features rock climbing, canoeing, rafting, and more.

Memphis University School
6191 Park Avenue
(901) 260-1300
www.musowls.org

Since 1893 MUS has existed with three goals: preparing boys for competitive colleges, providing them with a well-rounded liberal-arts education, and helping them to develop into cultured gentlemen.

On 94 rolling acres in East Memphis, MUS teaches boys in the 7th through 12th grades. The student-faculty ratio is 15 to 1. The school still has the same general goals, and the numbers tell the story. Some 32 percent of the school's 2003 graduates were National Merit scholars. Over five years the mid-range SAT and ACT scores were 30 percent above the national average.

Traditionally, connections made at MUS have continued into adult life, with about

70 percent of the school's alumni remaining in the Memphis area. Many of the city's movers and shakers, including AutoZone founder Pitt Hyde and many others, are MUS graduates.

St. Agnes Academy–St. Dominic School
4830 Walnut Grove Road
(901) 767-1356
www.saa-sds.org

St. Agnes Academy–St. Dominic School is a Catholic independent school with a history—at least in the case of St. Agnes—that predates the Civil War. St. Agnes, founded in 1851, is a college-prep school for girls. St. Dominic was founded in 1956 as a school for boys. The two were joined in 1978 but still retain some of their single-sex character.

The school provides coed education in early childhood and kindergarten, single-sex classes in grades 1 through 6, and coordinated classes in 7th and 8th grades. High school is for girls only. Total enrollment is about 860, with upper-school enrollment of 350.

As a college-prep high school, St. Agnes provides a well-rounded academic education and offers a number of advanced-placement courses. It is known to shine in liberal arts and language, and is one of only two high schools in the state at which the University of Tennessee will grant college credit for foreign language instruction, in both French and Spanish.

St. Agnes teaches from a philosophy of service and requires all upper-school students to perform community service as part of their education.

Virtually all of St. Agnes's graduates go on to college.

St. Benedict at Auburndale
2100 Germantown Parkway, Cordova
(901) 388-7321
www.sbeagles.org

St. Benedict started as a private school in 1966, founded by Stanley and Alice Smith, and was known as the Auburndale School System. They sold the 22-acre campus in 1988 to the Catholic Diocese of Memphis, which gave it the current name. It serves students in kindergarten through 12th grade.

St. Benedict is a college-prep school with a total enrollment of about 1,025, including 400 in the high school. The school emphasizes honors and advanced-placement coursework, along with foreign language, music, art, and computer instruction. Virtually all of St. Benedict's graduates are accepted to college.

In 2004 the school merged with St. Francis of Assisi Parish and added 26 acres for expansion. This allows for significant growth in the size of the student body at the elementary school and the high school.

St. Mary's Episcopal School
60 Perkins Road Extended
(901) 537-1405
www.stmarysschool.org

St. Mary's is a girls-only college-preparatory school in East Memphis that is academically rigorous and carefully sequenced from prekindergarten through 12th grade. Founded in 1847, St. Mary's now has a total enrollment of about 840, with a student to faculty ratio of 10 to 1.

St. Mary's graduates have a reputation for being able to analyze and act and are highly sought for the critical thinking skills they possess. The school emphasizes a classic, rigorous liberal-arts curriculum that is designed to allow each girl to reach her individual potential.

The rigorous program has paid off for St. Mary's students. In 2003 the school's 63 graduates included 4 National Merit semifinalists, 16 National Merit commended students, and 1 National Achievement semifinalist.

The school shares a 20-acre campus with Church of the Holy Communion, an Episcopal church in East Memphis.

Westminster Academy
2500 Ridgeway Road
(901) 380-9192
www.westminsteracademy.net

For a very different educational experience, there's Westminster Academy, a private nondenominational Christian school founded in 1996. It was one of the first schools in the nation to revive Trivium learning, the ancient Greek method of study founded by Socrates based on grammar, logic, and rhetoric. Today that's more commonly known as classical education.

Westminster, with almost 300 students in kindergarten through 12th grade, is affiliated with the Association of Classical and Christian Schools. Students are required to take three years each of logic and classic rhetoric, while Latin and classical Greek are also part of the curriculum.

What truly makes Westminster distinct is its approach. Students write papers every week, for each class, and defend their papers before the class. Discussion is considered central to learning, and history is woven into the subject of each class.

HOMESCHOOLING

Nearly 2,000 children in the Memphis area go to school at the kitchen table, in one of the most dynamic homeschool communities in the United States. This is partly as an outgrowth of the city's position in the Bible Belt, as many parents choose to homeschool for religious reasons.

Homeschool is almost a misnomer, because, through the Memphis Area Home Education Association, students can still participate in competitive sports, including basketball and cheerleading. They have field trips, dances, graduation ceremonies, even their own scholarship fund. For more information contact the Memphis Area Home Education Association (901–788–6432, www.memphishomeed.org). Other resources include Gateway Christian Schools (901–454–1606, www.gateway christianschools.com) and Home Life Academy (901–380–9220, www.homelife academy.com). The Tennessee Department of Education has certain requirements for enrolling homeschool students. For more information contact the agency at (865) 579–3749 or visit its Web site at www.state.tn.us/education/aahomsch.

CHILD CARE

Memphis is a very family-oriented city, and you'll find many providers of quality day care. There are nearly 400 licensed child-care centers in the Memphis area and probably twice as many unlicensed places that also provide care to children. The licensed centers include large national chains such as La Petite Academy and Kinder Care. But, in a city like Memphis, where churches play a central role in the lives of so many families, it's not surprising that church child care dominates the scene.

In finding care for your child, your best resources may be friends, neighbors, and coworkers with young children. You'll probably want to visit a number of child-care centers and take time to ask questions as well as observe how the care providers interact with the children. One good sign is participation in the Tennessee Department of Human Services' Star Quality program, a voluntary assessment of a center's staff, regulatory compliance, and other factors. Since it's voluntary, a center's participation tells you its operators are determined to go beyond the bare basics. Any facility that earns the top score of three stars will be proudly displaying the results, but a score of two or even one exceeds state minimum standards.

Also, many churches, including Calvary Episcopal Church in downtown Memphis and Christ the King Lutheran in East Memphis, operate excellent day-care centers that welcome children from outside their own flocks. Of course, if you choose to join a church, it may well offer day care, allowing you to leave the little ones with people you know. Also check out private schools; many of them have waiting lists, and by starting with their child-care center, it may be easier to get a slot a few years later when it's time for school to start.

Tennessee Department of Human Services
400 Deaderick Street, Nashville
(800) 462–8261
www.state.tn.us/humanserv

The Tennessee Department of Human Services is in charge of overseeing child care in the state. Under state law any child-care provider caring for more than four children must have a license from this agency. The department provides a free child-care resource and referral service, offering customized child-care listings, literature, and counseling.

Check out the Web site, which maintains a list of licensed and registered child-care centers, organized by zip codes within Shelby County and other nearby counties. It also has information on licensing and updates on proposed child-care rules and legislation.

If you are looking for a licensed child-care center for your little one, log on to the Tennessee Department of Human Services Web site at www.state.tn.us/humanserv. It has a listing of centers organized by zip codes so you can find one close to your home.

HIGHER EDUCATION

Memphis is home to a diverse group of colleges and universities, ranging from free-spirited Memphis College of Art and picturesque Rhodes College to the state's largest two-year college, Southwest Tennessee Community College.

Perhaps the most visible is University of Memphis, home of the Tigers and the second-largest university in the state. (So many Memphians have attended U of M throughout the years that you'll find Tigers fans all over town.) The state's leading medical school, University of Tennessee Health Science Center, is here, even though UT has its main campus in Knoxville. Other institutions of higher education here have a narrow focus, such as Memphis Theologi-

cal Seminary and Southern College of Optometry.

Most of the colleges and universities offer some form of evening and weekend classes, so that people who work full time can continue their education whether in pursuit of a diploma or for the pleasure of learning something new.

Among the public colleges and universities, the primary issue continues to be state funding. Tennessee ranks well below other states in terms of its financial support to higher education and due to state budget woes, more of the financial burden has been shifted to students in the form of higher tuition. One outcome of this funding squeeze has been the loss of faculty, especially from the University of Memphis and the medical schools, but that is easing as other states, faced with similar budget problems, aren't as able to woo away professors.

To address this issue and after much debate, Tennessee implemented a lottery in 2004. Since all proceeds go toward merit scholarships, the lottery is expected to help Tennesseans pay for college.

Christian Brothers University
650 East Parkway
(901) 321–3200
www.cbu.edu

CBU is a Catholic school in the tradition of the Christian Brothers of the LaSalle Order, and it's a common sight to see the brothers on campus and teaching classes. The college has a strong program of evening classes to accommodate working students as well as traditional daytime classes for full-time students.

U.S. News and World Report, in its Year 2004 Annual Guide of America's Best Colleges, ranked CBU number 28 in the top regional Southern colleges and as one of the top-50 schools in the nation offering bachelor's and master's degrees in engineering. CBU also offers degree programs in management and education, as well as an MBA and executive MBA programs. Enrollment is about 2,000. CBU is not to be confused with Christian Brothers High

School, which maintains its campus on Walnut Grove Road in East Memphis, although the LaSalle Order oversees both.

Crichton College
255 North Highland Street
(901) 367-9800
www.crichton.edu
Crichton (pronounced CRY-ton) is a non-denominational Christian college, known for intimate classroom experiences and fostering an attitude of service. It recently moved to a new campus on Highland Street. Enrollment is about 925.

LeMoyne-Owen College
807 Walker Avenue
(901) 774-9090
www.lemoyne-owen.edu
LeMoyne-Owen is a historically black, private liberal-arts college that was one of the original schools that formed the United Negro College Fund. Enrollment is about 1,000.

It is affiliated with the United Church of Christ and the Tennessee Baptist Missionary and Education Convention. The college is committed to providing a holistic education for the traditional and nontraditional student and to providing leadership and service to the Memphis and Mid-South community and beyond.

The school awards bachelor's degrees in arts, sciences, and business administration.

Memphis College of Art
1930 Poplar Avenue
(901) 272-5100
www.mca.edu
Nestled in the heart of Overton Park in midtown, the College of Art, as it's known locally, is one of the nation's leading art schools. It teaches traditional forms in sculpture and painting as well as computer graphic design, and it recently added a photography program. With an enrollment of about 250, the school awards bachelor's and master's degrees of fine arts. The school prides itself on its 11-to-1 student-teacher ratio.

MCA is a hip place, so there's great people watching in the area around the main building.

Students have showings throughout the year, including an annual holiday show and sale. The college's lobby is also the scene for some of the city's more inspired art shows.

Rhodes College
2000 North Parkway
(901) 843-3000
www.rhodes.edu
Rhodes is a private liberal-arts college, with a reputation for academic excellence. With an enrollment of about 1,500, Rhodes awards bachelor's degrees in sciences and arts and master's degrees in accounting. In addition to classroom work and extracurricular activities, students are required to perform public service in the community.

Rhodes (formerly known as Southwestern at Memphis) has a beautiful campus, with soaring stone buildings in the English tradition, and lots of trees in a residential area of midtown Memphis. About 75 percent of its students live on campus, which makes for a lively atmosphere.

The school has a 12-to-1 student-faculty ratio, which encourages students to get to know their teachers. About 60 percent of students participate in Rhodes's internship program, working at local businesses that include Federal Express, the Orpheum Theater, and the Memphis office of Ernst & Young.

In addition, the college's Meeman Center for Lifelong Learning offers adult classes on everything from art and theology to astrophysics.

Southern College of Optometry
1245 Madison Avenue
(901) 722-3216
www.sco.edu
SCO is a private college of optometry, awarding doctor of optometry degrees. It is one of the more competitive optometry schools in the United States, with an enrollment of about 480 in its four-year graduate program. The school estimates

that it has trained 14 percent of all optometrists in the United States.

The school also operates the largest optometry clinic in the city and in 2003 dedicated a new 46,000-square-foot, state-of-the-art eye and vision center on its campus to accommodate demand for eye care.

Southwest Tennessee Community College
737 Union Avenue
(901) 333-4368
www.stcc.cc.tn.us

Southwest Tennessee Community College was formed in 2000 with the merger of two community colleges, and people still refer to the midtown campus as Shelby State and the East Memphis campus as State Tech. Plans are to build a third campus, but in light of state fiscal problems, the plans may not get off the drawing board for some time.

Southwest is the largest two-year college in the state higher-education system. For now it has been energetically seeking places to offer classes and has satellite locations as far away as Fayette County. Currently it has seven off-campus sites in addition to the two main campuses.

A progressive community college, it's known for providing a nurturing, safe environment for students, many of whom are the first in their families to attend college. Local industry often turns to Southwest to develop specialized training for new

---

These days you don't have to go to a campus to work on your college degree. Southwest Tennessee Community College and the University of Memphis are part of the new Regents Online Degree Program, a state program that allows students to earn an entire college degree online. To enroll call University of Memphis at (901) 678-2000 or Southwest Tennessee at (901) 333-4000 or, for more information, check out www.tn.regentsdegrees.org.

---

processes for its employees. Enrollment is about 12,000.

University of Memphis
Central Avenue at Patterson
(901) 678-2000
www.memphis.edu

The University of Memphis is the second-largest university in Tennessee (after University of Tennessee in Knoxville), with enrollment of more than 18,000 students. The school's main campus covers more than a dozen city blocks near East Memphis. Classes are also available at other locations in Shelby County and West Tennessee. The university also is renovating the former navy hospital in suburban Millington as the anchor for a third campus. Most people call it "U of M," but don't be surprised to hear it called by its former name, Memphis State.

U of M is an urban commuter university, with only a fraction of students living on campus in a traditional college arrangement.

The university has nine colleges and schools that award bachelor's, master's, and doctoral degrees in multiple disciplines. It's also home to the Cecil C. Humphreys School of Law and the Fogelman College of Business and Economics.

The University of Memphis Tigers—both the basketball and football teams—help raise the school's visibility around town, and many alumni turn out to watch the teams play. (See the Spectator Sports chapter for more details.)

U of M has a particularly deep involvement within the city of Memphis, and local businesses also play a significant role at the university.

The city's largest employer sponsored the FedEx Technology Institute, a $25 million center for research at U of M, and Memphian Kemmons Wilson, the late founder of Holiday Inns, funded a school of hospitality management that includes a full-service hotel.

An example of community involvement is the Urban Institute, established at the university to coordinate the community projects of five departments. Examples of its work include a project that documents changes in social patterns in the area north of downtown, where a massive housing project is being torn down and replaced with a blend of subsidized and market-rate housing. The Urban Institute is tracking changes as part of a national project that aims to break the circle of welfare and cultural dependency.

University of Tennessee Health Science Center
800 Madison Avenue
(901) 448-5500
www.utmem.edu
Known as UT-Memphis, this school is the state's main medical school and training center, with an international reputation for its emphasis on hands-on training. Enrollment is about 2,000.

The goal of the College of Medicine is to get every student into a clinical environment in their first semester. Rotations also take med students through the pediatrics hospital, the trauma center, suburban and rural hospitals, and doctors' offices. Its philosophy, which is promulgated in every class, is that students must always understand that there's a patient who's affected by their education.

An innovative program to address the shortage of doctors in rural areas recruits young people from the underserved areas. Their communities support their education with the understanding that they will return and hang a shingle in their hometowns.

The big news these days is that UT-Memphis is aggressively developing itself as a research university, working in partnership with the city's two large health-care systems. Medical research in this country is being concentrated into just a few dozen universities, and UT-Memphis is committed to making sure it is one of those chosen few. Among the key components is the Hamilton Eye Institute, a new $64 million ophthalmology center combining academics, research, and clinical care.

The same multifaceted approach is behind the UT Cancer Institute, a $40 million center that broke ground in 2003.

The school also has a strong link to area health care, with more than 800 Memphis physicians teaching its students and with many of its faculty members practicing medicine. (See the Health Care and Wellness chapter for more information.)

The College of Nursing is equally responsive to the communities it serves. The school awards only graduate degrees, and so is designed for mid-career nurses who are already in practice. UT-Memphis also has programs in dentistry, pharmacy, allied health, and other health-related subjects.

Other Higher Education

The Memphis area also is home to a number of schools that offer specific technical or vocational training or a limited number of courses, primarily intended for adults seeking to advance their careers. Others offer degrees and instruction in religious studies or health care. In addition, there are some other community colleges located just outside the city in Mississippi and Arkansas.

Baptist Memorial College of Health Sciences
1003 Monroe Avenue
(901) 227-4330
www.bmhcc.org

Belhaven College
5100 Poplar Avenue
(901) 888-3343
www.belhaven.edu

Concorde Career Institute
5100 Poplar Avenue
(901) 761-9494
www.concordecareercollege.com

Embry-Riddle Aeronautical University
2990 Airways Boulevard
(901) 332-4300
www.embryriddle.edu

Harding University Graduate School of Religion
1000 Cherry Street
(901) 761-1352
www.hugsr.edu

ITT Technical Institute
1255 Lynnfield Road
(901) 762-0556
www.itt-tech.edu

Memphis Theological Seminary
168 East Parkway
(901) 458-8232
www.mtscampus.edu

Methodist Hospital School of Nursing
251 South Claybrook Street
(901) 726-8516
www.methodisthealth.org

Mid-America Baptist Theological Seminary
2216 Germantown Road South
Germantown
(901) 751-8453
www.mabts.edu

Mid-South Community College
2000 Broadway, West Memphis, Arkansas
(870) 733-6722
www.mscc.cc.ar.us

Northwest Mississippi Community College
5197 W.E. Ross Parkway
Southaven, Mississippi
(662) 342-1570
www.nwcc.cc.ms.us

Southeast College of Technology
2731 Nonconnah Parkway
(901) 345-1000
www.educationamerica.com

Union University/Germantown
2745 Hacks Cross Road, Germantown
(901) 759-0029
www.uu.edu/gtown/

University of Mississippi/DeSoto Center
5197 W.E. Ross Parkway
Southaven, Mississippi
(662) 342-4765
www.ole miss.edu

Vatterott College
6152 Macon Road
(901) 761-5730
www.vatterott-college.edu

William R. Moore College of Technology
1200 Poplar Avenue
(901) 726-1977
www.williamrmoore.org

RETIREMENT 🌴

etired Memphians—rather than retired New Yorkers, Michiganers, or other transplants—make up the majority of senior citizens in the city. As a result it's not surprising that the retirement amenities available in Memphis tend to focus on the people who live here already and are simply reaching the age at which they have different needs in terms of housing, recreation, assistance, and care. This situation is a contrast to that in Florida, the Ozarks, and other places in the Sunbelt, which attract retirees from other parts of the country.

Memphis is a place where people have strong ties to their neighborhoods, so one welcome trend is toward retirement communities geared toward local neighborhoods. Thus retirees who decide they need a little more assistance can still be close to familiar amenities and the neighbors they care about by choosing one of these communities. Many offer meals, transportation, activities, assisted-living services, and other amenities. That approach is exemplified by a $60 million, 35-acre suburban retirement community that began construction in late 2003 with a 2005 completion date. The Village at Germantown (901-737-4242) includes about 200 independent-living units as well as a skilled-nursing facility and some assisted-living units. Real estate developers, cognizant that the oldest of the baby boomers is approaching age 60, also see a growing market for condominiums and other smaller housing units, as retirees look to downsize but stay in their neighborhoods.

This concept differs from that in senior housing seen in the late 1980s, when a construction boom of retirement communities took place in Memphis and in many major cities in anticipation of a surge in demand that never materialized. These were centers with maintenance-free living, social activities, and personal assistance available on an a la carte basis. Many of them fell flat when it turned out retirees didn't flock to these types of residences immediately upon retirement.

Since then the retirement industry has retrenched. The great consolidator of retirement living in the region has turned out to be Wesley Senior Ministries, an affiliate of the United Methodist Church, which stepped in to take over distressed retirement centers. Presently Wesley serves 2,000-plus residents in more than 20 facilities, most of them senior-housing communities across three states. In addition, several large operators of assisted-living facilities have entered the Memphis market, including Atria.

Of course, retirees need more than just a place to live. Resources are plentiful in this area, and it's easy to find meals, recreation centers, volunteer opportunities, and a variety of activities. Local government agencies are important players, as are churches, as they often have programs, activities, and outreach for that segment of the population.

City life isn't for everybody, though, and those who prefer small-town life will find dozens of options within a short drive of Memphis. Many retirees and urban professionals are buying property in these small towns, the most celebrated of which is Oxford, Mississippi. *Money* magazine in 2001 named this college town as the best place to retire in the South, and it continues to hold many charms for retirees, particularly Ole Miss alumni, since it's home to the University of Mississippi. Oxford has a picturesque town square and a population of 11,800 (see the Day Trips chapter for more information).

SENIOR SERVICES

These local agencies serve as clearing-houses, with information on all types of services available to senior citizens. In some cases they operate their own facilities and programs.

Aging Commission of the Mid-South
2670 Union Avenue Extended
(901) 324-6333, (901) 525-CARE
www.agingcommission.org

The mission of the aging commission is to serve as the focal point for aging services and as a liaison between senior citizens and the agencies and programs that serve them. It coordinates and funds community services that promote independence and choice for retirees age 60 and older.

In partnership with other groups, the commission funds programs that provide housekeeping assistance, legal advice, and Alzheimer's day-care services as well as a retired senior volunteer program.

The county mayor's office on aging was recently merged with the Aging Commission, so this office now helps senior citizens with problems such as dealing with Medicare/Medicaid and social security, taking care of dental needs, and counseling. It continues to publish the *Senior Citizens Handbook*. Updated twice yearly, this valuable tool has a wealth of information on everything from a complete listing of available services to the warning signs of serious illnesses and advice on protecting one's self from fraud. There's also an information and assistance hotline (901-234-3399).

---

i *A great way to stay informed about what's going on in Memphis is the* Best Times, *a monthly newspaper for "mature Mid-Southerners." It's free on newsstands at supermarkets and other locations around town or available by subscription for $15 a year. For more information, call (901) 458-2911 or direct correspondence to Best Times, 3100 Walnut Grove Road, Memphis, TN 38111.*

Memphis Inter-Faith Association (MIFA)
910 Vance Avenue
(901) 527-0208, (901) 521-0536 for MIFA Meals
www.mifa.org

MIFA is a major provider of meals to seniors, serving 3,000 hot lunches every day both at central locations and through its home-delivered meals program. Through its Long-Term Care Ombudsman advocacy program, MIFA works to improve the quality of life and care in nursing homes and other long-term care facilities. Through other programs active, low-income seniors work as companions to frail seniors, and volunteers provide handyman services. MIFA also operates two senior centers.

Senior Services
4700 Poplar Avenue
(901) 766-0600, (800) 487-5207
www.memphisseniors.com

Although it's reaching out to other age groups these days as well, Senior Services can put you in touch with providers of an array of services, including stay-at-home assisted living, career assistance, and transportation. The organization also operates two senior activities centers, a nursing home, and a free information and referral service, available to the public and to professionals. A new service is the ScamBusters Hotline (901-323-7226), operated in cooperation with the district attorney's office and First Tennessee Bank. It offers advice on how to protect one's self from scams as well as what to do if you feel you've been the victim of a scam.

VOLUNTEER OPPORTUNITIES

Memphis Inter-Faith Association (MIFA)
910 Vance Avenue
(901) 529-4514
www.mifa.org

MIFA has an ongoing need for volunteers to staff its meals operation, Long-Term Care Ombudsman advocacy, and other programs.

RSVP
910 Vance Avenue
(901) 527-0208, ext. 229
RSVP (Retiree & Senior Volunteer Program) matches interested seniors with community needs. Under this local branch of the Corporation for National and Community Service program, more than 700 retired Memphians age 55 and older volunteer their time to help out in the community.

Volunteer Memphis
22 North Front Street
(901) 523-2425
www.volunteermemphis.org
This group recruits thousands of volunteers each year and refers them to area nonprofit organizations in Memphis and Shelby County. The volunteer assignments range from helping children as part of the Volunteers in Schools program to helping in the Memphis Brooks Museum of Art gift shop. Although Volunteer Memphis isn't specifically a retiree program, many of its participants are senior citizens.

SENIOR CENTERS

These centers, located in neighborhoods throughout the city, provide activities, a sense of community, and hot lunches to senior citizens. All of them are open Monday through Friday, except for holidays. The Frayser-Raleigh, Lewis, Orange Mound, and McWherter centers are operated by the City of Memphis Division of Park Services (901-454-5200 or www.cityof memphis.org for more information). Senior Services (901-766-0600, www.memphis seniors.com) runs the South Memphis and Hollywood centers, and MIFA (901-527-0208, www.mifa.org) operates the East and Metro Bickford centers.

East Senior Center
4221 Macon Road
(901) 763-1181

Frayser-Raleigh Senior Center
3985 Egypt Central Road
(901) 383-9101

Hollywood Senior Center
1560 North Hollywood Street
(901) 323-8634

Lewis Senior Center
1188 North Parkway
(901) 272-7408

McWherter Senior Center
1355 Estate Drive
(901) 761-2462

Metro Bickford Senior Center
232 Bickford Avenue
(901) 578-9546

Orange Mound Senior Center
2569 Douglass Avenue
(901) 323-3662

South Memphis Senior Center
1620 Marjorie Street
(901) 774-2000

RETIREMENT COMMUNITIES

When it comes to choosing a retirement home, you'll find numerous options in Memphis. There are more than 100 retirement centers and other residences for seniors in the city, ranging from independent-living residences to nursing homes.

Where to live during the golden years is a very personal decision, and one that requires careful research and thought. People have different ideas of what they're looking for in terms of amenities, food, and social activity. For example, a very sociable environment with loads of organized activities might be heaven to one retiree and hell to another. The chances of finding a fit are good, because the services of each center can be closely tailored to the individual needs of the resident. "Continual care" is a buzzword you'll hear a lot, and it means that when a resident needs more care or services, they're available.

Once you narrow down your choices to a few favorite candidates, go and spend time at each facility. Try the food, stroll the grounds, talk to the residents, and ask lots of questions. This way, you can be confident about your decision.

Remember that there are four categories of housing for senior citizens: senior housing (often called independent living), assisted living, homes for the aged, and nursing homes. In Tennessee assisted-living facilities, homes for the aged, and nursing homes are all licensed by the state Department of Health.

Senior housing is designed for independent living, sometimes with personal services. As the term can mean just about anything—including simply an apartment complex that doesn't allow families with children—it's always a good idea to ask what amenities are available. Assisted living is for those who are able to maintain their independence, thanks to help with such things as meals, housekeeping, monitoring of medicines, bathing, and dressing. Homes for the aged are a variation on assisted living, small with as few as four licensed beds. Nursing homes are for residents who need 24-hour licensed nursing supervision and assistance with most activities of daily living.

We list some of the city's best facilities for independent living and assisted living, but you may want to obtain a more complete listing of what's available, especially since new facilities are always in the works. Contact Aging Commission of the Mid-South's information and assistance hotline at (901) 324-3399 or try the *Best Times* at (901) 458-2911 for the annual listing of retirement living communities that appears in its November issue.

Belmont Village
6605 Quail Hollow Road
(901) 624-8820
www.belmontvillage.com
A village atmosphere, complete with neighborhoods and town hall, restaurant-style dining, and plentiful activities, has made this 120-unit assisted-living facility popular among seniors. Belmont has one-bedroom and studio units with kitchenettes if you want to cook, three meals served daily in its bistro if you don't. Activities include lots of outings to plays, art exhibits, restaurants, and attractions; services include transportation, help with daily-living chores such as dressing and bathing, and 24-hour-a-day emergency response. Other amenities include wellness and learning centers, exercise classes, library, and beauty salon. Belmont also has an Alzheimer's facility.

Carriage Court
1645 West Massey Road
(901) 763-3232
www.carriagecourt.com
Carriage Court is an East Memphis facility known for its lively staff and full schedule of activities. It had operated as Brighton Gardens, part of the Marriott Corp. chain, until being sold to Carriage Court in late 2003. The 115-unit assisted-living community offers a choice of one-bedroom or studio apartments and four levels of care. Residents can get assistance with the everyday tasks of living and eat three meals a day, ordering from the menu in the restaurant-style dining room. Activities and entertainment range from bridge and bingo to theme parties and outings to museums. Some of the units are in a special facility devoted to caring for residents with Alzheimer's or other related memory disorders.

Colonial Estates
2600 Colonial Tower Drive
(901) 382-8852
This suburban high-rise retirement community, located in Cordova at the Colonial

Country Club golf course, has a swimming pool, tennis courts, an activities program, a library, and a beauty shop. The 84 one-bedroom and two-bedroom apartments have balconies with views and satellite TV, and laundry and housekeeping services are available. Home health services and physician visits also are available.

Kirby Pines
3535 Kirby Road
(901) 365-3665
Its complete roster of services, good cooking, and well-planned activities program make Kirby Pines a standout for independent living. The retirement community, which offers continuing care, has 471 units, ranging from studio apartments to three-bedroom apartments or garden homes. Three meals a day and an array of services are available; special amenities include walking trails and a greenhouse. Kirby Pines requires a significant initial entrance fee, which starts at $53,800, but residents get a money-back guarantee and decorating allowance.

The Parkview Retirement Community
1914 Poplar Avenue
(901) 725-4606
www.merrillgardens.com
Situated on the western edge of Overton Park, the Parkview was built originally as a hotel in the 1920s and still has the lobby frescoes and the high ceilings of the era. This newly renovated independent-living facility, a favorite among retired midtowners, has about 130 apartments, ranging in size from efficiencies to three-bedroom units. There's an "anytime" dining policy, so residents can have their three meals a day as they wish, ordering from the menu. Daily activities are available, and services include transportation, weekly housekeeping, 24-hour nursing support, and an emergency response system. The Parkview offers only limited assisted-living services, but residents are free to hire personal sitters as needed. The property is gated, with 24-hour security.

Plough Towers
6580 Poplar Avenue
(901) 767-1910
There's a definite international flair at Plough Towers, an independent-living facility where many residents are Russian-speaking. The 11-story, high-rise facility has 150 one-bedroom and two-bedroom apartments and serves a noon meal five days a week. On the premises you'll find a computer center, library, convenience store, physical therapy center, and beauty shop. A full calendar of activities is available. There's also a full-time social worker on staff, and a doctor, podiatrist, and psychologist visit each week. Limited transportation services also are available, and because it's a government rent-assisted building, the monthly fee is determined by income. Plough Towers is overseen by the Memphis Jewish Housing Development Corp.

Town Village Audubon Park
950 Cherry Road
(901) 537-0002
www.townvillage.com
This independent-living village, built in 2002, prides itself on award-winning cuisine and its full calendar of activities, guest speakers, and cultural programs. Located in East Memphis near Harding University and the Dixon Gallery and Gardens, this gated community has 176 units ranging in size from studios to two-bedroom apartments, each with its own full-size washer and dryer. Town Village serves two meals a day and offers amenities including an indoor pool and spa, exercise center, convenience store, beauty/barber salon, and resident gardening areas.

Trezevant Manor Lifecare Retirement Community
177 North Highland Street
(901) 325-4000
www.trezevantmanor.com
Trezevant Manor, which began as independent-living apartments in the mid-1970s, today has about 160 independent-living apartments as well as 12 cottages,

The Memphis Area Transit Authority offers something for every senior, from discounts on bus fare (non-rush hours only) and trolley fare to special transportation services through its MATAplus program if you're disabled. To be certified for MATAplus, call (901) 722-7140, or for general information on the program, call (901) 722-7171. For other questions, call the MATA Hotline at (901) 274-6282 or visit www.mata transit.com.

25 assisted-living units, and a 104-bed nursing home. The residents may live in a cottage or apartment at first, then move to one of the other units if they require more care. This gated community, known for its elegant, traditional decor and excellent service, offers restaurant-style dining, transportation, housekeeping services, and daily activities that include parties, exercise classes, and on-the-premises concerts as well as excursions to plays or out to dinner. Amenities include a library, fitness center, chapel, grocery store, beauty shop, and bank. The apartments range from studios to three-bedroom units, and the cottages have either three or four bedrooms.

Wesley Highland Towers
400 South Highland Street
(901) 325-7810
www.wesleyhousing.com
Formerly University of Memphis women's dormitories, the two 10-story towers presently operate as an independent-living facility with 396 efficiencies and one-bedroom apartments. Wesley Highland Towers offers three meals a day in its cafeteria, a wellness program, transportation services, a beauty shop, and a sundry store. There are some activities and social functions, too. Rental assistance is available for qualified residents through HUD. Residents of the tower who need assisted-living or nursing-home care are given priority at Wesley's other facilities, where those services are available. Wesley is convenient to University of Memphis, a plus for residents interested in taking classes on campus.

MEDIA 📺

emphis media are much like those of other major urban centers, given their lineup of publications and stations. These days Memphis is a one daily-newspaper town, with the *Commercial Appeal* publishing seven days a week. Filling the role that otherwise would be played by a second major daily are two weekly newspapers, the *Memphis Flyer* and *Memphis Business Journal*. In addition, a number of suburban and small-town newspapers in the area focus on local politics, high-school sports, and other news of interest to their respective readerships.

The city's most visible magazine is *Memphis* magazine, which has been published since 1976. This glossy monthly has an urbane and sometimes offbeat take on the city and its cultural scene, personalities, and restaurants. You'll also find numerous free publications around town (look for racks in the foyers of local supermarkets or libraries), including *Downtowner* magazine (a monthly with news and features about downtown Memphis) as well as two monthlies (*RSVP* and *901*) with photo-packed coverage of society events. In recent years, a number of new publications have surfaced, including two glossy shelter magazines, *At Home in Memphis* and *MidSouthLiving*.

Memphis has the country's ninth-largest African-American population, which is served by *Tri-State Defender*, a weekly newspaper that focuses on civil rights and other issues of interest to that audience. The city's growing Hispanic population is served by two free Spanish-language weeklies, *La Prensa Latina* and *El Horizonte*.

The current editions of most local newspapers are available on newsstands as well as from individual vending machines. In addition, many have Web sites where visitors can access some or all of the newspapers' content as well as breaking news or other extra features.

Radio is the Memphis medium with the most colorful history, given its ties throughout the years to the music produced here. For example, WDIA was the first station in the United States to have an all-black format, with Nat D. Williams as its first black DJ. The station also helped to launch the careers of B. B. King, Rufus Thomas, and others. (See the Memphis Music chapter for more information.) Memphis DJs also were the first to play Elvis Presley's music, back when he was an unknown, and some, including Rick Dees, have become nationally known radio personalities. Currently the airwaves here offer a broad range of stations, and in 2003 Memphis ranked 48th among U.S. radio markets, according to Arbitron.

Memphis has seven television stations, including affiliates of the major networks and a religious broadcast station. The top stations compete for viewers by touting their local news coverage and the quality of their weather-tracking equipment (a good thing, given the storms and the occasional tornadoes that come through this area). Memphis had the 43rd-largest TV market, with 662,300 TV homes as of November 2003, according to Nielsen Media Research.

As with media in other markets, many Memphis television stations also make their news coverage and other offerings available on the Internet, so you can watch the news at your own convenience.

Many Memphians opt for cable television or direct satellite dish for a bigger selection of channels. Time Warner Communications has consolidated most of the local cable TV systems, and now serves much of west Tennessee, north Mississippi, and east Arkansas. The lone cable holdout is Millington CATV, which serves customers in and around Millington. DirecTV, Dish Network, and other companies are making inroads to this market, as is evidenced by the discreet dish receivers found on many Memphis rooftops.

PRINT PUBLICATIONS

Dailies

The *Commercial Appeal*
495 Union Avenue
(901) 529–2211
www.commercialappeal.com

The *Commercial Appeal,* or the *CA* as locals call it, is a morning daily newspaper with a circulation as high as 235,000 for its Sunday edition. Editorially, it has a definite liberal slant, and from a business standpoint, it's believed to be one of the most profitable papers in the E. W. Scripps Co. chain. The *Commercial Appeal* serves the Memphis metro area as well as surrounding counties in Tennessee, Mississippi, and Arkansas.

The paper dates from 1841, when Memphis was a rowdy 20-year-old river town, and it has been the city's only daily newspaper since 1979, when the evening paper, the *Memphis Press-Scimitar,* ceased publication. If you're used to a meaty, in-depth urban newspaper, you may find this one a bit thin. The quality is consistent with that of most Scripps-Howard newspapers. One high point was in 1994, when the *CA* won a Pulitzer Prize for editorial cartoons by Michael Raminez. Like most daily papers the newspaper carries a mix of local, national, and world news, as well as feature sections. The *CA* joined the trend among U.S. newspapers toward community journalism when Chris Peck, an advocate of that approach, took charge as editor in 2003. As a result, there has been more coverage of things such as the arrival of panda bears to the Memphis Zoo and community outrage over the death of a young child in a day-care van. Its new feature, Appeal, which focuses on individual neighborhoods, is a twice-weekly special section of the newspaper that replaces the weekly Neighbors section. While the changes have been well received, there have also been critics who say they would gladly swap the feel-good stuff for better news coverage. Each Friday's edition of the *CA* includes the Memphis Playbook, a pull-out section with details about entertainment and events scheduled for the weekend as well as listings of what's available at area museums, galleries, theaters, casinos, and other venues. The *CA* also provides thorough coverage of the Memphis music scene.

Much of the newspaper's content, as well as breaking news, is available on its Web site. You can also search the newspaper's archives, and although you can read the headline and first paragraphs for free, there's a charge for viewing or downloading the entire article.

The newsstand price for the daily edition (Monday through Saturday) is 50 cents, and $2.00 for the Sunday edition. A one-year subscription is $224.25 for both the Sunday and daily paper ($17.25 per four-week billing period), and $140.40 for Monday through Friday only.

The *Daily News*
193 Jefferson Avenue
(901) 523–1561
www.memphisdailynews.com

The *Daily News* publishes Monday through Friday with a circulation of about 2,500, with most readers being attorneys, real-estate agents, and others who track lawsuits, public notices, and property transfers. Although its strength is this information, which it culls from local government sources, it also runs business news stories. From its Web site you can look up all kinds of information without stepping into a courthouse or dealing with bureaucracy. The *Daily News* is 50 cents a copy on the newsstands and $80 for a one-year subscription.

DeSoto Times Today
8625 Highway 51
Southaven, Mississippi
(662) 393-6397
www.desototimes.com

DeSoto Times Today is the daily paper, published Tuesday through Saturday, for fast-growing DeSoto County, Mississippi. Its circulation is about 8,500 (around 32,000 for the weekend edition, which is also delivered to nonsubscribers). Under the guidance of editor Tom Pittman, the paper has taken an energetic approach to covering local government, politics, economic development, and lifestyle issues. And of course, there's local high-school sports. The cost is 50 cents on the newsstand and $108 for a year's subscription.

The *Evening Times*
111 East Bond
West Memphis, Arkansas
(870) 735-1010
www.theeveningtimes.com

The *Evening Times* is an afternoon newspaper that publishes Monday through Friday. It covers Crittenden County and eastern Arkansas, with a circulation of around 9,000. The paper's niche is the collection of small towns in Crittenden County, such as West Memphis, Marion, Crawfordsville, and Earle. The paper also extends its coverage to Hughes, in neighboring St. Francis County. The newspaper is 50 cents a copy on the newsstand and $75 for a year's subscription.

Weeklies

Bartlett Express
6187 Stage Road, Bartlett
(901) 388-1500
www.bartlettexpress.com

The *Bartlett Express* covers news and local sports in the bedroom suburb of Bartlett, located northeast of Memphis. The weekly paper, which comes out every Thursday, has a circulation of about 6,500. Cost is 50 cents a copy on the newsstand and $22 for a year's subscription.

Collierville Herald
148 North Main Street, Collierville
(901) 853-2241

The *Herald*, one of Tennessee's oldest newspapers, is distributed weekly with a circulation of about 7,200. Because the suburb of Collierville has a second weekly newspaper, local wags say it enjoys a more competitive newspaper scene than Memphis proper. The *Herald* also carries local sports and community news. Cost is 50 cents an issue, $18 for a year's subscription to a Collierville address, and $22 a year to an address outside the area.

Cordova Beacon
6187 Stage Road, Bartlett
(901) 388-1500

This suburban weekly, with a circulation of 3,000, covers news of interest to residents of the bedroom community of Cordova. The newspaper is 50 cents a copy on the newsstand and $22 for a year's subscription.

Covington Leader
2001 Highway 51 South, Covington
(901) 476-7116
www.covingtonleader.com

The *Covington Leader* is a weekly newspaper with a circulation of about 8,000. Its focus is local news, sports, and features in the city of Covington and surrounding Tipton County, north of Memphis. The cost is 75 cents on the newsstand and $23 for a year's subscription to an address within the county.

DeSoto County Tribune
8885 Goodman Road
Olive Branch, Mississippi
(662) 895-6220
www.dctribune.com

The *Tribune* is a weekly paper with a circulation of about 10,000 and covers local news, government, and sports for DeSoto County. Its greatest strength is in covering the eastern part of the county, especially in the boomtown of Olive Branch. The cost is 50 cents a copy on the newsstand and $18 for a year's subscription.

Fayette County Review
14750 Highway 64, Somerville
(901) 465–4042
fayettecountyreview.com

A weekly newspaper with a circulation of about 3,200, the *Fayette County Review* could be the next newspaper to suddenly expand. It covers the county just east of Memphis, which is seeing some of the most aggressive home building in the region. As the county becomes a major bedroom community for the metro area, the paper's coverage of local government, economic development, and sports will likely expand. The newspaper costs 35 cents a copy on the newsstand, $10 for a year's subscription to a local address, and $18 for a year's subscription to an out-of-town address.

Germantown News
7545 North Street, Germantown
(901) 754–0337
www.germantownnews.com

The *Germantown News* is a weekly paper published Thursdays with a circulation of about 6,700. The paper, published by Crittenden Publishing Co. in West Memphis, concentrates on news and features in the city of Germantown. The cost is 50 cents a copy on the newsstand and $25 for a year's subscription.

The *Independent*
151 North Main Street, Collierville
(901) 853–7060

The *Independent* is Collierville's other weekly paper and has a circulation of about 12,000, mostly distributed free. It competes with the *Collierville Herald* on local news. The newspaper, although free to the town's homeowners, is 50 cents a copy or $15 for a year's subscription.

Memphis Business Journal
80 Monroe Avenue
(901) 523–1000
memphis.bizjournals.com

Memphis Business Journal is a weekly newspaper with paid circulation of about 9,500 and readership of about 60,000, published every Friday. A must-read for the business community, this well-respected weekly is often first with many important stories. The paper's primary focus is covering local business: real estate, economic development, health care, education, tourism, and other segments of the economy.

MBJ was started in 1970 by journalists Deborah and Barney Dubois plus a group of local executives, and it immediately established its reputation as an aggressive newspaper that breaks a surprising number of local news stories. At present *MBJ* is one of about 40 city business newspapers owned and operated by American City Business Journals, headquartered in Charlotte, North Carolina.

In addition to its news coverage, *MBJ* also features weekly special sections that zero in on a particular industry plus exhaustive listings of tax liens, judgments, commercial property transfers, and other news of record. *MBJ*'s annual *Book of Lists*, published the last week of the year, is a valuable resource, and its Web site provides daily breaking news in addition to articles from the print edition of the newspaper. The cost is $1.75 a copy on the newsstand and $75.00 for a year's subscription.

The *Memphis Flyer*
460 Tennessee Street
(901) 521–9000
www.memphisflyer.com

Every week Memphians flock to nearby news racks or to one of the distinctive green dispensers around town for the latest issue of the *Memphis Flyer*. The attraction: both lively coverage of what's happening around town as well as stories that often are the most talked-about in town.

The *Flyer* is a weekly free paper that tries to fill a number of niches, from liberal alternative news source to exhaustive listings of restaurants, nightlife, and live music. It is part of Contemporary Media, Inc., which also publishes *Memphis* magazine.

The *Flyer* does some investigative reporting but specializes more in long,

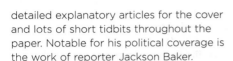

detailed explanatory articles for the cover and lots of short tidbits throughout the paper. Notable for his political coverage is the work of reporter Jackson Baker.

Because its advertising rates are favorable to small retailers, many people find the assortment of ads for small local business at least as valuable as the writing itself. The *Flyer* also does a brisk business in classified and personal ads; though most of the ads are middle of the road, some of them are the most risqué in Memphis.

Depending on your neighborhood the new issue is available on Wednesday or Thursday. The *Flyer* has a circulation of about 59,000 and readership of about 225,000.

The *Millington Star*
5107 Easley Street, Millington
(901) 872-2286
www.millingtonstar.com
The *Millington Star,* with a weekly circulation of about 6,000, focuses its coverage on this northern suburb and, to a lesser degree, on the smaller towns of Munford and Atoka. The paper has adapted to the changing life of Millington; a decade or so ago it was a U.S. Navy–base town, but it has now become a middle-class suburb, since the base has been replaced with a Bureau of Naval Personnel office and commuting Memphians have discovered the area. *Millington Star* reflects this transition and has become more of a community and lifestyle paper. The cost is 50 cents a copy on the newsstand, $22 for a year's subscription to a local address, and $28 for a year's subscription to an out-of-town address.

North Shelby Times
3518 North Watkins Road
(901) 358-8034
www.northshelbytimes.com
The *North Shelby Times* is a weekly paper that covers news and sports in the northern third of Shelby County. Ten thousand copies are circulated each week, by delivery and racks. It's free, both for single copies and for a subscription.

One of the greatest resources around is the Memphis Business Journal's *Book of Lists. Published in December, it lists the top players among large employers, banks, private companies, shopping centers, and some 70 other categories. To order a copy, call (901) 523-1000 or check out memphis.bizjournals.com. The cost is $35 for the book, although it's free with a subscription.*

Shelby Sun Times
7508 Capital Street, Germantown
(901) 755-7386
The *Shelby Sun Times* covers local news and events for a broad swath of East Shelby County but mostly covers Cordova and Germantown. It distributes 35,000 copies a week, mostly thrown into residential driveways. The newspaper is free if you pick it up, but you can subscribe for $20 a year.

Tri-State Defender
124 Patterson Avenue
(901) 523-1818
The *Tri-State Defender,* a weekly newspaper with a circulation of about 36,500, was formerly a part of the crusading Sengstacke newspaper chain, based in Chicago.

The *Defender* was known as a fearless force at the peak of the black civil rights era and served, along with black churches in Memphis, as one of the rallying points for the civil rights struggle. Those days are mostly in the past, but the *Defender* still takes a powerful, civil rights–oriented voice in other issues, from local schools to welfare reform. The paper in recent years has expanded its offerings of society and lifestyle news and information as it seeks to become both an urban community paper while maintaining its political edge.

The newspaper is 75 cents a copy on the newsstand or $28 for a year's subscription.

Monthlies

Best Times
3100 Walnut Grove Road
(901) 458-2911
This monthly newspaper for mature Mid-Southerners has loads of information about things to do, volunteer opportunities, and issues of interest to seniors. Each year its November issue includes a comprehensive listing of retirement-living options, a valuable resource for anyone shopping around for that type of living arrangement. Single copies are free, and a one-year subscription is $15.

Memphis Parent
460 Tennessee Street
(901) 521-9000
www.memphisparent.com
This monthly newspaper calls itself the newsmagazine for today's active family. Published for the parents of children of school age and younger, *Memphis Parent* contains lots of practical information, with articles about how to protect kids from lead paint or how to encourage a love of reading, for example. Each issue includes an events calendar with a comprehensive listing of activities and events going on for children and families.

Magazines

At Home In Memphis
6263 Poplar Avenue
(901) 684-4155
www.athome-memphis.com
This glossy new monthly magazine is more style than substance, featuring lavish spreads on beautiful homes in the area. The articles and advertising provide a look at not only homes but also what's new in the city's boutiques, spas, and galleries. Circulation is about 25,000, a portion of which is paid circulation. The cost is $3.50 a copy or $19.50 for a one-year subscription.

Life Design
3181 Poplar Avenue
(901) 327-0342
www.lifedesignmagazine.com
This glossy magazine features weddings and more, with spreads of the latest wedding-gown fashions, wedding announcements, and articles that range from bridal bouquets to redesigning your kitchen. Check it out if you are planning a wedding, since it has lots of practical information about selecting reception halls, booking bands, and so forth. Single copies and subscriptions are free.

Memphis
460 Tennessee Street
(901) 521-9000
www.memphismagazine.com
This glossy monthly was started in the mid-1970s with an eye toward celebrating the popular culture, the important issues, and the culinary landscape of Memphis. It continues this mission, providing a witty and informed take on what's happening around the city. *Memphis* magazine also has probably the most complete listing of restaurants in the city, as well as reviews of both new eateries and perennial favorites. Newcomers to Memphis should check out the magazine's *City Guide,* published in August. Its *Restaurant Guide,* published in January, has a listing of the restaurants chosen as favorites by the magazine's annual readers' poll, as well as features about what's hot on the culinary scene. Both are for sale on the newsstands all year. The magazine, published by Contemporary Media, Inc., is a sister publication to the *Memphis Flyer.*

The company also publishes *Bartlett, Collierville, Germantown,* and *Midtown* magazines at least once a year. *Memphis* magazine is $3.50 on the newsstand and $15.00 for a one-year subscription.

Memphis Downtowner
408 South Front Street
(901) 525-7118
www.memphisdowntowner.com

Since 1991 this neighborhood magazine has been both chronicler and cheerleader as downtown Memphis has developed. It has features and news about goings-on, mainly downtown but more broadly, too. Free on news racks around the downtown area or $15 for a one-year subscription.

MidSouthLiving
6915 Crumpler Boulevard
Olive Branch, Mississippi
(662) 890-3359
www.midsouthliving.com

Like *At Home In Memphis,* this is a lavish color magazine featuring gorgeous homes. *MidSouthLiving,* though, comes out six times a year and includes coverage of the entire Mid-South area, and its advertising and articles are more narrowly focused on homes, and products and services for homes. The magazine also sponsors a yearly Home & Garden show. Circulation is about 35,000. The magazine is $2.95 a copy or $15.00 for a year's subscription.

Specialized Publications

Memphis has a wide array of specialized publications, often with a very narrow focus. The *Contract Bridge Bulletin* is a monthly magazine for bridge players, published by the American Contract Bridge League, with a circulation of more than 140,000.

Ducks Unlimited, a wetlands conservation group, publishes its bimonthly magazine, *Ducks Unlimited,* in Memphis, with a circulation upwards of 660,000. Other publications include two quarterly magazines, *Puddler* with 65,000 copies, and *DULeader* with a circulation of more than 90,000.

Auto Trader and sister publications such as *Big Truck Trader* have a combined circulation of more than 40,000, while *National Hardwood Magazine* and *Cotton Farming Magazine* reflect the city's prominence in those industries.

Spanish-Language Publications

El Horizonte
P.O. Box 751482
(901) 507-9106

This free weekly newspaper, which covers both the Memphis and Jackson, Mississippi, markets, consists mainly of articles about current events and sports in the Caribbean, Mexico, and other areas of Latin America. It also features advertising and classified advertising targeted at the Hispanic market.

La Prensa Latina
995 South Yates Road
(901) 751-2100
www.laprensalatina.com

The city's other free Hispanic weekly considers itself bilingual, publishing some articles in both Spanish and English. *La Prensa Latina* features local, national, and Latin American news. It, too, runs ad for goods and services targeted at the city's Hispanic population. The publisher is Memphis-based Mendelson & Associates. Circulation is 38,000.

TELEVISION

In the Memphis market you'll find the major networks represented through local affiliates, which also deliver local news, weather, and some local programming.

The stations' news departments compete on the big local stories, often hyping them on the air to attract viewers. All the major network affiliates feature local newscasts between 5:00 and 6:30 P.M. and again at 9:00 or 10:00 P.M. Most of them also do a local early morning show, which leads into network morning shows. Although the stations brag a lot about their weather-forecasting and tracking equipment, the truth is that they all have pretty similar resources.

WMC-TV 5, with Action News 5, is generally considered the news leader in this market, with the most professional anchors and reporters. The station's top anchors in news, sports, and weather have held their positions for more than 25 years, earning them a loyal viewership over the years and building a reputation for dependability for the station.

WREG-TV 3, which calls itself News Channel 3 On Your Side, also has a solid reputation, positioning itself as an advocate for the people of Memphis and making weather coverage its top priority. Viewers enjoy the station's "Does It Work?" feature, in which a reporter tries out a gadget and reports on the experience. This station is a bit more promotional than its colleagues, and more likely to hold contests in which viewers can win money or prizes. It's the CBS affiliate in town.

Both these stations, in terms of news and some programming, attract viewers in the 50-plus age group, although they angle for younger viewers, too.

In contrast Fox 13 and ABC 24 WPTY attract a younger audience. ABC 24 and UPN 30, which share a newsroom, anchors, and reporters, revamped their news operation in 2003. Not only is this the youngest news operation in terms of longevity (started in 1996), it also has the city's most youthful anchors and reporters, a reflection of its audience demographics.

The more experienced Fox 13 news team was affiliated with ABC until the mid-1990s, when both stations underwent major changes.

UPN 30 WLMT, the number-one rated UPN station in the country, gears its coverage toward the region's African-American viewers. You'll find more news stories about the city's African-American community and leaders and a programming lineup with shows featuring African Americans. It's also where you can watch University of Memphis basketball, a great favorite among Memphis viewers.

WKNO-TV Channel 10 is the PBS affiliate, which features not only PBS standards such as *Frontline* and *Nova,* but also has some strong local programming. *It Matters* is a series that offers an in-depth look at

topics of local interest, and *Beyond the Parkways* is a popular and oft-aired documentary on the history of Memphis streets. WKNO broadcasts the annual W. C. Handy Awards, the Memphis ceremony recognizing excellence in the blues. More than 70 percent of the station's operating budget comes from local supporters and viewers.

WPXX-TV Channel 50 is part of the PAX-TV network, committed to what it calls "family-friendly television."

Television Stations

WHBQ-TV Channel 13 (Fox)
www.fox13whbq.com

WKNO-TV Channel 10 (PBS)
www.wkno.org

WLMT-TV Channel 30 (UPN)
www.upn30memphis.com

WMC-TV Channel 5 (NBC)
www.wmctv.com

WPTY-TV Channel 24 (ABC)
www.abc24.com

WPXX-TV Channel 50 (Pax)
www.paxtv.com

WREG-TV Channel 3 (CBS)
www.wreg.com

RADIO

A quick spin of your Memphis radio dial will turn up every kind of station, from National Public Radio to hip-hop, talk radio to Christian to album-oriented rock. This is the 48th-largest radio market in the United States, and the 13th-largest black radio market, according to the industry's 2003 Arbitron rankings. In addition to entertaining and informing listeners, Memphis radio has produced some well-known and influential disc jockeys. The most recent is Isaac Hayes, the legendary Memphis musician who has his own syndicated radio show featuring "hot-buttered love songs." Memphis radio launched the careers of Elvis crony George Klein and radio personality Rick Dees, who created the hit "Disco Duck" while a Memphis DJ in the mid-1970s. In the 1950s WHBQ disc jockey Dewey Philips was instrumental in getting Elvis and other musicians onto the airwaves. In 1948 WDIA was the first radio station in the country to adopt an all-black format, and it continues to be one of the top urban adult-contemporary stations in Memphis. Blues Caravan, a popular public-radio program, is produced here and often taped on Beale Street.

In recent years Memphis radio has seen a lot of consolidation among radio and television stations, as have other U.S. media markets. As a result many of the top stations are owned by one of four large companies. Of the public companies Clear Channel Communications owns six Memphis radio stations plus two TV stations, whereas Infinity and Entercom own three stations apiece. A local private company, Flinn Broadcasting, owns six stations.

Arbitron ratings reflect the strength of the African-American radio audience here: A contemporary gospel station, WHAL-FM, was the number-one-ranked radio station, while three of the top five stations were urban contemporary, according to late 2003 figures.

Note: Don't be surprised if you tune into a station listed as country and hear adult-contemporary Top 40 instead. As in other markets new radio stations are constantly appearing as old ones fade away, and stations often change formats, rushing to cash in on the latest hottest trend.

RADIO STATIONS

ADULT CONTEMPORARY

WJCE-AM 680
WMC-FM 99.7
WQOX-FM 88.5
WRVR-FM 104.5
WVIM-FM 95.3

Beloved among Memphis radio listeners is Weevil (aka WEVL-FM). Its disc jockeys are volunteers who bring their own records and CDs to the studio for their one-hour shows. The programming includes probably the city's best blues listening, Cap'n Pete's Blues Cruise, and other shows ranging from gospel to World Music Dance Party. Tune in to 89.9 or visit www.wevl.org for a schedule and other information.

CHRISTIAN AND GOSPEL

KWAM-AM 990
WAVN-AM 1240
WBBP-AM 1480
WCRV-AM 640
WHAL-FM 95.7
WLOK-AM 1340
WOOM-AM 1380

CLASSICAL

WKNA-FM 88.9
WKNO-FM 91.1 (NPR)

COUNTRY

WGKX-FM 105.9
WYYL-FM 96.1

JAZZ

WJZN-FM 98.9
WUMR-FM 91.7

NEWS/TALK

WMC-AM 790 (sports talk)
WREC-AM 600

OLDIES

WRBO-FM 103.5 (urban R&B)
WSRR-FM 98.1

ROCK

WEGR-FM 102.7 (classic rock)
WMBZ-FM 94.1 (alternative)
WMFS-FM 92.9 (album-oriented rock)
WOWW-AM 1430 (Disney)

SPANISH

WGSF-AM 1030

SPORTS

WHBQ-AM 560
WTCK-AM 1210

URBAN

KJMS-FM 101.1
KXHT-FM 107.1 (hip-hop)

WDIA-AM 1070
WHRK-FM 97.1
WKRA-FM 92.7

OTHER

WEVL-FM 89.9 (diversified alternative programming)
WYPL-FM 89.3 (reading service to the blind)

WORSHIP 🙏

Given its location well within the nation's Bible Belt, it's not surprising that Memphis is richly endowed with churches and other places of worship. By one estimate there are at least 5,000 identifiable houses of worship in Memphis, and there may be many more than that. These range from the mammoth Bellevue Baptist Church, which claims 27,000 members, to tiny community churches that might consist of the preacher and a handful of followers.

You may find the prevalence of the Christian religion in this area to be a bit startling if you are moving here from outside the Bible Belt. Around here, it's not unusual to see giant billboards or television commercials advertising a church, as houses of worship embrace the same marketing techniques that businesses use. As you get to know Memphians, it's likely you'll find that a large number of them attend church. In fact, for many, their religion is such a fundamental part of their lives they have difficulty imagining someone who's not religious at all or who embraces another form of worship. They put their money where their faith is, too. Giving generously to their church or temple is a key reason Memphis ranked fifth among large urban areas in terms of charitable giving, according to the *Chronicle of Philanthropy.*

Of course, if you are moving here from elsewhere in the Bible Belt, you may feel right at home with this type of atmosphere. But wherever you are coming from, if you're looking for the right house of worship, you will find a remarkable variety of options from which to choose. (See the Where to Find a Place to Worship section of this chapter for some ideas on how to begin your search.)

Protestant Christian churches may dominate the scene, but that's not to say there aren't other faiths represented here.

Memphis has a number of Roman Catholic churches; Jewish synagogues, which include the largest Orthodox congregation in the country; and Hindu, Muslim, and Sikh temples. You'll also find Quakers, Korean Baptists, Buddhists, and Scientologists (singer Isaac Hayes is well known in Memphis for his involvement with Scientology).

The importance of worship is reflected in the cityscape as well. As you drive around Memphis, you'll see churches in every part of the city. There are historic downtown churches that date from the 1800s, clustered in the area north of Jefferson Avenue. These include Calvary Episcopal Church, well known for its "street ministries" to aid the homeless and other outreach. Also downtown is Clayborn Temple AME Church, a meeting place during the 1960s for civil rights activists, and Beale Street Baptist Church, the first brick-constructed, multistory church in the United States built for African Americans (today it's the First Baptist Church Beale). In midtown there are a lot of churches built in a 1950s suburban style. A real standout in that part of the city is the Cathedral of the Immaculate Conception, one of the most beautiful of the many Roman Catholic parishes in the Memphis area. While many churches thrive in the central part of the city, other churches and most synagogues have left that area for the suburbs, following the families who make up their congregations as they've moved eastward.

WHO'S WHO AMONG MEMPHIS CHURCHES

Memphis is home to several very famous churches. The most popular among visitors and music lovers is the Full Gospel Tabernacle, where singer Al Green is pastor. After his chart-topping successes of the 1960s and early 1970s, this Grammy-winning performer was called to start his own church. He is known for his charismatic preaching and, needless to say, the music at the services is fantastic. Mason Temple is where Dr. Martin Luther King Jr. delivered his "I've Been to the Mountaintop" speech the evening before he was killed in April 1968.

Memphis also is the seat of the Church of God In Christ, a predominantly black denomination that has its annual convocation in Memphis. The COGIC gathering brings thousands of "saints" to the city each year, and it's actually the biggest convention of the year in Memphis. Other important black churches include Mississippi Boulevard Christian Church, the largest Disciples of Christ congregation in the country, and the Christian Methodist Episcopal Church, which has its headquarters in Memphis. In general, churches and their pastors play an important leadership role in the African-American community, which traditionally has had more faith in its churches than, say, the government. The churches of Memphis, in fact, were an important source of grassroots support during the difficult days of the civil rights movement and other times of crisis. In 2004 pastors stepped in to help negotiate a solution when an impasse developed between city mayor Willie Herenton and city council members.

The various branches of the Baptist church seem to dominate Protestant faith in the city, but you'll also find numerous Methodist, Presbyterian, Episcopal, Unitarian, and Lutheran churches, just to name a few. The religious right also has a presence here. Adrian Rogers, pastor of Bellevue Baptist Church, is a leader in the Southern Baptist Convention generally credited with bringing the organization back to its conservative roots. Memphis is home to the ultraconservative Religious Roundtable, founded by Ed McAteer with the aim of bringing biblical principles into public policy.

Memphis also has a long tradition of independent worship. So you'll find a growing number of community churches, in which a pastor is answerable only to his congregation. Because they aren't affiliated with an organized religion, these houses of worship don't have to worry about a church hierarchy. This type of worship appeals to Christians who find church policies too liberal, as well as to Christians who find established churches too conservative and confining.

OTHER FAITHS FLOURISH

The reform, conservative, and orthodox movements of the Jewish faith are well represented in Memphis, with six synagogues. About half of the Jews who attend services go to Temple Israel, a reform congregation with some 1,800 families. It's also the city's largest and oldest congregation, founded in 1853. Baron Hirsch has the largest Orthodox congregation of any synagogue in the United States There are other synagogues that include a Hasidic gathering, Eruv of Memphis. In general, the city's Jewish community is a mixture of native Memphians, many of whose families have worshipped here for generations, and Jews who are newcomers to the city.

The Muslim faith is represented here by at least four mosques. March 2004 was declared Muslims in Memphis and Shelby County Month, part of a push by area Muslims to educate the larger community about their faith and its history. You'll also find a number of Buddhist temples, includ-

If you are interested in how the Bible came to be, you should visit the Biblical Resource Center and Museum in Collierville (901-854-9578, www.biblical-museum.org). The museum, which moved into a newly renovated historic building in 2004, features an interactive exhibit entitled "How We Got the Bible" as well as replicas of the archaeological artifacts that were key in translating the Bible.

ing the colorful Tinh Xa Ngoc Vietnamese Buddhist Temple on Jefferson Avenue in midtown. There is also Dharma Memphis, an umbrella group that describes itself as a collective of Buddhist groups in the Memphis area. Also represented in the area is the Hindu faith, with a temple in nearby Eads that serves some 6,000 worshippers of Hindu deities. A Sikh community also is active in Memphis. Many of these faiths are growing as the city continues to become more international.

A HISTORY OF COMING TOGETHER

A notable characteristic of the Memphis worship community is that leaders from different religions tend to pull together during times of crisis. When the city was in turmoil after the assassination of Dr. King in Memphis, it was a small group of priests and pastors whose impromptu march to city hall helped to break the impasse between city leaders and striking garbage workers. (See the Close-up in the African-American Heritage chapter for details about this time in the city's history.) Churches further banded together as the riots following Dr. King's death threatened to tear the city apart spiritually. A lasting result of this coming together has been Metropolitan InterFaith Agency (MIFA), a charitable organization that today provides meals and other services to some 60,000 people. More recently, an ecumenical group of local religious leaders united in the wake of the events of September 11, 2001, praying together. Some churches, too, made a point of supporting the city's Muslims against backlash during that emotional time. In 2002 on King's birthday, a group of churches and congregations publicly committed themselves to fight against racism.

Even when there's not a crisis, there's interconnection among faiths. This can be seen in the Memphis Ministers' Association, a group of religious leaders that has met quietly for decades, and in other organizations, including Shelby County InterFaith, which is made up of diverse religious and community groups and committed to developing affordable housing and addressing other community needs. This is also exemplified by Calvary Episcopal Church's annual preaching series, which includes pastors from other denominations as well as Temple Israel's highly regarded senior rabbi.

CURRENT TRENDS IN MEMPHIS WORSHIP

In Memphis, like many areas of the country, a lot of churches are wrestling with how they can meet the needs of their traditional worshippers and at the same time attract new members who prefer more casual and contemporary worship. For that reason, it's not unusual to see even mainline churches offering varied forms of worship that might include live rock bands, blue jeans and other casual attire, and in some cases take place outdoors or some other place that's very different from the stained-glass-windows-and-organ-music environment of a traditional church sanctuary. A good example is Christ United Methodist, a large church in East Memphis. It offers an entire menu of worship options, so on Sunday churchgoers could attend a traditional service, a contemporary service, or a service that's a blend of the two, in addition to a special service for families with children. Plus, there's a high-energy Saturday-night service with live music.

Contemporary worship tends to be more established at the larger, more-conservative churches, but today other churches are catching up, adding come-as-you-are services with nontraditional music lest their flocks stray elsewhere for those offerings.

One trend that continues is movement farther away from the city proper, so you see lots of congregations building large suburban churches. They're mainly looking to keep pace with their members, who themselves are moving farther out as Memphis continues to grow and develop. The brick-and-mortar churches these congregations leave behind offer opportunities for others, and it's interesting to see the variety of vibrant, new congregations eager to move in. (Of course, some of these churches, sadly, are torn down and replaced with shopping centers and such.)

As for the new suburban churches, many are so large they are in fact campuses, with sanctuaries as well as classrooms, gymnasiums, ballparks, and other secular amenities that might even include a school. These facilities are made to order for families who build their lives around their chosen house of worship. They have grown to expect not just worship services, musical programs, and education, but also social events, sports leagues, workout facilities, and many other activities that reach beyond simply worship.

WHERE TO FIND A PLACE TO WORSHIP

Probably the best and most inclusive source for information on local houses of worship is, believe it or not, the Yellow Pages. There are four categories in the phone book, so look under Churches, Synagogues, Mosques, or Temples, depending on the type of worship you are seeking. The Churches listing is particularly extensive, organized both by geographical area and by denomination. If you call, you'll find most are glad to answer questions and may offer to send you information about their programs. Ask if they have a Web site, too, since many houses of worship these days maintain a presence on the Internet. Of course, there's no substitute for visiting the place to see if it "feels" right. As for other sources of information, the Saturday edition of the *Commercial Appeal* has religious news and some listings of churches with information about services and also carries regular columns on faith as well as issues of interest to the worship community. The Web site www.memphisareachurches.com features a limited listing of area churches.

Finally, as is true with other aspects of settling into a new place, your best source of information might be coworkers and neighbors. It's sometimes a good idea to stress, though, that you are "just looking," as sometimes people with the best of intentions can be a bit heavy-handed in plugging their own place of worship. Don't forget to look around your new neighborhood, too, for a house of worship that looks inviting.

INDEX

A

A. Schwab, 129, 132, 154
Abe Scharff YMCA, The, 209
    accommodations, 31–50
    bed-and-breakfasts and country inns,
        47–49
    hotels and motels, 33–47
Acupuncture and Acupressure Center, 256
adult contemporary radio, 283
adult recreation leagues, 191–93. *See also*
    recreation
Africa in April Cultural Awareness
    Festival, 164
African-American heritage, 110–16
    attractions, 132, 148–50
    Beale Street, 111, 113–14, 115, 148–49
    civil rights and Martin Luther King Jr.,
        114, 116
    history, 111–13, 115
    today, 116
after-hours spots, 97. *See also* nightlife
Aging Commission of the Mid-South, 270
Agricenter International, 49
Agricenter International Farmers'
    Market, 125
airlines, 14
airport shuttles, 16
AirTran, 14
air travel, 14–16
Alamo/National, 15
Al-Anon, 251
Albers Fine Art Gallery, 174–75
Alcenia's Desserts & Preserves Shop,
    78–79
Alcoholics Anonymous, 251
Alex Haley House Museum, 226
Alex's Tavern, 88
Alfred's, 83
alternative medicine, 255–56. *See also*
    health care and wellness
Amber Palace, 71
American Airlines, 14
American Cancer Society, 251
American Diabetes Association, 251
American Dream Safari, 146

American Heart Association, 251
American Lung Association, 251
American restaurants, 52–53. *See also*
    restaurants
America West, 14
AmeriSuites, 40
Amtrak, 16
amusements and activities, 158–59. *See
    also* kidstuff
Anderton's, 78
Anna's Steak House, 80
annual events, 162–70
antiques, 119–21. *See also* shopping
apartments, 243–44
Arcade, The, 68, 160
area overview, 3–12
Arkabutla Reservoir, Mississippi,
    190–91, 196
Arkansas day trips and weekend get-
    aways, 198–99, 219–20, 226–28
Arlington, 236–37
Arlington Resort Hotel & Spa, 227–28
Art Museum of the University of Memphis,
    137–38, 176
arts, 171–83
    art museums, 176–77
    classical music, 178–80
    dance, 177
    film, 177–78
    galleries, 172–76
    support groups, 183
    theater, 180–81
    venues, 181–83
Art Village Gallery, 172
Asian Palace, 53–54
Asian Palace Express, 53–54
Asian restaurants, 53–57. *See also*
    restaurants
At Home In Memphis, 280
attractions, 131–50. *See also* kidstuff
    African-American heritage, 132,
        148–50
    Beale Street, 115, 132, 145, 148–49,
        154–55
    Downtown, 152–54

general attractions, 132–37
kidstuff, 152–58
Memphis history, 142–45
Memphis music, 145–48
museums, 137–42
music, 107
tours, 132, 146
Audubon Municipal Golf Course, 200
Audubon Park, 185
Automatic Slim's Tonga Club, 60, 85
Auto Trader, 281
AutoZone Liberty Bowl Football
    Classic, 169
Avis, 15

B
B. B. King's Blues Club, 83–84
Babcock Gifts, 126
Backstreet Memphis, 95
Ballet Memphis, 177
Bally's Casino Tunica, 230
Bangkok Alley, 54
Baptist Heart Institute, 248
Baptist Memorial College of Health, 267
Baptist Memorial Health Care Corp.,
    248, 254
Baptist Memorial Hospital/Collierville, 248
Baptist Memorial Hospital/DeSoto, 248
Baptist Memorial Hospital for Women, 248
Baptist Memorial Hospital/Memphis, 248
barbecue primer, 56
barbecue restaurants, 57–60. *See also*
    restaurants
Bar-B-Q Shop, The, 57–58
Bari, 72
Barnes & Noble Booksellers, 121, 158
bars and clubs. *See also* nightlife
    Beale Street, 83–85
    country-and-western, 94
    Downtown, 85–87
    East Memphis and suburbs,
        89–91
    gay, 95–96
    Midtown, 88–89
    sports, 96
    wine, 97
Bartlett, 237
Bartlett Area Chamber of
    Commerce, 244
Bartlett Express, 277
Bartlett Lanes, 191–92
Bartlett Performing Arts and Conference
    Center, 93, 182
baseball, 211–12. *See also* spectator sports
basketball, 212–14. *See also* spectator
    sports
Bayless Greenhouses, 125–26
Beale Street
    African-American heritage, 111, 113–14,
        115, 148–49
    attractions, 115, 132, 145, 148–49,
        154–55
    bars and clubs, 83–85
    music, 98–99, 114, 145
Beale Street Music Festival, 164–65
Beale Street New Year's Eve
    Celebration, 170
Beale Street Visitors Center, 154
Beale Street Zydeco Festival, 163
Bear Trace at Chickasaw State
    Park, The, 204
Beauty Shop & Dō, 60
bed-and-breakfasts and country inns,
    47–49. *See also* accommodations
Beethoven Club, 179
Belhaven College, 267
Bella Notte, 126
Belle Air Biplane Rides, 146
Bellevue Tennis Center, 208
Belmont Village, 272
Belz Factory Outlet, 118
Best Suites, 44
Best Times, 270, 280
Bhan Thai, 54
Biblical Resource Center and
    Museum, 286
Bickford swimming pool, 208
Big Hill Pond State Park, 188
Big Truck Trader, 281
Billy Hardwick's All Star Lanes, 192
bistros and eclectic restaurants, 60–65.
    See also restaurants
Blue Monkey, The, 85, 88
Blue Plate Café, 68
Blues City Café, 84
Blue Suede Service, 15
boat travel, 16
Bogie's Delicatessen, 66–67

Bogie's Delicatessen Midtown, 66–67
Bogie's Downtown Deli, 66–67
Bol a Pasta, 72, 160
Bonne Terre Café, 69
Bonne Terre Country Inn and Café, 47
books about Memphis, 30
Bookstar, 121
bookstores, 121–22. *See also* shopping
Borders Books Music and Cafe, 91,
  121, 158
Boscos Squared, 76, 91
Bottom Line, 89–90
bowling, 191–92. *See also* recreation
boxing, 214. *See also* spectator sports
Boxing on Beale, 214
breakfast places, 68–69. *See also*
  restaurants
brewpubs, 91. *See also* nightlife
Briarcrest Christian Schools, 260
Bridgewater House, The, 47–48
Brontë, 52, 160
Brooklyn Bridge Italian Restaurant, 72
Brother Juniper's College Inn, 68
Brushwork, The, 60
Buckman Performing and Fine Arts
  Center, 182
Buckstaff Bath House, 227
Budget, 15
Buffalo National River, 194
Buffalo River, 194
Buntyn Café, 79
burgers and pub grub, 76–78. *See also*
  restaurants
Burke's Book Store, 121
Burkle House, 115, 149–50
business, 7, 11, 26–27
bus service, 16
Butcher Shop Steak House, The, 80–81
Butler Street Bazaar, 125

C
Café, 69
Café Francisco, 91–92
Café 1912, 69
Café Ole, 74–75
Café Samovar, 61
Café 61, 60–61
Café Society, 69
Café Soul, 85

Cajun/New Orleans cooking restaurants,
  65–66. *See also* restaurants
Calvary and the Arts, 178
Cannon Center for the Performing
  Arts, 182
canoeing/paddling, 193–95. *See also*
  recreation
Capriccio Grill, 72–73
Carabella's, 126–27
Carnes Pool, 208
Carnival Memphis, 166
car racing, 215–16. *See also* spectator
  sports
car registration, 245
car rentals, 15
Carriage Court, 272
Carriage Tours of Memphis, 146, 152
car travel, 13–14, 16–18
Cash, Johnny, 101
casinos, 229–32
Cat Head Blues and Folk Art, 218 219
Cayenne Moon, 65–66
Center for Southern Folklore, 85, 115,
  132–33, 139, 145, 172
Central Avenue (Hot Springs,
  Arkansas), 227
Central Avenue (Memphis) antiques dis-
  trict, 120
Central B B Q, 58
Century 21 River Oaks, Inc., 241
chambers of commerce, 244–45. *See
  also* relocation
Chao Praya, 54
Chapel in the Woods at Graceland, 139
Charles W. Baker Airport, 16
Charlie Morris swimming pool, 208
Cheapskates, 207
Checker Cab, 16
Cherokee Valley Golf Club, 201–2
Chewalla Lake Recreation Area, 198
Chez Philippe, 69–70
Chickasaw State Park, 188–89
child care, 263–64. *See also* education
childhood immunization clinics, 248
children's activities. *See* kidstuff
Children's Museum of Memphis, The, 138,
  152, 155–56
Chinese Acupuncture Center, 256
Chocolate Soup, 122

Choice Hotels U.S. OPEN Racquetball Championships, 214
Christian and gospel radio, 283
Christian Brothers High School, 260
Christian Brothers University, 264–65
Chucalissa Archaeological Museum, 142–43, 156
Chucalissa Indian Village, 190
Church Health Center, 255
Church of Scientology Mission of Memphis, 256
Ciao Bella da Guglielmo, 73
Cielo, 61
Circuit Playhouse, 180, 181
City of Memphis Division of Park Services, 184
City of Memphis Web site, 4
Civil Defense, 251
civil rights, 27–28, 114, 116
Claire's, 159
Clarion Hotel Airport, 45–46
Clarksdale, Mississippi, 218–19
classical music, 178–80. See also arts
classical radio, 283
climate, 5, 188
clothing and accessories, 122–25. See also shopping
    kids' apparel and toys, 122–23
    men's apparel, 123
    women's apparel/boutiques, 123–25
Clough-Hanson Gallery, 175
Club at Big Creek, The, 202
Club at North Creek, The, 202
Club 152 on Beale, 97
coffeehouses, 91–93. See also nightlife
Coldwell Banker/Hoffman-Burke, Inc., Realtors, 241
Coleman-Etter, Fontaine Realtors, 241
Coletta's, 73
Collierville, 237–38
Collierville Chamber of Commerce, 244
Collierville Herald, 277
Collierville Soccer Association, 193
Colonial Estates, 272–73
Comfort Inn Downtown, 33
Commercial Appeal, 4, 175, 272, 276
Complex, The, 193
Concerts at Lindenwood, 178

Concerts International, 179
concert venues, 93–94. See also nightlife
Concorde Career Institute, 267
Confederate Park, 187
Consignments, 120
Continental Airlines, 14
Contract Bridge Bulletin, 281
Cooper-Young Festival, 168
Cordova, 238
Cordova Beacon, 277
Cordova Bowling Center, 192
Cordova Cellars Winery, 133
Cordova Minor Medical Center, 254
Cordova Skating Center, 207
Corky's Ribs & BBQ, 58
Cotton Bowl Lanes, 192
Cotton Farming Magazine, 281
Cottonwoods Golf Course, The, 204
country-and-western club/bars, 94. See also nightlife
country inns and bed-and-breakfasts, 47–49. See also accommodations
country radio, 283
Courthouse Square, 223
Courtyard by Marriott, 40
Covington Leader, 277
Cozy Corner Restaurant, 58
Crichton College, 265
Crisis Center, 251
Crittenden Memorial Hospital, 249
Crossroads, 95
Crump, E. H. ("Boss Crump"), 24–25
Crye-Leike, Inc., 241–42
Cupboard Restaurant, 79
cycling/mountain biking, 196. See also recreation

D
Daily News, 276
dance, 177. See also arts
dance clubs, 94–95. See also nightlife
Dan McGuinness Irish Pub, 86
Davey Crockett Municipal Golf Course, 200
David Lusk Gallery, 175
David Mah Studio, 175
Davies Manor Plantation House, 143
Davis-Kidd Booksellers, 121–22, 158
Days Inn at Graceland, 46

day trips and weekend getaways, 217–28
    Arkansas, 226–28
    birthplace of the blues, 217–20
    Clarksdale, Mississippi, 218–19
    Helena, Arkansas, 219–20
    Holly Springs, 223–24
    Oxford, Mississippi, 222–23
    road to Shiloh National Military Park,
        225–26
    Tupelo, Mississippi, 221–22
    West Tennessee, 224–25
D'Edge Gallery, 172–73
Deliberate Literate, 92, 122
delis, 66–68. See also restaurants
Delta Airlines, 14
Delta Axis at Marshall Arts, 173
Delta Blues Museum, 218
Delta Cultural Center, 219–20
Delta Medical Center, 249
Delta Medical Physician Referral, 251
Delta Queen Steamboat Company, 16
demographics, 6–7
Denny's, 68
DeSoto County, Mississippi, 240
DeSoto County Family YMCA, 209
DeSoto County Tribune, 277
DeSoto Times Today, 277
diners and breakfast places, 68–69. See
    also restaurants
Dino's, 73
disc golf, 197. See also recreation
Dixon Gallery and Gardens, The,
    138–39, 176
Dockery House Bed and Breakfast, 48
Doe's Eat Place, 219
dog racing, 216. See also spectator
    sports
Dollar, 15
Doubletree East Memphis, 40–41
Douglas swimming pool, 208
Downtown
    attractions, 152–54
    bars and clubs, 85–87
    galleries, 172–74
    hotels and motels, 33–39
    relocation, 234
Dr. Martin Luther King Jr.'s Birthday, 163
driving ranges, 205. See also golf
Ducks Unlimited, 281

Ducks Unlimited Great Outdoors
    Festival, 167
DULeader, 281
Durden Gallery, 173
Dyers Bartlett, 76
Dyers Burgers, 76, 160
Dyers Cafe, 76

E

Earnestine & Hazel's, 86
East End Skating, 207
East Memphis
    bars and clubs, 89–91
    galleries, 174–76
    hotels and motels, 40–44
    relocation, 235–36
East Memphis YMCA, 209
East Senior Center, 271
Edmund Orgill Golf Course, 200–201
education, 257–68
    child care, 263–64
    higher education, 264–68
    homeschooling, 263
    private and parochial schools,
        259–63
    public schools, 257–59
Edwin Watts Golf, 129
Eleven Point River, 194
Elfo, 61
Ella, 123
Ellen's Soul Food, 79
El Porton, 160–61
Elvis-abilia, 129–30. See also shopping
Elvis Presley Automobile Museum, 134
Elvis Presley Birthday Celebration, 163
Elvis Presley birthplace and museum, 221
Elvis Presley's Heartbreak Hotel, 46
Elvis Week, 167–68
Embassy Suites, 41
Embry-Riddle Aeronautical
    University, 268
Emerald, The, 54
emergency numbers, 251
Empire Coffee Company, 92
Enterprise, 15
entertainment centers and laser games,
    159–60. See also kidstuff
Equestria, 52
Erika's, 70–71

Erling Jensen, The Restaurant, 61–62
Evangelical Christian School of
    Memphis, 260
Evening Times, 277
Ewing Children's Theater, 180
eye exams, 252

F

Fairfield Inn, 44–45
Fair Oaks Golf Club, 202
farmers' markets, 125. *See also*
    shopping
Fat City, 67
Faulkner, William L. (MD), 256
Fayette County, 239
Fayette County Chamber of
    Commerce, 244
Fayette County Review, 278
FedExForum, 93
FedEx St. Jude Classic, 166
Felicia Suzanne's, 52–53, 86
festivals. *See* annual events
film, 96, 177–78. *See also* arts; nightlife
Fino's from the Hill, 67
Fire Museum of Memphis, 139, 152
First Church of the Elvis Imperson-
    ator, 139
fishing, 197–99. *See also* recreation
Fitzgeralds Casino/Hotel, 230–31
Five Spot, 53
Flashback, 120
flea markets/thrift shops, 125. *See also*
    shopping
Flying Saucer Draught Emporium, 86
Fogelman Downtown YMCA, 209
Folk's Folly, 81
football, 214–15. *See also* spectator
    sports
Fordyce Bathhouse Museum, 227
Fort Pillow State Historic Park, 226
Four Way Restaurant, 79
Fox & Hound English Tavern, 96
Fox Meadows Municipal Golf
    Course, 200
Fox Meadows swimming pool, 208
Frank Grisanti's Italian Restaurant, 73
Frayser-Raleigh Senior Center, 271
Frayser swimming pool, 208
Frayser Tennis Center, 208

French restaurants, 69–70. *See also*
    restaurants
Front Street Delicatessen, 67
Full Gospel Tabernacle, 145–46
Fun Quest Lanes, 192
Funquest Skating Center, 207

G

Gaisman swimming pool, 208
galleries, 172–76. *See also* arts
Galloway Municipal Golf Course, 200
Gamblers Anonymous, 251
Gap Kids, 159
garden shops, 125–26. *See also* shopping
Garibaldi's, 161
Garland's, 62
Garrett Lake, 197
gay bars, 95–96. *See also* nightlife
General DeWitt Spain Airport, 16
German restaurants, 70–71. *See also*
    restaurants
Germantown, 238
Germantown Arts Alliance, 183
Germantown Chamber of Commerce, 244
Germantown Charity Horse Show, 166
Germantown Commissary, The, 58
Germantown Community Theatre, 180
Germantown News, 278
Germantown Parks and Recreation
    Department, 184
Germantown Performing Arts
    Center, 93, 182
Germantown Soccer Club, 193
Gestures, 127
Ghost River (Upper Wolf River), 195
Gibson Guitar Factory, 107, 146–47
gift shops, 126–27. *See also* shopping
Glass Onion, 76
Gold Strike Casino Resort, 231
golf, 199–205. *See also* recreation
Golf and Games Family Park,
    159–60, 205
Gooch swimming pool, 208
Gordon Biersch Brewery, 77, 91
gourmet stores, 127. *See also* shopping
Grace, 114
Graceland Mansion, 107, 133–34, 135, 147
Graceland Plaza, 129
Graceland Too, 224

Grand Casino, 231
Greater Memphis Arts Council, 183
Greater Memphis Soccer Association, 193
Greek restaurants, 71. *See also* restaurants
Greenbelt Park, 187
Greyhound Bus Lines, 16
greyhound racing, 216. *See also* spectator sports
Grill 83, 53
Ground Zero Blues Club, 218
Grove Grill, The, 53, 90
Gus's Fried Chicken World Famous, 79–80, 226

H

Half Shell, The, 77
Hampton Inn—Medical Center Midtown, 39
Hampton Inn—Perkins Road, 45
Hampton Inn—Poplar, 41
Hampton Inn & Suites at Peabody Place, 33
Hampton Inn & Suites Shady Grove, 41
Handy, W. C., 99, 114
Harding Academy, 260–61
Harding University Graduate School of Religion, 268
Hard Rock Café, 84, 161
Harrah's Casino & Hotel, 231
Harry's Detour, 62
Hawthorn Suites, 42
Healing Arts Center, 256
health care and wellness, 246–56
    alternative medicine, 255–56
    health department, 247–48
    history, 247
    hospitals, 248–54
    walk-in clinics, 254–55
Helena, Arkansas, 219–20
Herb Parsons State Park, 196
Heritage Tours, 110, 132
Hertz, 15
Hickory Hill, 236
Hickory Hill swimming pool, 208
Hickory Ridge Mall, 118
higher education, 264–68. *See also* education
hiking, 205–6. *See also* recreation
Hilton Memphis, 42
Hi Records, 105

historical sites, 142–45. *See also* attractions
Historic Elmwood Cemetery, 115, 143
historic sites, 115
history, 19–30
Hi-Tone Café, 88
Hobson Co., Realtors, 242
hockey, 215. *See also* spectator sports
Holiday Inn, University of Memphis, 39
Holiday Inn—Mt. Moriah, 45
Holiday Inn Select Downtown, 34
Holiday Inn Select Memphis Airport, 46–47
Holiday Inn Select Memphis East, 42
Hollis Art Studio/Gallery, 173
Holly Springs, Mississippi, 223–24
Hollywood Casino Tunica, 231–32
Hollywood Senior Center, 271
Holy Rosary Elementary School, 259
homeschooling, 263. *See also* education
Homestead Studio Suites, 43
Homewood Suites by Hilton, 43
Hope and Healing Center, 255
Horizonte, El, 281
Horn Lake, 207
horseback riding, 206. *See also* recreation
Horseshoe Casino & Hotel, 232
Horseshoe Lake, 198
hospitals, 248–54. *See also* health care and wellness
hotels and motels, 33–47. *See also* accommodations
    Downtown, 33–39
    East Memphis, 40–44
    Medical Center/Midtown, 39–40
    Southeast Memphis, 44–45
    South Memphis/airport, 45–47
hotel shuttles, 16
Hot Springs, Arkansas, 226–28
Houston's, 53
Huey's, 77, 86, 88, 90, 167
Huey's Downtown, 77
hunting, 206. *See also* recreation
Hutchison School, 261

I

immunization clinics, 248

Imperial Bowling Center, 192
Independent, 278
Independent Walk-in Clinic, 255
Indian restaurants, 71–72. *See also*
    restaurants
India Palace, 71–72
Indie Memphis, 177
indoor activities, 158–60. *See also*
    kidstuff
Interstate Bar-B-Q & Restaurant, 59
IRIS: The Orchestra, 179
Isaac Hayes, 86
Isabella, 124
Italian restaurants, 72–74. *See also*
    restaurants
ITT Technical Institute, 268

J

J. P. Coleman State Park, 191
J. Wag's, 95
Ja Ja's Cuisine of Thailand, 54–55
James Davis, 123, 124
Jarrett's, 62–63
Jasmine Thai and Vegetarian
    Restaurant, 55
Jason's Deli, 67
Java Cabana, 92
Jay Etkin Gallery, 173
jazz radio, 283
Jerry Dover Memorial Classic, 212
Jillian's, 86–87, 158–59, 192
Jimmy Graham Interior Design, 120–21
Jim's Place, 71
John Green & Co., Realtors, 242
Johnson, Robert, 100
John West Kyle State Park, 191
Joseph, 124
Joysmith Gallery, 173
juke joints, 96. *See also* nightlife
July 4th Fireworks, 167

K

Kennedy Park, 185–86
kids' apparel and toys, 122–23. *See
    also* shopping
kidstuff, 151–61
        attractions, 152–58
        kid-friendly dining, 160–61
        rainy-day activities, 158–60

King, Martin Luther, Jr., 112–13, 114
King's Palace Café, 84
Kirby Pines, 273
Kirkwood National Golf Club, 204–5
Kress Suites, 34
Kroger St. Jude and the Cellular South Cup,
    163–64
Kudzu's, 87
Kullison Park, 207
Kwik Check Food Store, 67–68

L

L.E. Brown swimming pool, 208
Lakeland, 237
Lansky's 126, 123
La Playita Mexicana, 75
LaQuinta Inn & Suites, 43
LaserQuest, 159, 160
LaserRock hotline, 142
Las Tortugas Deli Mexicans, 75
La Tourelle, 70
Laurelwood Shopping Center, 118
Lausanne Collegiate School, 261
Lawrence Johnson Realtors, 242
Leaderboard Golf, 203
Le Bonheur Children's Medical Center,
    249–50
Le Bonheur Urgent Care, 254
Le Chardonnay, 77, 97
Leftwich Tennis Center (East
    Memphis), 209
LeMoyne-Owen College, 265
Lester swimming pool, 208
Lewis Senior Center, 271
Libertyland Amusement Park, 159
libraries, 245. *See also* relocation
Lichterman Nature Center, 134–35, 138
LifeBlood: Regional Blood Center, 251
Life Design, 280
Lisa Kurts Gallery, 175–78
Little Lambs and Ivy, 122
Little Tea Shop, 80
lottery, 11
Lounge at Gibson Beale Street Show-
    case, The, 87
Lulu Grille, 63

M

M. L. King Jr. Municipal Golf Course, 200

Madison Flame, The, 95
Madison Hotel, 34–35
magazines, 280–81. *See also* media
Magevney House, The, 143–44, 145
Magnolia Grove Bed and Breakfast, 48
Main Street Trolley, 18, 135–36, 152–53
Mallard Pointe Golf Course, 205
Mallory-Neely House, The, 144
malls and major centers, 118–19. *See also*
    shopping
Mantia's, 63, 127
maps, 17
Marena's Gerani, 73–74
Marlowe's Ribs and Restaurant, 77–78
married, getting, 139
Marriott Residence Inn, 44
Martin Luther King Jr. Riverside Park,
    186, 187
Marx & Bensdorf Real Estate & Investment
    Co., 242
Mason Temple, 115
Mason YMCA, 209
MATA (Memphis Area Transit Authority),
    18, 274
Mayuri Indian Cuisine, 72
M-Bar & Lounge at Melange, 88
McEwen's On Monroe, 63
McWherter Senior Center, 271
Med-Emergency Clinic, 255
media, 275–84
    print publications, 276–81
    radio, 272, 282–84
    television, 281–82
Medical Center/Midtown hotels and
    motels, 39–40
Medical Center YMCA, 209
Meditation Garden at Graceland, 134
Meeman-Shelby Forest State Park, 184,
    189, 197
Melange, 63–64
Melos Taverna, 71
Memphis, 62, 280
Memphis and Shelby County Health
    Department, 247–48, 251
Memphis Antique Guide, 120
Memphis Area Transit Authority (MATA),
    18, 274
Memphis Belle, 25, 144, 156
Memphis Blues Rugby Football Club, 193

Memphis Botanic Garden, 122, 136,
    138, 139
Memphis Brooks Museum of Art, 122, 138,
    139–40, 176
Memphis Business Journal, 272, 278
*Memphis Business Journal's Book of
    Lists,* 279
Memphis Chamber Music Society, 179
Memphis College of Art, 176, 265
Memphis Convention & Visitors Bureau,
    4, 34, 163
Memphis Dance Group, 177
Memphis Downtowner, 280–81
Memphis Explorations, 132, 146
Memphis Film Forum, 177
Memphis Flea Market—The Big One, 125
Memphis Flyer, 175, 278–79
Memphis Futbol Club, 193
Memphis Graceland KOA, 49
Memphis Grizzlies, 212
Memphis Inter-Faith Association
    (MIFA), 270
Memphis International Airport, 14–15
Memphis Kemet Jubilee, 165
Memphis Light Gas & Water, 251
Memphis Marriott Downtown, 35
Memphis Marriott East, 45
Memphis Motorsports Park, 215–16
Memphis music, 98–109
    attractions, 107, 145–48
    current music scene, 106–9
    early blues singers, 99–100
    Elvis Presley and rockabilly era,
        102–3
    Robert Johnson and post-
        Depression blues, 100
    rock-and-roll glory years, 105–6
    soul era: Stax and Hi Records,
        103, 105
    W. C. Handy, Beale Street, and Birth
        of the Blues, 98–99
Memphis Music & Heritage Festival, 168
Memphis Music (shop), 130
Memphis Parent, 280
Memphis Parks Commission, 151, 184, 185
Memphis Park Services, 199–200
Memphis Pizza Cafe, 74, 161
Memphis Plan, 255
Memphis Police Museum, 140, 154–55

Memphis Queen Riverboats, 136, 153
Memphis Redbirds, 211–12
Memphis Regional Chamber, 4, 244
Memphis Restaurant Association, 62
Memphis RiverKings, 215
Memphis Rock 'n' Soul Museum, 107, 147
Memphis/Shelby County Public Library, 158, 245, 272
Memphis Symphony Orchestra, 179
Memphis Theological Seminary, 268
Memphis Ultimate Frisbee Team, 193
Memphis University School, 261–62
Memphis Vocal Arts Ensemble, 179–80
Memphis Zoo, 136, 138, 152, 156–57
men's apparel, 123. See also shopping
Methodist Healthcare, Inc., 250, 254
Methodist Healthcare/North Hospital, 250
Methodist Healthcare/South Hospital, 250
Methodist Hospital School of Nursing, 268
Methodist-Le Bonheur/Germantown Hospital, 250
Methodist Medical Complex-Robinsonville, 254
Methodist Med Search Physician Referral, 251
Metro Bickford Senior Center, 271
Metro Cab, 16
Mexican restaurants, 74–76. See also restaurants
Mid-America Baptist Theological Seminary, 268
Mid-South Center for Natural Medicine, 256
Mid-South Coliseum, 216
Mid-South Community College, 268
Mid-South Fair, The, 168–69
MidSouthLiving, 281
Midtown
    bars and clubs, 88–89
    galleries, 174–76
    hotels and motels, 39–40
    relocation, 234–35, 240
Mikasa Japan, 55
Millington, 238–39
Millington Chamber of Commerce, 245

Millington Family YMCA, 209
Millington Star, 279
Ministers in a Minute, 139
Mississippi
    day trips and weekend getaways, 218–19, 220–24
    state parks, 190–91
Mississippi River, 185, 197, 230
Mississippi River RV Park, 49–50
Mister B's, 66
Mockingbird Inn, 221–22
Mojo's Greek and Mediterranean, 71
Molly's La Casita, 75
motels. See hotels and motels
motor vehicle registration, 245
mountain biking, 196
movies, 96, 177–78. See also arts; nightlife
Mud Island Amphitheater, 93
Mud Island River Park, 137, 153
Muse, 124
museums, 137–42, 176–77. See also arts; attractions
music. See also arts; Memphis music
    Beale Street, 98–99, 114, 145
    classical, 178–80
music and musical instruments, 128. See also shopping

N
Napa Café, 64
Narcotics Anonymous, 251
NASCAR, 215
Nashoba Plantation Colony, 22
Natchez Trace Parkway, 222
National Association of Recording Arts and Sciences, 109
National Bird Dog Museum, 225
National Civil Rights Museum, 115, 138, 140, 149, 153–54
National Hardwood Magazine, 281
National Ornamental Metal Museum, 122, 139, 140–41, 176
Neely's Bar-B-Q, 59
Newby's, 88–89
New Daisy Theatre, The, 93–94
New Era Tickets, 182
New Orleans/Cajun cooking restaurants, 65–66. See also restaurants

newspapers, 276–80. *See also* media
news/talk radio, 283
nightlife, 82–97
    after hours, 97
    bars and clubs, 83–91
    brewpubs, 91
    coffeehouses, 91–93
    concert venues, 93–94
    country-and-western club/
      bars, 94
    dance clubs, 94–95
    gay bars, 95–96
    juke joints, 96
    movies, 96
    sports bars, 96
    wine bars, 97
North Memphis, 236
North Shelby Times, 279
Northwest Airlines, 14
Northwest Mississippi Community
    College, 268

O

Oak Court Mall, 118
Oak Hall, 123, 124
Oaklawn Park, 226, 227
Odette, 127
oldies radio, 283
Ole Miss campus, 223
Olive Branch Catfish Company, 78
Olive Branch (Mississippi) Chamber of
    Commerce, 245
One More, 95
On Teur, 64
Opera Memphis, 180
Orange Mound Senior Center, 271
Orange Mound swimming pool, 208
Oren F. Dunn Museum, 221
Orpheum Classic Movie Series,
    The, 178
Orpheum Theater, The, 94, 182–83
Otherlands Coffee Bar, 92
Outdoors Inc., 129
outfitters/sports stores, 129. *See also*
    shopping
Overeaters Anonymous, 251
Overton Park, 184, 186
Overton Park Municipal Golf
    Course, 200

Owen Brennan's, 66
Oxford, Mississippi, 222–23

P

P. F. Chang's China Bistro, 55
paddling/canoeing, 193–95. *See also*
    recreation
Paint-a-Piece Pottery, 158
Palladio Antique Market, 120
Paradiso, 96, 178
parking, 17–18
Park Place Hotel, 44
parks, 185–91. *See also* recreation
    city, 185–86
    county, 187–88
    Mississippi state parks, 190–91
    river, 186–87
    Tennessee state parks, 188–90
Parkview Retirement Community,
    The, 273
Patio Gallery, 174
Pat O'Brien's, 84
Patrick's, 90
Paulette's, 70
Payne's Bar-B-Q, 59
Peabody, The, 35–36, 37
Peabody Ducks, The, 37, 137, 154
Peabody Hotel Lobby Bar, The, 87
Peabody Place Entertainment and Retail
    Center, 118–19, 159
Peabody Place Museum, 141, 176–77
Peanut Shoppe, The, 161
Perry Nicole Fine Art, 176
Pete and Sam's, 74
P&H Café, The, 89
Phillips Grocery, 224
Pho Hoa Binh, 55
physician referral services, 251
Pickett, Greg, 200
Pickwick Landing State Park, 189
Piggly Wiggly, 27
Pine Hill Municipal Golf Course, 200
Pine Hill swimming pool, 208
Pink Palace, The, 27, 141–42, 157
Pink Palace Museum, 138, 141, 157
Pink Palace Museum Crafts Fair, 169
Pinocchio's Book Store, 158
Plantation Golf Club, 202–3
Playhouse on the Square, 181

Plough Towers, 273
pools, swimming, 207–8
Poplar Tunes, 128
pottery studios, 158. *See also* kidstuff
Power House, 174
Precious Cargo Exchange, The, 92–93
Prensa Latina, La, 281
Presley, Elvis, 102–3, 104, 105–6, 146, 221.
    See also Graceland Mansion; *headings
    beginning with Elvis*
Prudential Collins Maury, Inc., Realtors,
    242–43
pub grub and burgers, 76–78. *See also*
    restaurants
publications, print, 276–81. *See also* media
public transportation, 18
Puddler, 281
Pumping Station, The, 95–96
Putting Edge, 159
Pyramid Arena, The, 94

Q

Quail Ridge Golf Course, 203

R

racing, 215–16. *See also* spectator sports
racquetball, 207, 214. *See also* recreation;
    spectator sports
Racquet Club of Memphis, 214
radio, 272, 282–84. *See also* media
Radisson Hotel Memphis, 36
Radisson Inn Memphis Airport, 46, 47
Raiford's, 94
rainy-day activities, 158–60. *See also*
    kidstuff
Raleigh Springs Mall, 119
Raleigh swimming pool, 208
Raleigh Tennis Center, 209
Range Master, 206–7
real estate, 240–44. *See also* relocation
recreation, 191–209. *See also* parks
    adult recreation leagues, 191–93
    canoeing/paddling, 193–95
    cycling/mountain biking, 196
    disc golf, 197
    fishing, 197–99
    golf, 199–205
    hiking, 205–6
    horseback riding, 206

hunting and shooting, 206–7
    racquetball, 207
    skating and skateboarding, 207
    swimming, 207–8
    tennis, 208–9
    YMCAs, 209
Red Cross, 251
Red Roof Inn, 40
Reelfoot Lake State Park, 190
Regents Online Degree Program, 266
Regional Medical Center at Memphis,
    251–52
relocation, 233–45
    chambers of commerce, 244–45
    libraries, 245
    motor vehicle information, 245
    neighborhoods, 234–40
    real estate, 240–44
RE/MAX at Mallard Creek, 243
RE/MAX Elite of Memphis, 243
RE/MAX On-Track, 243
Rendezvous, The, 59–60
rental housing, 243–44
Residence Inn by Marriott Memphis
    Downtown, 38
restaurants, 51–81
    American, 52–53
    Asian, 53–57
    barbecue, 57–60
    bistros and eclectic, 60–65
    Cajun/New Orleans cooking, 65–66
    delis, 66–68
    diners and breakfast places, 68–69
    French, 69–70
    German, 70–71
    Greek, 71
    Indian, 71–72
    Italian, 72–74
    kidstuff, 160–61
    Mexican, 74–76
    pub grub and burgers, 76–78
    seafood, 78
    Southern home cooking, 78–80
    steak houses, 80–81
retirement, 269–74
    retirement communities, 271–74
    senior centers, 271
    senior services, 270
    volunteer opportunities, 166, 270–71

Rhodes College, 265
Richland Elementary School, 257
RiverBarge Excursion Lines, 16
River Bend Golf Links, 204
Riverbluff Walkway, 155
river parks, 186–87. *See also* parks
River Records, 128
Rivertown Gallery, 174
Riverview swimming pool, 208
Riverwalk, 155
Robinson Gallery/Archives, 174
rock radio, 283
Ronnie Grisanti & Sons, 74
Rowan Oak, 222–23
RSVP, 271
Rum Boogie Café, 84
RV parks, 49–50. *See also*
    accommodations

S

Saigon Le, 55–56
Saint Francis Hospital, 252
Saint Francis Physician Referral, 251
Salsa, 75
Sam's Town Tunica, 232
Sam Stringer Nursery and Garden
    Center, 126
Santi Lodge Bed and Breakfast, 48
Sassafras Inn, 48–49
Saunders, Clarence, 27
Sawaddii, 57
schools. *See also* education
    private elementary/middle,
        259–60
    private elementary/secondary,
        260–63
    public, 257–59
seafood restaurants, 78. *See also*
    restaurants
Sean's Deli and Smooth Moves, 161
Seasons at the White Church, 64
Second Floor Contemporary, 174
Second Hand Rose, 120
Seize the Clay, 158
Sekisui, 57
Sekisui Downtown, 161
Sekisui International, 132
Sekisui Pacific Rim & Sushi Bistro, 57
senior centers, 271. *See also* retirement

Senior Services, 270
SENSES, 94–95
Shack Up Inn, 219
Shangri-La Records, 128
Sharpe Planetarium, 142, 157–58
Shelby County, 236–39
Shelby County Municipal Golf Course,
    200–201
Shelby Farms, 155, 184, 187–88,
    196, 206
Shelby Farms Public Shooting
    Range, 207
Shelby Sun Times, 279
Shellcrest, 49
Sheraton Casino & Hotel, 232
Shiloh National Military Park, 224–25
Shooters Five-Star Honky-Tonk, 94
shooting ranges, 206–7. *See also*
    recreation
shopping, 117–30
    antiques, 119–21
    bookstores, 121–22
    clothing and accessories, 122–25
    farmers' markets, 125
    flea markets/thrift shops, 125
    garden shops, 125–26
    gift shops, 126–27
    gourmet stores, 127
    malls and major shopping centers,
        118–19
    music and musical instruments, 128
    outfitters/sports stores, 129
    souvenirs, including Elvis-abilia,
        129–30
Shops of Saddle Creek, The, 119
Sidecar Café, 90
Side Street Grill, 89
Signature Flight Support, 16
Silky O'Sullivan's, 84–85
Silver Caboose Restaurant & Soda
    Fountain, 68–69
Sincerely Elvis Museum, 134
Sip Coffee and Conversations, 93
Skateland Summer, 207
skating and skateboarding, 155, 207. *See
    also* recreation
Slave Haven Underground Railroad
    Museum, 115, 149–50
Sleeping Cat Studio, 181

Sleep Inn & Suites at Court Square, 38
Sleep Out Louie's, 87
soccer, 192–93. *See also* recreation
Social Security Administration, 251
Southaven (Mississippi) Chamber of
    Commerce, 245
Southeast College of Technology, 268
Southeast Memphis hotels and motels,
    44–45
Southern College of Optometry, 252,
    265–66
Southern Heritage Classic, 168
Southern home cooking restaurants,
    78–80. *See also* restaurants
Southern Poison Center, 251
Southland Greyhound Park, 216
Southland Mall, 119
South Memphis
    hotels and motels, 45–47
    relocation, 236
South Memphis Senior Center, 271
South Tipton County Chamber of
    Commerce, 245
Southwest Tennessee Community
    College, 266
souvenirs, including Elvis-abilia, 129–30.
    See also shopping
Sowell and Co. Realtors, 243
Spaghetti Warehouse, 161
Spanish-language publications, 281
Spanish radio, 284
spectator sports, 210–16
    baseball, 211–12
    basketball, 212–14
    boxing, 214
    football, 214–15
    hockey, 215
    racing, 215–16
    wrestling, 213, 216
sports bars, 96. *See also* nightlife
sports radio, 284
sports stores, 129. *See also* shopping
SpringHill Suites by Marriott, 38
Spring River, 195
Square Books, 222
Stage Stop, The, 90
St. Agnes Academy-St. Dominic
    School, 262
Stanky Creek, 196

St. Ann-Bartlett Elementary School, 259–60
Starbucks Coffee, 93, 159
statistics, vital, 8–10
Stax, 103, 105
Stax Museum of American Soul Music,
    107, 115, 139, 148, 150
St. Benedict at Auburndale, 262
steak houses, 80–81. *See also* restaurants
Stella, 64
St. Jude Children's Research Hospital,
    252, 253
St. Mary's Episcopal School, 262
Stonebridge Golf Club, 203
Stone Center for Wellness, 256
story hours, 158. *See also* kidstuff
Strange Cargo, 130
Strings and Things, 128
Studio on the Square, 96, 178
suburbs
    bars and clubs, 89–91
    relocation, 236–40
Summer Quartet Drive-In, 178
Sun Studio, 107, 148, 149
Sweeney YMCA, 209
Swig, 87
swimming, 207–8. *See also* recreation

T

T. J. Mulligan's, 90–91
T. O. Fuller State Park, 190
T. O. Fuller State Park Golf Course, 201
Talbot Heirs Guesthouse, 38–39
Taqueria Guadalupana, 75–76
Tater Red's Lucky Mojos and Voodoo
    Healings, 130
taxis, 15–16
television, 281–82. *See also* media
Tennessee Department of Human
    Services, 264
Tennessee Department of
    Transportation, 17
Tennessee state parks, 188–90
Tennessee Wildlife Resources
    Agency, 197
tennis, 208–9. *See also* recreation
Texas de Brazil, 81
theater, 180–81. *See also* arts
Theatre Memphis, 181
Theatre Works, 181

Thomas B. Davis Family YMCA, 209
Three Oaks Grill, 70
thrift shops, 125. *See also* shopping
Thrifty, 15
Ticketmaster, 182
Timbeaux's on the Square, 66
Tipton County, 239–40
Toad Hall Antiques, 120
Tom Lee Park, 155, 187, 208
Tom Sawyer's Mississippi River RV
    Park, 50
Tonic, 124–25
Top Brass Sports, 207
tours, 132, 146. *See also* attractions
Tower Records, 128, 159
Town Village Audubon Park, 273
train service, 16
transportation, 13–18
    air travel, 14–16
    boat travel, 16
    bus service, 16
    car travel, 13–14, 16–18
    public transportation, 18
    taxis and hotel shuttles, 15–16
    train service, 16
Trees by Touliatos, 126
Trezevant Manor Lifecare Retirement,
    273–74
Tri-State Defender, 114, 279
Tsunami, 64–65
Tunica Lake, 198
Tunica National Golf & Tennis, 205
Tunica Queen, 230
Tunica River Park, 230
Tupelo, Mississippi, 221–22
Two Way Inn, 97

U

Ultimate Memphis Rock 'n' Roll
    Tours, 132
Union Planters IMAX Theater, 141–42, 157
Union University/Germantown, 268
United Express, 14
Universal Art Gallery, 174
University of Memphis, 266–67
University of Memphis Tigers, 213–15
University of Mississippi, 223
University of Mississippi/DeSoto
    Center, 268

University of Tennessee Health Science
    Center, 267
Upper Wolf River, 195
Urban Gardener, 126
urban radio, 284
U.S. Airways, 14
USA Racquetball, 214
UT Medical Group Physician
    Referral, 251

V

Vatterott College, 268
venues. *See also* arts; nightlife
    arts, 181–83
    concert, 93–94
Veterans Affairs Medical Center,
    252, 253
Victorian Holiday Walk, 144
Victorian Village, 144
Viking Culinary Arts, 127
Village Toymaker, 122
Volunteer Memphis, 271
volunteer opportunities, 166, 270–71.
    See also retirement

W

W. C. Handy Blues Awards, 165
W. C. Handy House, 107, 115, 148, 150
walk-in clinics, 254–55. *See also* health
    care and wellness
Wall Doxey State Park, 191, 197
Wally Joe, 65
Washington Street Bistro, 65
weather, 5, 188
Wedgewood Golf Club, 203
weekend getaways. *See* day trips and
    weekend getaways
Weevil (WEVL-FM), 283
Wellford's Antique Collection, 121
wellness. *See* health care and wellness
Wesley Highland Towers, 274
West Memphis (Arkansas) Chamber of
    Commerce, 245
Westminster Academy, 262–63
West Tennessee day trips and weekend
    getaways, 224–25
Westwood swimming pool, 208
WEVL-FM (Weevil), 283
Whitehaven Tennis Center, 209

Wild Bill's, 96

Wild Oats Market, 256

William R. Moore College of Technology, 268

Williams-Sonoma Outlet, 127

Willis Gallery, 174

Willows Sporting Clays, The, 207

Willow swimming pool, 208

Wilson Air Center, 16

Winchester Bowl, 192

Winchester Minor Medical Center/ Le Bonheur Urgent Care, 254

wine bars, 97. *See also* nightlife

Wolbrecht Tennis Center (East Memphis), 209

Wolfchase Galleria, 119

Wolf River Bottomlands, 206

Wolf River Singers, 180

Woman's Exchange, 80, 123

women's apparel/boutiques, 123–25. *See also* shopping

Wonders: The Memphis International Cultural Series, 137, 142, 177

Wooddale Tennis Center (Parkway Village), 209

Woodruff-Fontaine House, 144

World Championship Barbecue Cooking Contest, 56, 165

wrestling, 213, 216. *See also* spectator sports

Wright, Francis, 22

Wyndham Garden Hotel, 39

Y

Yarborough's Music, 128

Yellow Cab, 16

yellow fever, 22–23

YiaYia's Eurocafe, 65

YMCA at Schilling Farms, 209

YMCAs, 209. *See also* recreation

Young Avenue Deli, 89

Z

Zinnie's East, 89

ABOUT THE AUTHOR

Nicky Robertshaw is a freelance writer who's also the Dining Out columnist for *Memphis* magazine. Born in Mississippi, she moved to Memphis in 1993 to write for *Memphis Business Journal* after spending a number of years as a reporter in New York and Washington, D. C. She lives in midtown Memphis with her husband, Chris, and daughter, Maddie.

HELP US KEEP THIS GUIDE UP TO DATE

Every effort has been made by the author and editors to make this guide as accurate and useful as possible. However, many things can change after a guide is published—phone numbers change, facilities come under new management, etc.

We would love to hear from you concerning your experiences with this guide and how you feel it could be improved and be kept up to date. While we may not be able to respond to all comments and suggestions, we'll take them to heart and we'll also make certain to share them with the author. Please send your comments and suggestions to the following address:

> The Globe Pequot Press
> Reader Response/Editorial Department
> P. O. Box 480
> Guilford, CT 06437

Or you may e-mail us at:

> editorial@GlobePequot.com

Thanks for your input, and happy travels!

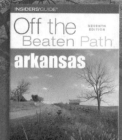

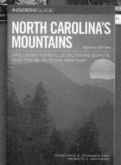